Grierson on Documentary

John Grierson (at the National Film Board of Canada, 1945)

TWENTY-SEVEN

GRIERSON
ON
DOCUMENTARY

Edited by Forsyth Hardy

REVISED EDITION

UNIVERSITY OF CALIFORNIA PRESS
Berkeley and Los Angeles, 1966

University of California Press
Berkeley and Los Angeles, California
English edition
Faber and Faber Ltd
London, England
First American edition: Focal Press, 1947
© *1966 by The Regents of the University of California*

Library of Congress Catalog Card Number: 66:14091

Printed in Great Britain

Acknowledgements

Much of the material comprising this volume appeared in journals in which Grierson had a close personal interest: *Cinema Quarterly*, *World Film News*, and *Documentary News Letter*. Details of the published sources are set out in the Appendix: grateful acknowledgements are due to the editors and publishers concerned.

Stills appearing in the volume are acknowledged individually to their production companies. I am particularly indebted to Paul Rotha for permission to use several stills from early documentaries not obtainable from any other sources in this country; and to Ernest Lindgren who kindly made available the resources of the National Film collection. I have also been able to draw on the stills library of the Edinburgh Film Guild. For the stills from war-time documentaries I am grateful for the assistance given by the Ministry of Information and the National Film Board of Canada.

Contents

Contents

Illustrations

11

Illustrations

Introduction

In the early thirties a new word and a new name began to appear with some regularity in the public prints of the English-speaking world. The new word was 'documentary' and the new name John Grierson. The word documentary made its first appearance in a review written by Grierson for the New York *Sun* in February 1926. It derived from *documentaire*, a term applied by the French to their travel films. Grierson used it to describe Robert Flaherty's *Moana* which, he wrote, 'being a visual account of events in the daily life of a Polynesian youth, has documentary value'. Later he defined it as 'the creative treatment of actuality'. It came to represent in the next twenty years a vast and far-reaching use of the film for social comment.

To that development many men and many minds contributed. Flaherty, in *Nanook of the North*, first drew world-wide attention to the film's power of imaginative natural observation. It was from Grierson, however, that the main driving force and inspiration of the movement came and it has grown most sturdily where he has happened to be. He had the imagination to see the service films may render to our moods of resolution as well as to our moods of relaxation. His understanding of the medium has been perceptive enough to give skilled and persuasive form to his ideas. As a teacher he has stimulated film-makers to intense effort and earned their implicit loyalty. And as a politician he has fought documentary's battles, overcoming suspicion and incomprehension through his unwavering integrity.

This is the story of the man and the movement he founded.

*　　　*　　　*

John Grierson was born in 1898 at Deanston, a village on the Stirlingshire-Perthshire border in Scotland. His grandfather and his forebears were lighthouse men and a love of ships and the sea came easily and naturally to Grierson, even at his inland home among the hills. His father, schoolmaster at the Stirlingshire village of Cambusbarron, was 'a good dominie of the old school', who believed that learning was power and who took his job seriously. Grierson has described how his father pioneered in the development of social amenities at the beginning of the century and how he brought to the village school the first film show ever given in educational circles. He had reservations, later to be strengthened, about his father's individualist philosophy in education; but there is no doubt about the stimulating impact of his father's energy and example. There was the further stimulus of a large family which delighted in the argument characteristic of many Scottish homes of the period and perhaps Grierson's agility in debate owes something to the grounding of these lively family discussions.

Grierson made what has been described by one of his professors as a brilliant entry to Glasgow University in 1915. Almost immediately the demands of war carried him off to mine-sweeping in the North Sea with the Royal Naval Volunteer Reserve. It confirmed him in his love of ships and the sea and in other respects it was inevitably a toughening process. 'I have been in and out of every sea loch from Cape Wrath to the Mull of Kintyre and in every sheltering harbour east and west from the Butt of Lewis to Barra Head,' he wrote. 'Nor can there be many islands in the great highland galaxies that I haven't been to, and that includes St. Kilda and the Flannans, North Rona and the Monachs. I have been on ships the world over but there have never been ships again for me like the highland and island ships.' With this experience behind him, Grierson returned in 1919 to Glasgow University from which he graduated in 1923 with distinctions in English and Moral Philosophy. After a short period of lecturing at Durham University he was awarded in 1924 a Rockefeller Research Fellowship in Social Science.

The next three years Grierson spent in the United States studying the press, the cinema, and other instruments affecting public opinion. What he learned about the sources of their power over men's minds determined his outlook for the future. Men like Walter Lippmann were saying at the time that the older expectations of democratic education were impossible, since they appeared to require that the ordinary citizen should know every detail of public affairs as they developed from moment to moment. With Lippmann, Grierson agreed that the view of education which assumed that stuffing the citizen with facts would enable him to act intelligently according to his interest was untenable in a complex society. But Grierson did not share Lippmann's apparent discouragement. For the indiscriminate transmission of facts, Grierson opposed the possibility of a selective *dramatization* of facts in terms of their human consequences. Interpretation through the dramatic media could give individuals 'a common pattern of thought and feeling' with which they could usefully approach the complex issues of modern living. The power to tap the springs of action had slipped away from the schools and churches and had come to reside in the popular media, the movies, the press, the new instrument of radio, and all the forms of advertising and propaganda. Grierson proposed to study the dramatic and emotional techniques by which these media had been able to command the sentiments and loyalties of the people where many of the instruments of education and religion had failed.

Grierson's ideas on education and mass communication found their first response in the field of the motion picture. Newspaper editors and film critics were stimulated by his approach and he was invited to write as a guest critic for several journals, notably the New York *Sun*. In the spate of discussion which followed, Grierson's film contacts widened. Soon he was in Hollywood, studying production at first hand and meeting Chaplin, Sternberg, von Stroheim, and the other leading film figures of the day who, with their own creative existence at stake, were also concerned to reason out the problem of putting the emotional power of the film at the service of mature thinking.

Seeking the sources of that power, Grierson began to write on film aesthetics 'as a hobby' and to analyse the reactions of the film-going masses as measured at the box-office. He also began to study and compare the film achievements of other countries. Two events had an important influence on him at that time. One was the appearance in America of Eisenstein's *Potemkin*, a reconstruction of an episode from the 1905 Russian Revolution which had tremendous propagandist power. The other was a meeting with Robert Flaherty, who had already shown in *Nanook* and *Moana* his use of the camera to bring alive everyday people and normal happenings. Here were two related methods which could be used to enlist the sympathies of masses of people in social themes.

It is important to remember that Grierson's interest was first aroused in the cinema, not as an art form, but as a medium for reaching public opinion. He has never sought to disguise this approach and has often firmly emphasized it. In 1933, for example, he wrote:

'I have no great interest in films as such. Now and again shapes, masses and movements so disport themselves that I have a brief hope that something of the virtue of great painting may one day come into cinema; but I have but to consider the economic bases of production to suspend the hope indefinitely. For the absolute pleasures of form a

15

man would more wisely look to painting and be done with it. Outside considerations of commerce do not so frequently distort; the skill is more intense because more confined; and the artist, on a cheaper canvas, can more easily command the bewildering perfections of harmony. I look on cinema as a pulpit, and use it as a propagandist; and this I put unashamedly because, in the still unshaven philosophies of cinema, broad distinctions are necessary. Art is one matter, and the wise, as I suggest, had better seek it where there is elbow room for its creation; entertainment is another matter; education, in so far as it concerns the classroom pedagogue, another; propaganda another; and cinema is to be conceived as a medium, like writing, capable of many forms and many functions. A professional propagandist may well be especially interested in it. It gives generous access to the public. It is capable of direct description, simple analysis and commanding conclusion, and may, by its tempo'd and imagistic powers, be made easily persuasive. It lends itself to rhetoric, for no form of description can add nobility to a simple observation so readily as a camera set low, or a sequence cut to a time-beat. But principally there is this thought that a single say-so can be repeated a thousand times a night to a million eyes, and, over the years, if it is good enough to live, to millions of eyes. That seven-leagued fact opens a new perspective, a new hope, to public persuasion.'[1]

I have given this quotation at length because it summarizes aptly the conclusions Grierson was reaching and the attitude towards the cinema which was hardening during those years of intense investigation in the United States. When he left Britain cinema for him had been merely one aspect of a fascinating subject; when he returned in 1927 he was deeply absorbed in the possibilities of its use as a medium of education and persuasion. Before he could put his ideas to the test it was necessary to find a government department which might be convinced of the service films might render. This he found in the Empire Marketing Board which was already using posters, newspapers, exhibitions, and school classroom walls, and was fumbling over its first approaches to the cinema.

Sir Stephen Tallents has described how, one day in February 1927, Grierson called on him 'brimming with ideas'. As a result of the interview he became Films Officer to the Empire Marketing Board, sharing the position for a short time with Walter Creighton. His first preparatory work consisted of writing memoranda about foreign cinematic experience and arranging a series of film displays illustrating

[1] *Sight and Sound*, Winter, 1933–34.

what other countries had done, or were doing, to put their achievements on the screen. In due course the E.M.B. felt sufficiently qualified and confident to advance into action. As Tallents has recorded:

'At this point a justly cautious Treasury had to be wooed and won over. We noted with a strategic eye a fortunate combination of circumstances. The Financial Secretary of the day was the greatest living authority on the fascinating records of the British herring industry. Grierson had served a tough apprenticeship to the sea in mine-sweepers during the War. We baited our hook with the project of a film to illustrate the North Sea herring fisheries. The Treasury swallowed it, and Grierson set out to make his first film. During the next few months he and his cameraman[1] had some rough passages on the North Sea. So, metaphorically, had his project in London. But faith prevailed. Our anxieties were dispelled on a late autumn afternoon of 1929, when *Drifters* was included and warmly applauded in a programme of the Film Society.'[2]

In considering *Drifters* it is important to appreciate not only its contemporary reception but also its long-term effect. *Drifters* aroused immediate interest because of both its subject-matter and its technique. In the studio-bound British cinema, whose most daring expedition was into a West End theatre to photograph an Aldwych farce or a Co-optimists' show, a film which drew its drama at first-hand from real life was something revolutionary. Grierson's simple story of the North Sea herring catch brought what were then new and striking images to the screen: drifters swinging out to sea from small grey harbours; nets flung wide from restless vessels; fishermen moving about their everyday tasks. Here was workaday Britain brought to the screen for the first time: what has become familiar today through a thousand documentary films had then the impact of startling discovery. In technique also *Drifters* struck a note which was new in Britain. Grierson had studied the work of the Russian directors—had indeed helped to prepare the version of *Potemkin* shown in America—and he applied to his own film the principles of symphonic structure and dynamic editing evolved by Eisenstein and Pudovkin. *Drifters* might have broken new ground in its theme and remained technically dull; in fact its form was little less exciting than its content.

So much for the immediate reaction to *Drifters*. More important were the long-term results of its success. It vindicated Grierson's belief that in the film he had found the most useful medium for his purposes

[1] Basil Emmott.
[2] *Spectator*, 19 November, 1937.

as a sociologist. The documentary film movement, he has written, 'was from the beginning an adventure in public observation. It might, in principle, have been a movement in documentary writing, or documentary radio, or documentary painting. The basic force behind it was social not aesthetic. It was a desire to make a drama from the ordinary to set against the prevailing drama of the extraordinary: a desire to bring the citizen's eye in from the ends of the earth to the story, his own story, of what was happening under his nose. From this came our insistence on the drama of the doorstep. We were, I confess, sociologists, a little worried about the way the world was going. . . . We were interested in *all* instruments which would crystallise sentiments in a muddled world and create a will toward civic participation'.[1]

The success of *Drifters* made it possible for Grierson to further his ideas. Instead of directing other films he devoted his energies to building up a film unit and training its members. The young men he gathered round him were of like mind: Basil Wright, Arthur Elton, Stuart Legg, Paul Rotha, John Taylor, Harry Watt, Donald Taylor, Edgar Anstey, and others; they were also men who preferred 'the dog-biscuits of E.M.B. production to the flesh pots of Elstree and Shepherd's Bush'. They were united by a common enthusiasm and a common aim. Grierson, whose energy seemed endless then as now, was an exacting teacher but hard and constant work did not seem to affect the eagerness of the film-makers he was training. There was, at the E.M.B. Film Unit during those early thirties, an energizing and inspiriting atmosphere which affected everyone who made contact with it. One was aware both of an unselfish devotion to an ideal and a sense of vital urgency in the effort towards its realization.

Much of this feeling derived from Grierson himself and from the disinterested direction he gave to the British documentary film movement. 'The documentary film', he maintains, 'was, in spite of all foreign aids and instances, an essentially British development. Its characteristic was this idea of social use, and there, I believe, is the only reason why our British documentary persisted when other aesthetic or aestheticky movements in the same direction were either fitful or failed. The key to our persistence is that the documentary film was created to fill a need, and it has prospered because that need was not only real but wide. If it came to develop in Britain there were three good reasons for it. It permitted the national talent for emotional under-statement to operate in a medium not given to under-statement. It allowed an adventure in the arts to assume the respectability of a public service.

[1] *The Fortnightly Review*, August 1939.

Introduction

The third reason was the Empire Marketing Board and a man called Tallents. . . . Without him we would have been driven exhausted into the arms of Hollywood or into the practice of a less expensive art. Tallents marked out the habitation and the place for our new teaching of citizenship and gave it a chance to expand. In relating it to the art so variously called "cultural relations", "public relations" and "propaganda", he joined it to one of the actual driving forces of the time and guaranteed it patronage.'[1]

Between January 1930 and July 1933, the E.M.B. Film Unit grew in man-power from two to over thirty; it moved from a cellar in the Charing Cross Road to an attic in Wardour Street and thence to an office of normal dimensions in Oxford Street; and it produced over a hundred films. The most memorable were those comprising a group of seven which followed *Drifters* into the theatres and which demonstrated conclusively Grierson's quality as a producer. They included *Industrial Britain*, made by Robert Flaherty who lent his knowledge and skill to the unit for a time during its formative period; Wright's *Country Comes to Town*, on London's market services, and *O'er Hill and Dale*, an account of a day in the life of a Border shepherd; and Elton's *Up-Stream*, about the salmon fisheries in Scotland, and *Shadow on the Mountain*, on Professor Stapledon's pasture experiments at Aberystwyth. For everyone concerned these were experimental and exploratory films: for Grierson they were his first contribution towards the task of bringing Britain and the British Commonwealth alive; for their young directors they were first films, with both hope and heartbreak in them; for the cinema showmen they were a new and strange product, reluctantly accepted; and to the audiences which applauded them all over the country they offered a different and refreshing experience. What had begun with one man and one film was beginning to grow into a movement.

Grierson's leadership of the movement took several forms, any one of which might have absorbed a normal man's energy. In Whitehall, with Sir Stephen Tallents, he was planning how films could help to communicate the new concept of the Empire as a Commonwealth of Nations. As producer he was actively concerned with the day-to-day progress of perhaps twenty films at a time. He stimulated the establishment of the Empire Film Library at the Imperial Institute whose resources, built up from material drawn from all over the Empire, were soon strained to meet the constant flow of requests from schools and societies. In addition, Grierson's was the chief voice raised in ex-

[1] *Ibid.*

19

position of the documentary idea. He did not spare himself in lecturing all over the country—to learned bodies, film societies, discussion groups, at universities, conferences, schools. Similarly, and simultaneously, he wrote tirelessly about documentary theory, addressing his articles to the growing group of realist film-makers in Britain and abroad. He spoke for the most part through *Cinema Quarterly*, the Edinburgh journal founded by Norman Wilson and myself, which Grierson later expanded into a monthly magazine, *World Film News*. He also enlisted the active support of critics and journalists, not only in London but also in the English provincial cities and in Scotland.

It was in a sense a two-way process. Some of us who were writing regularly about films at that time were often impatient of their meagre mental standard and were always on the alert for anything that would push the cinema a little nearer to its unrealized potential. Documentary provided one proof that the medium could be used with intelligence and imagination on a more demanding mental wave-length than trivial escapism. The result was that each new film as it appeared was responsibly analysed, each change in the direction of the movement noted. Thus the articles of, among others, W. A. J. Lawrence in *The Times*, Charles Davy in The *Yorkshire Post*, Ernest Dyer in The *Newcastle Chronicle*, Robert Herring in The *Manchester Guardian* (and, Grierson insists, my own writing in The *Scotsman*) were more than film reviews: they stimulated and, I imagine, on occasion guided Grierson; and they kept the achievements of the movement before the public. Since the films Grierson was making, or wanted to make, were on public issues, the more they made news the better his purpose was served.

In 1933, when the Empire Marketing Board was dissolved, the documentary film movement was too soundly established to disappear with it. Already members of the unit had made films, under Grierson's guidance, for one or two Government departments and a number of enlightened industrial undertakings. But it was important that the unit Grierson had established should continue as a training school and as a clearing-house for documentary theory and practice. 'With our new found relationship between film making and public affairs, there were so many fields open to us beyond the E.M.B.', wrote Grierson, 'that the disappointment could only be momentary. The first one that offered itself was the G.P.O. We grasped it eagerly, for the story of communications was as good as any other and in one sense it was better. When the E.M.B. Film Unit was invited to go with Tallents to the Post Office—or Tallents insisted on it—we had at least the assurance of imaginative backing. It was never easy in the first place to bring a measure of beauty and dramatic significance from materials which no art had touched before. Nor is it easy for a merely analytic or literary or publicity mind to follow a process of discovery with which it has little in common. With Tallents behind it, the documentary idea prospered at the Post Office and in surroundings which seemed at the beginning singularly unpromising. One remembers looking at a sorting office for the first time and thinking that when you had seen one letter you had seen the lot. Yet the exercise in public communication which we were called to perform was challenging, and significant of all communication between the citizen and his corporate servants.'[1]

Grierson took up this new challenge with vigour and imagination. Although his terms of reference may have appeared narrower—the 'bringing alive' of the Post Office rather than the British Commonwealth and Empire—he succeeded in widening the field to include the whole story of communications, national and international. 'We gradually began to see, behind the infernal penny-in-the-slot detail in which the Post Office is so symbolic of our metropolitan civilization, something of the magic of modern communications. We saw the gale warning behind the Central Telegraph Office, the paradox of nationalism and internationalism behind the cable service, the choral beauty of the night mail, and the drama tucked away in the files of the ship-to-shore radio service. Most significant of all, in a film called *Big Money*, Cavalcanti achieved the singular feat of getting under the skin of the Accountant-General's department and bringing the routine clerk in most human terms to the screen.'[2]

During this period Grierson was experimenting as much with new techniques as with new subject-matter. The G.P.O. Film Unit had acquired its own sound equipment and this gave him an opportunity of demonstrating his belief that the sound-track need not simply provide the obvious accompaniment in dialogue and music to the visuals but could make an individual and different contribution. *Song of Ceylon, Night Mail, Pett and Pott, Coal Face*—these and other films demonstrated imaginative uses of sound which were far in advance of contemporary studio thought or achievement. Cavalcanti, director of *Rien que les Heures*, had been invited from France as a guest producer. He remained to put the stamp of his brilliant craftsmanship on many of the G.P.O. films and to earn the gratitude of a generation of young film-makers. W. H. Auden, Walter Leigh, Benjamin Britten, William Coldstream and Cavalcanti's countryman, Maurice Jaubert, were

[1] *Ibid.*   [2] *Ibid.*

among others who lent their special talents to the experimental work in progress. Len Lye was given an opportunity of developing his ideas in the use of abstract colour images in such films as *Colour Box* and *Rainbow Dance*. Some of the films made during these middle thirties appear self-consciously stylized and pretentious today; but together the films of this period represent the most considerable achievement yet recorded in the imaginative use of sound and they did much to keep the G.P.O. Film Unit in the foreground of public attention in Britain and to win recognition for British cinema abroad.

As a producer Grierson imposed no rigid pattern on the directors who worked under him. The style of the films was largely influenced by the subject-matter. 'The documentary idea, after all,' he has written, 'demands no more than that the affairs of our time shall be brought to the screen in any fashion which strikes the imagination and makes observation a little richer than it was. At one level, the vision may be journalistic; at another, it may rise to poetry and drama. At another level again, its aesthetic quality may lie in the mere lucidity of its exposition.'[1] Towards the end of Grierson's period of control at the G.P.O., however, a general change of style became apparent in the films. It was heralded by *The Saving of Bill Blewitt* (directed by Harry Watt), a story film set in a Cornish village using real people as characters, and it was confirmed in *North Sea* (also by Harry Watt), a story of the ship-to-shore radio service which again used real people.

More important than this change of style was the change of emphasis. Sociological observation became more and more an integral part of the films. This was apparent in the G.P.O. productions—*We Live in Two Worlds* and *Forty Million People*, for example; but it was more obvious in the work done outside the Unit by the directors Grierson had trained. It was noted first in such films as *Workers and Jobs*, *Housing Problems* and *Enough to Eat* and among those whose influence on this trend will always be acknowledged was Ruby Grierson. Her sympathetic handling of people living in depressed conditions in the slums of London brought a new warmth and feeling into documentary and after *Housing Problems* the films were never again quite so detached and impersonal. Compare, for example, the work of Basil Wright in *Song of Ceylon* and *Children at School*. John Taylor, who had worked on several of the films with Ruby Grierson, showed in *The Londoners*, made to celebrate the Jubilee of the London County Council, how the personal interview technique could be effectively used with direct commentary, verse and studio work. Many of these films were sponsored

[1] *Ibid.*

by industries and organizations outside the Government which were beginning to use films on a large scale; and they were produced by the rapidly growing number of documentary units founded by members of the original Grierson group. The directors carried with them a sharpened sociological awareness; and in most cases they found a sympathetic and enlightened understanding in the public relations departments they served.

When Grierson resigned from the G.P.O. Film Unit in June 1937, there was already a larger volume of documentary production outside than inside Government sponsorship. The need for a central advisory body had been obvious for some time and Grierson met it by setting up Film Centre, in association with Arthur Elton, Stuart Legg and J. P. R. Golightly. His aim was to provide a consultative and policy-forming centre for a movement now rapidly expanding in many directions. Film Centre was not a producing unit: it undertook investigation and research, offered advice on the use of documentary film, and supervised production. Grierson could again act as a power-house of ideas and initiative for the whole movement.

As one example of his many activities at Film Centre, and because it was a personal service rendered to his native country, I might isolate his work for the Films of Scotland Committee. Set up by the Scottish Development Council in consultation with the Secretary of State for Scotland, the Committee had as its aim the projection of a country in terms of film. For a long time there had been acute dissatisfaction with the screen picture of Scotland; and the stirring of national feeling in advance of the Empire Exhibition in Glasgow appeared to give an opportunity for a corrective. Working closely with Niven McNicoll, then Public Relations Officer at the Scottish Office, Grierson drew up a production programme of seven films, describing in vivid summary the country's character and traditions, its economic planning for industrial development, its agriculture, education, and sport. Although the films were produced by different units and used different styles—emotional, factual, poetic—Grierson's production genius ensured for them a uniform high standard. They remain a unique and remarkably comprehensive record of a country's achievement and outlook.

The Scottish films were among those involved in what Grierson has described as 'the battle for authenticity' which reached its peak in the year before the outbreak of war. Documentary in Britain had not achieved its comparative freedom in social comment without meeting considerable opposition. Most of this had been concealed from the public and much of it had been overcome by Grierson's tenacity and integrity of purpose. It was brought into the open, however, by the selection of films for the New York World's Fair. The selection was in the hands of the British Council's Film Committee, with the late Philip Guedalla as Chairman, and the films chosen to represent Britain reflected the Council's somewhat exclusive belief in the importance of tradition and ceremonial. Documentaries dramatizing Britain's struggle to solve her social and industrial problems were excluded. The resulting controversy was bitter, touching as it did the core of all that Grierson stood and had striven for. He had the support of the Press in Britain and the United States and ultimately, in response to a direct request from the World's Fair for the authentic documentaries of Britain, the films were sent from Film Centre and shown, not as part of the official British exhibit, but in the American Science and Education pavilion. Grierson's purpose was achieved.

By the end of the thirties, the public affairs of Britain were being discussed extensively and eloquently on the screen, both in the cinemas and on the far-reaching non-theatrical network. A movement had been founded with its roots in the public need to learn the facts of modern living and in the need of government and industry to provide these facts. One of the first consequences was that on the outbreak of war there was in Britain a pool of film-makers trained in the use of the film for informational and inspirational purposes. The wartime record of British documentary, from *Target for Tonight* and *Desert Victory* to the hundreds of small functional films which taught us how to dig for victory and put out fire bombs, is a straight development from what had been created at the E.M.B. and the G.P.O. Thanks to the movement Grierson founded, Britain was in this sphere well equipped for the struggle for national survival.

The British documentary example began to have world-wide effect as early as the middle thirties. In the United States Pare Lorentz made his three great films, *The Plow that Broke the Plains*, *The River*, *The Fight for Life*—and with such other film works as Joris Ivens's *Power and the Land*, Paul Strand's *The Wave*, Van Dyke and Steiner's *The City* and, later, Flaherty's *The Land*, the phrase 'documentary film' edged its way tentatively into the American vocabulary. But these films were isolated efforts, not part of a movement as in Britain. The main difficulty was lack of adequate enlightened sponsorship. Public institutions such as the Rockefeller Foundation and the Museum of Modern Art Film Library did what they could to make documentary as practised in Britain more widely understood. But industry was not convinced that this new form of public relations would sufficiently serve

Introduction

their ends. The U.S. Government was equally reluctant. Under the New Deal, Pare Lorentz was briefly authorized to set up the U.S. Film Service, designed to produce films to meet the needs of government departments, but the agency was quickly decapitated by Congress on the ground that it had never been authorized. Meanwhile there were stirrings elsewhere in North America—stirrings which were to mean much for Grierson and the documentary movement.

Among the many young men who made the G.P.O. Film Unit a regular point of call in London was Ross McLean, private secretary to the Canadian High Commissioner, Vincent Massey. Appalled at the paucity of film material about his country, he prepared a report concluding with the recommendation that Grierson should undertake a survey in Canada and prepare a plan for the development of Canadian government film production. It was several years, and only after much pressure by Vincent Massey, Lester Pearson and others, before action was taken; but eventually in May 1938 Grierson sailed for Canada to begin his task.

The field was not entirely bare. There was a Government Motion Picture Bureau which had its origins in 1914 and was theoretically responsible for all Canadian government film-making, although much of it was carried out for departments contracting direct with commercial producers. There was also the National Film Society of Canada, a co-operative organization of educationists and laymen led by Donald Buchanan which had helped to create an informed and enthusiastic film audience. On the one hand there was what has been described as 'the slow peaceful production of mediocrity' and on the other a desire among the film enthusiasts to see films used progressively in the national interest.

Working as always at speed, Grierson produced a report which 'resembled other reports about as much as a machine-gun resembled a plastic pistol'. In broad summary it recommended that all Canadian government film work should be handled by one body and that a single all-embracing distribution network should be established. In October 1938 Grierson was invited to return to Canada to consult with departments and help to prepare the necessary legislation. His recommendations were approved *in toto*. In March 1939 the bill to create a National Film Board was introduced at Ottawa and on 2nd May the National Film Act was given the Royal Assent and the National Film Board had a legal existence.

This was, of course, only the beginning. There was a Film Board but as yet no Film Commissioner and no staff to translate recommendation

Introduction

into achievement. Stuart Legg, already in Canada to make two films on youth training, was invited to help to draft a film programme. Grierson himself was committed to visit Australia and New Zealand at the invitation of the Imperial Relations Trust and was in Hollywood on his way to Canberra when Hitler marched into Poland. He returned to Washington for consultations at the Embassy with Lord Lothian and while there was asked to go to Ottawa to discuss whether or not he would accept the position of Film Commissioner. He was reluctant to do so, both because of the immediate commitment in Australia and also because he was anxious to return to Britain; but he was even more reluctant to see an organization he had helped to create falter at the outset. And so he accepted the appointment in October 1939, although it was at first for only six months.

The organization, in Grierson's phrase, was 'pulled off the sky'. It was set up in an old sawmill in Ottawa and the original staff consisted of Grierson, Stuart Legg and Ross McLean, with two secretaries. To these he added Stanley Hawes and Raymond Spottiswoode from London, two young Canadians, Donald Fraser and James Beveridge, and a young Scot, Norman McLaren, who was to make one branch of the Film Board's work known and admired throughout the world. Later they were joined by Tom Daly, Sydney Newman, Guy Glover and a few others. As before Grierson gathered round him assistants of like mind and temperament. Among them were Evelyn Spice, Gudrun Bjering (now Parker) and Margaret Ann Bjornson (now Lady Elton). When suitably provoked, Grierson will maintain that 'The National Film Board was a matriarchy'. The Frenchman Alexander Alexeieff, the Dutchman Joris Ivens and the American Irving Jacoby were later to work with Grierson in Ottawa.

Meanwhile the lingering disputation between the National Film Board and the Motion Picture Bureau ended with the disappearance of the latter body and, with Grierson's appointment confirmed and extended, the way was clear for action. It is possible to see in Grierson's activities in Canada an extension of the ideas and experiments he was developing in Britain. In his conception the National Film Board was using films 'as they have never been used before, in a planned and scientific way to provide what might be described as a supplementary system of national education'. There were two major series of films, *Canada Carries On* and *World in Action*, each issued once a month to the theatres. Most of the other films were for showing in schools and factories, and by travelling projectionists in the vast rural areas of Canada, even into the Arctic.

26

Introduction

The two major series of films had clear and specific purposes. *Canada Carries On* was devoted to Canadian achievements—'what Canadians need to know and think about if they are going to do their best by Canada and themselves'. This was in the tradition of the films Grierson made in Britain. The important difference was that, with no inhibiting departmental restriction, he could draw freely on a whole country's activities to build up a comprehensive and co-ordinated picture. What he had been able to do for Scotland on one special limited occasion he could do continuously for Canada as a matter of course. The other series, *World in Action*, looked outward on world affairs which affected Canada in common with other countries. While in Britain, Grierson acted as consultant for a period to *March of Time* and the screen analysis of the broad trend of events behind the news was a form which had a strong appeal for him. He much admired the work of Louis de Rochemont and warmly acknowledges the influence it had on him. His interest in *World in Action*, however, went beyond the journalistic style in films. He saw the prestige value for Canada of a series of films surveying world affairs on the world's screens. At its peak of distribution, the series was shown in some 7,000 theatres in Canada, the United States and Britain. Perhaps more importantly, he saw that a series of films on world affairs which gave to Canadian achievements and aspirations no more prominence than was their due was the most effective antidote to narrow nationalism. Here, in other words, was Canada's window on the world.

Another Canadian development unmistakably in line with Grierson's policy was the extension of the non-theatrical field. Grierson had always been aware that there was a greater seating capacity in schools and village halls, in church halls and community centres, than there was in the cinema theatres and he kept the non-theatrical use of films in the forefront of his activities. At the E.M.B. he founded the Empire Film Library. At the G.P.O., non-theatrical audiences rose to over five million a year. In Canada he developed the field still further, by establishing film depositories across the country, arranging industrial circuits, sending travelling units into the far-flung rural areas and Arctic territories, and by devoting more than half of his production programme to films for this audience.

The National Film Board gave Grierson the advantages of centralized and co-ordinated control of a nation's film activities and the use he made of them underlined the quality of his social conscience and vision. 'The main thing', he wrote, 'is to see this National Film Board plan as a service to the Canadian public, as an attempt to create a

27

better understanding of Canada's present, and as an aid to the people in mobilising their imagination and energy in the creating of Canada's future. . . . A country is only as vital as its processes of self-education are vital.'

This is the outside image. What did it seem like from inside? For this impression I am indebted to Marjorie McKay: 'The Board itself was a strange mixture. At the top, and no one was in any doubt, was John Grierson—a fiery, aggressive, brilliant Scot, sometimes domineering, sometimes hard and cynical, sometimes sentimental—with one object, to build an organisation as fast as possible to carry the government's message as effectively as possible to every Canadian and to people of other countries. In a mere six years he created the National Film Board and increased the staff from about 40 to almost 800. Grierson was not a Canadian, but in his ceaseless and restless travels across the country he soon knew more of its feelings and moods than most Canadians. He talked with university people in every province, with the editors of newspapers and magazines, with writers and broadcasters, with teachers and adult education workers, with people engaged in every activity. He had an insatiable curiosity about, and interest in, people—what they did, how and why they did it, and what they thought about it and everything else. . . . The production staff had one thing in common, and that was youth. Most of them were in their twenties. The world was their oyster and Grierson was going to help them open it. There was going to be a brave new world after the war, and they would have a part in it. . . . Here was hope and opportunity. Here was excitement and probably most of all, a sense of doing something which mattered.'

What happened after the war to the National Film Board and the young men trained and inspired by Grierson is not my immediate concern here. Grierson himself felt that he had made his contribution and decided to resign his position as Film Commissioner in October 1945. He was acutely conscious, in the post-war months, of a recession in international understanding which he felt had to be fought arduously. To some extent the *World in Action* series had provided him with the widely circulating medium he sought for the discussion of international affairs; but he wanted to go further than Canadian government sponsorship could carry him. His immediate aims were to produce for showing in the cinemas a fortnightly series of films on world affairs and to discover an economic basis for a real international flow of films devoted to matters of common international interest.

In a letter he wrote to me shortly before his resignation, Grierson made clear his attitude towards international communication by film. He was referring to his earlier decision to leave Britain and also to his newly announced intention to develop a world circulation of films. 'What determined my decision to extend the range of documentary', he wrote, 'was the realisation that our work could not depend on a single national sponsorship, however strong, but only on the international reality created by the common interests of the common people everywhere. That reality is being gradually articulated as the documentary film forces, under the inspiration of the British and Canadian examples, get under way in America, Australia, New Zealand, Holland, China, France and elsewhere. Since I left Britain, I hope I have done something to make of documentary not only an international force but also a force for internationalism. That, in any case, would be the measure of the wisdom of my choice.'

This conception of documentary as a force for internationalism has always been in Grierson's mind and during the years of documentary's growth he has been moving, stage by stage, towards its realization. On the way he has resolved a difference in viewpoint which is reflected in this volume of his writings. Generally speaking, documentary's concern has been to inform and educate our generation in the nature of the modern world and its implications in citizenship. In the earlier phases of the movement, much effort was spent on the exposition of aesthetic theory and in particular the G.P.O. films reveal a preoccupation with considerations of form. In later phases, as the times became more urgent and the areas of interest widened, there was greater emphasis on the quantity of production and the extent of circulation. Under Grierson's direction, the Canadian Film Board offered the best illustration of this attitude. There were no large films, and none pretentious, but there were hundreds of them a year, short and simple, humble and honest, progressively covering the whole wide field of practical civic interest.

At this period, the end of his spell as Canada's Film Commissioner, there was an impatience with aestheticism *per se*. It was not that the aesthetics of documentary film had gone out of the window but that their practice was resisted. Grierson, combining the zeal of a practical reformer with the imagination of a creative artist, is as well equipped as any man to hold the aesthetic case; but, in his own words, he has resolved his difference 'in the idea that a mirror held up to nature is not so important in a dynamic and fast changing world as the hammer which shapes it. . . . It is as a hammer, not a mirror, that I have sought to use the medium that came to my somewhat restive hand.' In reaching this conclusion Grierson adds that it would be stupid to deny the aesthetic argument, far less forget it. 'There are things beyond even the urgency of the times, continuities deeper than our immediate civic duty, horizons that reach out beyond our most progressive effort, to remind us of the nature of tragedy and the nature of clowns, and finally of the humility that is the crown of wisdom.'

*   *   *

And so Grierson moved to New York, with Stuart Legg and Raymond Spottiswoode, to establish International Film Associates. Ideas and energy were not in themselves enough to command success for the new company. About the need for information and enlightenment on world events there was no doubt. Perhaps the cinema medium, with its inevitably slow and cumbersome distribution methods, was not the right one for Grierson's purpose. Perhaps he was already feeling towards television, with its immediacy and mass audience. The three series he announced could be duplicated in many television networks today: *Worldwise*, 'explaining and interpreting great events upon the international scene'; *Wonderfact*, 'relating the marvels of scientific discovery and technological development to the welfare of the man-in-the-street in every land'; *Venture*, 'highlighting the perfection of human skills in the realms of sport and outdoor achievement, in the settings of the great natural backgrounds of the earth'; and *Wonderworld*. Such were the ambitious plans of Grierson and his colleagues. There were resistances to their realization and after a year's effort they were forced to withdraw.

But it was defeat in method only. Grierson, who once said that 'good films are international and good film-makers are internationalist', was still concerned to resist and fight the recession of international understanding. As a new battle headquarters, he had in mind the United Nations organization and when in February 1947 he was invited by Julian Huxley, Director-General of U.N.E.S.C.O., to be the Organization's Director of Mass Communications and Public Information, he accepted the post and the opportunity it provided for achieving the international communication for which he had striven. In his work he had as associates J. B. Priestley and Ritchie Calder, Britain's members of the Working Party on Mass Communications at the U.N.E.S.C.O. conference in Mexico City where its programme in the field of film, radio and press was formulated, and in Paris Jean Benoit-Lévy who helped to plan a series of internationally commissioned films.

Introduction

I saw Grierson on a number of occasions during the year in which he held the post and was conscious of a perpetual tug-of-war between idea and realization. Here seemingly was the ultimate opportunity to realize the potentialities of the film as an international force. Here film could be used in the most constructive way to help the war-devastated and under-developed countries. Certainly Grierson saw the opportunity—'to help outweigh the tensions, the prejudices and antipathies, and to help build in their place a stronger sense of world community among all peoples'. He was also conscious of one of the short-comings of the Organization which, he believed 'can become a truly world movement only when the ordinary people take an active interest and share in its work'. It was easier at U.N.E.S.C.O. to prepare plans than to see them fulfilled. With consultative procedure involving forty member States added to the comparatively slow tempo of film-making, the experience had more frustration than reward for Grierson. There was money for the promotion of ideas but no money to carry them out.

In the spring of 1948, Grierson returned to Britain as Controller of the film operations of the Central Office of Information, although he continued to be associated in a voluntary capacity with the work of U.N.E.S.C.O. He was invited to take overall charge of the planning, production and distribution of Government films and to co-ordinate the work of the C.O.I. and the Crown Film Unit. As the Crown Film Unit was in direct succession from the E.M.B. and the G.P.O. Film Units, it was in a sense a return to the work he had begun some twenty years before; but the circumstances were different, as different as they could be.

During the war the documentary film had served Britain in a hundred ways, from simple information for servicemen and civilians to Churchillian exhortation in films like *Britain Can Take It* and *Target for Tonight*. Leading this great outpouring of films and setting a standard of sustained excellence not equalled anywhere at that time was the Crown Film Unit. Here there was no need for contrived enlargement of the themes, as had sometimes occurred when the basis was the communications theme at the G.P.O. The challenge of size was there and it was met. And in Humphrey Jennings (trained at the G.P.O. Film Unit) there was a film-maker of genius to find poetry in looking at and listening to Britain at war.

Some of us thought that Britain at peace would equally produce themes to stretch and challenge the film-makers. The subjects were there; but, with rare exceptions, the challenge was never accepted in the way it had been in the thirties. When Grierson returned there was

31

a mood of despondency. The powerful flow of wartime film-making directed with a sense of purpose and conviction by the Ministry of Information had been diverted into narrow departmental channels. The most imaginative films emerged not from the Government but from the large industrial concerns like Shell which had taken up with fresh vigour their film-making experiments interrupted by the war.

I believe Grierson hoped he could give fire and conviction to the Government's film-making effort. There was no doubt about the impact he made and the change in mood under his leadership. The men he had trained in documentary were among those who had pressed for his return: they had indeed petitioned the Government. Some fine films were made, among them *The Cumberland Story* and *Family Portrait* (Humphrey Jennings), *The Undefeated* (Paul Dickson), *Life in Her Hands* and *Out of Tune* (Philip Leacock), *Children of the City* (Paul Rotha and Budge Cooper) and *Waverley Steps* (John Eldridge). There were also disasters, blamed by the film-makers on interfering bureaucracy and by the departmental civil servants on creative failure. It was a frustrating period for Grierson, and increasingly so. There was so much which might have been done. The task was beyond the resources of one man even when he had the understanding help of such colleagues and former associates as Niven McNicoll and Charles Dand.

In June 1948 Grierson visited Glasgow to receive from his old University its Doctorate of Laws. In his citation Professor Boyd said: 'Mr. Grierson is an alumnus of this University, who has won worldwide recognition by his development of the film as a potent educational and social instrument. He is the creator of the documentary with which his name will always be linked. . . . It is, however, as a social philosopher rather than as an artist that Mr. Grierson has given himself to the films. He is conscious of this medium as a potent means of mobilising men's imagination and energy in the creation of the future. To devote himself to these wider aims he retired from his Canadian appointment, returned to this country and has since sought to further the film as an international force which will manifest to mankind the common interests which should bind them together.'

Film as an international force was always at the forefront of Grierson's thinking and while at the C.O.I. he lent his vision to every development which would extend the use of film internationally. One of these efforts which I saw at first hand was the film committee of the Brussels Treaty Organization whose work was later taken over by Western European Union and is being continued, and greatly extended today, by the Council of Europe. Grierson enjoyed these international gatherings, not only because of the films like *The Open Window* (Henri Storck) which resulted but also because of the opportunities they provided for meeting creative film people in many countries.

Grierson's experience at this time, allied to his genius as a teacher, made him more and more conscious of the limited opportunities there were in Britain for documentary film-makers to extend the range of their work—to do in Britain what the younger film directors in Italy and France apparently found it so easy to do. The British film industry was in an unstable condition: the upsurge of war and immediate post-war years had spent itself, the volume of production was haphazard and uneven, and the climate was unfavourable to experiment and change. Conscious of this malaise and prompted by Harold Wilson, the Labour Government took a number of steps, among them the appointment (1949) of the National Film Finance Corporation, an organization equipped with the power and money to make loans for film production.

While in general the N.F.F.C. was designed to assist and not to initiate production, the Government recognized that this was not enough and that there must be some positive means of encouraging young film-makers and giving them an opportunity to gain experience. The Corporation therefore decided to finance Group 3, conceived as a training ground for young directors in making comparatively low budget films, intended to be shown in the cinemas as second features. In 1951 Group 3 was set up, with John Grierson and his friend John Baxter in joint control.

It was Grierson's first experience of making fictional films—although inevitably the films were strongly realistic in character—and he approached the new problems with typical gusto. If it is possible to generalize about films which were so varied in style and content, I would say that they were vigorous and lively, unpolished and anti-establishment. A location outside London was also a common characteristic. *Brandy for the Parson* was made in Cornwall, *Laxdale Hall* on the west coast of Scotland, *The Oracle* in Northern Ireland. Did they fulfil their main purpose of giving young men a chance? Philip Leacock, who had made two documentaries, *Out of Tune* and *Life in Her Hands* at the Crown Film Unit, directed *The Brave Don't Cry* and later, for the Rank Organization, *The Kidnappers*. Cyril Frankel, whose training was also in documentary, took his chance with *Man of Africa*. And there were others directors like John Eldridge, John Guillermin, Wolf Rilla and Pennington Richards and writers like Montagu Slater, Don Sharp and James Forsyth—who grasped the opportunities which

C 33

Group 3 offered. The films made by Grierson and Baxter also provided outlets for new actors. Kenneth More was contracted by Alexander Korda after a viewing of the uncompleted *Brandy for the Parson*. Peter Finch made his first appearance in Wolf Mankowitz's *Make Me an Offer*. *Orders Are Orders* launched both Peter Sellers and Tony Hancock. Group 3 was doing its job.

What working with Grierson at this time meant was well expressed by Cyril Frankel, writing about his work on *Man of Africa*: 'Without doubt Grierson's great strength and contribution to the younger generation is as a *teacher*. By the word "teacher" I do not mean an administrator or dispenser of knowledge—Grierson does not try to do this. But he leads you to the threshold of your own mind, and then when you enter on the adventure of discovering something for yourself, his joy is to share the adventure with you, lending his advice and criticism. As a true teacher, he neither demands nor desires imitation: he does not look for a reflection of himself—he wants you to tear out of yourself what you are best able to express. This is by no means an easy experience to undergo—it is frequently painful and Grierson is certainly a man of extremes! And unpredictable! But then he reaches for the heights—and even to glimpse the heights you need to understand the depths.'

Of the Group 3 films, Grierson got most satisfaction out of making *The Brave Don't Cry* in 1952. This was a reconstruction of the mine disaster at Knockshinnoch in Ayrshire, scripted by the versatile Montagu Slater who, among other poems and novels, wrote the libretto for Benjamin Britten's opera, 'Peter Grimes'. In the size and nature of its idea—man's bravery in the face of disaster—it stood nearest to our conception of a Grierson film. It took courage to include in the Group 3 programme a film of this potential. The courage was Grierson's and he it was who stood behind the idea from the beginning and saw it through. I know how much he personally contributed to it, in effort and stimulus, and he had the satisfaction of seeing it selected, in the face of the toughest opposition, overt and concealed, to open the Edinburgh Film Festival in 1952. It is still being shown today, as is also one of the Group's other Scottish films, *Laxdale Hall*.

In terms of opportunity and stimulus, Group 3 was a success. From the outset it was opposed, for paradoxical reasons, by elements in the film industry and the lack of an adequate distribution outlet meant that the films were struggling economically. They cost between £40,000 and £70,000 and to recover this in the short term it would have been necessary for them to be shown on the circuits as first or co-features.

This did not happen, mainly because of the elements opposed to the idea of Group 3, and the films had to find their revenue by slower and more uncertain methods of distribution. Eventually they recovered their production costs and made a profit; but long before that time continuous production by Group 3 had ceased (July 1955). According to David Kingsley, then managing director of the National Film Finance Corporation, the only film to recover its cost by that date was *The Conquest of Everest.*

This problem of achieving adequate distribution for films was much in Grierson's mind as television, already a commonplace in the United States, was spreading across Britain and the independent service was under discussion. How his mind was working is well conveyed in this extract from an article written in 1953: 'I am, of course, involved in the argument as any film-man must be. Television can do all sorts of things on its own, and ably too. It can give an immediate sight of public events. It can provide a living magazine about wonderful places, and things and people. It can give you stage shows of all kinds. But when all is said, it is just another way of presenting films, without the cumbersome process of carting them around in cans and projecting them with fuss, expense and danger in theatres all over the country.

'The film world has one great virtue. It is, I say with affectionate exaggeration, a world of fly men, fast men, and thoroughly vulgar men. You might say that if it is publicly responsible, it is only for a buck. You might also say that if it ever does anything good, it is only because the innate goodness of mankind occasionally creeps up on it through a producer, a director or a writer, or through the odd workings of the Almighty in the public taste itself. But the film world is vital in the sense that it isn't smarmed over with deceptive words and attitudes. It doesn't choke goodness with lip service and make it sick with professionalism. It isn't holier than thou because it isn't holy at all. It isn't removed from the people. It lives where the people are. Its consequent great virtue is exuberance.

'But there isn't a lot of room for producers and directors in the film industry. There can't be. On the competitive level now established films are costly. There is also a limit to what we make because the theatres only need so many films. Some of us suspect that they need far, far fewer than they presently get. There is, you say, always room at the top. But you have to be a majority producer—or writer, or director—to get there and stay there. I make the necessary reservation that some great goods come in small bulk. It means, of course, that television provides now, and will more and more provide, an outlet for

35

the creative talent which does not make, or want to make, the grade of commercial cinema. . . .

'Since television represents the alternative basic economy for film-makers, the more certainly must they turn to it. Their case is important because the renegades from the commercial cinema may conceal much of the great visual talent to come. They must have in their reserve the special visual talents—particularly the poetic talents—which the majority cinema cannot easily use. I conclude from this that the future of television in Britain means life or death to a great part of the art of cinema itself. Any form of television which diminishes its vital development means therefore a loss to the creative life of the nation. Any or, rather, every form of television which, for whatever reason, or by whatever accident, nurtures it is a gain.'

As is clear from this quotation Grierson was thinking more and more about television. He saw it as a means of continuing in the new media the work he had been doing in the cinema, a means of bringing the documentary idea to a new audience. His opportunity to do so came when, after talks with his fellow Canadian, Roy Thomson (now Lord Thomson), of Scottish Television, a programme called *This Wonderful World* was introduced in October 1957. It was an immediate success.

For someone who, twenty-five years before, had said 'I look on cinema as a pulpit, and use it as a propagandist,' here was a new congregation to be reached—to be introduced to 'the wonderful things, the strange and beautiful things the camera has discovered'. Grierson drew on his uniquely wide knowledge of world film-making and, with his flair for selection and arrangement, built up a series of programmes which attracted and held a steadily growing audience. The qualities which distinguished *This Wonderful World* from other magazine programmes were the qualities which Grierson himself brought to it. He was a film-maker, talking from experience about films and able to illumine the particular achievement of other film-makers. He had travelled all over the world and could invariably make an informed personal comment on the setting or subject of the film. And the selection revealed not only the extraordinarily wide range of his sympathies but also the picaresque background of his mental living. It was, I think, this capacity to surprise which gave his programme a magnetic appeal. He could, and did, introduce into his programmes films, which, because of subject or treatment, would have been considered too difficult for showing in cinemas; but because he had gained the confidence of his audience, he was able to persuade them to accompany him on

Introduction

journeys into unfamiliar mental or aesthetic territories. Television had made it possible for him to reach a mass audience, composed of thousands of small family groups to whom he could talk in an intimate, persuasive way.

For his programme Grierson saw thousands of films, sifting through miles of celluloid to find the strange and beautiful things of the camera's discovery. He became a familiar figure at European film festivals and regularly visited the main film-producing centres in Europe and farther afield. He met the young men who, in Poland and Czechoslovakia, were experimenting with film form as the British documentary film-makers were in the early thirties. Grierson was conscious that the urge to experiment in documentary had passed from Britain to these countries where the younger film-makers were encouraged and stimulated at film schools. It is a tragedy that his great gifts as a teacher, acknowledged even by his enemies, should not have been employed during these years in Britain.

Grierson was, however, able to serve his own country again in a way which only he, with his knowledge and experience, could do. When the Films of Scotland Committee was reconstituted in 1955, Grierson agreed to join the body. As a voluntary organization without call on central funds, its potential operation was limited in comparison with the National Film Board of Canada; but those who served on it were, like Grierson, men eager to devote sustained effort for the good of their country. There soon began a flow of films projecting Scottish life and achievement. I have the best of personal reasons for knowing how much Grierson contributed to these in advice and guidance: his ability to cut through the verbiage of discussion to the heart of the matter was as unimpaired as his capacity to see the larger opportunity. To several of the films he made a personal contribution at least as individual and productive as any in his long record. He wrote and spoke the commentary for a film on hydro-electric development in the Scottish Highlands. He wrote the treatment for *Seawards the Great Ships*, the film on Clyde shipbuilding directed by Hilary Harris which won an Oscar in Hollywood in 1961. And he prepared the outline for *The Heart of Scotland*, the film on his native county, Stirlingshire, directed by Laurence Henson who had worked with him for two years on his television programme. His contribution to Films of Scotland was therefore something more immediate and involved than that of a committee member. It was recognized, with his many other services to Britain and the Commonwealth, when he was made a Commander of the British Empire in July 1961.

37

Introduction

Ceremonial recognition sits a little uneasily on the conception of Grierson as a down-to-earth realist. The unease is apparent in accounts I have heard of the twenty-fifth anniversary celebration of the National Film Board of Canada. A trumpet fanfare, the entry of the small greying figure of the grand old man of documentary, a reception from friends, film-makers and civil servants that was 'warm and a little reverent'. 'Don't believe the love feast,' Grierson said after the speeches were over and the film-makers proper got together. 'They treat me like I was up in the sky. I thought at least someone would ask me for an autograph. I feel like Hindenburg when he got a bit too old: I'd sign anything.' Impatient as he may have been with the pomposity inseparable from all anniversary ceremonial, he must have been gratified that the organization he launched in the most difficult and demanding circumstances had prospered so impressively and had become the largest and strongest of its kind in the world.

It does not occur to me to think of Grierson as an old man: I see too much evidence of his unquenchable vigour. He is still the most penetrating mind, the most commanding voice, in any company. If this is old age it is the better part of it. On a radio occasion which I shared with him, Grierson was talking about the film of Picasso at work. 'I found it one of the great privileges of my life', he said, 'to be present with Picasso drawing and painting *ad infinitum*. To see a great master at work, to see his mind move, is surely a compensation for all the mediocrity of life—and one's own life in particular.' How many there must be in half the countries of the world who have this feeling when they think of John Grierson.

*   *   *

I have attempted in this introduction to provide links for the story of Grierson's individual building-up of the realist film movement and to indicate the constants in his changing Odyssey. For the heart of the matter we must turn to his writings. It would be interesting to assess just how much Grierson's lucid and compelling exposition of its aims has contributed to the development of documentary. Certainly they have been a source of stimulus and enrichment for those who were outside the immediate range of his personal influence. Individually they have enunciated principles which have conditioned the whole trend of the movement and set a pace for it. Together they constitute the most solid and penetrating analysis yet made of the film as an instrument affecting public opinion.

38

Introduction

In this book I have made a selection from Grierson's vast volume of writing on mass communication. The earlier chapters include some of the film reviews contributed by Grierson to various journals in the early thirties: a few of the films may have gone out of currency but the criticism retains its lucidity and pungency. The most important statements on documentary principles follow: they have been widely quoted and reproduced in many languages. Grierson's wartime writings on the interrelations of education, propaganda and democracy are included. The chapters added to the volume since its first appearance in 1947 include his annual surveys of world documentary and his analysis of television.

Part I

BACKGROUND TO DOCUMENTARY

While at Glasgow University Grierson was a regular contributor, in prose and verse, to the University magazine and although these contributions did not include formal film criticism, several of them revealed his interest in the cinema, particularly in Chaplin. It was during his first visit to the United States that he began to write regularly about films and on his return to Britain he contributed film criticism to a number of weeklies, monthlies and quarterlies. From the first it was vivid, penetrating criticism with a value and validity beyond the fleeting moment; and yet it was always a by-product of his main work. The films were seen and the articles written during a period of intense and demanding activity. In some of them he drew on his experiences in Hollywood where he met many of the leading directors of the thirties—Chaplin, Stroheim, Von Sternberg, Vidor and Flaherty among them. In all his criticism he had a capacity to cut quickly to the heart of the matter. Critics as well as film-makers were influenced by his writing. In her autobiography *Thank You For Having Me*, C. A. Lejeune of the London *Observer* wrote: 'Grierson taught me how to look at films and see them whole; how to judge each one on its own merits; not seeking in it for some quality that was not intended to be there. He was a sharp and brilliant critic.'

The articles I have assembled here are drawn in the main from his writings during the early thirties. He had a special affection for the clowns of the cinema. His friendship with Chaplin enabled him to write with informed understanding of his films—their shortcomings as well as their virtues. He knew the minds behind production in Hollywood and was in a better position than most other critics to evaluate the films and explain how they came to be made. There was, of course, nothing of apology in his writing. Friendship was no shield for criticism when Grierson felt it to be necessary, as is often apparent in the reviews which follow. As a film-maker himself he could appreciate technical achievement and could relate skill in direction, photography and editing to a film's total accomplishment. Many of his judgments have entered into the common currency of film criticism: 'When a director dies, he becomes a photographer.'

Grierson never forgot that the cinema is a mass medium. In his criticism of fiction films he was not trying to turn it into something else but rather to influence its direction along more worth-while paths. His criticisms of the early work of Alfred Hitchcock and Anthony Asquith were trenchant, not because their films were lacking in technical merit but because they were so often on trivial themes and lacking in any real contact with the life of the country. He was essentially a humanist critic, as becomes increasingly clear from his comments on American films and on the work of the Russian directors. These were the movie influences which formed the background to his work for the documentary movement.

Grierson's attitude towards the role of the critic was most zestfully expressed in an article he wrote for the London-published magazine, the *New Clarion*:

'Of every film and of every film talent I ask a modicum of revelation. It may be a novelty of fact, or an angle of beauty, or an efficiency of technical demonstration. These will serve in the absence of better things. . . . But there are greatnesses beyond these things: the sort of greatness that comes with Chaplin and Pudovkin, and every now and again from people like Hitchcock and Asquith and Lachman and Vidor and Sternberg and Flaherty and Roland Brown. It is my old-fashioned opinion that nothing less will serve us finally in our attention on cinema. It would be foolish to expect a lot of it, for revelation will remain, as ever, a difficult and a rare experience; but consciously or not, we do ask a little of it every so often. Even a medium of professedly popular entertainment cannot quite escape that demand.

'As I understand it, the first job of a critic is to stand as sensory instrument to the world of creation, and register this revelation as it comes along, and point people to it and, it may even be, do something to underline or elucidate it.

'I look to register what actually moves: what hits the spectator at the midriff: what yanks him up by the hair of the head or the plain boot-straps to the plane of decent seeing. I see no reason why, because a film is made for the populace and made for money, we should exempt it from the ordinary duties of art.

'But it is never a question, this criticism, of our seeing all things alike. If I am a Scotsman with an origin in the Black Sabbaths of the North, my judgment is bound to be more hard-bitten and even ruder on certain issues than that of an Englander. But the Englander, on the other hand, will be a far better guide to the metropolitan graces. This sort of thing you must expect with any critic. The asses' ears of particular, and sometimes indefensible, predilection, haunt even the philosopher.

'Cinema is, by permission of our queer lop-sided and undisciplined system of society, a very haphazard affair, the effects and achievements of which are almost always dictated by the mind of the profit-monger. To any body of men interested in the better shaping of the world its influence is a serious matter. By romanticising and dramatising the issues of life, even by choosing the issues it will dramatise, it creates or crystallises the loyalties on which people make their decisions. This, in turn, has a great deal to do with public opinions.

'I do not mean that the critic must examine in every film its social implication or lack of it. It is enough if a critic is conscious of the general question and does his utmost to have the honours of life decently distributed. He has, of course, every opportunity of developing his distinctions. Along come the Russian films with their emphasis not on the personal life but on the mass life, their continuous attempts to dramatise the relation of a man to his community.

'The documentary films at their best may push up similar issues of man and his environment, and often honour the common things of life which are beneath the silly notice of the studios. And as for the ordinary commercial film, it so often hides mere cheap showman's intention behind its excitement and its spectacle, that the critic must stand ready at all times to pass a scalpel (or a dollop of carbolic) over it. I am not sure how much we effect by so doing but there is one consolation. The decent intention is the only one that can be publicised, and even the commercial showmen may yet hear of it.'

F. H.

1 The Logic of Comedy

Chaplin has always been a wayward clown to follow in criticism. One might prove a logic of comedy for Grock, the oldest Fratellini, the Marx Brothers, Laurel and Hardy, and very particularly for Raymond Griffith and Harry Langdon. One has only to begin the task in the case of Chaplin to find his Charlot pirouetting on a left foot round the corner of the Law.

I have heard Griffith and Langdon and Chaplin all discuss the figures they attempted to be and, in the Hollywood I knew, Griffith and Langdon were far from being the lesser figures which the accidents of voice and capital have since made them. They were the real threats to Chaplin's supremacy, for their ideas in comedy were clear. Griffith was fed on Shaw, but had added a certain toughness of his own. The fun he created was the fun of satire, shading between the inconsequential of pure slapstick and the inconsequential which was a fine considered impertinence. It was satire, with a courage of comment which extended strangely to the princes and revolutionaries of Britain, the national and domestic gods of America, the economic considerations behind the Civil War, and laid longing eyes on such sacramental subject matter as the Arctic flights of Byrd and the Big Parade. There was a superb scenario going the rounds by which *Arms and the Man* was transferred to the battlefields of France, and another in which *Androcles and the Lion* was transferred in crazy fashion to the campus of an American University, with cheer leaders for the lions and cheer leaders for the Christians. Neither was made.

Langdon was another mind in comedy altogether. He called his clown the Christian Innocent and was certain in his own head of the texts that fitted it. He wandered pleasantly from picture to picture, braving in perpetual fairy tale, as a child might, the fearful romances of penny banks and Saturday afternoons and colds in the head and women who spoke to him in the street. He survived precipices, tornadoes, and wives, in a fashion which was not so much astonishing as expected, and even by Holy Writ promised to his kind. His very finest was a film called *The Strong Man*, in which, with a faith that was

45

almost historical for Hollywood, Langdon somehow contrived to become the agent of the Lord in shattering the Walls of Jericho and confounding utterly the Wicked within it. He finished up, deservedly, as the village cop.

Chaplin also referred himself to religion. In one discussion with Donald Ogden Stewart, which gives effectively the measure of his comic conception, he upheld the Christian clown very brightly against the clown of the Anti-Christ. The comedy which was rooted in failure was set against the comedy rooted in superiority. Stewart mentioned the moment in *Hands Up*, when Griffith in the course of being hanged by the neck loosed an unforgettable grin on his executioners. Chaplin stood by the Testament, partly in consideration of the fun to be got by inflicting Christian innocents on the world, but more particularly for the tragedy latent in the idea. He was not quite so sure as Langdon that innocence proved its own reward. It could also be inadequacy, and failure, and futility.

But Chaplin has never in his films been quite so simple or straightforward as this. His Charlot is respectability in straits, suburbia in tatters, a *petit-bourgeois* Ulysses against the horizon. He is also at odd moments the complete romantic, the dreamer, the tramp, whose strange Additions are stricken out by the most plain laws of Arithmetic. Or again, he is the corner boy of more proletarian persuasion, with the blackbird cleverness of the gutter in him, a streak of cruelty, and not a little common envy and hatred. These elements, if illassorted, can yet in some measure be held together in the imagination. If the way of the wandering is something of an Odyssey, and the construction is picaresque rather than dramatic, Charlot may at least be as complex in his make-up and as various in his reactions as Poldy Bloom.

Unfortunately, the spirochaete of drama has been operating in Charlot ever since the litterateurs discovered him, and indecently flattered him by their discovery. Chaplin has been searching for rounded stories for his clown; and rounding his stories he has reduced somewhat the high abstraction of his Charlot. For engaging Charlot too intimately in the pursuit of women and wealth, Chaplin is in a fair way to debasing him. The real disappointment about *City Lights* is that the noble tramp we knew has equated our common frustration to the meaner frustrations of sex; and our down-and-out of *Sunnyside* and *The Pilgrim* has sufficiently lost his independence to slobber over a matter of cash.

The central story of *City Lights*, which ought to be the whole story, is on an intimacy between Charlie and a millionaire which persists only when the millionaire is drunk. There is noble fun in the situations it provokes. The kaleidoscopic changes between impossible luxury and the disillusionment of mornings-after are helped out by a musical commentary which is as intelligent as anything in the structure of the film. There is even a *leit-motif* for the laws of arithmetic.

The good life of Charlie and his millionaire is wearily complicated, however, by another story about a blind girl which, in effect, spoils all their fun. Chaplin takes it seriously, and Charlot, under compulsion, takes it so very seriously that he is persuaded to send the blind girl to Vienna and cure her. So in a sad and sorry finale she gazes through her bright new eyes on the man of her dreams: tattered and torn for her, convicted and imprisoned and even shot-at-by-the-peashooters-of-small-boys for her. It is doubtful if at this peak of concentrated and manufactured tragedy Charlot survives. For you may reasonably observe that it is one thing to found comedy on the Christian myth and another thing altogether to compete with it.

It is possible, on a second viewing, to forget the implications of the tale and enjoy the incidental gags for what they are. They are always skilful, and the fine calculation of Chaplin's unmatchable craftsmanship has been written into them. It takes Chaplin to measure the nude detail of a piece of sculpture. But even the lesser moments of liquor swallowings, whistle swallowings and spaghetti swallowings have their little brilliancies of observation. The correction of a wine glass angle when the whole bottle is pouring to perdition, the passing of the public attack of hiccoughs through the stages of apology, misery, desperation and anger: there are a thousand gems of the sort tucked away in corners. Chaplin's hands too, are still unique in pantomime. The mask may have lost some of its quality, but the hands with their little tensions and uncertainties slip through a syllogism as easily as ever. If only Chaplin's story-telling, with its cliché figures and cliché symbolisms, were as delicate!

One sequence of *City Lights* deserves to be recorded separately because it is likely to become as classical a movement in comedy as the starvation sequence in *The Gold Rush*. Boxing scenes have been done a thousand times in slapstick, and Chaplin has appeared in at least two before now. This version is brilliant. It becomes, by an uncanny piling of gag on gag, colossally funny. But it has also the complete rhythm of ballet. Chaplin has always been at his greatest when he approached ballet, and *City Lights*, with its many disappointments, does have its roots in this original power.

*　　*　　*

Chaplin carries in his name so much of the history, tradition and past brilliance of cinema that it is difficult to criticize *Modern Times*. Personal affection is the death of good judgment. Many criticisms of the film have reflected the difficulty.

The theme—in so far as there is a theme—is that our rationalized world is crushing the individual—and that there is no place for a free and lively spirit in the world of machinery, big business and police. Chaplin is as much of a misfit with the workers as he is with the bosses. He fears the workers only a little less than their masters. Positively, there are many superb gags and enough of Chaplin's brilliant dance and mime to make any film distinguished. Negatively, it is disconnected and, in its overtones, sad, sentimental and defeatist.

Chaplin has taken life seriously enough to make an indictment against its present slaveries, and must be judged as seriously as the issue he raises. His sympathies are fiercely against exploitation, but he proves himself the loosest of thinkers. His position is that of the romantic anarchist. His hatred of capitalist machinery and organization gets mixed up with the anarchist's hatred of all machinery and organization together.

It is recognized that the only solution Chaplin could offer is a call to personal bravery. Taking to the high road is as near to suicide of the will as makes no matter.

Funny situations succeed each other and demonstrate great comic invention and execution. They become curiously more depressing as this romantic and trifling issue begins to emerge. Critics have said that Chaplin made the mistake of putting his best laughs in the first part. This is a wrong estimate. The truth is that you cannot laugh very heartily with a corpse in the house. This is not a reflection on the comedy but on the atmosphere. Chaplin himself chose it.

Chaplin's usual collection of stock characters and sentimentalities— the waif held for vagrancy, the dying father, the children begging for bread, the stealing of a loaf—look somewhat mannered. We may endorse his sympathies but not his clichés. His maintenance of pure mime with background music seems equally old-fashioned and uninspired.

Avoiding the possibilities of sound—and there are other possibilities than dialogue—he merely demonstrates that he has lost interest in the technique of his art. He has, under the new régime, discovered nothing and created nothing out of its vitalizing powers. In this, Chaplin proves yet again how near the anarchist may be to the die-hard Tory.

48

Animal Crackers (American, 1931)
  With Harpo Marx. Produced by Paramount: directed by Victor Heerman

City Lights (American, 1931)
  Produced by United Artists: directed by Charles Chaplin

Dead End (American, 1937)
  Produced by United Artists: directed by William Wyler

Stage Coach (American, 1939)
  Produced by United Artists: directed by John Ford

The Logic of Comedy

So, in spite of Chaplin's unique claim to our respect, and the basic genius of his comic figure, *Modern Times* proves to be doubly depressing. In his social statement and in his technical statement he has no progressive sense of belief to offer either his public or himself. He is funny but not gay. When his brilliance should inspire, he only dispirits. Chaplin has failed to bring forward his creative power into these Modern Times. He is out-of-date. Paradoxically, *Charlie at the Rink* and *Charlie the Champion* are as fresh as ever.

*   *   *

I was not in Hollywood when *The Woman of Paris* was made, but I sat around when its successor *The Woman of the Sea* was under way. *The Woman of the Sea* (aliases: *The Sea Gull*, etc., etc.) has become a mysterious item in film history because, immediately after its production, it passed into limbo. By a minor accident I must be one of the few outsiders who ever saw it or can tell the sad, sad story of its demise.

Chaplin wrote the successor to *The Woman of Paris* for Edna Purviance and, as Von Sternberg had just then fallen foul of Metro in the production of *The Exquisite Sinner*, Chaplin gave him the job of directing it. I heard Von Sternberg's idea about the film and I heard Chaplin's, and it was fairly clear that the two minds were as separate as could be.

The story was a real Chaplin story, throwing a contrast between the woman who went from the fishing village to the big city and the woman who stayed at home. Sternberg was not yet the Sternberg of *The Docks of New York*. He was still a bit afraid of actors and actresses, and a trifle young and sentimental about art values. He played the story, not for its humanities, but for all the decorative values he could pull out of nets in the sunshine, waves on the shore, and so forth. It was, in an accurate sense, a rather lovely film.

Then on a pink carpet, I heard Chaplin describe the story as he had intended it to be. Chaplin, who understands decorative values not quite so well as my private jackdaw, laid all the emphasis on those elements which Sternberg had quite strictly missed: the homeliness of a fishing village, the sweat and the smell of a fishing village, the intimacy of one man with another, the accumulation of little intimate things which would make village life seem genuine and human against the abstract relationships of the city. Under the power of his description the carpet went insanely pinker.

Appreciating the Sternberg view, I could still understand fairly well

D   49

why Chaplin did not allow the film to appear. However beautiful, it was not a film that had anything to do with the story he felt, or indeed with any story he could ever feel. Chaplin is above all a humanist. He is not a great film architect, and by no means an exponent of the purely visual values (of design, tempo, etc.) to be obtained in cinema. But he has a power over the significant detail of character and of situation which has to be experienced to be believed. *The Woman of Paris* itself was no great shakes as a story, but it all shakes together as a story well and intimately told. Film characters were at last characters: breathing and distinct: individual to their last braces' button.

René Clair's *Sous les Toits de Paris* does perform a similar sort of miracle. The story is slight and one that would look rather dull if you set it down in print. But you have to see Clair take a monosyllabic *Non* out of a Paris midinette to know what film direction should look like. He likes people, he likes Paris, he likes flirtations on stairs, and whispered requests that receive monosyllabic *Nons* from midinettes. He likes people who sell popular songs and use assembled crowds to stage a bit of honest pocket-picking. He likes the peoples of the cafés, and the garrets, and one-roomed, two-roomed joints in which they live. He likes the glimpses one can get of fat women and thin men and somewhat un-baptist young ladies through skylights and street windows. He likes them all with a gusto which is French, but which is so admirably good-natured and so wisely informed, that what would be given an air of tom-peepery by the average director, has only the genius in observation of a de Maupassant or a Chaplin. 'By a single word, give me to understand wherein one cab horse differs from fifty others before and behind it,' was the test-piece in art set by Flaubert. René Clair can do it.

*   *   *

I am not sure where to place Laurel and Hardy. Indeed I am not sure if they should be placed at all. The case of Chaplin is a warning. The pundits have had their will of him, and his comedy has distressed itself with the responsibilities they have laid upon it. It would be a pity if critical analysis spoiled yet another gift of honest slapstick.

But the higher comedy is important stuff and is worth distinguishing. When comedy is merely a matter of artificial situation and expert gags, as in the case of Harold Lloyd and, to some extent, in the case of Buster Keaton, you laugh and are done with it. They are clever fellows to work their way through such amusing scrapes, but they mean no more. Keaton shows admirably the distinction between the higher and the lower comedy. His mask is a very significant thing with its dumb registration of things felt. It might pass through life registering a heap of things most deeply felt. But it does not. In every Keaton story the action whoops in reel five to allow Buster Keaton the clown to become Mr. Keaton the romantic achiever of all things, and the fun of his face sums up nothing but a temporary pretence.

Clowns are the world's incompetents. They are bound to the wheel of incompetence or they cease to be clowns.

Chaplin once, in *The Gold Rush*, broke the underlying significance of his role and spoiled a great film. He forgot Charlot the outcast to become a millionaire and marry the girl, like any John Gilbert or Ronald Colman. Clowns cannot possibly stoop to such romance. They are, in essence, super realists: that is to say, they are tragedians in disguise. Their endings are happy for everybody but themselves.

Chaplin's ancient endings were true clown endings, when he walked down an endless road in *Sunnyside*, and planted impossibly endless fields in *A Dog's Life*, and straddled the hopeless boundary of slavery and death in *Pay Day*. My point is that clowning, when it passes beyond the naïvetés of the fun of the fair, becomes an infernal responsibility to its practitioners. It becomes an art, subject to discipline, subject I am afraid to idea. Anyone can be foolish. The test of your great clown is whether, with all his fooling, he means something.

Laurel, as you know, is a quiet man and Hardy a robust and fat one. They are famous for the world they tumble about them. They have but to touch the garden gate and it collapses in ruins before their eyes. Do what they will, the bricks of their houses dislodge on their inoffensive and embarrassed heads, the water-butt leaps up to meet them, the window slams on their fingers. It is no wonder if sometimes in desperation they give up the impossible task of staving off chaos and, in an orgy of destruction, welcome it.

They are perhaps the Civil Servants of comedy. Nothing on earth would please them better than a quiet permanence in all things. The garden gate, the water-butt, and the window smooth on its roller, are their symbols of ease.

Laughing Gravy starts with a hiccup in the middle of the night. They are disturbed by it, disturbed by the hiccup itself, disturbed by the fact that it will wake the landlord. They represent the vast multitude in this world who worry about hiccups and about landlords.

The hiccup goes on its way. It wakes the dog and the dog most certainly wakes the landlord. The landlord, who has forbidden dogs, throws the dog into the snow. Laurel and Hardy, boobs that they are, pity it. Hardy goes in his nightshirt to bring it back, and the door, of course, slams behind him. He tries to get back in a knotted sheet and it drops him in yet another water-butt. He splashes the icy water in futile fury. He is definitely not one of the innocents whom angels guard. Few are.

So from step to step, in the simple continuity of an ordinary suburban night, one destruction follows another. They wash the dog furtively to wake no one, and spill the water and drop the bath to wake everyone. The landlord, maddening under the strain, breaks down his own precious door and smashes his own precious window. By the end, suburbia is in tatters.

Yet through it all there remains the curious continuity of two figures, one thin and one fat, which deplore the disturbance they are creating. They hate it, and would avoid it if they could. They are men of peace. But in this case the meek are not blessed. They do not inherit the earth. They inherit chaos. Chaos most active and violent and diabolical takes advantage of their inhibitions.

I find Hardy an improving clown. His gestures grow large. He begins to appeal hopelessly to his audience in the classical fashion of clowns. He begins to demonstrate a large and splendid selection of angers and petulances. He was once the minor partner, but now looks like becoming the major one.

Laurel improves into blankness. He can do nothing right and never will. Hardy, with a fine optimism, will try and fail. Laurel, poor devil, knows he has failed before he tries.

There is no wonder the life they lead goes to the heart of the multitude. A few million commuters in London alone will find good reason to laugh at them. There is not a gag of suburban fear and suburban futility in Laurel and Hardy they will not appreciate.

*   *   *

The quintessential virtue of buffoonery is discovered in the hangover. The merely funny causes its eruption of belly-laugh and is soon done: the larger idiocy engages the conscience. It is a head laugh and invokes a certain subconscious pondering. In it—the pundit Kant would say—the Imagination is related to the Faculty of Ideas, under a subjective presupposition of the Moral Feeling in Man. This arduously but more authoritatively means the same thing. There is a hangover. Of associations and appreciations which are a trifle profound.

The Logic of Comedy

I believe the philosophical explanation of it is that your born buffoon plays old Harry with the categories of reciprocity. They are the local daemons who preside over all habitation of the flesh: the laws of sense, the laws of consequence, the laws of fol-di-rol and fol-di-ree and other formulae of Philistia. You cannot bust them, but so blessed is the mind of man, that you can conceive of busting them. Your buffoon urges your fancy to an impossible emancipation, and this is your only clue in life for a really good laugh. You are kidding yourself to death.

In fact, you are quite literally kidding yourself to death, for obviously if such emancipation were realized you would perish: if, like Langdon, you jumped over a precipice and trusted the gods; if, like Chaplin, you set forth into the Arctic with an N.S.E.W. scribbled on a hunk of paper; if, like the oldest of the Fratellinis, you did not appreciate the difference between your shadow and your enemy. If, to put it very plainly, you hated your physical company so far as to will its destruction. The eldest Fratellini fights with his shadow fiercely, and screams, with possibly a note of agony. It is very funny as you see it, but something more.

I introduce this dissertation as a species of advance applause for the Three Marx Brothers, late of *The Coconuts* and now of *Animal Crackers*. They are great clowns, and may yet, like Grock, Chaplin and the Fratellini, become historical ones. If, that is to say, the commercial cinema permits them to polish their roles, and refine the Idea that is in them. It is, I admit, a good deal to ask of an institution which has destroyed Langdon and cast away Raymond Griffith. What rare and noble clowns these two might have been!

As it is, the Marx Brothers are a howling success. Their roles and methods are similar to the ones they took in *The Coconuts*, but I fancy somewhat developed. Groucho, the talker, plays fast and loose with every conversational convention there is: puns outrageously, but makes speeches which get brilliantly nowhere; destroys every continuity of expression or thought presented to him; and insults his polite listeners to the rollicking satisfaction of every suppressed desire in the bosom of man.

Chico, the Wop, is the villain as before, a dark scheming villain bubbling over with joy for the infinite desire of villainy within him. 'I don't want you to steal it,' says the girl. 'Then I can't take it,' says Chico. And certainly he can't. It must be villainy or nothing. He is an Iago, a bare-faced Iago, with the ambition in villainy of Macbeth—blessedly disproportioned to all possible existence.

But Harpo, the dumb member, is the greatest emancipator of all. His

53

capacity for pocket-picking is prodigious in its skill; his capacity at cheating at cards is prodigious in its nakedness; and to this he attaches the bright-eyed devilry of a mischievous child. The first two, by the extravagance of their emancipation, are absurd. Harpo, however, achieves the complete syllogism of emancipation. He is also insane. Capable, as it turns out, of most cheerfully murdering the entire cast, friend and foe alike, and himself into the bargain.

That, I submit, in all psychology, is a clown equipment which is more fascinating in its fact than in its possibility than any we have seen since Chaplin. If I understand Chaplin aright he takes comedy to the point of tragedy by reminding one that the little man, the *homme moyen*, who so brilliantly succeeds against odds, can only impossibly do so. Harpo comes near to proving, as Prince Myshkin did before him, that the place for all fun (as for all innocence), when it grows really prodigious, is a booby-hatch.

Animal Crackers is of course not an exercise in the logic of comedy. There are a few perfect examples like Langdon's *Saturday Afternoon* and *The Strong Man*, Grock's act, and Chaplin's *Pay Day* and *The Pilgrim*, but, as a rule, the logic gets lost in other matters and the presentation of the idea is incomplete. So there are some dud leads in *Animal Crackers*. Harpo, for instance, should not interpolate a serious harp solo, even if it happens to be a good one; and Chico should carry his villainy quite completely into his piano work. In *Animal Crackers* there is a beginning to that, but no doubt it will go further. Groucho, too, should be tireless in his talking, to the last bell. He is not.

The one supreme moment to record is the last one. There is a nymph whom Harpo has been pursuing like any satyr throughout the film. In the last bright murderous scene he hunts among his victims till he finds her, arranges himself appropriately and with the final and complete satisfaction of absolute lunacy gives himself the necessary knock-out. It is the prettiest happy ending since Langdon, the Cop and Hero, stumbled and was led forth on patrol by the blind girl.

*   *   *

The Marx Brothers have a sense of continuity in their comedy. From *Coconuts* and *Animal Crackers*, the Brothers graduate into *Monkey Business*. They insist on the jungle. This, of course, is very right of them. They are wild men, who, if they did not find a jungle ready to hand, would certainly invent one.

It is, I take it, the particular function of comedy to destroy the more trifling dignities of this earth: quality varies with the shape and size of the dignities it destroys. Pantomime goes with a whack to the seat of the pants; slapstick goes with peel or pie to any section of the anatomy which presents itself; Shaw, a Mack Sennett of the Parlour, trips up the prejudices. The quality deepens till, in Swift, you tumble up the human race itself. In this event, the laughter of mankind at its own sorry self is liable to echo down a couple of centuries.

The Marx Brothers are moderately solid clowns. They have the single weakness of taking their music seriously. Chico the Wop is liable to pursue his piano keys as if he really meant them. Harpo the Lunatic slips back miserably into sanity when he addresses the harp. But, taking the Brothers all in all, they do get through a large amount of necessary destruction. They are guerrilla warriors and lack the more solid sense of artists like Chaplin, but they are smart around the rocks.

In *The Coconuts* they turned the respectable Rotarian state of Florida into the sports ground of a booby-hatch, and very little was left of its vaunted climate and real estate when they had passed through it. In *Animal Crackers* they proceeded to the palatial interiors of Long Island. In *Monkey Business* they arrive as stowaways to devastate an Atlantic liner. There is a story somewhere of a gangster feud and an ocean romance, but since it is the job of a Marx Brother to destroy all such evidence of social equilibrium, you will catch only passing glimpses of either. The rest is anarchy.

Groucho attends, as usual, to the verbal continuities of life. He eliminates them, and, of course, talks incessantly. He sees to it that no idea gets anywhere, or, if somewhere, that its final destination will be of the maximum unimportance to the human race. In this Groucho brings to cinema America's strange genius for nonsense. He belongs to the tradition which has produced Bugs Baer and Ted Cook among the columnists, Robert Benchley and Donald Ogden Stewart among the writers. But there are a thousand exponents of varying talent in and around the newspapers, magazines and music-halls. They represent together a brilliance of idiocy which is quite easily America's most civilized contribution to this section of the century. The only weakness of it is that it is frothy stuff. This may be due to a national mind which has not yet got down to the job of social criticism. It is in its first fine youthful stage of making fun of anything and everything, quite indiscriminately. Stewart once confessed to me that his *Crazy Fool* was as good as *Candide*, and he spoke in good faith. The difference, of course, is in the skittles they skittle. Voltaire went for Leibnitz. *The*

Crazy Fool just failed in the bubbling of its enthusiasm to go for Big Business.

Poor old Groucho's chief distinction is that he is the world's best murderer of party manners.

Chico the Wop is, unfortunately, not quite so much in evidence in *Monkey Business*. There was a certain desperate villainy in him in *Animal Crackers* of which one hoped all things. He had all the makings of a comic Ishmael. One could conceive of him harbouring deep and dire stratagems for seizing this Atlantic liner, or firing it, or scuttling it. No such deep stratagems are given to him.

The largest part of the Marxian effort comes, of course, from the Brother Harpo. He is Mad Hatter altogether, with fairy tale in him. The others, for all their craziness, belong to this world. Harpo, in some fashion best understood by children and their fellow-innocents, belongs to another. It is difficult to separate him from the gang, but I find him individually the most considerable clown, apart from Chaplin, in the whole of cinema. There are patches of him in *Monkey Business* of a brilliance which not even Chaplin has touched since *The Gold Rush*. He is, like Chaplin, silent. Like Chaplin he has a capacity for sudden mad bursts of comedy. The classical example is the pillow scene in *The Gold Rush*, but Harpo's whoopee with the passports is not a bit inferior.

Such moments belong exclusively to the great clowns. I can think only of Chaplin and Grock and the Fratellini and Herb Williams as having the power of them. I commend you in this regard to an examination of Harpo's invasion of the Punch and Judy Show in *Monkey Business*. Like the best of Chaplin, it climbs in comedy, till, in a last crazy shot, it goes out of sight altogether. The last crazy shot in question is of Harpo disappearing on a scooter like some fairy figure from Grimm's.

It is best to be doubtful always of where the screen's comedians will take us. There is something in the mechanics of the business—Box Office Control and Committee Production—which destroys the good things cinema creates. In cinema the geese that lay the golden eggs are quite invariably done to death in the name of scientific and mass production. Other clowns have shown similar powers and have gone in a year or two in oblivion. The history of cinema is full of ideas and roles well started, which have been lost in the day-to-day whimmery of cheap showmen. Chaplin is unique. He has had the capital power, as well as the ability, to develop his role.

The Marx Brothers, to judge from a music-hall appearance, are powerless by themselves. They need not only the capital for production but also a director who will stay with them and bring the idea that is in them to greater power and point. But whether any commercial company is capable of seeing to this, I doubt. Comedy when it begins to be really good, is, like tragedy, too large an affair altogether for the commercial conditions which determine the film business.

*　　*　　*

The best of the week is Buster Keaton's *Passionate Plumber*. Jimmy Durante, the Schnozzle of ferocious sighs and four-syllabled excitements, is with him. The film adds little to the Keaton myth, but it is a good hour's fooling. The virtue of Keaton is that while he does not reach for the more cosmic honours of clowning, he is never feeble. I hear the world about me complain for the days when the frozen-faced comedian was silent. They speak of the mask which was essentially of silence, of the greater courage and more desperate self-discipline which that mask implied. I am afraid you will see little of this in *The Passionate Plumber*. It is another loss you must put down to the talkies.

In the silent days every comedy had to be a comedy of situation. The visual emphasis of the medium made action and event necessary for any considerable effect. Verbal play, however snappy, is no equivalent. It may get the laughs as they say, but this arithmetical computation of laughter is a poor guide to fun. It is one of the fallacies of the commercial philosophy, that 'they count 'em'. The tragedy in this case is that Keaton had once a reputation for greatness. Now, when situation has been buried alive in wisecracks, he is merely another good comedian.

Here I should record a question asked me recently by Alfred Hitchcock. 'Is cinema, then, so much a matter of violence?' For the argument in which it was put, I answered 'Yes'. Hitchcock went on to say that once he believed there was nothing in the novel which cinema could not do: the continuity of story, the description of character, the atmosphere behind, and the leisurely commentary on all three. He had come to doubt it. Those of you who have followed Hitchcock's work will appreciate the significance of both the question and the explanation. They explain a great deal, if not all, of that skilful but sometimes ineffective meandering which has unspeeded so many of his films.

Hitchcock asked his question rhetorically, with the air of one who for a year or two had been making a slow and bitter discovery. Action, of course, is the ultimate material in cinema. The first movies were introduced to the pavement crowds with the stentorian cry of 'They

57

move, they move.' We forget that original truth periodically and always come back to the rediscovery of it. We have rediscovered it with the Westerns, with the epics, with the *Vaudevilles* and the *Potemkins*; and we are rediscovering it now with the Disneys. Always it is the same old story of visible event: in a new guise and in response to a new deadening influence. Of which, as you can imagine, the talkies with their everlasting verbal flipflap, are the most deadening of all. The great pity is that comedy, which was once in slapstick so much a matter of movement, has been tempted more than any other genre. It was more than any other vulnerable to the specious attraction of the wisecrack: and the wisecrack is smothering it.

I hope I do not muddle the issue by talking in the same breath of violence, movement and situation. I only mean that cinema with its capacity for event should keep things happening: pulling its tension in drama from the violence (and in complement, from the suspense) of happening. The recommendation of Aristotle was that action comes first and the characters after. 'The end aimed at in drama is the representation not of qualities of character, but of some action.' The distinction will serve even better for cinema. If we try, either in Hitchcock incident or in Hollywood verbalism, to emphasize the mere detail, the unity and the drive of event which make a film important are being destroyed. And masks, the greatest of all the gifts of the silent comedy, are become mere faces again.

2 Directors of the Thirties

Joe Sternberg is one of the few directors whose every work one sees as a matter of course. He stepped rather suddenly into the film world in 1925 with a film called *The Salvation Hunters*, which he had financed with his last five thousand dollars. He has been interesting ever since. *The Salvation Hunters* was a young man's gamble. His stars were taken from the ranks of Poverty Row extras; his story was right outside the Hollywood tradition. It was a sad romantic affair of how a young man tried to escape from the dreary existence of a dredger. The dredger with its slime was, of course, symbolic. The ending, with its two young lovers moving off into the rising sun, was equally symbolic. Sternberg began with a great hankering for good things.

The simple, rather naïve and sentimental idealism of that first effort should be remembered when *Shanghai Express* is considered. Dietrich stars. Like that exotic and meaningless lady herself, the film is a masterpiece of the toilette. That only. Its photography is astonishing; its sets are expensive and detailed to an ingenious and extravagant degree; its technique in dissolve and continuity is unique. The film might be seen for its good looks alone. But it is cold-bloodedly lacking in every virtue which made Sternberg a lad of promise.

A great deal must have happened over the years to turn the simple romanticist into this sophisticated purveyor of the meretricious Dietrich. I wish I knew what it was. I knew Sternberg just after his *Salvation Hunters* and liked him immensely. He had made a fine picture for Metro called *The Exquisite Sinner*, and had been heaved off the pay roll for adding some genuine local colour to a Breton scene.

It struck me that sensibility of his peculiarly intensive and introspective sort was not a very healthy equipment for a hard world, and, in face of his strange progress, I am sure I was right. There is, as you can imagine, no place for the introspectionist in a commercial film world which is as objective in its conceptions as in its accounts. A director of this instinct is bound to have a solitary and (as commerce goes) an unsuccessful life of it. Sternberg, I think, was weak. Hating the notion of this commercial unsuccess, he has thrown his sensibility to the winds and accepted the hokum of his masters. His aesthetic conscience is now devoted to making the hokum as good-looking as possible. It is, indeed, almost pathologically good-looking, as by one whose conscience is stricken.

I detail this Sternberg saga because it tells more clearly than any personal story I know how even great spirits may fail in film. The temptation of commercial success is a rather damnable one. There are dollars past dreaming and power and publicity to satisfy every vanity, for anyone who will mesmerize the hicks of the world.

I watched Sternberg make still another picture, *The Woman of the Sea*, for Chaplin. The story was Chaplin's, and humanist to a degree: with fishermen that toiled, and sweated, and lived and loved as proletarians do. Introspective as before, Sternberg could not see it like Chaplin. Instead, he played with the symbolism of the sea till the fishermen and the fish were forgotten. It would have meant something just as fine in its different way as Chaplin's version, but he went on to doubt himself. He wanted to be a success, and here plainly and pessimistically was the one way to be unsuccessful. The film as a result was neither Chaplin's version nor Sternberg's. It was a strangely beautiful and empty affair—possibly the most beautiful I have ever seen—of net patterns, sea patterns and hair in the wind. When a director dies, he becomes a photographer.

Something of strength is missing in Sternberg's creative make-up. If one cannot by taking thought add a cubit to one's stature, one can no more by great gifts of photography add power to a feeble story. All Sternberg's stories seem to fade off into almost pathetic unimportance. There is, I think, no doubt that he makes his own choice, for almost always the central character is a figure who, like Jannings in *The Blue Angel*, and Esther Ralston in *Lena Smith*, has been specially wronged by the world. This affection for the outcast is the trade-mark of Sternberg's cinema. But, except in the *Lena Smith* case, the personal tragedy is always somehow too adventitious for the greatest effect. It is felt sympathetically, but not built into that world of accepted fact which alone can make tragedy real. Jannings, in *The Blue Angel*, was an old fool of a professor whose physical inhibitions overcame him when honest men are in dignity digging their graves. Dietrich, in *Shanghai Express*, is a lady of the very slimmest social justification.

I always regard Sternberg as the most Jewish of directors. 'The Jew is either at your throat or at your feet.' It is a distinction those who know Jews in the world of art can readily appreciate. More objective than most, they can be more subjective than most. Sternberg is a curious combination of the extremes. I have known him, I think, personally, and a man of finer sensibility I never met. But this side of him mingles strangely with a colossal respect for the more ordinary grandeur of the world. The combination explains *Shanghai Express*. Vast settings are there most splendidly produced, and Dietrich is at the centre of them, an outcast after the Sternberg heart, seeking your sympathy. It is doubtful, however, if you feel her case very directly. When cases are serious, an advocate should be simple. Sternberg is too successful and, I am afraid, too pretentious a director to be simple.

With *Shanghai Express* Joe Sternberg has become the great Josef von Sternberg, having given up the struggle for good : a director so successful that even Adolf Zukor is pleased to hold his hand for a brief condescending moment. He has made films with Jannings and George Bancroft : *Paying the Penalty, Docks of New York*, others of equally exquisite hokum; and Paramount has blessed his name for the money they made. Once from the top of the tree he made a last desperate gesture to his past in *The Case of Lena Smith*, a fine film which failed; but that is now forgotten and there will never be a repetition. He has found Dietrich and is safe for more dollars, more power, more success than ever. What irresolute director would not launch a thousand cameras for Dietrich, giving up hope of salvation hereafter? Sternberg has. He has the 'Von' and the little warm thankful hand of Adolf Zukor for his pains.

Shanghai Express follows the progress of a train from Peking to Shanghai, finding its story among the passengers as *The Blue Express* did. Dietrich is Shanghai Lily, a lady of no reputation. Clive Brook is an old lover meeting her again; hating her past, but still very much in love with her. They fall into the hands of Chinese revolutionaries and Dietrich saves Clive, and Clive saves Dietrich; and in that last mutual service the dust is shaken out of the Lily's petals and the doubter damns himself for having doubted. This high argument is staged with stupendous care, stupendous skill, and with an air of most stupendous importance.

I remember one shot of the Shanghai express pulling into a wayside station in the early evening. It is one of the half-dozen greatest shots ever taken, and I would see the film for that alone. It is, however, the only noble moment in the film. The scenes of Chinese life are massive, painstaking to the point of genius in their sense of detail and presented very pleasantly in dissolve; the minor acting fine; but the rest is Dietrich. She is shown in seven thousand and one poses, each of them photographed magnificently. For me, seven thousand poses of Dietrich (or seventy) are Dietrich *ad nauseam*. Her pose of mystery I find too studied, her make-up too artificial, her every gesture and word too deliberate for any issue in drama save the very gravest. Sternberg perhaps is still after that ancient intensity. When themes are thin it is a hankering that can bring one very close to the ridiculous.

*   *   *

Eric von Stroheim is the crazy man of the film world. He cut *Greed* to sixty reels and defied Hollywood to make it less, at which they sacked him and hired an infidel to bring it down to a humble ten. They are always sacking von Stroheim. The infidel cut and cut and gave up at twenty-five, and, when he too was fired, explained that Stroheim's sixty was a masterpiece, anyway.

Of course, Hollywood respected von Stroheim for his stand at sixty. Anyone who will threaten to entertain you for twelve hours on end is plainly in the grand manner. They gave him yet another and yet another film to do. Each time the story has been the same. Stroheim has gone whoopee and shot to the moon, and found himself unemployed before the picture hit the headlines.

He paid himself into the *première* of his own *Merry Widow*, though *The Merry Widow* went on to make a fortune. *The Wedding March* which followed became one of those traditional productions, which company after company fail on. It soared into the millions. I saw great slices of it shot and great hunks of financiers' hair torn from the roots in the process. But not a frame of what I saw appeared in the final version. When Paramount bought and finished the film, Stroheim was on the outside as before.

Yet for most of us von Stroheim is the director of all directors, and I think largely because of this superlative disregard for the financiers who back him. If he feels like shooting, he shoots, and damns the pennies. If he wants one last detail on a set, he will hold up the world at a thousand dollars per tick to get it. If the gesture of a single tenth-rate extra is to be perfected, he will rehearse it for a couple of hours and hold every star in the cast waiting till it is done. The public issue of the film means nothing to him in comparison with its issue of craftsmanship.

The principals in the desert scene of *Greed* he put into hospital by actually shooting the scene in Death Valley and sweating them under the Californian sun till they achieved the realism he wanted. That sort of thing does not, I know, prove him a great artist, but it does demonstrate a virtue which is necessary in some measure to every director. Surrounded by a thousand technicians and a thousand interests which conflict with this job of pure creation, a director has to have something of Lenin in him to come through. Strangely enough, there is not an artist who ever appeared under him who will hear a word against von Stroheim. In a world of commercial flip-flap he does stand so surely for the larger intensities of art.

The Lost Squadron uses him as an actor only, in yet another of those sinister Teutonic roles he made famous. The interesting point is that he is cast as the crazy film director he is supposed to be: with such a passion for realism that he pours acid on control wires and sacrifices the lives of his stunt airmen for a movie effect.

This sort of thing, of course, is not quite the measure of von Stroheim the director; for if he did smash things to pieces to get his stuff, be sure he took the biggest wallop himself.

Just for a minute, however, you do get something like a genuine picture of the man: when, standing dreadfully erect before the set, he screams 'Cameras!'. I have seen him do that with very similar passion and I have seen him go off the hoop as he does subsequently, and be very much the blood-curdling creature of temperament he demonstrates. It is worth seeing. He is the villain of the piece in this case, but you may believe with me that a single gesture of such villainy is worth a great deal of more flat-footed orthodoxy. 'What are a few deaths to the art of Benvenuto?'

*   *   *

The case of William Wyler is a rather curious one. He is an odd member of the Laemmle tribe: origin Swiss; and, like every other member of the tribe across the world, he has answered the tocsin of Uncle Carl and joined the family at Universal City. But there must be something in the Laemmle blood, because Wyler has taken a line of his own. He is very nearly the most serious of Hollywood's directors, and almost certainly the best poet. I have a notion he will become the director we once expected Vidor to be. Like Vidor he wanders in strange country but, unlike Vidor, he has the courage of it.

Hell's Heroes, a film of the early thirties, told the queer story of three bad hombres who sacrificed their lives to deliver a child to a frontier town, and Wyler directed it magnificently. With its perverse parallel to the tale of the Three Wise Men, the delivery of the child on Christmas Day, and the last man falling dead as the local choir broke into the carol of 'Holy Night', the story itself missed hokum by a hairbreadth. Only a director of unusual ability could have steered it past into genuine emotion.

In *A House Divided*, Wyler lives dangerously again. Here, the story concerns the father and son theme which Eugene O'Neill made great in *Desire under the Elms* and Douglas in *The House with the Green Shutters*. In this case the son is weak and the father is strong, the father takes a new wife, and wife and son fall in love with each other. The story is set against a background of sea. Walter Huston plays the father.

I saw Huston play the father role in the New York Theatre Guild's production of *Desire Under the Elms*. He played it for the great and intense thing it is, and caught the Calvinist passion of the role with a certainty that seemed a trifle bewildering in the atmosphere of Metropolitan America. When Calvinism has disappeared from its own country, dare one expect to find it honoured among the Philistines? But if that was strange, it is stranger still to find the outlook and the issue reappearing in a Hollywood film.

I am all for this William Wyler; he has a taste for the greater gestures and is still steering them past the hokum they so easily invoke. It is difficult to stage a tough old warrior of the Calvinist school, and achieve sympathy for him. If there is kindness in him, he would not show it; and 90 per cent of the slovenly little humanities which people expect will wither under his discipline. But Wyler and Huston put him over. It is not often that the ancient virtue of pity and terror creeps into a film. Here it does.

*   *   *

Cecil B. de Mille is the sort of prophet who has honour in his own country. He has been an enormous success ever since that first bright moment in his cinema career when, pressed for an alibi for some unusual photography, he invented the term 'Rembrandt lighting'. He got away with that one and, for that matter, has got away with most things since. After Rembrandt it was Moses and *The Ten Commandments*; after Moses it was a certain carpenter of Nazareth in *The King of Kings*.

De Mille is a showman in the grand manner. He shrinks at nothing —at no importance, at no dramatic issue either side of the Styx—in his passionate ambition to tell the world about something or other. He loves size, and the bigger his subject the greater the gusto in putting it

Directors of the Thirties

over. The birth of Israel, the birth of Christianity, the birth of Soviet Russia (in *Volga Volga*): come as large as they like, de Mille will spit on his hands and make a rollicking showman's job of them. He is the Jack the Giant Killer of the cinema world and, like his original, he works by guile. He reduces everything he handles to the same good old melodramatic formula—Pleasures, Passions, and the Price to Pay. And no matter what it is—the story of Moses, the story of Mary Magdalene or the story of the Revolution—having once lured them on to that beanstalk, he slays them easily.

The latest in Pleasures, Passions and the Price to Pay is *Dynamite*. I enjoyed this film but I would not happily see it twice. De Mille is so good a craftsman that he is always worth watching, and his slightly Hebraic sense of splendour is always inclined to be vivid. There is no bathroom like a Cecil de Mille bathroom. His plumbing, as a New York newspaperman once reported of the new seventeen million dollar Paramount Theatre, is palatial. All technicians of the ball and plug trade will please note.

This *Dynamite* film covers a heap of territory. It has (1) a prison with prisoner awaiting execution, (2) a high society lady in her high society world with (*a*) a swimming-pool and bathing belles, (*b*) a battalion of female archers, (*c*) a regiment of Aero Wheel racers, (*d*) a bemillioned interior with cocktail bar, cocktail party, petting party, bathroom and other offices complete. The society lady married the murderer to get the cash on grandpapa's will. Last-minute confession scene. Murderer (incidentally miner) gets off. Story spreads via super-chromo'd ten-cylinder to mining town. Three shots to do justice to the proletarian world of coal, all three of them bad; but for makeweight a speech by hero about coal turning to diamonds in so many million years. Cecil B. de Mille records the fact proudly. It brings him closer to his subject so to speak, and the tale proceeds, as you guessed, to a grand old explosion among the future diamonds. The third party to be eliminated (Conrad Nagel as the Price to Pay) is thereby eliminated, the high society lady loves her labourer, and capital and the proletariat go into a personal fade-out.

The crazy thing about all this is that it takes you everywhere and gets you nowhere. You have a great deal of life under observation but see nothing graciously and nothing well. De Mille is careful to make his miner despise the social luxury, but the terms are not real. Nothing is real, not even the miners. They have explosions, they disappear on impressive rescuing expeditions, but not a brass scuttleful of coal is heaved during the entire proceedings. Nothing ordinary is worth a

E   65

foot of film for de Mille—only the murders and the confessions and the cocktail parties and the dying children and the explosions among future diamonds. And let him do these things ever so well, as he often does, unreality is in their bones from the beginning.

* * *

It is a long time since I had so brave and powerful a film as *Kameradschaft* to write about. We scribblers on cinema wander about for the most part making the best of second-class jobs. Some are slick, some are able, some are good fun. We whoop them up in criticism rather desperately. We know that the only thing that matters is evidence of a fine purpose and a great imagination; it is the single and only measuring stick of painting and sculpture and the other arts. But what can we do? Cinema is a popular medium and one of the incomprehensible heresies of our social order is that the old *vox populi* is the voice of a second-rate god. The big ones come seldom.

I hate to do it, but I must lean out from the pulpit in this way to get *Kameradschaft* into its proper category. I do not think it is a world shaker; it is not as big in size as *Storm over Asia,* or as important among the classics as *Turksib,* or as fine in its quality as *Earth,* but it does belong to the greater company.

First, for its theme. It tells how disaster comes to the miners on the French side of the Franco-German frontier and how, in the shadow of that disaster, national distinctions are wiped out, and frontiers are broken down, in the common effort to save the men entombed. The theme has size. It reaches out from the usual smaller issues to a larger one in which the lives of men and women and families and villages and nations are given dramatic substance. Drama ripples out from the exploding pit in sea circles. That is what the dropping of a great theme into a slice of life must inevitably do.

Pabst, who made the film, is a very able director. He can manage crowds with grandeur and hold the difficult details of half a dozen stories and sub-stories in the pester and movement of his crowds; and he can keep his thematic emphasis through the lot. But I have one objection to his work. He is sentimental, as every Teuton (except possibly Bach and Heine and Frederick the Great) has been before him. He cannot leave his theme be. Here you will find the point about brotherhood emphasized far too much. The frontiers are broken down too much; the contrast of the war is played too much; the symbolic hand-clasp is held for exactly four seconds too long. You will hear that the brotherhood of workers is greater than the brotherhood of nationals. You will hear a lot about that and so far so good. You may ask yourself logically at that point what they are being brothers about. If they are uniting, what are they uniting for, and what against? Pabst will not tell you. The film finishes (as significantly for director Pabst as for Franco-German relations) in the re-establishing of the frontier barrier that was broken down so magnificently four reels before.

Looked at in this way, he has merely told us splendidly that when men are dying there is no nationality. But we know that already: even, curiously enough, in the war. One of my strongest recollections is of a ship shot to pieces by a submarine and a wounded crew bound up by the submarine commander himself. Perhaps you want international sentiment to develop a little further. Perhaps, in Marxian fashion, you would prefer an economic basis for the development, and good solid machinery to establish it. Pabst, I am afraid, takes us no further than the submarine commander.

You must see *Kameradschaft*. It is the grandest story of international bandaging ever made. It will bring tears to your eyes and honour to your bosom. You will like the men and women (fine people all of them) who mill and mass and struggle through breaking props and piling gases to give body and bravery to the film. You will salute a thousand well-turned episodes and a thousand really noble photographies. And you will realize at the end that this Pabst is a great director and *Kameradschaft* a great film. I merely emphasize the other aspect in case Socialists of more sentimental persuasion find their internationalist conscience satisfied by it. They are, often, so easily served!

If you answer me and say that this international bandaging is all one can expect from a film, I shall probably agree with you. Even as it stands *Kameradschaft* is superb propaganda for international understanding. No one can see it without realizing the futility of frontiers and the common aspirations of common people the world over. Perhaps, after all, the further move is not with the film-makers but with the politicians. Let Pabst and the film directors do the sentiment and the politicians the organizing. . . . If only the politicians would do the organizing!

*　　*　　*

On a swift generalization, it is remarkable how Fritz Lang's instinct runs to bigger ideas than any other director; but it is just as remarkable how little he ever makes of them. *M* is in the grandiose manner Lang established in such films as *Metropolis*. Its theme is taken from the Dusseldorf murders. Its hero is a sex pervert who murders little girls.

By its subject-matter the film is unusual in all conscience, but I doubt if, on examination, it proves to be anything more than a plain thriller. Lang's photography is always excellent, of course, and his description of a mood or situation can often be brilliantly brief. In this example the murder of one child is followed in the adventures of a toy balloon; and the approaching, growing and finally commanding mania of the murder is translated in the simple whistling of a motif from Grieg. But, if we look behind to the theme itself, we find that Lang's inspiration is only second-rate.

Metropolis, for all its pretension of setting and high flying issue between capital and labour, concluded sillily and sentimentally that 'it was love that made the world go round'. As H. G. Wells pointed out at the time, it was an infant conception without knowledge of society or science. Lang, I think, only ever peeps into the great problems. Looking into the hinterlands of space and time and the mind itself—in *The Girl in the Moon*, in *Metropolis*, in *Mabuse*, and in *M*—he is satisfied in the end with the honours of melodrama.

The concluding scene of *M* is in the basement of an old battered distillery. The murderer has been run down, not by the police but by the thieves of the town, who find that the now desperate activities of the law are spoiling their business. To effect his running down, the thieves have organized the city beggars to watch every quarter, every street and every section of a street. But with the murderer crushed and cringing before the underworld, the whole drama is climaxed in a trial scene in which thief and pervert argue the relative merits of their case. It is a fantastic way of bringing so derelict a spirit as the Dusseldorf murderer into the realms of sympathy, but obviously not a tragic way.

It may possibly be asked if the whole idea of the film is not a little perverse: if anything is to be gained by creating sympathy for such a character. The test is always in the telling. Whatever the derelict—a creature of jealousy like Othello, or ambition like Macbeth, or of madness like this man from Dusseldorf—it makes no odds in theory to the writer of tragedy. As a human figure, both possible in fact and relatable in fact to the warring issues of existence, he can be brought to sympathy and made an instrument of great appreciation and great art. The sociological argument is beside the point. If he must be kicked from the social midst—hung, imprisoned, or shut in a padded cell—the sociologist may be done with him. The artist is not. By that very fate he becomes for the tragedian the broken, incomplete figure of man who gives him his occasion and his opportunity.

When Peter Lorre, who plays the murderer, screams out 'I couldn't help it!' you will probably be moved. That is the centre of the piece, the theme itself; terrifying and, in the usual curious way, uplifting. But in that poignant moment one appreciates all the more the opportunity that has been lost. If this was the story, if this possession by devils and most foul destruction by devils was the story, the film's theatrical excursions into underworld organization, housebreaking and the like are irrelevant. Lang has, as usual, peeped into his big subject and been satisfied with a glimpse. The best that can be said for the film is that no other director one knows would have thought of the Dusseldorf murderer for his hero. In this Lang shares honours with Dostoievsky and the best of them. But Lang has only thought of his subject; he has not felt it. *M*, like *Frankenstein*, is a full-blown tragedy that has been diminished in the creation to a mere 'sensational'.

*   *   *

Ernst Lubitsch is one of the master craftsmen of the cinema. Consider, for example, *The Man I Killed*, the tragic anti-war story of the French youth who, conscience-stricken for his killing of a German youth, goes to make peace with the German's people. You may consider the story sentimental in its substance—for, war or no war, we do a lot of killing in our day—but you will have no doubt at all about Lubitsch. I cannot remember a film so beautifully made, so completely fine in its execution.

Perhaps I can indicate its quality better by describing a simpler illustration. Before Flaherty went off to the Aran Islands to make his *Man of Aran*, I had him up in the Black Country doing work for the E.M.B. He passed from pottery to glass, and from glass to steel, making short studies of English workmen. I saw the material a hundred times, and by all the laws of repetition should have been bored with it. But there is this same quality of great craftsmanship in it which makes one see it always with a certain new surprise. A man is making a pot, say. Your ordinary director will describe it; your good director will describe it well. He may even, if good enough, pick out those details of expression and of hands which bring character to the man and beauty to the work. But what will you say if the director beats the potter to his own movements, anticipating each puckering of the brows, each extended gesture of the hands in contemplation, and moves his camera about as though it were the mind and spirit of the man himself? I cannot tell you how it is done, nor could Flaherty. As always in art, to feeling which is fine enough and craft which is practised enough, these strange other world abilities are added.

Lubitsch does not often depart from comedy to make serious films. His last one was *The Patriot* in the late days of the Silents: with Emil Jannings as the mad Czar Paul. It was a huge performance with great acting, intense action, and some amazing camera movements in the corridors of the Palace.

The Man I Killed is a simpler film, lower in key, with none of the mad happening of *The Patriot* to build on. The youth, praised by the Priest, goes on his journey. The German family, living on the memory of their dead son, receive him as a friend of the son, and he finds it impossible to make the confession he intended. There are scenes of the old citizens of the German town at their beer; there are some homely interiors; and the only happenings are that the old father comes to like this foreign youth and turn from his hatred of the French, and the German youth's girl falls in love with the man he was killed by. Little enough, if you like, to make movement of, or make climactic intensities of. But Lubitsch's camera glides magically in and out of these ordinary scenes, taking the details of expression and character and essential story on its way. Watch it particularly in the last scene, as it goes from the youth playing his violin to the girl, to the old couple, and watch how there is expectation, and expectation surprised, in every foot of the gyro's passage. The actors are Lionel Barrymore, Phillip Holmes, and Nancy Carroll. As always happens under Lubitsch direction, they were never so modulated or so good.

Lubitsch sketches his character with a single pose, or a single gesture, taken in the camera's stride. He does his work so easily that you hardly know it is being done.

*   *   *

Only half a dozen directors make a personal contribution to their work which is recognizable and unique. René Clair is one. He may not be as solid a performer as Pudovkin nor as slick a one as Lubitsch, but for his power to do something new and fine and entirely his own he stands as high as any of them. He has power of fantasy and fairy tale; he can jumble sound and sight together to make a crazy quilt of good sense; and he is, above all, French.

For sheer brilliance of direction I begin to think that there are only two directors worth recording: Clair himself and Lubitsch. Lubitsch perhaps has an advantage on the big sets, but when it comes to the intimacies, none can pull a face out of a crowd or build up a sequence of tenement detail like Clair. And, in liking his neighbours as he does, he has the unique distinction of liking them all equally, whether they are artists or apaches or policemen or thieves or doctors or duns, or moral or not.

Le Million is a bright and brilliant film, full of wit and fun, and very, very ably directed. The story is a delightful trifle about an artist who wins a million francs in a lottery but whose winning ticket is stolen with his coat and passed from hand to hand over the length and breadth of Paris. The pursuit of the coat is a slapstick affair with Clair squeezing each sequence of studio and underworld and police station and opera house for its every detail of fun. In lesser hands *Le Million* would have been a comedy. In Clair's it has become a fairy tale. There is magic in it.

Clair's *A Nous la Liberté* is, as one might expect, full of cleverness and good humour, and has a merrier idea at the centre of it than either *Le Million* or *Sous les Toits*. The scene is a super-rationalized gramophone factory, the director of which is an escaped convict. It is in every essential respect—from the militarized labourers to their bullying section bosses—an exact replica of the prison he escaped from. Unfortunately the director does not realize the slavery he has built, and it takes a brother convict to bring him, most literally, back to earth. This gramophone Napoleon throws his Napoleonic hat to the moon, his Bois de Boulogne wife to the Bois de Boulogne, his dinner parties to the streets, and his factory to all the dogs of slapstick.

It is all very grand and, when they walk out finally to the ancient decencies of hoboism, they leave the world to a symbolic scramble for the factory's wealth. But as Willie Gallacher used to say, in a famous peroration of his, 'When the wee alarm clock goes ting-a-ling-a-ling you will go off to your work tomorrow just the same.' It is very fashionable to slam the slaveries of machinery and sing heigh ho for the high road. I am for combining both in the common sense of a three-speed all-weather spring-saddled and mass-produced push-bike!

*   *   *

Hitchcock is the best director, the slickest craftsman, the sharpest observer and finest master of detail in all England. There is no doubt about this. He has these qualities so abundantly that in their sum they give him a style which is his and no one else's. A Hitchcock film is a Hitchcock film—and never a bad one—and this, if you will believe me, is an achievement of character where so many hands, grubby and otherwise, contribute to the final result of a film.

Yet for all these virtues Hitchcock is no more than the world's best director of unimportant pictures. Not one he has made has outlasted a couple of twelvemonths, or will—unless something radical happens to change his standard of satisfaction and give his talents something solid to be bright about.

As the credit and future of British cinema rests very much in Hitchcock's hands it would be best to make a job of the analysis. Here is *Murder*, a story of a young lady falsely accused. She is a poor benighted creature (Norah Baring) who works her hands around in a Baring way and cannot remember anything. She cannot remember anything and the usual potent court room atmospherics emphasize the blank. She is sentenced to death and so far so good. At this crucial point in the lady's career, however, it is plain that we must proceed to set her free again. We do so. With ins and outs, sometimes interesting, not often urgent, but with due Hitchcock regard for the absolute in-and-outness of this world, we do so.

We find a hero in the person of an actor-manager who is also a knight. Your attention is thereby directed to the magnificence of the apartments of the actor-manager-knight class. It is also directed to the sentiments of one who would, on his own confession, use the technique of his Art to unravel the tangles of Life. (*Sic.*) We find an aide for our hero in the person of a poorish stage manager. Your attention is thereby directed to the comic table manners of poorish stage-managers when eating with resplendent actor-manager-knights. We proceed on our quest. Our hero shaves. This directs your attention to the possibility (unique to the talkie) of uttering the thoughts of a face. In fact we make a high spot of it by uttering the thoughts of two faces, to wit the face shaving and the face reflected. Moreover we make the radio the excuse for an undercurrent of commentary music.

The heart of our hero is, by this novel use of talkie technique, cheered in his murder researches. He proceeds to the place where the body lay and spends his night in a lodging house. There is no reason why he should, but your attention is thereby directed to the plague that a landlady's children can be to an awaking plutocrat. And so sensitive has Hitchcock become to the comic horrors of poverty, your attention is directed most ably. A child squalls and squawks throughout the scene. This too is novel, for where is the theatre that can guarantee the like? We proceed to find our true murderer as trapeze act in a circus. This is especially lucky, for it not only directs your attention to the cinematic possibilities of a trapeze-act (originally exploited in *Vaudeville*) but it presents you incidentally, if there be such a mental distinction in the Hitchcock philosophy, with elephants, clowns, dwarfs and dressing-rooms. The murderer hangs himself with his own trapeze-rope and outwits the censor. The benighted lady is set free. Our proposition is complete.

I believe I am putting the matter fairly and with due regard for the film's excellences. My criticism is that the excellences are incidental excellences. They dress out the banal issue so that the separate scenes hold you as they would not, under a lesser director, come near to doing. But the issue pokes its empty face at you, at every turn.

I am not saying that the life of a lady means nothing as an issue: I am suggesting that in this case it never ceases to be anything but a trumped-up occasion for Hitchcock's cleverness. It may be because Hitchcock is too intelligent to take an affair like that seriously. It may also be that Hitchcock thought it was a serious affair and engaged himself at the midriff to do his deepest by it. In that case *Murder* is a flop all ends up for Hitchcock as a large-size director.

Now catalogue the talkie novelties, for you will hear much of them in the parlours of the highbrow.

(1) The scene in the jury-room. Sir John is the last juror to hold out against the verdict of Guilty. The mental pressure from his fellow jurors is built up in mass and tempo by cutting-in the faces and phrases with growing close-up and loudening voice; the faces have their characteristic phrases, they are repeated, quicker and quicker; a chorus of 'What do you think of that, Sir John?' mounts up through the sing-song babel. This sort of technique has been used by the advanced play-writers (Rice, Connelly, Dos Passos, etc.), and has been developed by the B.B.C. The principle of construction is sound, but the value of each demonstration depends of course on the variety and suggestion value of the sound images which go to the making of it, that is to say on the imagination which goes to the choice of the sound images. In this case they are obvious and ordinary.

(2) The shaving scene already mentioned. The mind speaks off stage. In this case the voice is straight. It was a husky whisper and dramatically opposed to the straight voice in one of the high spots of *Hell's Heroes*. The *Hell's Heroes* job was stronger.

(3) The death sentence. This is not seen. It is plain that we have had enough of the courtroom—and other movie courtrooms—already, and

73

have exhausted the visual interest. The silent film would have had to repeat. The talkie need not. The death sentence is heard. The visual accompaniment is the meandering of a caretaker through the deserted jury-room, picking up an odd cigar, wiping a desk, etc., etc. This is fine and the best thing in the film. By its weight of understatement—that is to say, apart from its technical novelty—it almost makes the gim-crack death sentence solid.

There remains to add that Hitchcock is the only English director who can put the English poor on the screen with any verisimilitude. Perhaps as time goes on and success comes over him, Hitchcock tends to love them less and exploit them more, to see them strictly from the outside and be snobbish. He finds it more a matter of regret that they have no dinner jackets than that they have no dinners. But apart from that he is the one director who is familiar with them to the point of genuine observation.

I write so much about Hitchcock for the good reason that he is the only English director worth writing so much about. One large dis-turbance in the slats of his ambition, such as I am attempting to give him, and he would be a great director indeed. At the moment he resembles too much the luxury forward line at Stamford Bridge: he is pretty to watch in front of the uprights but somewhat apathetic about the issue thereof. Will Hitchcock, for a change, take counsel of Arnold Bennett, and give us a film of the Potteries or of Manchester or of Middlesbrough—with the personals in their proper places and the life of a community instead of a benighted lady at stake? That is something not only worth doing but, for the sake of the commonweal, some-thing urgent to be done. It is already within his scope; it stands, however, as a challenge to his depth.

* * *

A new Hitchcock film is something of an event in the English year. Hitchcock has a personal style of his own direction, which can be recognized. He has a long record of good work, with large slices here and there of supremely intelligent work. He is known to have a freer hand than most in direction and to have odd thoughts of greatness. It is no wonder, therefore, if in criticism we exalt him a trifle. With a national cinema growing up under our eyes, we need strong and indi-vidual directors more than anything else. Financiers and impresarios you can buy two a penny. Directors who have something to say and the power to say it, you can only close your fingers and wish for.

Rich and Strange is the story of a young couple who cross the earthball on a holiday, and drift, in shipboard fashion, to new loyalties. An adventuress so-called disrupts the male and a colonial planter disrupts the female. In the main it is a meandering tale built up on the slim behaviourism of two or three characters and the minutiæ of their relationships. The end of the story is that the couple are shipwrecked and saved by a Chinese junk. In that oddest of all spots in the world they discover the great mercy of having a baby.

The most important thing about the film is not so much the story. It is the sudden emphasis it lays on weaknesses in Hitchcock's make-up. I have guessed before that these existed, but have never seen so clearly what new opportunities of direction must be given him if he is to build up his talent to the very grand affair we expect it to be.

In trying new material Hitchcock has found himself outside both his experience and his imagination. He has already proved himself as a director of London types and Londonesque melodrama. This new and greater canvas of seven seas and half a world has caught him short.

Think of the theme for a moment. You have in the background the journey across the earthball, and Marseilles and Suez, and Colombo and Singapore to play with. That must surely mean something to the story. You may think of it more deeply as a demonstration of the fact that even the world and its wonders can only teach people to be themselves. Whatever you think, you cannot avoid the background. It is the material of your drama and your cinema both.

The success of the film as a study of people and as a slice of cinema depended, therefore, on Hitchcock's ability to make that journey live. He fails, and entirely because his mind does not quite appreciate the wonders of the world he is trying to use. He is in this sense the supreme provincial your true-born Londoner tends to be. He knows people but not things, situations and episodes but not events. His sense of space, time, and the other elements of barbarian religion, is almost nil.

The shipwreck is like the ship itself, a fake and a frost, composed of half a dozen studio effects. The scenes abroad have nothing that in-fluences the story even by a trifle. They cannot be rich and strange because not one of them is newly observed. It would have been good to have added to the film some sense of strange trafficking and curious merchandise, but if anything, the greater weakness is the weakness of the ship. By its very nature a ship is a living thing, worth the grace of cinema, and in missing it, Hitchcock has very literally missed the boat. It is not as Hitchcock makes it just a collection of rails to look over, and evening skies to go mooney about. It moves; it passes with not a little triumph through an entire ocean, with all sorts of things stowed away in its mysterious belly.

But let me indicate the charm of Hitchcock's direction of his separate episodes. You will have heard before now of 'the Hitchcock touch'. This consists in his great ability to give a novel twist to his sketch of an episode. The man and woman are quarrelling desperately in some Oriental room: Hitchcock punctuates that episode with the apologetic entry of a Chinaman who wants to sweep the floor. The man, again, has just clinched his appointment for a first essay in infidelity: he walks idiotically into a ventilator. The film is full of details of the kind, sometimes amusing, always clever, sometimes merely clever.

I would suggest that Hitchcock's concentration on such details is at least a part of his worry in the world. Reaching for the smart touch, as often as not he irresponsibly destroys the characters he has been building up and throws away his sequence. In Chaplin you do not mind the beaded story of moments and episodes. In a dramatic director like Hitchcock you must. A film is not like the celebrated Rosary, an affair of moments to be counted over, every one apart. It is a procession of people and events that march along: preferably, of course, going somewhere.

I believe the highbrows, in their praise of him, have sent Hitchcock off in the wrong direction, as they have sent many another: Chaplin, for example. They have picked out his clever little pieces, stressed them and analysed them till they are almost everything in his directorial make-up. We have waited patiently for the swing of event (preferably of great event) to come into his films, something that would associate him more profoundly with the dramatic wants of common people. Something serious, I am afraid, will have to happen to Hitchcock before we get it.

* * *

Tell England is the work of Anthony Asquith and Geoffrey Barkas. From internal evidence it would seem that Asquith is responsible for the interpretation of the story; Barkas for the organization of the scenes of mass warfare. Asquith, again, within the limits usually attached to directors in commercial production, is probably responsible for the cutting. Who was responsible for the final scenario, and who for the final condition of the film, I cannot guess. The film, I calculate, has been shot round a thousand and one winders in the making. It carries the customary evidence of studio uncertainties.

You will gather from this the suggestion that Asquith has had a certain burden to bear in acting knee-wife to Raymond's rather sissified story of English heroism on the shores of Gallipoli.

Yet *Tell England* is undoubtedly the biggest job so far performed in the history of English cinema. There have been better jobs and more finished jobs, but not bigger ones. Looking back over a long sequence of minor efforts, the last attempt to add an element of importance to an English film was, curiously enough, in the film which gave Barkas his reputation: *Q Ships*. You will remember how in that picture one of the German officers acted as a sort of recording angel for the dead submarine commanders. He assumed a size in tragedy which, in fact, made *Q Ships*, not the epic of the British Navy it was meant to be, but the epic of the German U boats.

Since then we have inclined so much to Blackmails and Murders that one had almost come to forget that importance had any possible relation to English cinema. *Tell England* is a brave effort to stop the rot. It is a young man's effort. It is the effort of a man whose ideas of human importance are not mine. But if you have any sense of proportion in films you are bound to take it seriously. It is in a higher category altogether than other English films, however you place it in that higher category.

I make these nice distinctions because I have had a great deal of trouble in coming to a critical conclusion about *Tell England*. I have had to see it twice, and should properly, no doubt, see it twice again. The difficulty has been to separate the intelligence of Asquith as a technician and his great ambition as an artist from the thoroughly false importances which either the Raymond story or Asquith's own mind has imposed on the fabric of the film.

Of skill there is no doubt whatever. Some of the connectives between scene and scene are classical in brevity and point. The variations in the treatment of the three separate advances on the peninsula indicate an intelligence in visuals which is for anyone to study. The handling of rhythms is not so strong, but the percussive cutting of one shot-and-shell sequence is better than anything of the sort from Russia.

But it is when you have granted these things, when you come to the cause it celebrates, the sentiments that inform it, the stuffing with which it is stuffed so to speak, that the trouble starts. For to be plain, admiring the film, I do not like it: I would as quickly put it on the tumbril as any film I ever saw. For what is the upshot of this Gallipoli of Asquith's? It is in part a filthy massacre, and that part of the story is well told. But in its other part it attempts, as Tragedy must, a justification of that massacre. Tragedy, however, is no Tragedy unless the justification is just. It is no Tragedy unless the human dignity that arises above the death and destruction is a deep-laid dignity, and the human vision which throws death back into its true proportion to life is a vision of something fairly ultimate. *Tell England*'s ultimate will not bear a great deal of examination.

To be blunt about it, Asquith's rather trifling hero dies specifically for—(i) Fay Compton, (ii) a couple of swans, and (iii) afternoon tea on the domestic lawn. He dies for an England which may indeed be Asquith's England, but which is hardly an England worth dying for. For on its own evidence, it is a leisure-class England which has lost contact with fundamentals, with the toiling earth and the men who go with it. It is a complacent and effete England, which—if it exists—one would rather die to wipe from the map in a more local war.

Unfortunately, these false choices extend to Gallipoli. In the presence of death officers commanding and men commanded reach an uncommon equality, or Shirley would be no poet. And gunfire of the splendid fury illustrated by Asquith comes certainly within the category. But the old English film tradition prevails. Officers are heroes and men are comic relief. Officers die, with personal wonderings, worryings, and all evidence of being human about it. O.r.'s are content to fall anonymously in a welter of pseudo-proletarian jokes that a self-respecting village idiot would be ashamed of.

Undoubtedly the strongest thing about *Tell England* is something that emerges quite accidentally from it. It is not Asquith's young Rupert Brookes who wonder and worry and die for the immaculate lawns of England, but the battalions of poor devils who, without wondering or worrying, do a great deal of dying to provide a background for them.

I have thus far been blaming Asquith for the false emphases which ruin *Tell England*, but I am probably wrong. The false emphasis can all be traced back to the Raymond book, and it was folly, not in Asquith but in his principals, to attempt to build a Gallipoli on its tawdry foundations. A film of Gallipoli to be genuine must be either a rollicking cynical farce like *Shoulder Arms* or a drab tragedy which finishes not in honour but in futility. For a brief second during the film Asquith himself thought so. The box-office wallahs, no doubt, prevailed. As it is, Asquith really has set his hand manfully to the most impossible job that was open to him.

*   *   *

Directors of the Thirties

I have seldom seen an English film that gave me so much pleasure as *Dance Pretty Lady*. If you would see how movement should be put together and most ordinary exits and entrances turned into a poetry of movement, you will find a whole curriculum in this film. And more. One of Asquith's great talents is his power of giving conversational point to action and character. He slips in details of observation which are, on their own account, a running commentary on both. Plastered hair, a stiff collar, or a room's decorations become in his hands a character sketch; the window of a hansom cab underlines a period. There is no other director who can do it so well; there is no other director who can even do it.

Always, too, looking at Asquith's films, you realize how well he knows his painters. I suppose the little references to one or another, the consciousness in this case that Degas should not be shamed in his own subject, can mean little to some audiences. Asquith can at least defend himself on the Kantian maxim, that one may only appreciate as one would wish the whole world to appreciate. It is a maxim never, never in evidence in the film world, but heaven knows cinema could do with a little of it.

Dance Pretty Lady is a delight to the eye: be assured of that. I cannot, however, say so much for its appeal to the imagination. It represents filigree work, most delicate, on a story that could not possibly make a big film. A little ballet dancer (much too young to be allowed to fall in love with anybody) falls in love with a sculptor. She will not let him have her 'because she would feel a sneak'. The sculptor goes off in a tantrum, lets another man, 'a dirty rotter', have her instead. The sculptor comes back for a quick and sudden and quite banal happy ending.

That is the tiding of great joy which Asquith (of Balliol and I know not what other traditions of English leadership) has spent a year in fetching us. A more cynical and shameful waste of time I cannot imagine. I may tend to over-emphasize our need for leadership and the film's great capacity for giving it, but was there ever another film director trained so specifically and deliberately and cold-bloodedly for the job as Asquith? This is it, bless you. Claptrap about a virginity. Why, the entire sentiment that makes a plot like that possible went into discard with the good, prosperous, complacent old Victoria. It was, relatively, an important matter then. But it is mere infant fodder now when you consider the new problems we carry in our bellies, and think of the new emphases we must in mercy to ourselves create out of our different world.

79

Flaherty was sitting with me at *Dance Pretty Lady*, and he is a good judge. He was as fascinated as I was myself. But his summing up was this: 'If that boy ever gets a story you will see the film of your life.' It is a trouble to know whether Asquith is denied the big story by his masters, or is by his own nature powerless to find it.

I think, myself, that like many other brilliant young men of his training and generation, he is a damned sight too remote from ordinary things to discover it easily. It is not enough to recognize bigness by its classical reference (for this Asquith can do on his head); it must be recognized, without reference at all, out of one's own most private sense of importance, if there is to be power of revelation. I cannot tell you what the secret is, but it should be plain on the fact of it that there are more powerful spirits to be called from the deep than you are likely to get from stories of this sort.

* * *

Quick Millions is a very remarkable film. It is so much tougher than its gangster predecessors that *Scandal Sheet* and *The Front Page* seem bedtime stories in comparison. Indeed it gets so close to the hoodlums it deals with that it has all the flavour of a personal experience. It is, strangely enough for Hollywood, realist to the bone. It does not romanticize its racketeering; it describes it. It even explains it. It is on the way to being, apart from its drama, a sociological document.

Behind the racketeering story, of course, is the story of private enterprise gone riot. *Quick Millions* reaches through to it bitingly. The toughest article present is not the chief gangster, nor even the hench-man who finally puts him on the spot; it is the writer and director of the film, Roland Brown. He presents each factor of the racketeer game, the buying and selling and grafting in high places which make it possible, without batting an eyelash. He makes big business in its American version a big joke.

In the tale a truck driver undertakes to get rich at the expense of society, and he does so with a facility which only to Englanders will seem bewildering. He works a garage racket, which means that under pain and penalty of one destruction or another he levies a weekly protection fee from garage proprietors. Being an intelligent organizer he smashes a few cars in the street and sees to it that co-operating garages are supplied with custom. He works the building racket, which means that for a weekly tribute he refrains from (*a*) bombing, (*b*) killing and (*c*) otherwise sabotaging on the premises in question. His hench-

Turksib (Soviet, 1928)
   Produced by Vostokfilm: directed by Victor Turin

Earth (Soviet, 1930)
   Produced by Vufko-Kino: directed by Alexander Dovzjenko

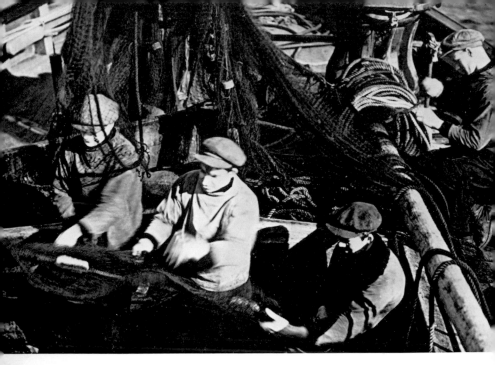

Drifters (British, 1929)
  Produced by E.M.B. Film Unit: directed by John Grierson

Aero Engine (British, 1933–4)
  Produced by E.M.B. Film Unit: directed by Arthur Elton

man, when he breaks from the decency of his principal's control, edges in on the milk racket and the cloak and suit racket. A machine-gun play on a few milk-cans, a mud spray on a few dresses, pave the way for both.

The police are impotent, for their chiefs are either bought outright or scared of some private revelation. Their personal scandals are on file in the racketeer's palatial office. Superior organization, as he explains lucidly, is everything. In a world in which social purpose is strictly lacking in society's managers, and everyone is impeachable, it is definitely everything.

This is not a fantastic picture of American life, but the nearest thing to bald-headed revelation the movies have ever given us. In one American city recently I sat in on a detective sergeant's description of the city management, which had every one of these elements detailed. Public authority is going to pieces everywhere. Prohibition is a cause. It has done everything to make law-breaking an honoured and established pursuit. It has brought honest citizens into a direct dependence on hoodlums. They would be inefficient hoodlums if they did not improve their grip. But Prohibition is not the whole cause. The silly scramble for wealth, the utter lack of ambition outside the scramble for wealth, the fact that leadership has become divorced from a primary loyalty to the State, the fact that the State has lost the power to create a loyalty to itself, make order impossible. You cannot educate a people in grabbing while the grabbing is good—and no Prosperity speech by an American President has meant anything more since Roosevelt —and expect the grabbers to confine themselves to the ranks of High Finance.

Quick Millions will tell you much of this and it will tell you in a manner which is altogether unique. This is Roland Brown's first film and he has begun his technique where Hollywood and the Germans and the Russians left off. This is a faster film than a Russian, and without recourse to the click-clack and eyestrain of the *montage* business. It is so fast, and moreover so smooth in its quick continuity, that it makes the *montage* business look crude and old-fashioned. And if anyone still remembers *Berlin* with an unwarranted affection he had better see *Quick Millions* demonstrate how *Berlin*, without loss of omplexity, might have been made articulate. Poor Milestone, who with his *Front Page* was supposed to create something of a revolution in the tempo of tale-telling, is a dullard alongside this new and very amateur director. Brown does not know what to do with an actor when he sees one. So long as he makes the gesture that gives Brown

F   81

his continuity, he can be as good or as bad as he likes. But what continuity!

You will find blemishes in the film: notably a couple of impotent speeches by reformers and a more impotent resolution by big businessmen to do this, that and the other thing. Forget them and concentrate on this director's demonstration of how to start a story in forty-five seconds and end it in twenty. The subtlety of attendant detail I leave you to examine for yourselves. More often than not it makes the very acting unnecessary.

*   *   *

King Vidor's *Hallelujah* is an all Negro film. This is to the good, for the Negroes, like any other spontaneous species of the human race, have a great deal in them that is cinematic; in both the visual novelty of their bodies and the rapt emotionalism of their ways of expression. Moreover, Vidor is a serious director. I saw something of him in Hollywood and liked him for that seriousness, and I would not miss anything he did. He is an intimate and unofficial disciple of Chaplin: no man can be that and be tawdry.

The principal virtue in *Hallelujah* is in the intention, for glorifying the Negro is not the easiest of tasks in paleface America. For the rest I was disappointed. I was so anxious to see the film that I went to its very first appearance, and disappointment may take colour from too much expectancy; but there it is. It is difficult to knock a film like that for, heaven knows, it is better than most and required a labour in the making one should respect. I must, however, on your behalf insist on superlatives.

The trouble with *Hallelujah* is that setting out to glorify the Negro it does much less than it might. The film tells you about a Negro of honest and pleasant home-town associations who falls for a vamp, takes to religious revivalism, falls once more for the vamp, is cuckolded, murders, does time, and arrives back for a fade-out on the plantation again. All of which is rather threadbare. In cinema the big opportunities are the cotton picking, the delivery of the cotton at the market, the Negro cabaret, the revival scenes, the lumber yard to which the Negro, as renegade preacher, descends. All of them admit of song and sound most rhythmic, and none of them achieves it. The film is badly cut, almost without knowledge of Russian achievement in that field, and almost any big mass scene in, say, the *Village of Sin* (Russian), *Storm over Asia* (Russian), or in the *New Babylon* (also Russian) would shame *Hallelujah*.

I apologize for this judgment and again you must see this film rather than others. I was perhaps too acutely conscious of the possibilities of the original material. I have not seen too much of the American Negro, but I have certainly seen better cabaret stuff, better revival scenes and heard better renderings of Negro songs than the film gave me. The point is that the intensity which is instinct in everything Negro did not come through. I question, too, if this rather sordid preoccupation with vamps and Aimée Macpherson evangelism, represents the dramatic truth of the Negro. I note, from a publicity puff, that Vidor freed the Negro from misunderstanding just as Abe Lincoln freed him from slavery. Both statements are exaggerated.

*　　*　　*

Tabu is a South Seas film in the *Moana* tradition. It went into production with the very proudest and most classical story the world's drama has ever evolved. A boy and a girl love each other—the gods sanctify the girl and make her tabu—the boy breaks the tabu—the gods destroy him. In one version or another it is the story which made Socrates and the Greek Tragedies and Corneille and Racine. If you remember the futile academics of your youth, it was as each dramatist solved the problem: for the gods or against the gods: for society and against the personal or for the personal and against society: that he was allowed by the professors to carry the banner of classicism or romanticism.

I myself was schooled by Calvinism to the classical version and have been content to see the gods obliterate the little tabu-breakers: the Antigones and Hippolytuses and Horaces. And who would not be, who has heard an audience at the Comédie Française roar their welcome to the 'qu'il mourut' of Horace itself? Unfortunately, the Murnau-Flaherty work is not to be ranked with Corneille. To defy the gods is a terrible thing, and they have failed to make it terrible. The standard is there for everyone to see.

One should, I suppose, be grateful for South Sea settings and Polynesian maidens and the sterling rhythms of the hula-hula. The photography, when it is not fussy and finicky and too dam' beautiful by half, is the wonderful photography which says what it wants to say. The Polynesian bodies when they are not overposed are the decent god-like bodies *Moana* taught us to expect. The hula-hula dance I found at first a trifle exhibitionist, lacking by a hairbreadth in spontaneity and, therefore, in purity. It was not the dance of Moana. But

83

it stays in the head. There is a moment in it when the youths and maidens glide into the ring of villagers which must be as great a split second as there is in all cinema. And more than that. In the middle of the ceremonial the boy moves to the girl he is losing. Their faces light up as they infect the dance suddenly with their happiness. The danger infects it and the beat of the dance gathers and increases about them. This is true dance, for it is drama.

I must say less of the efforts of the director to pursue the lovers to their fate. The thunder and lightning, which the original dramatic proposition calls for, is seriously absent. The film fuddles. Murnau leaves a long and arduous sub-title to describe the escape to another island across 'a raging Pacific'. This is a mistake from which the film never recovers. You may not in cinema mention a raging Pacific in a footnote.

When retribution comes, it comes clumsily by way of dance halls and drink and some episodic pearl diving. I cannot myself swear to the sequence of events: I could not follow it through the heel-tapping of guitar and accordion numbers. I can only record that high tragedy in this case is not the steamroller affair it used to be. There is no little red flag marching ahead of it. It lacks the note of the inevitable.

There is, on the whole, relief when the messenger of the gods drops off a schooner (its name is *Moana*) and beats Tahiti and civilization to the job of destroying the protagonists. When heroes get muddled and forget to be heroes, destruction is obviously the best thing for them. The quicker the better.

You will gather that *Tabu* is not quite a masterpiece. The drowning of the boy in the last sequence is good: the old messenger of the gods is a grand tragic figure at all points, indeed the only protagonist worthy of buskins; there is, too, some considerable dramatic value in the notion of Fate striking and missing in the shark sequence. With the last part of the dance, they belong to that larger world of cinema which one hardly ever glimpses in the commercial movies. They are worth collecting. And you must see *Tabu*, if only to realize how very great and pure a film *Moana* was.

It is difficult, of course, to tease out from the final account the individual contributions of Flaherty and Murnau. My own opinion is, that all the good things come from Flaherty and all the bad ones from Murnau. They were the wrong people to work together. Flaherty is a naturalist director, with an eye only for the spontaneities and the decencies, and a mind only for stories that go to the heart of things. Murnau was a studio product, a manipulator of artificial effects, a manager of exaggeration, introspective, perverse: an artist who never smelt an honest wind in his life. Flaherty was an explorer in the South Seas; Murnau was at worst a tripper, at best an exploiter. *Tabu* must have been a dogfight!

3 Hollywood Looks at Life

Hollywood has always had the good sense to loose an occasional salute to the common life. Behind its luxuries there has always been a suggestion of origin in Kanka Kee or Kalamazoo. Behind the gowns and gauderies there has been a frank allowance that the lady inside them started under honest parents as a shop girl. Tales of the Frontier and the Railroads and the Gangs and the War have remained still more faithful to the notion that rank was but the guinea stamp and a man was a man for a' that.

The manhood may have been romanticized, but behind it, dimly, has been the presupposition that common things have virtues and that straight-up braveries are the essence of nobility. It is this presupposition which has made me prefer American films to English ones. I imagine most people are with me.

Say what you will of the Americans: they do not take their subjects and settings from one silly stratum of near-society. They use the stuff in front of their noses, even if they colour it with the baby pinks and baby blues of happy endings and luxury finales. Not one of us but knows their soda fountains better than our own cafés, their cops better than our police, their department stores better than our shops, their newspapers and business offices better than Fleet Street and the City.

There is a limit, of course: the limit reflected in the baby blues and baby pinks: the showman's fear of introducing the sordid. Hollywood has made a dream world even of its realities. I know there may be a case for filling the world's head with dreams, but one finds it a relief when a story of commoners stays rooted to the solid earth. We want it romanticized just the same, but we want our romance with the sweat and the smells thrown in. It is a better romance.

One great effort to break through to this braver world was King Vidor's *The Crowd*. It failed commercially, because people were too accustomed to the usual halcyon treatment of human life to stand it. It told the story of two young people, who married with all the hopes and intentions outlined in American magazines and movie philosophy and finished up as most folk do, cultivating their back garden on five pounds a week and a family. It cut across Hollywood's world audiences like a whip. It hurt them.

As well offer bread and meat to a dope-fiend as give movie audiences the plain honour of families and affections. So it seemed. But I am not sure that the dope is working quite so well as it used to do. *Bad Girl* came along some time ago and made a great success. *Taxi*, which pursues the same tradition of *petit bourgeois* trials and tribulations, is careful to mix its family drama with a gangster feud, and spice it with three solid killings. You will like the film, however, for James Cagney's very decent presentation of a hard-boiled young taxi-driver, and for the friendly detail of his house and home.

The Champ brings King Vidor back into the big lights, after the sad adventures of *The Crowd* and *Hallelujah*. Vidor is a good director who takes films seriously, his one fault being a tendency to equate seriousness with pessimism. This fallacy is very common in America: I leave the sociologists to guess why.

With *The Champ* he is on safe ground. He has Jackie Cooper and Wallace Beery, and a tale about a prize-fighter, ex-champion of the world, who tries to come back for his son's sake. Beery kills himself in the process. It is told with a great deal of skill, and the relations of the derelict father and worshipping son are sketched with a good deal of humour. You must be left, however, to endure the heart failure of the final episode as best you can. It means that Jackie can be taken at long last to a nice home, a good education and a fitting environment. The film tells you so, and presumably romance is thereby satisfied. There is one scene in *The Champ* where Beery arises after a dirty night and goes through the odd gestures of coming properly to life again. From the chorus of reminiscent chuckles around me, I was led to believe that Beery had made a masterpiece of it. The reminiscent chuckles are passed on for your consideration.

*   *   *

Street Scene is from the play by Elmer Rice: a sad, pessimistic play describing the domestic tangles of a tenement building in downtown New York. That is the old town, where the aristocratic quarters of fifty years ago are the slums of today. There, racial elements are mixed as only metropolitan America knows how to mix them: in this case Russian Jews with Italians with Irish with Swedes with Germans. If you knew Halsted Street, Chicago, you would call that a simple mixture, but it is sufficient to make *Street Scene* the first in-seeing picture of American life we have had.

Here is the real America, where a thousand bewildered foreign peoples dig in their toes and fight desperately for a foothold in the promised land. There are economic footholds and spiritual ones. This is about the spiritual ones.

Elmer Rice, before he wrote *Street Scene,* wrote a superb skit on Hollywood, calling it in the Swiftian manner, *A Voyage to Puerilia.* He knows Hollywood, and he has taken no chance on the infantile adaptations served out to intellectual dramatists. He adapted the play himself. It is so faithful a reproduction that the film, like the play, is confined to the single tenement set in which the protagonists laugh and fight and dream and weep and murder each other. The only variants for film purposes are the cuttings from close-up to close-up, the long tracking shots to and from the doorway, and the odd surrounding details of elevated railroads, roofs, and passing traffic.

This may sound very dull to those of you who are keyed to the swooping and swinging of movement, which is regarded as the essence of film. But, after all, it is an account of people and of what may happen to them in a day or a night on their own doorstep. Both Rice and Vidor, the director, were wise not to be tempted beyond their thesis. Even as it stands it is a better job than the stage production. The variety of the movement within the limits set is a feat of great skill, and I think only Vidor of all directors could have brought it off. The music, too, with its Blues commentary on the story, and its fragments of jazz (the folk-songs of these very American tenements) adds a quality to the film which the play could not attempt.

I found myself stirred by *Street Scene,* simply because it was serious about something and stuck to its gesture. Yet in the ultimate I am as out of sympathy with it, as I am with Rice's earlier *Adding Machine.* In America, to be serious is to be pessimistic, and I cannot follow the process of thought. In this case misunderstandings happen and murders happen, and everyone is more or less derelict in a world he cannot master. The Russians call this 'defeatism' and class it as the sin against the Holy Spirit. In that, they are strangely true to the classical tradition of dramatic values, where—whatever happened—the potential or the promise of life was also indicated, and the true balance kept.

The Blues are bad medicine when they are of the Gershwin variety. I believe they are even shallow medicine. Better the Negro rendering, where the horn goes heroic. *Street Scene* is pure Rhapsody in Blue.

* * *

Hollywood Looks at Life

Seldom does cinema provide so captivating and wholesome a film as *Three-Cornered Moon*, the story of an American family's fortunes during the depression. Some films are clever, some funny, and all too many bear the thin excellence of technical skill; but a fine observation is the rarest of qualities in this mass art of ours. It prefers to stumble through the wider hoops of romance and sensation: afraid of the minutiæ of living things and living people: incapable, seemingly, of the themes which touch the common routine of our affections. Compare *Three-Cornered Moon* with the films which deal, in the Cabell phrase, with the 'regions beyond life': where the ordinary is not sublimated but side-stepped, and the ambition (not always, nor altogether commercial) is to take the plain citizen 'out of himself'.

What relief to come back from the pyrotechnics of super spies, super crooks, and super monsters to the even more sensational pyrotechnics of an ordinary household, where the plain citizen can be 'inside himself' again, and where the trials and triumphs, though they are small, are blessedly recognizable as his own. The Rimplegars, in Gertrude Tonkonogy's story, are a rich Brooklyn family reduced by the depression to a bank remainder of one dollar sixty-five. They are, like every family in the world, an incredible mixture. The mother, brilliantly played by Mary Boland, is incapable of anything except affection; but it is enough to make her a great lady indeed. The daughter, Claudette Colbert, is bright as a blackbird, but senselessly involved in an affair with an æsthete—who is a pretty foul specimen of an æsthete. One brother is muddling through a law apprenticeship, another through an athletic career at Yale, another through the mad preliminaries of theatrical hope. With wealth behind them, they might tumble along till doomsday: ridiculously concerned in their own inconsequent affairs: quarrelling and fighting to their hearts' content: the delighted mother dancing equally inconsequent and equally inefficient attendance on their squabbles and their stomach-aches. It is, in other words, that rarest of all good things, a family seen from the inside: and so accurate in its detail and affectionate in its drawing that it is, without a doubt, autobiographical.

When the crash comes, what a masterpiece of half comic, half desperate self-sacrifice the family becomes. There is no nonsense about the uprising affection the situation produces, and that is the film's principal attraction. But it is there, working them all to death, in shoe factories, public baths, public libraries, second-rate touring companies, as inefficient, as free in complaint and, with pretty judgment on the part of the author, just as ridiculous as before. You are not asked to

89

sympathize with their fallen fortunes, for that would have been the weakest of gambits. You are merely asked to observe the strange and incomprehensible fact that blood is thicker than water: even when, as in this case, it is of plutocratic density.

You will like the Rimplegars. Their family fortitude will not, I hope, lull you into a false state of satisfaction regarding the depression for all the family fortitude in the world will neither excuse it nor solve it. Here, however, are people drawn from the life and drawn so ably that they have the presence and importance of personal acquaintance. That is so rare a feat in cinema that I give you *Three-Cornered Moon* as very much the film of the year. The honours of it go to the author. She has done her people proud.

*   *   *

I went searching for Tom Mix the other week. I wanted to see how the ancient tougheries were standing up against the Cagneys, the Gleasons, and the Tracys. With Cagney in *The Picture Snatcher*, Gleason in *Orders is Orders*, Tracy in *Private Jones*, all parading their more fashionable braveries to the moon, academic research in this very important matter seemed an ordinary critical duty. If I also wanted to slide off the metropolitan pavement into a cool stretch of Wyoming foot-hills, I make no apology for a rustic's nostalgia.

Mix was riding the wind in *Rustlers Round Up* at Camberwell; in *The Fourth Horseman* at Herne Hill; in *Rough Riding Romeo* at Walworth Road; in *Death Valley* (or was it *Defiant?*) at Forest Hill. Indeed, I gathered that our West End emphasis is not altogether shared by a very large number of citizens beyond the Elephant and Castle. There is something to be said for their preference.

The Western saga is simple, but there are some curious and precious qualities in it. Behind the paraphernalia of good hombres and bad hombres, ranch conspiracies and banditries, rustlings and rides to the rescue, there is so plentiful a splashing of hills and horses and fresh air that one only realizes on seeing it again how cabined, confined, and claustrophilic our other films are. In a world so plain in its villainy and diffident in its heroism, the belly-aching spiritual (or only sexual), which is nine parts of the West End emphasis, seems more than remote. It is clear that Mix, at the first whimpering smell of it, would shift from one foot to the other, mutter illiterate apology, and take his leave. You may reckon indeed that the persisting diffidence is something of a persisting decency shying away from all such sickness in the blood. It represents the instinct of common men, to free themselves not only from complications but also from complexes. The world it rules may be a simple world, where the principles of law are understood even by cow-punchers, and I am not sure that the technique of lying and deceit in which all of us so proudly graduate is not better suited to the particular villanies we fight, but the other has dignity.

It is this quality more than any other that the Cagney heroes lack. They are bravos in their own way, though obviously the world has become too deep for them. The Western's straight to the mark solution for bandits and bad men has become a posturing protest in, say, *Private Jones*. Jones thinks the war is bunk and persists against odds in toughly saying so. Mix would have said very little. He would merely have shot a couple of politicians and woven some magical hemp round several profiteers. I notice that our metropolitan toughs roll into action only on the more orthodox occasions. They will push a moll in the face, smack her garter a yard high, tip a drink down her blouse, and square up on all possible personal occasions. So much for a general belief in direct action. But it is kindergarten stuff. You may regard it as commendable after a surfeit of Christian propriety and social complacency; you may even think it significant of a new and rising temper in the world by which ordinary men will again liquidate the smells they register; it is, on the other hand, too uncertain of itself, too ineffective, to give any considerable satisfaction. If dignity attaches to the Western hero, there is this deeper reason for it: that he does also carry protest to an active conclusion.

This larger argument apart, there is still nothing in cinema to compare with the movement which these Westerns so easily and consistently command. The horses are fine in themselves, but pressed in the crescendo of rides to the rescue, and cross-timed with the events they hasten to help, they give you the simple essence of good cinema. The Western moves; it delights the eye with progressive and developing movement; it stirs with most visible happening. It is superior to everything except event; and it plays its story against a landscape noble in itself. Its avoidance of the more complex, and possibly more reasonable, versions of personal romance need not bother you. It would be better, I know, if the little girl looked more like a rancher's daughter and less like a dolled-up stenographer, and you may even find that in this regard the cow-puncher's diffidence is overdone; but in *Rustlers Round Up* you will find a note of compensation. Where in any more sophisticated rendering (outside D. H. Lawrence) have you heard a

91

proposal of marriage fortified by a speech in praise of stallions? The boys and girls of Camberwell were delighted.

*   *   *

Cimarron takes a tough young newspaper editor through those generations that saw the building of Oklahoma, from the opening of the Indian Reservations and the first rush for the land, through the building of city and State, up to the last mad discovery of oil. That is recent history and a matter of two generations or three at most; but it gives you themes in space and time and creation.

Hollywood, which knows what to do with space and also—occasionally—with creation, has never been very strong on Time. You may remember the effort of Lillian Gish to rock a cradle through the ages in Griffith's *Intolerance*. The Massacre of the Hugenots was there, if I remember, matched in modern history with a trial for murder in twentieth-century New York. *The Vanishing American*, a later effort, began splendidly with the passing of tribe after tribe across the prairies and the wiping out of each by its successor, but fell down on a modern episode where Noah Beery (sheriff and villain) pinched a bit of land from Richard Dix (Indian and hero), and Dix, being an Indian and coloured, couldn't marry Lois Wilson, the local lipsticked schoolmistress. The Indian infants in a touching if rickety scene waved penny flags and repeated the Oath of Allegiance.

It used to be one of the copy-book headlines that you couldn't get the hang of the local event and give it its reference in history. This is particularly true of a tribe like the Americans. They have Mencken but no prophet: The *American Mercury*, but no criticism.

But *Cimarron* is a step ahead, even if it slips up a trifle on logic. Dix (again Dix), the symbolic hard-baked American of the Oklahoma land rush, the hard-baked editor who lays down the law and defends an editorial from both hips, remains the everlasting hunter of new-fangled enterprises. The war with Spain. The Great War. The opening of the Oklahoma oilfields. Just like that, uncritically and any-old-how, following the fashion in whatever is new and tough, and leaving the old lady at home to build up the *Oklahoma Gazette* and prosper on the want-ads.

I am not sure myself if the Oklahoma land rush, the building of Oklahoma, the Spanish-American War, the Great War and the Oklahoma oilfields, make a straight flush—and you may agree with me—but the film does get across that particular stretch of history and does make it feel like history. That is the accident I refer to. This film has the size of time, and that is the most wonderful and the most difficult thing on God's earth to get into any job. With even a hint of that you may forgive a film anything.

Chang, which ran a trifle to expert showmanship in sections, achieved it by the odd patience with which Burmese natives started hacking down trees at the end to rebuild the homes they built laboriously enough at the beginning. The quality of ease and patience made the show. Time is in character: mostly in ease, mostly in patience, seldom in dramatics: in a handful of corn thrown into the earth generation after generation through all the less pertinent sequences of disaster and death. The Greek sculptors avoided the peak of action.

Cimarron, if it has anything, has a hint of this continuity of essential character. It is good that men should ride off to war and things, and leave their ladies on the domestic watch tower. You and I may, in a sense, want to investigate the wars a little and discover what the gesture is all about; for you never know about wars and the gesture may be a fake one. Even the garden patch can be a long way from home. Apart from that, the principal truth stands and any sense of tribal criticism at all will pick you the real deaths from the dud ones. *Cimarron*'s director is Wesley Ruggles. He is, I understand, young and coming.

*   *   *

Variety, best of all the cinema gossip papers, tells us we must expect more gangster pictures. After seeing *Enemies of the Public* I am not so sure that this is the bad news it sounds. The Westerns created Epic by repeating themselves: by the very threat of monotony escaping into bigger things. Few of the movie subjects have suffered a similar transmutation because they were done with before they were well started.

One of the stranger curses of the game is that, like other female worlds, it follows the fashions. A hit in horror films or animal films is followed with a rush by others of the species: quickly conceived and as quickly executed to exploit the newly discovered taste. The public mind is thought of rather pathetically as some citadel fortified and defended against an enemy. One little breach in the walls and our entertainers are piling pell-mell after each other to seize the advantage.

This superficial outlook has been disastrous because the weakness of the repetitions is liable to kill a field of material for years. A batch of sea films flop (because they are bad films, of course, not because they are sea films), and the word goes round that sea films are 'out'. Or a plenitude of war films puts war films 'out'. So, innocently, is the plain fact of the matter lost sight of—that a good story with the original issues of life in it emerges from any material whatsoever.

This is a long but necessary introduction to *Enemies of the Public*. We have had gangster films by the dozen over the past year, and this is yet another of them. But it is a good film—good in itself—and all question of fashion is immediately beside the point. I found myself liking it much better than my fellow-critics, and you will have to make your own careful judgment on its merits.

My impression was that there was something at the heart of it more solid than any gangster film before has shown. Not the shootings: there were better in *Beast of the City*. Not the continuity: *Quick Millions* makes it look ragged. The achievement of *Enemies of the Public* is that it gets closer to the person of the gangster, to the mind that works behind the gangster, to the possibility of the gangster, than any previous film of the sort. It does make him credible, and that represents a very noteworthy exercise in the higher revelation.

For this, one must be grateful to a story which contains some of the pertinent social facts. Most of us are guided in our film theory by the notion that cinema has nothing to do with the novel and a very great deal to do with the short story. We look for an action begun, executed, and resolved, with a certain directness. We are enslaved to the Greek conception of Unity in Time, as the dramatists who follow Greek theory have never been.

Enemies of the Public takes the big plunge and follows a life history spasmodically through its several ages. The boy becomes the pool-room youth, the pool-room youth the consequent tough, the tough the gunman, the gunman the bright and burnished 'big shot' himself. It all really happens. That is to say, we do in a fashion grow up with the youth, and, as familiars must, we find him as possible an acquaintance at the end as he was at the beginning.

This is something different from our detached acceptance of the 'big shots' in the average gangster film. They are melodramatic set-ups. This, because we have seen it grow, is more nearly a living gangster. A living character, of course, is the first necessity of a living drama. What happens to him is immediately important. What fate befalls him has not only life and death in it, but is as liable to have the elementary laws of philosophy in it.

I shall not put the matter too high, but *Enemies of the Public* noses sufficiently into the larger world of appreciation to command your attention. Cagney lives and perishes as the gangster, and such sterling dames as Joan Blondell and Jean Harlow walk casually in and out of the picture. It is whispered down Wardour Street that the censor has had his way with them. This may account for the strange poppings of their exits and entrances.

*　　*　　*

The Mayor of Hell follows the sociological line and describes an experiment in self-government in an American reformatory. The reformatory is a studio set-up, and the boys are ordinary little Hollywood actors, registering mass emotion to the crack of a directorial whip. Fortunately the theme is better than the film, and I, for one, shall say nothing to discourage Hollywood in the pursuit of other social problems of the sort. Play them as they may, it is better to have them romanticizing reform than romanticizing rackets.

Far too little justice has been done to the side of American life which this reformatory theme represents. No country, in its universities, has studied the liberal aspects of social service so carefully and so laboriously; and it is good to remember that Chicago produced Clarence Darrow, the finest of all humanitarians in our day, at much the same time as Al Capone. The principles of reform laid down by American liberals may appear somewhat sentimental and tender-minded. You may even believe that Darrow's belief that crime is illness is not deep enough, and that Judge Lindsay's psychological clinic for children in Denver does not sufficiently comprehend the economic sources of crime, but the justice they represent is wiser and, to some extent, it works.

So with the film. Its conclusions are easy, but, in its plea for children's courts from which the penitentiary atmosphere is eliminated, and for reform schools that really reform, it does a magnificent piece of propaganda for the more sensible treatment of wayward children.

What happens is something like this. Cagney, a young war heeler, is given a job as deputy commissioner to a reform school. In the American municipal racket it means that for services rendered—gangster services at polling booths—he is given the right to take a rake-off on contracts. No more is expected of him. But he falls in love, and listens to his lady's ideas of reform, and puts them into practice. The boys are let loose to do the things they want to do: to do woodwork if they are natural carpenters, to draw if they are made that way, to run their own stores, organize their own affairs, and administer their own laws. All this, as one might expect in a Hollywood film, they immediately do, with only minor casualties. They become, indeed, decent law-abiding little citizens, and potential pillars of the *status quo.*

It may be that *Mayor of Hell* was inspired by *The Road to Life*, which dealt similarly with a bunch of ragamuffins. If so, it raises a pretty distinction in sociological argument. I found the uplift note pretty strong in *Mayor of Hell*; and, if anything, the toughery of Cagney makes him a more plausible reformer of boys than the scout-master approach of his counterpart in the other film. But *The Road to Life* had a stronger argument. Its notion of boys learning to be useful, learning to make things, learning to take a creative part in society is no different in principle, no higher in aim, than the theme of this American film. The superiority lies in the fact that the boys are offered a role and a régime they can genuinely believe in and enjoy. I doubt, for example, if you can really exercise the smash and grab spirit in youth when smash and grab—in only slightly different forms—is the most honoured practice of society. And I doubt if you can, with any final success, teach youngsters to be useful when every snob value in the land is associated with uselessness. *The Mayor of Hell* gracefully skips any such considerations.

* * *

With *Gabriel Over The White House* Hollywood makes a first hurried and hectic dash into the field of politics. I hear that there is great concern in America lest by adding its weight in this way to direct propaganda cinema may upset the balance of politics; but you will be wise to reserve your judgment on the principle till you have viewed the product. As you might imagine, Hollywood is liable to pursue the sensations and romances of political issue and is hardly likely to face the ordinary realities of political construction. In this example, Holly-wood's political conclusions are, to say the least, simple.

You will appreciate how very simple if I give you the line of the story. A new American President has just been elected, and it is plain that his high-winded election promises will pass into limbo in the usual way. He is a good party man, a roysterer, a 'good-fellow', in the old-time American sense: more than likely to use the spoils of office for the personal benefit of himself and his friends. He is involved in a motor-car accident, suffers concussion, and emerges as a New Man. At frequent intervals, he casts up his eyes in a northerly direction (inspiration from God) and listens queerly to ghostly choruses (heavenly choirs by

Berlin (German, 1927)
    Produced by Fox-Europa, Berlin: directed by Walter Ruttmann (from the Paul Rotha Collection)

Rien que les Heures (French, 1926)
    Produced by Néofilm: directed by Alberto Cavalcanti (from the Paul Rotha Collection)

The River (American, 1937)
  Directed by Pare Lorentz

  Both films produced by the Resettlement Administration

The Plow that Broke the Plains (American, 1936)
  Directed by Pare Lorentz

Cosmopolitan Productions Inc.). On special occasions, a trumpet solo off stage witnesses the presence of Gabriel himself.

All this is dandy. As the mistress of his roystering days very gravely puts it, 'There is the old Judd . . . there is this great gaunt ghost who is the new Judd . . . and there is the THIRD BEING . . .'. With this holy trinity in charge at the White House, the political fireworks are all set for a Hollywood fiesta. Are you surprised that the cleaning up of (*a*) America and (*b*) the World, is carried out forthwith! I was not; for, in student days, I walked the wards of an asylum and, once a week, saw the self-same miracle performed under the self-same conditions. Eyes were turned upwards, ghostly voices spoke, Gabriel played a two-fingered exercise on his cornet; and dictatorships were achieved, and the ills of the world were solved, by the Perfect Faith of raving lunacy.

I found the sequence of events exciting to a degree. The new President has Quixote lashed to the mast in the matter of easy solutions. The Secretary of State baulks him, so he fires the Secretary of State; and, for good measure, he sacks the rest of the Cabinet as well. Congress criticizes; he adjourns Congress. The unemployed march on Washington; he forms a labour army in which the unemployed (forgetful of labour doctrine) happily accept a soldier's pay. When the gangsters challenge the White House itself, they are wiped out by a dozen armoured cars and a firing squad. Last miracle of all, the statesmen of the world are brought together in holy harmony, and the Peace of the World is achieved. And how, my pretty politicians, how? By assembling the might of America's navy and America's air force, and telling said statesmen they will be blown to hell if they don't do as America tells them. In the English version a diplomatic alteration has been made. It is an Anglo-American combine of navies and aircraft which bullies the world into peaceful submission. Wheesht, Stalin!

You will not wonder that on achieving so swift and satisfactory a millennium, our Mr. President Judd collapses under the strain. And you will be delighted, as I was, to hear him, with returning consciousness, speak in the roystering accents of the good old days. He calls, as anyone would, for his Pendy; the concussion has passed away. But do you think the film allows us to utter the gargantuan peal of laughter which is trembling at our gizzards? Not on your life! The film, not weary with well-doing, murders the President off, lest, by the odd chance of returning sanity, this strange millennium be embarrassed. Depressing the necessary button with his heavenly forefinger, Gabriel fades out on a high C.

It would be scurvy of me to set against this fairy tale of politics the

G
97

thought of the ordinary realities which politics involve, of the day-to-day building of organizations, of the persistent wars between constructive and destructive forces, wise and stupid and plain ordinary forces, which prevent easy conclusions and slick results. Perhaps the business is altogether too dull and painful for the easy manipulations of cinema romance; and original sin (or original incapacity) is too sorry a deterrent to the halcyon endings which cinema demands. I do not, therefore, object overmuch to the fairy-tale form. It is dangerous, like other drugs, but not half so dangerous as the underlying suggestion, in this case, that a benevolent dictatorship can curb rapacity, and that peace can be commanded by a jingo display of war power.

*   *   *

Arrowsmith is about publicity—which is the little rather snuffy-nosed brother of Propaganda. It tells, as you probably know from the Sinclair Lewis novel, the sad story of an American who once upon a time hated publicity. He was a research worker and discovered a serum and went to the Caribbean to demonstrate it in a plague of bubonic. The serum came through, and the medical came back to New York to shun publicity as a plague even worse than bubonic. With any great instinct in research he might have discovered a serum for publicity, too. But he did not think of that. He merely humped into melodramatic gestures of personal integrity, and shunned it. Here I am not so sure what the issue is, but I liked the film very well for the fine acting of Colman as the medical, for the superb direction of John Ford (a great director at all times) and for the unusually fine art direction. It is a good film: slick to a degree in its sequence and beautifully shot.

I see there are objections to the Caribbean sequence, which is supposed to be—in heavy contrast to the rest of the film—too 'studio'. I thought it all 'studio' and the Negro spiritual effects, which accompanied the bubonic in the jungle, no more unreal in drama than the fantastic laboratory settings, and the strange laboratory habits of the research worker, Colman, and the miraculous muddlings among the beakers and test-tubes. Happily one does not expect realities in such a film. One accepts the studio props and the studio presentation and hopes that within these artificial limits something real and live will issue.

In this case I think it does. It is unusual to see an honest worker made a hero of: and it is almost revolutionary in a Hollywood film to see him heroicized in terms of his work. This is so much a matter for praise that one can forget the little snail tracks of box-office intention which emerge from time to time.

As for that ultimate issue between the honest worker and the publicity merchant, I wonder if it is the desperate affair the film would have us suppose. It is bad to have scientific results prostituted for a headline. But how otherwise can scientific results be spread to the populace except by simplifying them and dramatizing them? And how otherwise can public institutions establish their necessary public relations, except by translating their plans and results into the vernacular of luncheons and news stories?

That is my single objection to a good film. Sinclair Lewis is always bludgeoning some fake villain, and you must expect it from him.

*   *   *

'Just a rough diamond in a platinum setting—in tights, tiaras, tea gowns—singing songs that will make the town gasp. . . .' As a tired businessman myself, I felt the invitation to the Carlton was a personal one. Then I saw strange things indeed. Beside me were two benevolent, grey-haired old ladies. They chortled and chuckled and dug each other in the ribs at every wisecrack. A couple of rubber-tyred spinsters behind me raved. Young women in scattered singles stood off from their swains in sudden access of sophistication. Mae West was plainly not the dame for dithering men I expected of her, but something quite opposite. She was the woman who fulfilled not the first desire of males, but the last desires of females: who showed her weaker sisters how to 'find them, fool them and forget them'. The vicious streak in that curious cocktail was obviously going to the sisters' heads.

And why not? The character Mae West has created is the darling of every mill girl's and every duchess's dreams. She gets her man and plenty of them and plays the lot for the suckers they undoubtedly are. She demonstrates what every woman knows and only lacks the courage and the coolness to exploit to the maximum: the fact that the muzzier moments of the male are pretty muzzy. What matter if she is old and fat if she can hold them! Is it not part of this exquisite female romanticism that she holds them despite both age and fattery? No need indeed to fiddle and fuss, no need to belly crawl with a hundred and one abdominal titivations and facial falsifications, if a steady eye on the muzzier moments and a cool grip on the emotional occasions can out-countenance the victim.

I imagine women feel as proud of Mae West as men feel of Tom

Mix. She is the two-handed gunman of the parlours and the bold bad bandit of the bedrooms: as heroically unashamed as the other is heroically unafraid. I submit the feat to your attention as worth considerable applause. Mae has succeeded where D. H. Lawrence, in a lifetime of hard writing, failed most miserably. If D.H. had known his subject half as well as he professed to, he would have left it to the honky tonk girls from the start.

Apart from these profound considerations you will get a great deal of fun out of *I'm no Angel*: in Mae, in the original wise-cracks of Mae, and in the equally original movements of Mae. She is a thoroughly bad actress in a thoroughly bad story but, as a turn, she is worth the hour and a half she devotes to herself. On any ordinary ruling the Censor should have stopped her innuendoes in her throat. On a Rabelaisian ruling they pass with honours. 'It isn't the men in my life I am worried about: it's the life in my men,' says Mae—and very justly. I only wonder what the family trade will say about her. Will the ladies stir with pride and possibilities like the Carlton lot, and let danger be damned; or will the sickly look of recognition in their attendant males warn them to let sleeping dogs lie? Maybe it were better. Mae may find 'em and fool 'em, and so do they all in their fashion. But the wiser course is not to crow about it. The only weakness of Mae West's set-up is that she crows her head off. In so doing, she gives more than the game away; and no doubt women, on further thought, will spot the weakness. The female she presents is female enough; the manner of presentation, with its rip-roaring exhibitionism and self-certainty, is male. The thought may give pause to her female admirers, and I expect it presently will. I am afraid Mae is in for a short life though—bless her—a merry one. In the meantime 'let her glory shine', as they say among the Holy Rollers. May her every hip wriggle be priced in gold, her every shoulder shimmy above rubies. What honky-tonk queen should cost less?

4 The Cinema of Ideas

Great writers have had bad luck with cinema. Herman Melville's
Moby Dick, greatest of all sea stories, became a sentimental vehicle for
John Barrymore's profile, and the malice of the Great White Whale
was suppressed at last in a hide of indiarubber. The only importance
of *Peter Pan* and *A Kiss for Cinderella* in the history of the cinema was
that they lost a great deal of money and abolished whimsy for ever
from Hollywood's repertoire. *The Admirable Crichton* prospered, but
in the disguise of *Woman to Woman*. Mr. Shaw, with *How He Lied to
Her Husband*, turned out to be a poor scenario writer in a medium
which demanded action. The size of Anna Karenina escaped the Garbo,
and the devil of Dostoievsky was not in *The Brothers Karamazov*. The
single blessing of *Don Quixote* was that the butchery of its manufacture
produced *La Douce France*, one of the best satires ever written on the
movies. Only Shakespeare has done well. There was life in the Fairbanks account of *The Taming of the Shrew*, and something of the
ancient flash came through the Hebraic spectacle of *A Midsummer
Night's Dream*. Not even in alien accent does poetry completely perish.

There is a difference about Mr. Wells's entry into cinema. Hearing
perhaps of these other strange transformations, he has had the courage
to attend on the movie world in person. He has himself turned his book
into the terms of movie. And lest anyone, seeing the film, doubt what
he intended it to be, he has published his treatment. It is *Things to
Come*. Arriving so far, he has at least beaten the example of Mr.
Maeterlinck, who, after a luxurious passage to Hollywood and an
equally luxurious welcome, was told that they hoped, with patience, to
make him as great as Rex Beach. Maeterlinck did not finish. Hollywood found to its horror that his leading lady was a bee.

I hope I am not prejudiced by the professional reading of scripts, but
I find the published version of *Things to Come* fascinating and easy and
vivid to read. For anyone with eyes to see and a mind's eye to conjure
up the images he is meant to see, a film description has many advantages over plain narrative. Events, characterizations, and the argument
of the drama are whipped into a running shape more precisely and

101

with less meandering than the narrative form permits. Something certainly is lost. Those sandwiched encyclopædic slices of fact which give size to *Moby Dick*, and the rolling introductions which 'establish' the stories of Scott, must unfortunately go by the board. The deviations of description and commentary and plot within plot are impossible. But a mounting action and a tempo'd climax of argument and event give the film description its own virtue. For this alone *Things to Come* must be a revelation to most people. Here they will see the stuff of which films are made, and, by its origin, it is big stuff which has not often come the way of a film director.

One thing about Wells is that he lives and learns to the minute. I have seen Shaw sink dully, and, for once, dumbly, before a description of the possibilities of cinema. Against this is the vision of Wells sitting watching, month after month, the wildest experiments the London Film Society could conjure up for him. In so far as he has confessed in my own theatre at the G.P.O. that he was in course of 'learning' from us, I may, I hope, claim the right to examine him on his first result.

Let me set down the story in brief and be done with it. In his introductory word, Wells calls it a 'spectacle'. It is not, like the book *The Shape of Things to Come*, 'a discussion of social and political forces', but a 'display' of them; for 'a film is no place for argument'. The subsequent arguments of its readers and spectators were not the less violent for that. The spectacle is certainly a strange one.

It is 1940 or perhaps a little before, and the good families of Everytown are preparing for Christmas. War breaks out and disrupts the families, dragging out from 1940 to 1970. Civilization disappears and Everytown reverts to medieval conditions. The technique of our era of science is lost. The Black Death comes. In the stage of final desolation the reversion to the primitive is complete. Mechanical knowledge is vaguely remembered, and buying and selling is a matter of old clo' bazaars where the effects of the ancient gentry are the prize of bandits' mistresses. The great patriots' war goes on under the leadership of petty chiefs and savage gangsters.

At this point the old Wellsian finger wags, and out of Basra comes a new dominating force which restores civilization and the world. It is, of course, as every Wellsian knows, the power of the technicians and scientists, mobilized and regimented to reorganize what the politicians and the soldiers, with their imbecile nationalism, have destroyed. As a saving qualification, however, even with the dictatorship of the technicians, perfection does not altogether come. The question of the haves

102

and the have-nots they solve. The deeper question of the do's and the do-nots remains. There is revolution in the Utopia of 2055: on the question of whether two young people should be sacrificed by science in a journey to the moon. That revolution is not resolved, and the film ends, as Wells promised, 'in a note of interrogation among the stars'.

The story goes with a clip, making light of marching armies, landscapes of tanks and poison gas, and scenes of death and desolation as vast as London Town. The chronicle rips over the years of Everytown with the destructive gusto of a tornado making for Miami. 'The Tower Bridge of London in ruins. No signs of human life. Seagulls and crows. The Thames, partly blocked with debris, has overflowed its damaged banks.' This, one effect in thousands, gives every assurance of spectacle. But one problem drums in my head. Can patriotism be mobilized to its own evident destruction over thirty years? Is the human spirit so craven as to endure the destruction of civilization in the name of whatsoever patriotism? On a more practical and political level, would an armed proletariat stand for it? Wells was not in the war of 1914–18, or he would have sensed how near the breaking-point men can be not in thirty years but in three. The facts are there to guide political philosophy. The Russians broke in three, the Germans in four, and there were, shall we say, certain difficulties appearing among British, French, and Italians alike.

It is an important issue for the film, for I doubt if any thesis can sell so vast a dereliction of the human spirit as these thirty years of death and desolation represent. Few at heart will believe in it, and where there is no belief there is only melodrama. On a first impression of the treatment I would say that too much of one's common experience is left out of account. I remember a certain Peter Kerrigan magnificently challenging a crowded St. Andrew's Hall in Glasgow to 'pit him oot' and receiving no answer. There are no Peter Kerrigans in *Things to Come*—not at least for thirty years—nor flywheels of Russian example to hold the desolation in check.

On a lower level there are other doubts, particularly about these technicians who take the place of the proletariat of Marxist theory and create the first liquidating dictatorship. This is to put faith in a class of society which in the past has shown no inclination to serve any but the highest bidder, and as a class has demonstrated no political consciousness at all. The experts walked out of Russia with their masters. It is an axiom of Marxism that only the proletariat know the burden of Fascism and war, and may be trusted to destroy the system responsible. This one may at least comprehend. That a privileged and honoured class like the experts should find fire and determination enough to give new laws to society is a trifle more difficult to appreciate.

These are the essential issues of *Things to Come* and more important than any mere question of film treatment. Being important issues they, of course, affect the treatment considerably. As a result of this lack of faith in the common people there are, for example, no common people in the film, save as soldiers and victims, and no braveries or humanities of common people. A photographic art is, in the last resort, an art of the ordinary. It may by its many fantastic devices create vision and spectacle, but a shot of a child or a spontaneous gesture will bring you slap bang into cinema's own essential virtue. These scenes of war and pestilence, of a craven or non-existent people, these star-finding technicians, have not the life's blood of such common observation. They are rather the projection of an argument which one feels is itself out of touch with common observation.

The film reflects this difference. There are marchings and counter-marchings of time—abstract, spectacular, melodramatic, fantastic—but they are no more humanly true than the effects of *Metropolis*. It is a great story and a great tract, but, if I may say the worst, it is no more intimate in its human reference than a spectacle by de Mille.

There is, of course, the argument that it is high time the spectacles of de Mille found the quality of a great writer and time that we had a great tract in cinema. That miracle has certainly come to pass. There will be more thinking over *Things to Come* than over any film since *Deserter*. There is a greater sense of social warning and a better instruction in citizenship than in any previous film whatsoever. It is perhaps the measure of *Things to Come* that it sets out in most popular fashion to make the millions think. The important thing is that the first of our great writers has taken this medium of millions and studied it and used it to address the world.

I will not say that Wells is as good in the cinema medium as he is in his own. It would be foolish to expect this, for the idiom of the cinema is a young man's idiom asking even newer complexities of mould than Joyce himself. Wells gives the show away in pretty fashion when he tells us that the music specially written by Arthur Bliss for the film may be had on gramophone discs. Any real film man will laugh at the possibility of such a divorce, and suggest mildly that where there is so much of pure music there must be less of pure film. In yet another direction I do not find any of these heartbreaking qualities of

104

time and suspense with which a more poetic Pudovkin introduces his great scenes and sets them against the far horizons of drama.

But these are academic points. What I greatly admire is that this brave old master has out-faced us all with the size and scope of his vision, and that this clever old master has seen a way, within the vicious limitations of commercial cinema, to advance a great social argument. Before these two major facts I do not care how unsubtle his sound band is. The mental band is all right, and when, pray, did cinema ever give consideration to *that*?

*   *   *

Don Quixote is still the greatest of the enchanted wanderers and, whatever film is made of him, something of the idea must inevitably be left to excite the imagination. In Pabst's film something does remain and, sorry rag that it is, it is enough to give the film an almost revolutionary distinction. We do not often take our films into the higher and wider adventures and never, except possibly in Chaplin, into the irrational regions of philosophy. Surfeited with the too, too local anecdotes of Shepherd's Bush and Hollywood, it is pleasant to remind ourselves that cinema may also deal with ideas.

The film itself is a triumph of photography, with a peak in the windmill scene which must delight everyone who respects the powers of the camera. The acting presence of Chaliapine, too, is something so unique in itself that it commands respect. But the film and the idea within the film: that is another story altogether.

Chaliapine needed a mountain top to give film proportion to his gestures; and the idea of Quixote needed wind and space and horizon to give it size in cinema. But no, the poor devil staggers through five hundred close-ups of face and posture, with a rabble of grotesquely inferior studio actors jostling him for each. Never, except in the final windmill scene, does the film begin to open out. Even the battle with the sheep and the freeing of the thieves are cabined and confined: with an over-filtered photography depriving them of their last vestige of air. A dropsical curse this super-photography sometimes is!

From a directorial point of view this lack of space has a disastrous effect on the whole film. How, except against images of isolation, is Quixote conceivable? The romantic lunatic as a hero might be a great subject, but his dream needs the detached substance of poetry to make him a figure of drama and not of a lunatic asylum. If sympathy is to

105

be got for him, or heroism or tragedy added to the tatterdemalion grandeur of his hopes, it is only against other-world horizons that he can properly be figured. And that, in cinema, is definitely not to be done by close-ups.

Don Quixote does not come over. We note the gestures of his knight errantry and, impossibly connotated as Cervantes makes them, they mean, or should mean, something real. The injustice which sleeps neither night nor day, the chastity which is the first rule of knighthood, the chains which must be broken, the giants, the magicians, even the lances and the helmets and the Rosinantes have reference in the common philosophy. But here, there is no deep familiarity in our contact with them, though every Tom, Dick, and Harry of us has waved his similar plumes. How, in jostling studio streets or scrappy close-set encounter of sheep, prisoners, wine bags and comic tournament, could there be!

One directorial occasion will suffice to indicate how *Don Quixote* goes dead. Quixote has emerged from the tourney and, raising his helmet, recognizes Carrasco as the fake adversary. It is a moderately important moment when he says pathetically: 'I have been tricked, they have made a fool of me': and a more important moment still when, with a last muster of essential dignity, he rides off through the jeering populace. That dignity meant everything to the representation of the idea. It should have been staged mountain high: the audience with Quixote, the laughter breaking in waves of the sea over him. But no: one far shot of Quixote riding off, and the crowd of monkey extras yelling their heads off into the camera! I never saw a great occasion so shoddily done, and that it came from a man of ordinarily fine understanding like Pabst I cannot understand.

Quixote, of course, is not necessarily this figure of tragedy. It is only one of the many possible ways of playing him. You may affirm that his pursuit of Romance in a world of two-times-two makes him more naturally a figure of comedy. You may follow the pundits and say that he is the pilloried representative of chivalry and a figure of satire. Or you may note the cumulative quietness and affection of the Cervantes narrative and say he is just as possibly a figure of picaresque or of fairy tale. On any one of these counts this Pabst-Chaliapine interpretation has equally failed.

Chaliapine has played the figure too high for either comedy or satire. He presents Quixote from the first as distraught and a madman, and holds this note of overwrought insanity to the end. Quixote is as heavily outlined as Boris Goudonov. So detached from ordinary recognition is he, so much a figure for certification, that you neither laugh at him nor make fun of him.

As for fairy-tale, the touch is not light enough, the vision too pedestrian. The wine bags are just ordinary wine bags, the sheep just ordinary sheep, the tourney just a plain bad tourney. You see them as such, and for all the director and the camera tell you there is nothing more. You might have seen them as Quixote saw them, for giants and magicians and fearful affrays, and captured that double vision of phenomena which is the essence of fairy-tale, but Pabst (Teuton though he is) has forgotten the possibility. Quixote is just a poor stick.

In spite of complaint the film stays curiously in the head. It may seem that Pabst has done a scurvy job by this English version and allowed a tenth assistant cameraman to cut it; but it is difficult not to sympathize with a poor benighted Pabst doomed to direct the notoriously undirectable Chaliapine and mix him with the somewhat unmixable Robey. The job may have been impossible from the beginning. In the problem of a German directing Chaliapine and Robey in a language which he (probably) and Chaliapine (almost certainly) did not understand may be found a sufficient excuse for the curiously undramatic and unmeasured wordage which accompanies the film. But whatever the final judgment on the film, it is certain to turn the molecules of criticism. And that is a unique distinction.

* * *

The Reverend Galsworthy's famous sermon on gentility, *The Skin Game*, has been turned into a film. Hitchcock is the new preacher, but the sermon remains very much as before. It is still the funny, rollicking yarn it always was.

If you remember, the Hillcrists, who are the landed gentry, are at outs with the Hornblowers, who are the industrial gentry. You never saw such a fight of hooligans. They storm and threaten and kick each others' shins; they accumulate every species of muck from rotten eggs to cods' entrails and slosh it over each others' heads; they turn to blackmail and reputation-dirtying with an ease which would astonish and even stagger the most hard-baked criminal. At the end of it, the Reverend Galsworthy asks his famous question: 'What's the use of gentility if it can't stand fire?' The operative word is 'gentility'.

I first heard that tag line years ago and have never ceased to find diversion in inventing answers for it. That, however, was in the days before the Raspberries (American and Hungarian) short-circuited criticism.

There is, of course, an issue between these landed and industrial gentries. The landed gentry, it seems, do not want the nasty chimney smoke drifting over their demesne. The industrial gentry, it seems, think the landed gentry a bunch of snobs. There is (for the moment) some question of whether a certain peasant's cottage will be held by the landed landlord or blotted out by the industrial landlord. There is also the very grave question of whether a proletarian damsel of doubtful origin can be the sort of person a landlord (landed or industrial) would care to have around. On this last matter, as you can imagine, both landlords are agreed.

If you like your fights faked, this one may stir you. Otherwise, I am afraid, you will find it a very unfunny farce indeed. For, of course, Mr. Hillcrist and Mr. Hornblower never fought at all. They fell into each other's arms seventy and eighty years ago. Mr. Hillcrist put his money in Mr. Hornblower's business and Mr. Hornblower bought some of Mr. Hillcrist's land and they have been as thick as thieves ever since. And well they might be. What birds of a feather they were, and are.

Can you really imagine Mr. Hillcrist worrying about the industrial smoke over his demesne? Why, it was the merriest thing in the world when he found coal under it, and no trouble of conscience at all to have it ripped up and slaughtered and uglied by workers' slums if the royalties were forthcoming. Can you really imagine Mr. Hillcrist worrying about the poor peasant in the corner field? Did he not put his fields to sheep and easy profits, and drive him into Mr. Hornblower's factories? Did he not otherwise burn him out of that very cottage and drive him to a wilderness overseas, Hillcrist himself not caring a hoot in hell where he went?

I can assure you of a fine time at *The Skin Game* if you have a neighbourly neighbour you can poke in the ribs and chuckle with: it is full of such jokes. It will give you all sorts of opportunities for casting your mind back on the other fruits of that English gentility which Mr. Hillcrist so splendidly represents. You will hear of the honest land-love the Reverend G. claims for him, and think of his criminal neglect of his drainage system. You will hear the Reverend G. blubbering about his sportsmanship, and think of the tenants he has rowed across the ferry. This was the Highland Hillcrist's equivalent for bumping off. The rest was hat-touching, forelock-pulling, fifteen shillings a week and a bag of meal.

As for Mr. Hornblower, he was so shocked when Chloe turned out

The Cinema of Ideas

to be a proletarian damsel of doubtful origin, that he left that part of
the country for ever: retaining only a controlling share in the local
company. It was strange for Mr. Hornblower to be so shocked, because
at that very moment he was pimp to a thousand Chloes in his very own
factories. It was hardly so strange that he should worry mostly about
the shock to his system and very little about poor Chloe herself. But
you may depend on it he got over what shock there was. In another
parish over the hill he set up his mansion with the rest of them, and
has been Lord Hornblower to this day.

No, you could not expect the Reverend Galsworthy to know these
more intimate details of the Hornblower family history. Like the other
literary toadies of his generation, he sobs on a short front.

The film itself I must proclaim for the fine job it is. It is a smooth
account, with all the ingenuity in character. But when, oh, when, will
Hitchcock get a theme that will match with his powers of production?
This has all the air of being more important than the previous ones,
but when you come to think of it, what a shallow and contemptible
theme it is!

* * *

All Quiet on the Western Front is Universal City's version of
Remarque's picaresque war novel. The film is built on a larger scale
than the book, and considering the crudity and naïveté, and the still
unmastered complexities of the sound film medium in which it is
presented, it is a braver and bigger piece of work than the original.

Not better. Writing a novel is a moderately simple business, and
simpler to do well. One man sees it through from start to finish,
without any more interference from an outside world than he cares to
stand for. At the worst he can, like Joyce or Lawrence, publish in
France: but always he has the will of his medium. His materials are
cheap.

With cinema it is very different. For every foot of film you shoot,
you may put down 6d.[1] for the material film alone. Your actors, sets,
and equipment, your regimental staff of cameramen, art directors,
electricians, carpenters, and the rest, come over and above. Your most
humble effort in cinema carries you therefore into a maelstrom of high
finance—a maelstrom in which the promoters, backers, bankers, and
other riff-raff of private enterprise tumble and curvet like so many
dogfish, snapping for dividends. They require safeguards for your
every move, and reduce the essential gamble of art to such vulgar

[1] Today the equivalent figure would, of course, be much larger.

109

certainty as their own minds command. They will not trust their funds into a world of art or inspiration, for that indeed would be trusting them out of their sight. By that fact is the film director limited. He is in strait-jacket to the devil. There are few occasions when he breaks through.

All Quiet is the exceptional occasion. The tracks of the companioning pig are to be found only at the theatre entrance. A lady with one leg naked to the hip stands over the doorway at the Alhambra bidding the vulgar suppose that the film concentrates on the higher nudities. The film, however, is consistently earnest and for quite considerable passages intelligent. I have heard that the director's ending was scrapped for an ending suggested by the favourite son of one of the bosses, but by that time you will be too grateful for a deal of honest directing to worry about the soft-headed symbolism of a single last shot.

The film handles war material a thousand times better than any previous Hollywood film has known how to. It gathers them up relentlessly, more detail and more, till the mass of detail registers the size and significance of war itself. Any private story there may be is cast strictly in proportion to the size and significance of that larger reality. This, you may well believe, is almost revolutionary in Hollywood film technique.

There is, however, something more in *All Quiet* than the bravery of the war scenes. There are passages of intimate feeling—intimate war feeling—which show quite unusual power of insight for a film production. These passages, I admit, are balanced at least equally by passages of mother love and youthful whimpering in which the insight is more nearly Hollywoodesque, but the greater moments are none the less real. In the best of these you might be sitting with Gorki, and I found some satisfaction in the thought that this best was provided by the long-lost Raymond Griffith. He is the French soldier whom the youth stabs to death in the panic of the retreat and, dying, he becomes a cynical mask of death that delivers in a flash all that any anti-war film could wish to say. The youth might well scream through the night watches in such a presence.

Oh yes, it is a good film, but, that justice be balanced, I shall put down certain qualifications. I did not like the whining mamma of the 'leave' episode; and I did not like the boy's prayers over the hospital death-bed of his friend. In moments of the greatest personal emotion there must be a decent limit to fluency, and no suspicion of exhibitionism. The stuttering Shakespearian model stands: 'Pray do not mock me . . . I am a very foolish blind old man . . .'. This film, like

The Cinema of Ideas

others, tends to take the high spots easily, and the sentimental and the slick are blood brethren in the field of art. The boy, for example, talks much too much when the mask of death is driving him mad. The essence of madness is surely silence, as any trip to a madhouse will testify. The silence may be broken suddenly and perhaps terribly, but the beastly thing about the business is that it sinks intolerably back into silence again.

Once or twice, however, the film does reach that final stabbing restraint: once when the boy kisses the hand of the little French girl (she of the higher nudity), once when he finds the last of his comrades dead on his shoulders, and once again when on a morning in spring, the boy himself is killed. On these occasions the Western Front is indeed most poignantly quiet.

This unevenness in *All Quiet* may or may not be due to a weakness or confusion in the idea controlling it. It is concerned, as the book was, with the futility of war and, to be sure, some wars are futile enough. But, complaining too much about the futility of a particular war, it carries over into a pacifist complaint against war in general. And that is dangerous ground for drama. The embittered protest of outraged youth becomes too closely associated with the quite different protest against all life-doctrine, and apt to set up a deal of whining. It may be dirty—as the film maintains—to die for one's country, but there must always, of course, be some country—define that country how you please—for which it is in the original sense good to die and to discipline for; the two processes being in principle identical.

In this case there is no ironsided assurance of one country or another, one positive life or another, behind the film; and the conclusion of futility is on the whole too easily bought. Youth dies without having lived or died for anything in particular. This is not true tragedy. The essence of that highest of all philosophic forms is that the size and articulation of death is only complementary to the size and articulation of the life that is set against it. Here death is terrible enough, but all that is lost is a rather sentimental undefined demonstration of youthfulness. The film deduces no considered or deepening reason why one should weep for it.

*　　*　　*

Frankenstein is the sensation of the day. It is not as I write the best film in London; but it will make more money than any of them. I watch the local intelligentzia go through the usual agonies of despite

111

when a popular crasher comes along, but away they toddle to see what it is all about. So, I imagine, will most people.

In *Frankenstein* we advance majestically from the sevenpenny novelette to the penny blood. It sets out to scare you to death and it succeeds. This may or may not be an important thing to do, but the yokel in you will snoop up to the Chamber of Horrors and plunk down the necessary penny. There is no use me saying that its direction is comical, its general level of acting atrocious, its romantic relief a last word in infantile imagining: when Frankenstein's monster is upon you, tearing and rending, and growling and whining, the yokel in you will rise and acclaim and tell me to take my criticism to the devil.

This only proves what one of my comrades-in-arms is forever telling me. Skill doesn't matter; cleverness certainly doesn't matter: only the idea matters. In *Frankenstein* the idea is altogether novel in cinema. What does it matter if it is presented idiotically, if the imagination that went to its making is the imagination of a rabbit: it is sensational enough in itself to emerge from any directorial murdering.

The film tells you of the strange manufacture of a human being and of what befell between this manufactured man and the world he stumbled into. He had a raw beginning. A crazy young doctor gathers corpses from graves and charnel houses and anatomists' slabs and moulds their dead pieces together. As men have done before him, he calls down fire from Heaven and pours life into this creature of his making. He is a strangely pathetic figure at first, raising stiff arms in wonder to the light, and taking orders like some great lumbering baby. But, gathering strength, he gets gradually out of hand. He murders his keeper, breaks from the watch-tower of Frankenstein, and terrifies an entire countryside with savage attacks on everything he encounters.

You may trust the film to tell you how awesome in sound and sight such an unnatural customer may be. When the bats fly low and night's in the sky, Universal Studios are at their best.

The finale is of a brute savagery in the pursuing mob which easily beats in subnormality the efforts of any single monster born or created. They drive him into a windmill and burn him, screaming and screeching, to death. As George Atkinson demonstrates, the film rises in glee to the foul sadistic excitement of an Alabama manhunt.

There are two moments in this film altogether magnificent: the gesture of the monster as he raises his eyes to the light for the first time, and his reaction to the first sight of a child. How anything of this beauty got into a film so crudely inspired, I cannot conceive. I can only think that the episodes were in Mrs. Shelley's book, and that Boris

Karloff, who played the monster, was bigger by a mile than Carl Laemmle junior and his scenario department.

Indeed I am sure of Karloff's part in the business, for he brings a curious beauty to the role which the script does not intend. The story is stacked against any sympathy with the monster; his brain is supposed to be a criminal brain; he is supposed to be a savage, congenitally wrong. But, seeing the film, I thought there was a greater human dignity in him than in all the miserable little Anglo-American fools who yapped round his great heels. I even found a certain perverse pleasure in his disembowelling of the idiots.

Of course, the whole trouble is that Hollywood has cheapened a great theme. This monster might be anything. It might be a symbol of every creation whatsoever, for each must inevitably take life to itself and pass beyond the power of its maker. It might be a symbol of machinery which, invented in good faith, becomes by the stupidity of its manipulators the degrading monster it is. It might, like any figure of Greek tragedy, represent the power from which some last gift of grace is lacking; or, in still another rendering, represent the Rogozhin to Prince Myshkim, the Hyde to every human Jekyll. Shakespeare made Caliban of such a figure, giving it the brutish reference of ancient eras and first strugglings from slime.

There is no end to the possible significances, except in the limits of your imagination. All Hollywood saw, however, was a bogey man and a chance to whoop up the boys with straw in their ears. I admit they have done it well. The scene where life is born (by aid of a 'ray beyond the violet ray', a ten-foot spark-gap, and a melodramatic thunderstorm) is good value for money; and the art director who created the sets deserves a special hand. The stumbling entrances, the off-stage whinings, the fantastic agonies of Karloff in the final flames, are quite physical in their effect. But here's to the straw in your ears! May you quake!

*   *   *

Like most people who work at cinema, I see too many films: respecting most of them for the labour and the ingenuity I know they contain and, in one way or another, learning from all; but it is seldom enough that a film bowls you over. *The Life of Emile Zola* is one of the fine ones which begin as a film and end as an experience: like *Potemkin*, *Earth*, *Deserter*, *Man of Aran*, *Pasteur*, and, with all its faults, *The Good Earth*.

On the sweeping canvas of late nineteenth-century France, Hollywood has staged in this life of Zola as dramatic a battle for truth as ever the cinema managed in fact or fiction. Most people will wonder how they came to be interested, but, considered as a form of expiation, there is good reason for its fire. No one would be more likely to appreciate the disintegration that goes on in the successful artist and the pains of the artist in the face of vested interests than the writers and directors of Hollywood.

The quality of the film derives from this feeling of secret auto-biography and, of course, from Paul Muni. As a piece of acting his account of the character of Zola is enormously skilled: jumping from age to age of the man; changing his gait, his speech, his idiosyncrasies, his mind: developing his literary character with such an uncanny sense of detail that, before we know it, we are facing a picture that so pleasantly reminds one of H. G. Wells that it cannot be far from the great Zola himself.

One sequence when Zola is a poor young man receiving his first fat cheque for *Nana* is a most moving little patch of film acting, and heaven knows what with. Another, when Zola makes his defence of truth at the Dreyfus libel trial, has the temerity to run eight hundred feet or so, or four times longer than the newsreels would allow our best political orators. Muni gets away with it. This I find queer enough. He has, at times, more annoying mannerisms than any actor I know, yet this power of settling into the clothes of his character amounts almost to transubstantiation.

The principal theme of the story is not, as we have heard, the Dreyfus trial. Hollywood and its directors have taken deeper account of the writer himself: the progressive writer successful, finally complacent, shocked into the old fire by the political scandal which the Dreyfus case represented. Whatever the literary accuracy may be, it is a story which feels good all the way and in the great trial scene when judges act like curs and generals like jackals, it becomes, for a moment, majestic. A curious point is that Cézanne has been made the driving force of Zola's life. He appears as a much lighter figure than the bearded tough of the portraits and a more romantic figure than the fierce old psalmist Cézanne actually was; but let it be registered as the most bewildering thing of the year. Hollywood has paid this tribute to the man who, more than anyone in the last half-century, despised everything that Hollywood stands for.

*   *   *

The Cinema of Ideas

Dead End was a serious and successful play on Broadway. It is equally serious and successful as a film. It is beautifully directed by William Wyler, who is not only one of the great directors, but one of the rare two or three whose sense of drama is as adult as his skill. It is profuse in human sympathy as it dives down into the tenements of East Side New York and discovers the teeming tragedy of the poor. What more can we ask? We have challenged the cinema to grow up and take stock of society, and here it does both. We have cursed its dream life and sugar-stick endings. Here is real life and—as one gangster generation dies of its own evil and a new generation is marched off to the reformatory—here is the spondaic ending of honest observation.

Yet, and in spite of watching the film with eagerness and respect, I dislike it intensely and it won't do at all. It is aquarium stuff. It looks at people distantly, like fish, and its sympathy is cold with distance. The poor, poor beggars, are poor; they are uncomfortable; they breed thieves and gangsters and a curse on the conditions that breed them; they struggle against overwhelming odds and what break are they given in achieving the good life? That is the theme and the thesis. It sounds all right; but who was it said that there was more reality in a louse on a dirty bagman than in all this sorrow for the working class? Granted the poverty, the discomfort, the struggle against odds, no slice of humanity is so dim and sad as *Dead End* observes. They laugh and fight and love one another and, except to the sympathizers from without, their dreams of escape are not more important than the rich grip on life they already signify. It is this that *Dead End* misses. It lacks gusto.

Perhaps I am no great shakes as a reformer, but I feel a trifle bewildered when I see anæmia made the price of reform. In *Dead End* the heroine, poor dear, wants a cottage in the country away from 'all this' and the architect hero, poor dear, feels so savage he could pull down 'all this' with his bare hands. Well, I say, let the L.C.C. boys and all such look to that; and they will. But who, except the dramatist and the poet, will see to it that the deeper virtues are not lost in the process? Here, emphatically, there is no contact with these deeper virtues. The poor fish swim round and round with sad eyes and no escape: as though escape were outside, along Riverside Avenue and into the Bronx, and not inside, laughing and loving one another and kicking up hell at injustice and being themselves.

I urge the point because there is one thing the cinema preciously possesses. It began in the gutter and still trails the clouds of glory with which its vulgar origin was invested. But as we ask it to go deep, be sure we are not just asking it to go middle class. And be sure that the next phase of cinema may not be to eliminate the Cagneys in favour of the Colmans, and indeed to Colmanize Cagney himself. Behind all the arguments about the future of British films there has been an alignment which reflects this fear, and it is far more important for the future than all the divisions over national *v.* international, small films *v.* large. Some of us say the future is where vitality is, and never mind the art of cinema for the present. It would be a pity if we achieved everything and lost our sense of smell.

*   *   *

Vessel of Wrath is the Somerset Maugham story of the beachcomber in the South Seas who in drunkenness and debauch defies the reforming zeal of a couple of English missionaries and finishes off by marrying the female member of the godly pair and keeping a pub in Sussex. Charles Laughton makes it a study of comic misbehaviour. There is great skill in his insolence and a nicely calculated vulgarity which is very near that gusto we have been missing so much in British films. Viewed as a comment, not on missionaries, but on those wretched Women's Leagues of America who have been taking the corpuscles out of American films, Laughton's performance has a certain importance.

A little more of this sort of thing and the British cinema will be able to challenge the American on the simple ground of sophistication. No one will be more sensible of the challenge than the Hollywood producer.

Like any first film from a new production unit, *Vessel of Wrath* is a problem child, and just because it is important one has to say so. *Henry VIII*, the epic of Royal bedsheets, produced no heirs male. This one may if its errors are realized and the Mayflower unit's arrangements tightened up accordingly.

For one thing the film does not drive through to its ending. The last third is no resolution of the first two and the film fails in narrative power. I think I know why. Hunt Stromberg once pointed to the fundamental necessity of having someone decide the mould of a film and see to it that all the participants fit their contribution into the mould. Here the mould has not dictated the part of the actors. They have spilled their business on and over and round about, with great generosity but a minimum of discipline.

In the first place, for reasons of economy Erich Pommer has acted as both producer and director—a silly thing to do as Pommer should know, better than anyone. Where the cold-blooded eye of the producer was wanted, the warm appraising eye of the director has taken command. Director and actor have produced a similar undisciplined situation. Because presumably Laughton was partner in this new venture he has been given more than his due, and I know of no more fearful spectacle under the sun than an actor footloose.

I do not blame Laughton but Pommer. After all it is in the nature of a good actor to be the worst of critics. Especially when he is good, no one will ever convince him that a medium which, like the film, can do so much of his acting for him, is not stealing his personal thunder.

I like Laughton very much, for he is a brilliant fellow, but I like the future of British films even more. He will not mind, therefore, if I suggest an elementary lesson in the categories. The trouble with Laughton is that he is good at several very different things. He has skill in tragedy and has an ambition to play King Lear. He speaks rhetoric with a flair almost unique among modern actors, and though there may be mannerism in the way he slides across a full stop, no one will forget his reading of the Bible in *Rembrandt*. He is, moreover, a dangerously good and upsetting showman in his capacity for lagging on a cue and exaggerating an acting trifle behind the back of his director. No scrum half ever played the blind side of a referee more knowingly. Add to these talents the equally various ones of being good at comedy and quite brilliant in slapstick and you have a deadly mixture of virtues.

In any single film you can't possibly have the lot. Lear cannot possibly at the same time act the Fool, and Macbeth take his place among the porters. That precisely is what Laughton is forever doing. He does not understand economy, and by the mere process of being everything by starts and nothing long, is the greatest saboteur a film could have. It may all come from his anxious desire to add everything of himself to the value of the film. But the damage is certain. Laughton one at a time would be the wonder of the day. Five at a time he is a producer's headache.

I have quarrelled a great deal with people over *Vessel of Wrath*. But I soon found we were quarrelling over very different things. I viewed it as principally slapstick and was prepared to forgive the odd departures into drama and sentiment. My arguers had viewed it as drama and were bewildered by the fact that it was mostly slapstick. See the film as, nearly, in the category of Laurel and Hardy, and you will see *Vessel of Wrath* at its best.

But this does not absolve Pommer and Laughton from making up their minds more decisively next time. Knowing Laughton a little, I think he should come through. A strategic retreat from his own talents is what is called for.

* * *

Captains Courageous, I am told, is the film of the month among the general releases, and I believe it, though I can never find my way in the idiotic labyrinth of *premières*, first runs, second runs, and the kind I see at the Crystal in the Borough. These, of course, are the best ones, for by the time a film gets to the Crystal the spit and polish have gone, the confidence trick of presentation and ballyhoo is an old damp squib of months ago, and *Lost Horizon, Mr. Deeds*, and the Hoot Gibsons, they all come even at last on the bill boards. They have to talk across the hard floors and the waste spaces of the peanuts to be good, with nothing to warm them except what is inside themselves, and that is as it should be. The Crystal is the place to pick the classics all right. Only the elemental survives under its last ironic timeless eye.

But *Captains Courageous*, I know, will pass down the line in triumph and, except for its miserable and indeed bloody last reel, it will be for the boys of the old Dover Road what the cinema was thirty-five years ago in the then abandoned skating-rinks. I cannot be a critic at all about this film. It has everything I asked for thirty-five years ago—the sea and the fishing-schooners and fog on the Grand Banks and fishing cod from a dory with hand lines one after the other—and then a race between the schooners in a high wind, with noses ploughing under and throwing water high over the fo'c'sle, and the hull heeling over till it seems impossible it will ever come back, and the mast straining under the bravery of brave men, till it cracks.

I confess I have been fortunate since. I have gone to sea as I vowed and fished cod one after the other with hand lines one after the other, and there isn't a whip of wind or water, or a hull heeling over so it didn't seem it would come back, that I couldn't match; and the reality was as good as the dream, as all realities are when you look into them. The only difference, perhaps, that it wasn't mostly on the Grand Banks and the only fish I ever loaded into a Grand Banks schooner was some raw bootleg liquor in the days of Prohibition. But here, with *Captains Courageous*, I fall for it as hard as ever and all over again, and will quite certainly join a schooner at Gloucester, Mass., as soon as I can get there, and in spite of the Swiss advertisements and the Travel and Industrial Association of Great Britain and Ireland, saving their presence.

118

The Cinema of Ideas

Maybe when I get to Gloucester, Mass., I shall not hold so strongly for racing till the foremast goes; and there is a point in navigational ethics in crossing a bank in a high sea, just to beat the other fellow, which I shall discuss at length, if not soberly, with the skipper. I have no doubt either, that we shall get by without losing the brave and noble Spencer Tracy when the mast goes and indulging in a long heart-to-heart talk with him before he finally disappears below the waves. I feel certain that at the end of our trip, when we unload our cod and sell them smart, that we shall not have a grand slam burial service for the hundreds of drowned sailormen we have left behind us, with weeping women and other nonsense stacked to the skyline, and a daft statue of an emaciated man-at-the-wheel towering over us, his eyes staring nowhere a good mariner's should. But all that is best in the film I shall have and easily; and that is how the sea is the one thing that never disappoints a man—and how good a sea film *Captains Courageous* is. A bit of exaggeration perhaps at the high spots, but basically all that a fishing film should be—with everybody in their right places round the table in the saloon, and the mixture of dirt, and discipline and ribaldry just right, and none of that sissy swagger that is coming these days into every ship afloat, what with education and the cruises and the pyjama parties on the Atlantic, so there is no sea tradition left, except in the stokeholds.

I should say that for this breath-taking reality of the sea—or, shall we say, the breath-taking reality of the romance of the sea made real— the film is better than Kipling, except that Kipling couldn't conceivably have made such an over-nauseating mess of that last reel. The Americans have handled the essential story well. The little prig of a boy who is due for salvation at the hands of fishermen is a very son of a bitch of a boy as played by Freddie Bartholomew, and his saving at the hands and heart of a Portuguese fisherman named Spencer Tracy is as nice and delicate a job of work as Spencer Tracy ever did. He even sold me a rather sappy address to the night sky and the angels and sang something about 'Don't cry little fish' in a harsh and horrible voice which, I confess, is my idea of singing on the Grand Banks off New-foundland. Only the long and dithering death of the man withdrew my loyalties. I can explain it only by saying that I don't mind old Captain Ahab dying as a hero should, when, as any fool can see, it is the time for Destiny and the Great White Whale to come for him. But watery graves, which happen by accident and only to be sad about them, are not good fishing, nor good film, but only bad Louis B. Mayer and melodramatic slobbering of the worst. When I get to Gloucester, Mass.,

Louis B. Mayer will quite positively not be present. He would drown anybody, including me, for his box-office.

Victor Fleming directed and I would like to hear his explanation of how so good a film—though, you will have gathered, simple-minded—managed to foul its lines so stupidly coming into harbour. For the death of our hero is but the signal for a general collapse in which Lionel Barrymore's seamanship, good film direction, and the tight little story of the making of a man, suddenly go off the earth together with Spencer Tracy. It is notorious that Americans, not content with the lugubrious sentimentality of Mothers' Day, have also created a Fathers' Day, and that is the trouble. What a people, what a people! The boy's father is brought in and there are dreadful goings on about fathers getting close to their sons, laying alongside their little hearts, close hauling their what-nots, and being pals to them, and other horrifying sickness of the sort, with the little hand finally closed in the fat sloppy hand of American paternity. Here, I regret to say, I leave the ship. Who does not know that fathers, like skippers, exist to slam hell out of their sons—and sons, fathers?

5 The Russian Example

In *One Family*, which sets out to bring our modern Empire alive, to seize and hold and shape the dramatic material of the Empire's commerce, the difficulty is to find a dramatic mould into which one can pour the ordinary business of orchard harvests, prairie harvests, plantation harvests and the like. It sounds easy as pie, I know, for these on the face of them are noble subjects, with the earth under, and the sky over, and a multitude of human lives in and around. The earth gives forth, the ships carry, the millions in the market place black each other's eyes for the profit and loss. Yes, but Canada and the Antipodes, Africa and the Indies—who will discover and map the common streams of dramatic life in a world so wide, and present them for the Congo rivers they are? That would be a large work indeed and in criticizing *One Family*, one should consider as much the size of the job involved as any tendency to shortcoming.

It may be—and what I understand of aesthetic bids me believe—that in making art in our new world we are called upon to build in new forms altogether. Fantasy will not do, nor the dribblings of personal sentiment or personal story. The building of our new forms has been going on, of course, for a long time in poetry and the novel and architecture, and even within such limitations of medium as one finds in painting and sculpture. We have all been abstracting our arts away from the personal, trying to articulate this wider world of duties and loyalties in which education and invention and democracy have made us citizens.

It would, I know, be easy to find a description of the problem as far back as Socrates. Was there not something to the effect that everything I have comes from the state, that in the state is my only self worth worrying about, and that my all must be for the state? I forget the lines, but where the state is so much vaster and more complex than the one-horse town of Athens, and the work of learning how to govern it decently is so important and so pressing, there is an urgency in the problem of articulating it to ourselves which is without parallel in the history of citizenship. What sentiments will we have in this new world

121

to warm and direct our will in it? How shall we crystallize them and teach them if we are to stave off chaos?

Do not believe it if people tell you we have only to go to the Russians for our guide. The Russians are naturally on the same job as ourselves, and more deliberately, and with less patience of the reactionary and sentimental Poets-in-Blazers who take the honours of art in our own country. But, looking at the core of the problem, what in fact have they given us? Pudovkin is only D. W. Griffith in Revolutionary garb, with the sensation of a Revolutionary victory by arms to balance the Ride of the Klansmen and the other fake climaxes of Griffith cinema. Who in the name of sense can believe in revolution as a true climax? As a first act climax perhaps, but not as a fifth. By these terms Pudovkin is, *qua* artist, no revolutionary at all. The pastures of his art are old pastures, eaten to the roots.

Eisenstein is something different, if on the whole not quite so successful. He plays the mass and thinks without a doubt in the mass, but again the fake climax of Revolution in *Potemkin*. And when he had a chance to make a climax of peace-in-the-mass instead of war-in-the-mass, he failed. *The General Line* is no less in its fundamentals a failure than Creighton's *One Family*. This is a hard saying with so many brilliant criticisms about on the subject, but I shall stand by it; and the Russians, I know, will take my point. Eisenstein does not get inside his Russian peasants nor, with true affection, inside the problem of co-operating them. He is looking at their peace drama from the outside, being clever about it, even brilliant about it, but from the outside. The struggle of their communal farms strikes no fire in him.

There is, I believe, only Turin and *Turksib* which for all its patches of really bad articulation is the single job that takes us into the future. *Turksib* is an affair of economics, which is the only sort of affair worth one's time or patience.

My only warning in that matter is that it makes the job of building its Railroad a great deal easier from the dramatic point of view, by its drought, its sandstorms, its icestorms, its rock-blastings, and its quite sensational railway ride. They are all handled supremely well, and no one before, of course, thought of making a high spot of either rock-blasting or an engine solo. But you will see one's difficulty in following out its method if I set you the problem of, say, London's commerce—today's London commerce—and not any special Christmas or Easter day of London commerce—and ask you to find the physical, that is to say the movie, equivalent for these droughts and sandstorms, etcetera. Turin had a desert, and we have a doorstep. Fundamentally it is no matter in art how far or near or easily romantic or difficultly romantic your subject is: the affair, if it is a real affair—an affair of State in the good sense of that phrase—can be dramatized somehow. But plainly, and I have been saying all this to say so, it is not easy.

I remember sitting with a couple of Russian directors discussing the set-backs which accompanied the production of *The General Line*. They knew, as I knew, how it had fallen short of expectations, but at the end of our talk the position of Eisenstein as a master of cinema had been unassailed. The size of the job, the difficulties of the job: these were the matters they talked of. I had a picture of a bunch of directors (the left-wing school of the Russian cinema) disagreeing in many things, achieving quite various successes and publicities, but working together as one on a problem they faced in common. We have no such grouping of directors in this country and no such grouping of dramatic loyalties where the cinema of public affairs is concerned. Any one of us who starts in on the job, starts in at scratch; the difficulty of our art, the size and life-giving power of our art ignored by the classes who have Power of the Militia (financial and all else) in this ribald State of England. We work ignominiously, half artists and half, for our living, errand-boys to the dickering doddering half-witted old Status Quo.

It would take a giant in such circumstances to produce anything comparable with the Russian films (and they are fools who expect it), for there would be no public thought or public urging behind the job. That is what we lack, and if the critics can create it, so much the better for all of us.

*   *   *

Dovzhenko's *Earth* is, I think, quite certainly one of the great films. I shall not guarantee that others will react to it as I did, but it may be decent to record that I have seen few films that have been responsible for the same renewal of cinematic energy. When I find a film that acts like a Salvation Army band on the weak and the wicked, I am content to avoid criticism and call it art.

Earth is a Russian film. It is tied to the Bolshevik idea as usual, but in some strange manner it manages to escape from it. There is just a possibility that the Russians accused it of Menshevik tendency and called for a more vigorous push on the Ukranian film front. The film tells the story of the struggle between kulak and peasant in the Ukranian villages: it is, in the upshot, rather more concerned with the Ukranian villages than with the struggle between kulak and peasant. The kulak, poor devil, who goes mad at the loss of his boundaries, is treated almost sympathetically. The local priest is for a brief but bright moment—before the Bolshevik code takes hold and forces Dovzhenko to make a 'heavy' of him—just the good stupid old village priest he was bound to be. Feeling a little out of it when the pagan youths order no prayer from him, unhappy, a figure—it is amusing to note—of Tchekov tragedy.

All this is rather fresh and with all my respect for Bolshevik ideology and the political righteousness with which it is pursued, I am tempted to take a step to the right and chortle for Dovzhenko's demonstration of the continuity of history. It means that Russian art threatens to leave melodrama and become—probably much too soon from a political point of view—humanist again.

Dovzhenko is a fine poet. His struggle between kulak and peasant is not really dramatic at all. The village people bring along a tractor; the tractor ploughs over the kulak's lands; the kulak shoots the fair-haired youth of the village in a crazy moment of drunken anger; and the young people of the village bury his body with hymns and speeches to the future. But all this will give you no idea whatever of the quality of *Earth*; and just because Dovzhenko is not a dramatist but a poet. The theme is right enough and good for deepening. It is in the deepening, however, in the attendant circumstances and accompanying image, that Dovzhenko shows his quality.

That other side of the film runs somewhat as follows:

It is autumn, apples are falling from trees, an old peasant is dying. The people of the village are gathered round him, talking easily, as peasants do, in the presence of death. The old man has laboured in the field for sixty-odd years, and should he not get a medal for that? He thinks he would prefer a pear. The sequence is quiet, and plainly done. Corn in three or four shots, apples in three or four more, the faces of the old man with only the faintest and subtlest changes of expression to carry the titles. A study in stills.

The villagers going off to fetch their tractor, low in the frame with a 90 per cent sky, the peasant ploughing with his solitary horse, high and heavy on the round of the hill for contrast. Space.

The tractor, after some trouble with radiators and a replenishment of radiators which is strictly censorable in England, arrives. The people in gala dress run to meet it, white and flashing in the sun, children young in the sun, dressed and decorative but with emphasis on light.

The tractor at work. Ploughing and reaping and threshing mixed up anyhow, and why not. Set against the stolid labours of a man with a scythe who refuses to be impressed. A fast sequence but no more

124

brilliant in cutting than many another. The speed picked up by inclusion of a man running, cut progressively faster and faster with the delving plough. A trick initiated by Turin.

Women bind the stooks high against the sky, laughing; the thresher is fed high against the sky, not too panchromatic and dropsical. There is wind and action and light, and a detail or two of bare peasant legs and blowing skirts. This, on the other hand, is Dovzhenko and important. He likes legs and blowing skirts and replenished radiators, rather decently. These details save the sequence from a certain lack of open spectacle. The women tie their stooks, standing to the camera, high, with their hands accurately in focus. This is one way of doing it and not the best. The emphasis, however, remains with wind, skirts, legs and sunlight.

The day is over and the labour done, and Dovzhenko is more at home than ever. The peasant youths stand statuesque in the dusk, each with his woman. From one point of view it is slightly implausible that youths and their women should so insist on the statuesque, for I cannot think that Russian ploughmen are inferior to our native ones, but with Dovzhenko the effect is right. The dusk is the coagulated sort of dusk which belongs to the country. Through it and down the road from the village the boy comes. He is foot-loose, he breaks into a dance, the dust swirls white under his feet.

The shot that kills him does not mean a thing in comparison. It is an excuse for a pagan burial, with apple trees brushing across the face of the dead and sunflowers in the background, with a bunch of youngsters singing about the future, an embryo commissar hitting up a peroration, and the older men, by the power of it, believing implicitly. The kulak who buries his head madly in the earth he has lost, who falls symbolically in a heap among the graveyard crosses of an older régime, is relatively unimportant. Even the old priest whose business is so tragically taken out of his hands is unimportant. The emphasis is on the apple trees and the sunflowers, and, lest there be any mistake about it, it remains there to the end.

The finale is of apples, of rain pouring crescendo on apples, of rain stopping and the sun brightening on apples. For 150 feet. The sequence is possibly the simplest example of easy dramatization in the history of cinema.

Technically it was for any of us to do this last sequence and we have not done it. This, I imagine, is the measure of Dovzhenko. There is nothing complex or difficult about his material, his method, or his mind; there is only a directness of sympathy and precision of method which one rather envies. Other films like *Turksib* have been more exciting technically; and they will have progeny more numerous than *Earth*. But none of them has been quite so satisfying since Flaherty walked out of *White Shadows* and lost himself in Samoa. For there is this similarity between Dovzhenko and Flaherty that both are lyricists. Dovzhenko is stagier and more apparently camera-conscious; but he is, on the other hand, more sensitive to the flash of action.

It is perhaps a pity that *Earth* is not an English film, for there is very little in it (except the faith in the future) which could not be paralleled in our own villages. I have known people talk as familiarly in the presence of death and behave in graveyards not dissimilarly to the old man who bent down his head to catch the words of the departed patriarch. For the rest we have all the apples, and corn, and peasants with bellies to the earth and heads to the sky, that any lyrical mind could wish for. We have also a history, of invasions and wars and plagues of one sort and another that have gone over the land and left the local gods of birth and death undaunted. We only lack the common faith in the future to complete our material.

It is an important lack, and it seems to a semi-alien like myself that the English mind will have to do something about it. It has lost the capacity for taking a chance on enthusiasms; so much so that even this emphasis on *Earth* will be suspect. It should have qualifications. It should leave a loop-hole in case of this, that, or the other thing; always unspecified. So with dearth of belief, action perishes, and the replenishing of radiators is impossible. The tractor cannot work and the village fête is a frizzle. And the English wind, of course, will not blow the skirts of the women with any decency, and English men and women will not stand to the camera statuesque in the dusk. For the little, England loses the lot.

*　　*　　*

With Dziga Vertov's *Man With the Movie Camera* we are at last initiated into the philosophy of the Kino Eye. Some of us have been hearing a great deal about the Kino Eye and it has worried us considerably. Only the younger high-brows seemed to know anything about it. They have dashed back from their continental rambles with hair more rumpled, neck more open, and tie more non-existent for gazing on it. But on the whole articulation has failed them, and it has been difficult to gather from their wild young words what particular mesmeric virtue this Kino Eye possessed.

126

The Russian Example

Now that Vertov has turned up in the original, it is easier to see why intelligent students of cinema were betrayed into their extremity. The Vertov method of film-making is based on a supremely sound idea, and one which must be a preliminary to any movie method at all. He has observed that there are things of the every-day which achieve a new value, leap to a more vigorous life, the moment they get into a movie camera or an intimately cut sequence. It is at that point we all begin; and, backing our eye with the world, we try to pick the leapers. The secret may be in an angle, or an arrangement of light, or an arrangement of movement, but there is hardly one of us but gets more out of the camera than we ever thought of putting into it. In that sense there is a Kino Eye. In that sense, too, the Kino Eye is more likely to discover things in the wide-world-of-all-possible-arrangements which exists outside the studios.

Vertov, however, has pushed the argument to a point at which it becomes ridiculous. The camera observes in its own bright way and he is prepared to give it his head. The man is with the camera, not the camera with the man. Organization of things observed, brain control, imagination or fancy control of things observed: these other rather necessary activities in the making of art are forgotten. *The Man With the Movie Camera* is in consequence not a film at all: it is a snapshot album. There is no story, no dramatic structure, and no special revelation of the Moscow it has chosen for a subject. It just dithers about on the surface of life picking up shots here, there and everywhere, slinging them together as the Dadaists used to sling together their verses, with an emphasis on the particular which is out of all relation to a rational existence. Many of the shots are fine and vital; some of the camera tricks, if not very new, are at least interesting; but exhibitionism or, if you prefer it, virtuosity in a craftsman does not qualify him as a creator.

The Man With the Movie Camera will, however, bring a great deal of instruction to film students. The camera is a bright little blackbird, and there are rabbits to be taken out of the hat (or bin) of montage which are infinitely magical, but . . . articulacy is a virtue which will continue to have its say-so. Here by the *reductio ad absurdum* is proof for the schoolboys.

I have just been watching an Atlantic liner putting to sea, from—I am happy to say—the liner's point of view. Shots have been cropping up for an hour that I would describe as sheer cinema. The patterns of men rolling up the cargo net, the curve of the rope shot in parabola to the tug, the sudden gliding movement-astern of the tug, the white

127

plume on the *Mauretania* high up in the dry dock, the massed energy
of the black smoke pouring in rolls from the funnel and set against the
rhythmic curve of the ship against the sky—they have all, possibly, a
visual virtue in themselves. But the dramatic truth, and therefore,
finally, the cinematic truth too, is that the ship is putting to sea. She
is in process and continuity of something or other. Say only that she
is setting out to cross an ocean and has the guts for it; or say, by the
Eastern European emigrants in the steerage, that a bunch of people
are going with hope to a new world; say what you like, according to
your sense of ultimate importances, the necessity is that you say
something. The Kino Eye in that sense is only the waiter who serves
the hash. No especial virtue in the waiting compensates for a lunatic
cook.

*   *   *

I have never set eyes on a film that interested me more than Vertov's
Enthusiasm, nor one that demanded more solid criticism. But I never
saw a film that was so fundamentally un-Bolshevik in its excitements.
If an amateur Bolshevik with a training in the studio leap-frog of Paris
had made it, it would have been comprehensible. It is all dazzle-dazzle
and bits and pieces, whoopee for this, whoopee for that—like any
masterwork of the close-up school. But body of thought or body of
construction it has none.

Enthusiasm is a hymn of praise for the Five-Year Plan in the Don
Basin; it praises the steel and stalwarts of the Don Basin. If the Five-
Year Plan is no clearer in the head than the praise of *Enthusiasm*,
heaven help the Russian workers. If the film is any guide, they will be
doing in year five the job they already did in year two; they will repeat
themselves endlessly. And they will have the darnedest job finishing at
all. For a thousand feet *Enthusiasm* tried to bring itself to a conclusion.
Uncertain of the success of its whoopee for steel, it tried a whoopee for
the land. Uncertain of that, it tried steel again. So far as I am concerned it is still trying.

There was a story in the Don Basin. There was a story of the
steelworkers laying a foundation of steel for the new Russia; that is to
say, doing something good and definite as *Turksib* did. There was an
alternative story: the story of Russian workers leaving the fake
enthusiasms of the Christian church for the more decent enthusiasms
of creative Socialism. The one story meant an epic of most definite
achievement. The other meant the creation of a new poetry.

I think Vertov tried the second issue. He demolished the mysticisms

128

Nanook of the North (Canadian, 1920)
  Produced by Reveillon Freres, New York: directed by Robert Flaherty (from the Paul Rotha Collection)

Moana (American, 1926)
  Produced by Famous-Players (Paramount): directed by Robert Flaherty (from the Paul Rotha Collection)

Louisiana Story (American, 1946–8)

Robert J. Flaherty Productions: directed by Robert Flaherty

Frances Flaherty,
Richard Leacock (camera)
Robert Flaherty

of the ancient religion at the beginning of his film and tried to build up a new mysticism in the relation between the worker and his machine. It was a job worth trying, and he has brought all his great power over camera angles, and all his sense of percussive cutting, to help him. But he has failed. And he has failed because he was like any bourgeois highbrow, too clever by half. He has given us ten thousand clever effects—of split lenses and tilted cameras and angled details. He has missed, however, the simple things which are the root of all poetry and mysticism. He has given us everything of the mechanicism and nothing of the people. He has described every beat in the industry of the Don Basin except the heart-beat.

At the same time I must indicate some of the amazing things there are in this film. It is so full of ingenuities that practitioners like myself will be feeding on its carcase years from now. Never were workmen so energized by a camera. It gets under and over them. It gyros to their movements with a growing intensity of movement which makes excitement of something most ordinary. Industrial happenings are generally so ponderous that it is the despair of a director to pace them. Vertov will show you how to under-emphasize and how to exaggerate. He will demonstrate how the most simple incidents (a girl with a pair of telephones or a couple of men on a two-handed hammer) can hold a whole sequence together. By sheer variety of observation—there never was such variety before—he turns a plain process into a fairy tale of excited happening.

As I suggest, it all leads nowhere, but it certainly leads furiously. Much the same sort of thing can be said of the sound effects. You will find sound cut in beats to the beat of the images; you will find it syncopating with the images; you will find most excellent passings of mechanical sound into musical sound : you will hear it distorted till it screams, and you will find feeling in it.

You will, however, still be dissatisfied. Whatever the band of buglers at its head, a film must march somewhere. This film is all bugling and marching and marching and bugling. The banners fly and the troops give the salute : the citizens cheer along the line of march ; the soldiers raise their voices in lusty chorus. There is Enthusiasm and no mistake. But I could not for the life of me tell you whether the enthusiasm is an empty one or a full one. Vertov has not told us.

*   *   *

Pudovkin's *A Simple Case* was a dreadful little film with an ingenious use of slow motion, a host of lovely images, and no point. *Deserter* is Pudovkin on the rebound: more complex in his effects, surer in his technical hand, and even stronger in his theme than he was in *The End of St. Petersburg.*

If you remember your Dostoievsky or your Joyce or your Melville you will know how leisurely the masterpieces may sometimes proceed: how, damning the audience, they may sometimes fly suddenly off the earth, or, by perversity, from off the earth back to terra firma again, without a by your leave: taking good pains to bore the lesser minds with inconsequent pondering on the guts of whales and the exact nature of disease and disaster. *Deserter* has something of this curious strength. If, in its hobbling from one odd chapter to another, as it freely does, the film extends your patience, you will respect it, as like as not, for the size it brings. Only the little fellows care what twiddling echoes go round your pipes and, sycophantically, measure the music to suit you. The big fellows call their own tune. You will certainly have time to consider this matter, for the film runs near a couple of hours: in innumerable acts and sub-divisions of acts: shifting from scene to scene in titles, and sometimes plain black-outs, as I cannot remember anything doing so variously since *Antony and Cleopatra.*

When you come to consider the continuing theme of the film you will be wise to look for none, but content yourself with the vast description it gives of the world today: of high-powered industry, of unemployment, of poverty, of the accumulating fire of public effort, of the stresses and storms between men and men which economic disaster has brought in its train. The net effect is of great tragedy, in which the beauties of blue sky and morning, ships and machinery, young faces and hopeful faces, are strangely stifled in the common disaster. For long passages there is argument: as of dictatorship, leadership, solution; and you will need to know Russian to know every turn of the dialectic. But you will regard even this as part of a necessary effort.

For my part, I shall only record that no film or novel or poem or drama has sketched so largely the essential story and the essential unhappiness of our time, or brought them so deeply to the mind.

*   *   *

It is a waste of time to consider what Eisenstein would have done with *Thunder Over Mexico*, if he had been allowed to cut it. The fact is that he was not allowed, and alibis that the cutting was done 'in exact accord' with Eisenstein's script are merely silly. One might as well talk of writing a George Moore novel from George Moore's notes; for with Eisenstein, as with Moore, the style is nearly everything. He is not a poet like Pudovkin, whose conceptions are themselves emotional and uplifting, nor a finely descriptive writer like Flaherty, whose observations are of themselves intimate. His raw material is common documentary, and sometimes very common. It is his power of juxtaposition that counts, his amazing capacity for exploding two or three details into an idea. It is not how his actors act, nor yet how the camera looks at them, that is important in Eisenstein, for his acting is often bad and his camera work meretricious: it is the odd reference he adds to his actors' presence that gives meaning and tempo to their lives. Say this for brief, that Eisenstein is detailed and cold in his shooting, and that he warms his stuff to life only when he starts putting it together. It is his method of approach; and there could be no genuine Eisenstein film without it.

Thunder Over Mexico might have been a good film with Eisenstein, or it might not; without him it is pretty dull stuff, without style, without ideas, and without construction. What I hear was intended to be a vast description of the Mexican spirit turns out to be a niggardly slow-told tale of how a peasant girl was raped by a feudal lord and how her peasant lover rebelled and was executed.

There is a symbolic sequence at the beginning which is meant to describe the age-long suffering of the Mexican people. It is full of dissolves, super-impositions and wipes, in a manner never before associated with Eisenstein, and I cannot understand its presence. If Eisenstein intended it, he has certainly deviated from his own stalwart doctrine. He was always an enemy of such vague methods of mental association as are represented by the draping of symbolic figures across the landscape; and I remember how he raged at the symbolic example of *Joan of Arc* when I once put it to him. This sequence, if it is anything, is just bad *Joan of Arc*. The tale of rape follows, in a setting of heavily filtered clouds and foreground cactus. The clouds and the cactus will pass for great photography among the hicks, but they are, of course, easy meat for anyone with a decent set of filters. The lovely moulding of form, the brilliance of near and intimate observation, which you get in *Moana*, say, are a mile away and beyond. These are superficial qualities only. But, as I suggest, one never looked to Eisenstein for great photography or intimate observation, and one's only disappointment is that Hollywood has fallen for these clouds and things and let the film go to the devil for the sake of its glycerined scenic effects. The types on the other hand are superb, for no one holds a candle to Eisenstein when it comes to picking faces. The acting, too, is much better than we have associated with Eisenstein in the past, though never as fine in its nuances of reaction as we get in Pudovkin.

But there you are and what of it? The significance that Eisenstein might have added to the tale is not there; and types, acting and glycerined clouds cannot turn a simple tale of village rape into the passion of a people. There were other things up Eisenstein's sleeve, or he is not the dialectician I have always taken him for.

Part II

A MOVEMENT IS FOUNDED

Grierson's articles on documentary theory helped to give direction to the movement he founded following the success of *Drifters*. His analysis of the work of directors using realist material in other countries—Cavalcanti in France, Ruttmann in Germany, Flaherty in America, Eisenstein and the other Soviet directors—contributed towards the evolution of a British school in documentary whose first characteristic was a sense of social criticism. The articles grouped here lay down the principles which guided documentary during its formative period and carry the story to the point at which the E.M.B. Film Unit, on the dissolving of the parent body, was transferred to the G.P.O.

F. H.

PART II

A MOVEMENT IS FOUNDED

1 'Drifters'

Drifters is about the sea and about fishermen, and there is not a Piccadilly actor in the piece. The men do their own acting, and the sea does its—and if the result does not bear out the 107th Psalm, it is my fault. Men at their labour are the salt of the earth; the sea is a bigger actor than Jannings or Nitikin or any of them; and if you can tell me a story more plainly dramatic than the gathering of the ships for the herring season, the going out, the shooting at evening, the long drift in the night, the hauling of nets by infinite agony of shoulder muscle in the teeth of a storm, the drive home against a head sea, and (for finale) the frenzy of a market in which said agonies are sold at ten shillings a thousand, and iced, salted and barrelled for an unwitting world—if you can tell me a story with a better crescendo in energies, images, atmospherics and all that make up the sum and substance of cinema, I promise you I shall make my next film of it forthwith.

But, of course, making a film is not just the simple matter of feeling the size of the material. If that were so every fool who fusses over a nondescript sunset, or bares his solar plexus to the salt sea waves on his summer holiday, would be an artist. I do not claim the brave word, though I would like to, but I think I know what it mostly means. It has very little to do with nondescript enthusiasm, and a great deal to do with a job of work.

In art, as in everything else, the gods are with the big battalions. You march on your subject with a whole regiment of energies: you surround it, you break in here, break in there, and let loose all the shell and shrapnel you can (by infinite pushing of your inadequate noddle) lay hands on. Out of the labour something comes. All you have to do then is to seize what you want. If you have really and truly got inside, you will have plenty—of whatever it is—to choose from.

So in this rather solid adventure of the herring fishery I did what I could to get inside the subject. I had spent a year or two of my life wandering about on the deep sea fishing-boats, and that was an initial advantage. I knew what they felt like. Among other things they had developed in me a certain superior horsemanship which was proof against all bronco-buckings, side-steppings and rollings whatsoever. I mention this because the limiting factor in all sea films is the stomach of the director and his cameramen. It is a super fact, beyond all art and non-art. Of my cameramen one also was an ex-seaman. The other, for all his bravery, was mostly unconscious.

In this matter I was altogether to blame. What I know of cinema I have learned partly from the Russians, partly from the American westerns, and partly from Flaherty, of *Nanook*. The westerns give you some notion of the energies. The Russians give you the energies and the intimacies both. And Flaherty is a poet.

The net effect of this cinematic upbringing was to make me want a storm: a real storm, an intimate storm, and if possible a rather noble storm. I waited in Lowestoft for weeks till the gale signal went up, and I got it. So did the cameramen. The wild Arabian breeze of the drifter's bilges did not help matters.

Taking the film as a whole I got the essentials of what I wanted. I got the most beautiful fishing-village in the world—I found it in the Shetlands—for a starting point. I staged my march to the sea, the preparations, the procession out. I ran in detail of furnace and engine-room for image of force, and seas over a headland for image of the open. I took the ships out and cast the nets in detail: as to the rope over the cradle, the boy below, the men on deck against the sea; as to the rhythm of the heaving, the run on the rollers, the knotted haul of each float and net; as to the day and approaching night; as to the monotony of long labour. Two miles of nets to a ship: I threw them in a flood of repetition against a darkening sky.

The life of Natural cinema is in this massing of detail, in this massing of all the rhythmic energies that contribute to the blazing fact of the matter. Men and the energies of men, things and the functions of things, horizons and the poetics of horizons: these are the essential materials. And one must never grow so drunk with the energies and the functions as to forget the poetics.

I had prepared against that as best I knew how. Image for this, image for that. For the settling of darkness, not darkness itself, but flocks of birds silhouetted against the sky flying hard into the camera: repeated and repeated. For the long drift in the night, not the ship, not the sea itself, but the dark mystery of the underwater. I made the night scene a sequence of rushing shoals and contorting congers. For the dawn, not a bleary fuss against the sky (which in cinema is nothing), but a winding slow-rolling movement into the light. Then a bell-buoy.

136

Then a Dutch lugger rolling heavily into the light. Three images in a row.

You can never have your images too great, and I think there are none of us poets enough to make cinema properly. It is in the end a question of suggesting things, and all the example of Shakespearian metaphor is there to tell you how short we stand of the profundities.

The most solid scene, I would say, was the spectacle of the hauling. Camera and cameraman were lashed on top of the wheelhouse, and the nets came up through the heavy sea in great drifts of silver. We got at it from every angle we could and shot it inside-out with the hand camera; and, put together, it made a brave enough show. But even then the fact of the matter, however detailed, however orchestrated, was not enough. The sea might lash over the men and the ship plunge, and the haul of the nets tauten and tear at the wrists of the men : it was still not enough. This business of horizons had to be faced over again. By fortune a whale came alongside to clean the nets, and I used it for more than a whale. I used it for a ponderous symbol of all that tumbled and laboured on that wild morning. It adds something, but it is possible that something else, had I but felt it properly, would have carried the scene still further to that horizon I speak of. Images, images—details and aspects of things that lift a world of fact to beauty and bravery—no doubt half a hundred passed under my nose, and I did not see them.

So through the procession into harbour, and the scenes in the market-place at Yarmouth—fact joined to fact and detail to detail. But here, of course, because of the size and variety of the scene, rather greater possibilities in the matter of orchestration. The gathering procession of buyers and sellers on the quayside, the procession of ships through the harbour mouth : the two processions interwoven. The selling itself, the unloading, the carrying : mouth work and shoulder work interwoven, made complementary to each other, opposed to each other as your fancy takes you. Rivers of fish, being slid into a ship's hold, cartfuls of baskets, girls gutting, barrels being rolled : all the complex detail of porterage and export dissolved into each other, run one on top of the other, to set them marching. It is the procession of results. Cranes and ships and railway trains—or their impressionistic equivalents—complete it.

The problem of images does not arise so plainly here, for cinematic processions, if you bring them off, are solid affairs that carry their own banners. Two, however, I did try. As the labour of the sea turned to the labour of the land, I carried forward a wave theme. It is played heavily for accompaniment as the ships ride in; but as life on the quayside takes charge of the picture, it is diminished in strength till it vanishes altogether. Through breaking waves the buyers and sellers go to their business. Count that, if you will, for an image of opposition. It is a far cry from the simple and solid labour of the sea to the nepman haggling of the market-place.

The last was of a similar type. As the catch was being boxed and barrelled I thought I would like to say that what was really being boxed and barrelled was the labour of men. So as the herring were shovelled in, and the ice laid on, and the hammer raised to complete the job, I slid back for a flash or two to the storm and the hauling. The hammer is raised on mere fish: it comes down on dripping oilskins and a tumbling sea. This notion I kept repeating in flashes through the procession of barrels and the final procession of railway trucks. The barrels of the dead pass for a second into the living swirl of a herring shoal, in and out again; the smoke in a tunnel dissolves for a moment into the tautened wrist of a fisherman at the net-rope.

I cannot tell you what the result of it all is. Notions are notions and pictures are pictures, and no knowledge of cinematic anatomy can guarantee that extra something which is the breath of life to a picture. If I raise this matter of images it is rather to give you some idea of how the movie mind works. It has to feel its way through the appearances of things, choosing, discarding and choosing again, seeking always those more significant appearances which are like yeast to the plain dough of the context. Sometimes they are there for the taking; as often as not you have to make a journey into a far country to find them. That, however, is no more difficult for cinema than for poetry. The camera is by instinct, if not by training, a wanderer.

2 Flaherty

A happy fortune has at last brought Robert Flaherty to England. Flaherty was the director of *Nanook* and *Moana*, the originator of *White Shadows of the South Seas*, the co-director, with Murnau, of *Tabu*. He was the initiator of the naturalist tradition in cinema, and is still the high-priest of the spontaneities. The happy fortune lies in the fact that of all distinguished foreign directors he is the one whose sympathies are most nearly English. Technically, he is American, but the major part of his life has been spent exploring or filming within the British Empire.

This long association, together with his explorer's hatred of Hollywood artificialities, makes him the one director whose cinematic persuasion is most likely to benefit our present England. He comes to London for the first time with an eye for its authority in the world, which adds fantasy to the most familiar. He has seen Eskimos travel a thousand miles to buy an English blanket which would last them a lifetime, when the shoddy article of more recent commercial tradition was at their igloo doors. He has eaten out an Arctic winter on the superior construction of English bully-beef tins, which refused to rust with foreign competitors. He has blessed the name of England ten thousand miles away for the one glue in the world which the tropics could not melt.

I knew Flaherty in New York, and he was the only man I knew there whom Babel did not enthral. This seemed to me a most perverse feat of the mind at the time, but in these later days I would more sensibly describe it as a feat of most necessary simplicity. It is only now apparent how the Blazonry of American ballyhoo was selling a generation into slavery. Flaherty used to say: 'They are a tribe of sharks preying on the weakness of their neighbours. This is their way of being ferocious.' He contrasted the public decency of Polynesians. Economics, of which he professes nothing, have most strangely found him right. I know not how many millions the American people will have to pay their irresponsible exploiters when prosperity comes again; for goods consumed.

139

Now in London I find Flaherty's eye for things as fascinating as before. He tells me that wholesomeness went out of American humour when Mark Twain died, and that behind all the flashing wit of American cross-talk is an essential unkindliness. He tells me that England is dirty and scrambled, that its humour is simple, but that this original human wholesomeness remains to it. He tells me that English faces retain an individuality which stands up to the buildings as American faces cannot. He contrasts the manicured landscape of the Continent with the informality and intimacy of the Chilterns. He praises, most unfashionably, craftsmanship.

These hints and emphases are very close to the problem we have to solve in our English cinema, for we are more than ever in search of the national certainties we are to proclaim. We have not yet evolved a *style*. We imitate Hollywood, and occasionally we imitate Neubabelsburg and Moscow. There is some original lack of affection for our own English worth, a lack of knowledge of it, a lack of bravery in it which prevents our bringing beauty, and convincing beauty, out of the films we make.

It is, I know only too well, difficult to be sure of one's attitudes in a decade like this. Can we heroicize our men when we know them to be exploited? Can we romanticize our industrial scene when we know that our men work brutally and starve ignobly in it? Can we praise it—and in art there must be praise—when the most blatant fact of our time is the bankruptcy of our national management? Our confidence is sapped, our beliefs are troubled, our eye for beauty is most plainly disturbed: and the more so in cinema than in any other art. For we have to build on the actual. Our capital comes from those whose only interest is in the actual. The medium itself insists on the actual. There we must build or be damned.

Flaherty's most considerable contribution to the problem is, as always, his insistence on the beauty of the natural. It is not everything, for it does not in the last resort isolate and define the purposes which must, consciously or unconsciously, inform our craftsmanship. But it does ensure that the raw material from which we work is the raw material most proper to the screen. The camera-eye is in effect a magical instrument. It can see a thousand things in a thousand places at different times, and the cunning cutter can string them together for a review of the world. Or he can piece them together—a more difficult task—for a review of a subject or situation more intricate and more intimate than any mortal eye can hope to match. But its magic is even more than this. It lies also in the manner of its observation, in the strange innocence with which, in a mind-tangled world, it sees things for what they are. This is not simply to say that the camera, on its single observations, is free from the trammels of the subjective, for it is patent that it will not follow the director in his enthusiasms any more than it will follow him in the wide-angled vision of his eyes. The magical fact of the camera is that it picks out what the director does not see at all, that it gives emphasis where he did not think emphasis existed.

The camera is in a measure both the discoverer of an unknown world and the re-discoverer of a lost one. There are, as everyone knows, strange moments of beauty that leap out of most ordinary news reels. It may be some accidental pose of character or some spontaneous gesture which radiates simply because it is spontaneous. It may be some high angle of a ship, or a crane, or a chimney stack, or a statue, adding some element of the heroic by a new-found emphasis. It may be some mere fore-shortening of a bollard and a rope that ties a ship to a quay in spirit as well as in fact. It may be the flap of a hatch cover which translates a gale. It may be the bright revelation of rhythms that time has worn smooth: the hand movement of a potter, the wrist movement of a native priest, or the muscle play of a dancer or a boxer or a runner. All of them seem to achieve a special virtue in the oblong of the screen.

So much Flaherty has taught us all. If we add to it such instruction as we have taken from Griffith and the Russians, of how to mass movement and create suspense, of how to keep an eye open for attendant circumstance and subconscious effect, we have in sum a most formidable equipment as craftsmen. But the major problem remains, the problem I have mentioned, the problem the critics do not worry their heads over, though creators must: what final honours and final dishonours we shall reveal in this English life of ours: what heroism we shall set against what villainy. The field of cinema is not only a field for creators but also for prophets.

The method followed by Flaherty in his own film-making might give us a most valuable lead. He took a year to make his study of the Eskimos and this after ten years' exploration in the Eskimo country of Labrador and Baffin Land. He took two years to make his study of Samoan life, and only now, after three more years in the South Seas, feels he could do justice to it. He soaked himself in his material, lived with it to the point of intimacy and beyond that to the point of belief, before he gave it form. This is a long method, and may be an expensive one; and it is altogether alien in a cinema world which insists on forcing a pre-conceived shape (one of half a dozen rubber-stamped dramatic shapes) on all material together. Its chief claim to our regard, however, is that it is necessary, and particularly necessary in England. We know our England glibly as an industrial country, as a beautiful country of this epic quality and that; we know it by rote as a maker of Empire and as a manipulator of world-wide services. But we do not know it in our everyday observation as such. Our literature is divorced from the actual: it is written as often as not in the south of France. Our culture is divorced from the actual: it is practised almost exclusively in the rarefied atmosphere of country colleges and country retreats. Our gentlemen explore the native haunts and investigate the native customs of Tanganyika and Timbuctoo, but do not travel dangerously into the jungles of Middlesbrough and the Clyde. Their hunger for English reality is satisfied briefly and sentimentally over a country hedge.

We might make an English cinema, as we might make English art again, if we could only send our creators back to fact. Not only to the old fact of the countryside which our poets have already honoured, but to the new fact of industry and commerce and plenty and poverty which no poet has honoured at all. Every week I hear men ask for films of industry. They want it praised and proclaimed to the world, and I would like to see their money used and their purposes fulfilled. But what advice can I give them? We can produce them the usual slick rubbish, some slicker, some less slick; but who of us knows an industry well enough to bring it alive for what it is? And what statescraft is willing to send a creator into an industry, so to know it: for a year, for two years perhaps, for the length of a hundred thousand feet of film and possibly more. Our businessmen expect a work of art to schedule, as the housewife expects her daily groceries. They expect it of a new medium. They expect it from raw material which they in their own hearts despise.

Flaherty, as an individual artist, cannot answer the whole problem. He knows his primitives and will do a job for them out of the strength of his affection. He could do a job for English craftsmanship and for the tradition of quality in English work, and for the native solidity in English institutions, and English criticism and character; but he is of a persuasion that does not easily come to grips with the more modern factors of civilization. In his heart he prefers a sailing barge to a snub-nosed funnel-after, and a scythe to a mechanical reaper. He will say that there is well-being associated with the first and none with the second, and in a manner he is right: right in his emphasis on well-being.

But how otherwise than by coming to industry, even as it is, and forcing beauty from it, and bringing people to see beauty in it, can one, in turn, inspire man to create and find well-being? For this surely is the secret of our particular well-being, that men must accept the environment in which they live, with its smoke and its steel and its mechanical aids, even with its rain. It may not be so easily pleasant as the halcyon environment of Tahiti, but this is beside the point.

I think in this other matter one may turn to the Russians for guidance rather than to Flaherty. Their problem, of course, is different from ours. The industrial backwardness of the country, the illiteracy of their people, and the special factors of Russian psychology make for a rhetoric in their cinema which we cannot blindly imitate. Apart from this national difference, which is in effect their *style*, there is an ardour of experiment in their treatment of industrial and social material. They have built up rhythms from their machinery; they have made their work exciting and noble. They have made society on the move the subject-matter of art. Their sense of rhythm is not necessarily our sense of rhythm. Their sense of nobility and sense of social direction need not be identical with ours. The essential point, however, is that they have built up this rhythm and nobility and purpose of theirs by facing up to the new material. They have done it out of the necessity of their social situation. No one will say that our own necessity is less than theirs.

When I spoke with Flaherty on the Aran Islands he was full of the possibilities of the British documentary cinema. If on these islands—only so many hours from London—there was this story of romantic life ready to the camera, how many more must there be! He mentioned the Hebrides and the Highlands, and sketched out a film of Indian village life. He spoke of the tales of fine craftsmanship which must be tucked away in the Black Country. But first, he emphasized, there must be the process of discovery and freedom in discovery: to live with the people long enough to know them. He talked with a certain rising fury of the mental attitude of the studio-bred producer who hangs a slicked-out story of triangles against a background of countryside or industry. Rather must the approach be to take the story from out the location, finding it essentially there: with patience and intimacy of knowledge as the first virtues always in a director. He referred to a quotation I once wrote for him in New York, when his seemingly tardy method of production was first an issue in the studios. It was Plato's description of his metaphysics where he says that no fire can leap up or light kindle till there is 'long intercourse with the thing itself, and it has been lived with'. No doubt the studios, with their slick ten- or fifteen-day productions of nothing-in-particular, still disagree with Flaherty and Plato profoundly. His idea of production is to reconnoitre for months without turning a foot, and then, in months more perhaps, slowly to shape the film on the screen: using his camera first to sketch his material and find his people, then using his screen, as Chaplin uses it, to tell him at every turn where the path of drama lies.

No director has the same respect as Flaherty for the camera; indeed very few of them even trouble to look through the camera while it is shooting their scenes. Flaherty, in contrast, is always his own 'first cameraman'. He spoke almost mystically of the camera's capacity for seeing beyond mortal eye to the inner qualities of things. With Fairbanks he agrees that children and animals are the finest of all movie actors, because they are spontaneous, but talks also of the movements in peasants and craftsmen and hunters and priests as having a special magic on the screen because time or tradition has worn them smooth. He might also add—though he would not—that his own capacity for moving the camera in appreciation of these movements is an essential part of the magic. No man of cameras, to my knowledge, can pan so curiously, or so bewilderingly anticipate a fine gesture or expression.

Flaherty's ideal in the new medium is a selective documentation of sound similar at all points to his selective documentation of movement and expression in the silent film. He would use the microphone, like the camera, as an intimate attendant on the action: recording the accompanying sounds and whispers and cries most expressive of it. He says the language does not matter at all, not even the words, if the spirit of the thing is plain. In this point as in others, Flaherty's cinema is as far removed from the theatrical tradition as it can possibly be. His screen is not a stage to which the action of a story is brought, but rather a magical opening in the theatre wall, through which one may look out to the wide world: overseeing and overhearing the intimate things of common life which only the camera and microphone of the film artist can reveal.

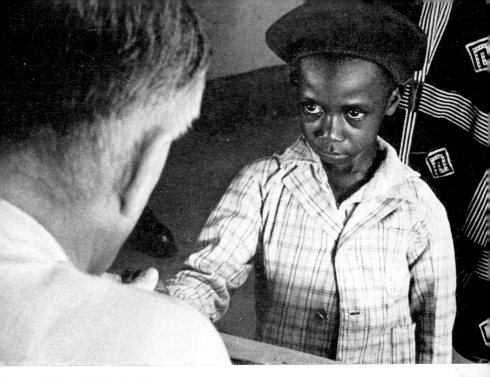

Daybreak in Udi (British, 1949)
  Produced by Crown Film Unit: directed by Terry Bishop

Man of Africa (British, 1953)
  Produced by John Grierson: directed by Cyril Frankel

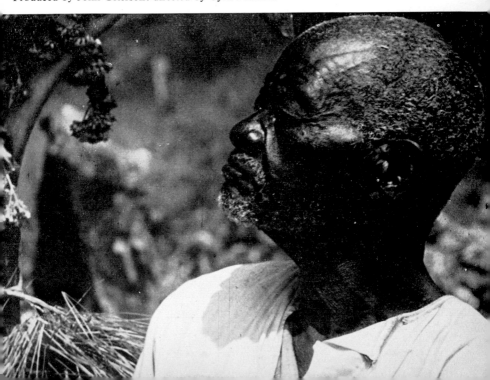

The End of St Petersburg (Soviet, 1927)
Produced by Mejrabpom-Russ: directed by V. I. Pudovkin

October (Soviet 1927–8)
Produced by Sovkino: directed by S. M. Eisenstein

3 First Principles of Documentary

Documentary is a clumsy description, but let it stand. The French who first used the term only meant travelogue. It gave them a solid high-sounding excuse for the shimmying (and otherwise discursive) exoticisms of the Vieux Colombier. Meanwhile documentary has gone on its way. From shimmying exoticisms it has gone on to include dramatic films like *Moana, Earth,* and *Turksib*. And in time it will include other kinds as different in form and intention from *Moana*, as *Moana* was from *Voyage au Congo*.

So far we have regarded all films made from natural material as coming within the category. The use of natural material has been regarded as the vital distinction. Where the camera shot on the spot (whether it shot newsreel items or magazine items or discursive 'interests' or dramatised 'interests' or educational films or scientific films proper or *Changs* or *Rangos*) in that fact was documentary. This array of species is, of course, quite unmanageable in criticism, and we shall have to do something about it. They all represent different qualities of observation, different intentions in observation, and, of course, very different powers and ambitions at the stage of organizing material. I propose, therefore, after a brief word on the lower categories, to use the documentary description exclusively of the higher.

The peacetime newsreel is just a speedy snip-snap of some utterly unimportant ceremony. Its skill is in the speed with which the babblings of a politican (gazing sternly into the camera) are transferred to fifty million relatively unwilling ears in a couple of days or so. The magazine items (one a week) have adopted the original 'Tit-Bits' manner of observation. The skill they represent is a purely journalistic skill. They describe novelties novelly. With their money-making eye (their almost only eye) glued like the newsreels to vast and speedy audiences, they avoid on the one hand the consideration of solid material, and escape, on the other, the solid consideration of any material. Within these limits they are often brilliantly done. But ten in a row would bore the average human to death. Their reaching out for the flippant or popular touch is so completely far-reaching that it dislocates something.

Possibly taste; possibly common sense. You may take your choice at those little theatres where you are invited to gad around the world in fifty minutes. It takes only that long—in these days of great invention —to see almost everything.

'Interests' proper improve mightily with every week, though heaven knows why. The market (particularly the British market) is stacked against them. With two-feature programmes the rule, there is neither space for the short *and* the Disney *and* the magazine, nor money left to pay for the short. But by good grace, some of the renters throw in the short with the feature. This considerable branch of cinematic illumination tends, therefore, to be the gift that goes with the pound of tea; and like all gestures of the grocery mind it is not very liable to cost much. Whence my wonder at improving qualities. Consider, however, the very frequent beauty and very great skill of exposition in such Ufa shorts as *Turbulent Timber*, in the sports shorts from Metro-Goldwyn-Mayer, in the *Secrets of Nature* shorts from Bruce Woolfe, and the Fitzpatrick travel talks. Together they have brought the popular lecture to a pitch undreamed of, and even impossible in the days of magic lanterns. In this little we progress.

These films, of course, would not like to be called lecture films, but this, for all their disguises, is what they are. They do not dramatize, they do not even dramatize an episode : they describe, and even expose, but in any aesthetic sense, only rarely reveal. Herein is their formal limit, and it is unlikely that they will make any considerable contribution to the fuller art of documentary. How indeed can they? Their silent form is cut to the commentary, and shots are arranged arbitrarily to point the gags or conclusions. This is not a matter of complaint, for the lecture film must have increasing value in entertainment, education and propaganda. But it is as well to establish the formal limits of the species.

This indeed is a particularly important limit to record, for beyond the newsmen and the magazine men and the lecturers (comic or interesting or exciting or only rhetorical) one begins to wander into the world of documentary proper, into the only world in which documentary can hope to achieve the ordinary virtues of an art. Here we pass from the plain (or fancy) descriptions of natural material, to arrangements, rearrangements, and creative shapings of it.

First principles. (1) We believe that the cinema's capacity for getting around, for observing and selecting from life itself, can be exploited in a new and vital art form. The studio films largely ignore this possibility of opening up the screen on the real world. They photograph acted stories against artificial backgrounds. Documentary would photograph the living scene and the living story. (2) We believe that the original (or native) actor, and the original (or native) scene, are better guides to a screen interpretation of the modern world. They give cinema a greater fund of material. They give it power over a million and one images. They give it power of interpretation over more complex and astonishing happenings in the real world than the studio mind can conjure up or the studio mechanician recreate. (3) We believe that the materials and the stories thus taken from the raw can be finer (more real in the philosophic sense) than the acted article. Spontaneous gesture has a special value on the screen. Cinema has a sensational capacity for enhancing the movement which tradition has formed or time worn smooth. Its arbitrary rectangle specially reveals movement; it gives it maximum pattern in space and time. Add to this that documentary can achieve an intimacy of knowledge and effect impossible to the shim-sham mechanics of the studio, and the lily-fingered interpretations of the metropolitan actor.

I do not mean in this minor manifesto of beliefs to suggest that the studios cannot in their own manner produce works of art to astonish the world. There is nothing (except the Woolworth intentions of the people who run them) to prevent the studios going really high in the manner of theatre or the manner of fairy tale. My separate claim for documentary is simply that in its use of the living article, there is *also* an opportunity to perform creative work. I mean, too, that the choice of the documentary medium is as gravely distinct a choice as the choice of poetry instead of fiction. Dealing with different material, it is, or should be, dealing with it to different aesthetic issues from those of the studio. I make this distinction to the point of asserting that the young director cannot, in nature, go documentary and go studio both.

In an earlier reference to Flaherty, I have indicated how one great exponent walked away from the studio: how he came to grips with the essential story of the Eskimos, then with the Samoans, then latterly with the people of the Aran Islands: and at what point the documentary director in him diverged from the studio intention of Hollywood. The main point of the story was this. Hollywood wanted to impose a ready-made dramatic shape on the raw material. It wanted Flaherty, in complete injustice to the living drama on the spot, to build his Samoans into a rubber-stamp drama of sharks and bathing belles. It failed in the case of *Moana*; it succeeded (through Van Dyke) in the case of *White Shadows of the South Seas*, and (through Murnau)

147

in the case of *Tabu*. In the last examples it was at the expense of Flaherty, who severed his association with both.

With Flaherty it became an absolute principle that the story must be taken from the location, and that it should be (what he considers) the essential story of the location. His drama, therefore, is a drama of days and nights, of the round of the year's seasons, of the fundamental fights which give his people sustenance, or make their community life possible, or build up the dignity of the tribe.

Such an interpretation of subject-matter reflects, of course, Flaherty's particular philosophy of things. A succeeding documentary exponent is in no way obliged to chase off to the ends of the earth in search of old-time simplicity, and the ancient dignities of man against the sky. Indeed, if I may for the moment represent the opposition, I hope the Neo-Rousseauism implicit in Flaherty's work dies with his own exceptional self. Theory of naturals apart, it represents an escapism, a wan and distant eye, which tends in lesser hands to sentimentalism. However it be shot through with vigour of Lawrentian poetry, it must always fail to develop a form adequate to the more immediate material of the modern world. For it is not only the fool that has his eyes on the ends of the earth. It is sometimes the poet : sometimes even the great poet, as Cabell in his *Beyond Life* will brightly inform you. This, however, is the very poet who on every classic theory of society from Plato to Trotsky should be removed bodily from the Republic. Loving every Time but his own, and every Life but his own, he avoids coming to grips with the creative job in so far as it concerns society. In the business of ordering most present chaos, he does not use his powers.

Question of theory and practice apart, Flaherty illustrates better than anyone the first principles of documentary. (1) It must master its material on the spot, and come in intimacy to ordering it. Flaherty digs himself in for a year, or two maybe. He lives with his people till the story is told 'out of himself'. (2) It must follow him in his distinction between description and drama. I think we shall find that there are other forms of drama or, more accurately, other forms of film, than the one he chooses ; but it is important to make the primary distinction between a method which describes only the surface values of a subject, and the method which more explosively reveals the reality of it. You photograph the natural life, but you also, by your juxtaposition of detail, create an interpretation of it.

This final creative intention established, several methods are possible. You may, like Flaherty, go for a story form, passing in the ancient manner from the individual to the environment, to the environment transcended or not transcended, to the consequent honours of heroism. Or you may not be so interested in the individual. You may think that the individual life is no longer capable of cross-sectioning reality. You may believe that its particular belly-aches are of no consequence in a world which complex and impersonal forces command, and conclude that the individual as a self-sufficient dramatic figure is outmoded. When Flaherty tells you that it is a devilish noble thing to fight for food in a wilderness, you may, with some justice, observe that you are more concerned with the problem of people fighting for food in the midst of plenty. When he draws your attention to the fact that Nanook's spear is grave in its upheld angle, and finely rigid in its down-pointing bravery, you may, with some justice, observe that no spear, held however bravely by the individual, will master the crazy walrus of international finance. Indeed you may feel that in individualism is a yahoo tradition largely responsible for our present anarchy, and deny at once both the hero of decent heroics (Flaherty) and the hero of indecent ones (studio). In this case, you will feel that you want your drama in terms of some cross-section of reality which will reveal the essentially co-operative or mass nature of society: leaving the individual to find his honours in the swoop of creative social forces. In other words, you are liable to abandon the story form, and seek, like the modern exponent of poetry and painting and prose, a matter and method more satisfactory to the mind and spirit of the time.

Berlin or the Symphony of a City initiated the more modern fashion of finding documentary material on one's doorstep: in events which have no novelty of the unknown, or romance of noble savage on exotic landscape, to recommend them. It represented, slimly, the return from romance to reality.

Berlin was variously reported as made by Ruttmann, or begun by Ruttmann and finished by Freund: certainly it was begun by Ruttmann. In smooth and finely tempo'd visuals, a train swung through suburban mornings into Berlin. Wheels, rails, details of engines, telegraph wires, landscapes and other simple images flowed along in procession, with similar abstracts passing occasionally in and out of the general movement. There followed a sequence of such movements which, in their total effect, created very imposingly the story of a Berlin day. The day began with a processional of workers, the factories got under way, the streets filled: the city's forenoon became a hurly-burly of tangled pedestrians and street cars. There was respite for food: a various respite with contrast of rich and poor. The city started work again, and a shower of rain in the afternoon became a considerable event. The city stopped work and, in further more hectic processional of pubs and cabarets and dancing legs and illuminated sky-signs, finished its day.

In so far as the film was principally concerned with movements and the building of separate images into movements, Ruttmann was justified in calling it a symphony. It meant a break away from the story borrowed from literature, and from the play borrowed from the stage. In *Berlin* cinema swung along according to its own more natural powers: creating dramatic effect from the tempo'd accumulation of its single observations. Cavalcanti's *Rien que les Heures* and Léger's *Ballet Mécanique* came before *Berlin*, each with a similar attempt to combine images in an emotionally satisfactory sequence of movements. They were too scrappy and had not mastered the art of cutting sufficiently well to create the sense of 'march' necessary to the genre. The symphony of Berlin City was both larger in its movements and larger in its vision.

There was one criticism of *Berlin* which, out of appreciation for a fine film and a new and arresting form, the critics failed to make; and time has not justified the omission. For all its ado of workmen and factories and swirl and swing of a great city, Berlin created nothing. Or rather if it created something, it was that shower of rain in the afternoon. The people of the city got up splendidly, they tumbled through their five million hoops impressively, they turned in; and no other issue of God or man emerged than that sudden besmattering spilling of wet on people and pavements.

I urge the criticism because *Berlin* still excites the mind of the young, and the symphony form is still their most popular persuasion. In fifty scenarios presented by the tyros, forty-five are symphonies of Edinburgh or of Ecclefechan or of Paris or of Prague. Day breaks—the people come to work—the factories start—the street cars rattle—lunch hour and the streets again—sport if it is Saturday afternoon—certainly evening and the local dance hall. And so, nothing having happened and nothing positively said about anything, to bed; though Edinburgh is the capital of a country and Ecclefechan, by some power inside itself, was the birthplace of Carlyle, in some ways one of the greatest exponents of this documentary idea.

The little daily doings, however finely symphonized, are not enough. One must pile up beyond doing or process to creation itself, before one hits the higher reaches of art. In this distinction, creation indicates not the making of things but the making of virtues.

First Principles of Documentary

And there's the rub for tyros. Critical appreciation of movement they can build easily from their power to observe, and power to observe they can build from their own good taste, but the real job only begins as they apply ends to their observation and their movements. The artist need not posit the ends—for that is the work of the critic—but the ends must be there, informing his description and giving finality (beyond space and time) to the slice of life he has chosen. For that larger effect there must be power of poetry or of prophecy. Failing either or both in the highest degree, there must be at least the socio-logical sense implicit in poetry and prophecy.

The best of the tyros know this. They believe that beauty will come in good time to inhabit the statement which is honest and lucid and deeply felt and which fulfils the best ends of citizenship. They are sensible enough to conceive of art as the by-product of a job of work done. The opposite effort to capture the by-product first (the self-conscious pursuit of beauty, the pursuit of art for art's sake to the exclusion of jobs of work and other pedestrian beginnings), was always a reflection of selfish wealth, selfish leisure and aesthetic de-cadence.

This sense of social responsibility makes our realist documentary a troubled and difficult art, and particularly in a time like ours. The job of romantic documentary is easy in comparison: easy in the sense that the noble savage is already a figure of romance and the seasons of the year have already been articulated in poetry. Their essential virtues have been declared and can more easily be declared again, and no one will deny them. But realist documentary, with its streets and cities and slums and markets and exchanges and factories, has given itself the job of making poetry where no poet has gone before it, and where no ends, sufficient for the purposes of art, are easily observed. It requires not only taste but also inspiration, which is to say a very laborious, deep-seeing, deep-sympathizing creative effort indeed.

The symphonists have found a way of building such matters of common reality into very pleasant sequences. By uses of tempo and rhythm, and by the large-scale integration of single effects, they capture the eye and impress the mind in the same way as a tattoo or a military parade might do. But by their concentration on mass and movement, they tend to avoid the larger creative job. What more attractive (for a man of visual taste) than to swing wheels and pistons about in ding-dong description of a machine, when he has little to say about the man who tends it, and still less to say about the tin-pan product it spills? And what more comfortable if, in one's heart, there

151

is avoidance of the issue of underpaid labour and meaningless production? For this reason I hold the symphony tradition of cinema for a danger and *Berlin* for the most dangerous of all film models to follow.

Unfortunately, the fashion is with such avoidance as *Berlin* represents. The highbrows bless the symphony for its good looks and, being sheltered rich little souls for the most part, absolve it gladly from further intention. Other factors combine to obscure one's judgment regarding it. The post-1918 generation, in which all cinema intelligence resides, is apt to veil a particularly violent sense of disillusionment, and a very natural first reaction of impotence, in any smart manner of avoidance which comes to hand. The pursuit of fine form which this genre certainly represents is the safest of asylums.

The objection remains, however. The rebellion from the who-gets-who tradition of commercial cinema to the tradition of pure form in cinema is no great shakes as a rebellion. Dadaism, expressionism, symphonics, are all in the same category. They present new beauties and new shapes; they fail to present new persuasions.

The imagist or more definitely poetic approach might have taken our consideration of documentary a step further, but no great imagist film has arrived to give character to the advance. By imagism I mean the telling of story or illumination of theme by images, as poetry is story or theme told by images: I mean the addition of poetic reference to the 'mass' and 'march' of the symphonic form.

Drifters was one simple contribution in that direction, but only a simple one. Its subject belonged in part to Flaherty's world, for it had something of the noble savage and certainly a great deal of the elements of nature to play with. It did, however, use steam and smoke and did, in a sense, marshal the effects of a modern industry. Looking back on the film now, I would not stress the tempo effects which it built (for both *Berlin* and *Potemkin* came before it), nor even the rhythmic effects (though I believe they outdid the technical example of *Potemkin* in that direction). What seemed possible of development in the film was the integration of imagery with the movement. The ship at sea, the men casting, the men hauling, were not only seen as functionaries doing something. They were seen as functionaries in half a hundred different ways, and each tended to add something to the illumination as well as the description of them. In other words the shots were massed together, not only for description and tempo but for commentary on it. One felt impressed by the tough continuing upstanding labour involved, and the feeling shaped the images, determined the

152

background and supplied the extra details which gave colour to the whole. I do not urge the example of *Drifters*, but in theory at least the example is there. If the high bravery of upstanding labour came through the film, as I hope it did, it was made not by the story itself, but by the imagery attendant on it. I put the point, not in praise of the method but in simple analysis of the method.

*   *   *

The symphonic form is concerned with the orchestration of movement. It sees the screen in terms of flow and does not permit the flow to be broken. Episodes and events, if they are included in the action, are integrated in the flow. The symphonic form also tends to organize the flow in terms of different movements, e.g. movement for dawn, movement for men coming to work, movement for factories in full swing, etc., etc. This is a first distinction.

See the symphonic form as something equivalent to the poetic form of, say, Carl Sandburg in *Skyscraper, Chicago, The Windy City* and *Slabs of the Sunburnt West*. The object is presented as an integration of many activities. It lives by the many human associations and by the moods of the various action sequences which surround it. Sandburg says so with variations of tempo in his description, variations of the mood in which each descriptive facet is presented. We do not ask personal stories of such poetry, for the picture is complete and satisfactory. We need not ask it of documentary. This is a second distinction regarding symphonic form.

These distinctions granted, it is possible for the symphonic form to vary considerably. Basil Wright, for example, is almost exclusively interested in movement, and will build up movement in a fury of design and nuances of design; and for those whose eye is sufficiently trained and sufficiently fine will convey emotion in a thousand variations on a theme so simple as the portage of bananas (*Cargo from Jamaica*). Some have attempted to relate this movement to the pyrotechnics of pure form, but there never was any such animal. (1) The quality of Wright's sense of movement and of his patterns is distinctively his own and recognizably delicate. As with good painters, there is character in his line and attitude in his composition. (2) There is an over-tone in his work which—sometimes after seeming monotony —makes his description uniquely memorable. (3) His patterns invariably weave—not seeming to do so—a positive attitude to the material, which may conceivably relate to (2). The patterns of *Cargo from Jamaica* were more scathing comment on labour at twopence a hundred bunches (or whatever it is) than mere sociological stricture. His movements—(*a*) easily down; (*b*) horizontal; (*c*) arduously 45° up; (*d*) down again—conceal, or perhaps construct, a comment. Flaherty once maintained that the east-west contour of Canada was itself a drama. It was precisely a sequence of down, horizontal, 45° up, and down again.

I use Basil Wright as an example of 'movement in itself'—though movement is never in itself—principally to distinguish those others who add either tension elements or poetic elements or atmospheric elements. I have held myself in the past an exponent of the tension category with certain pretension to the others. Here is a simple example of tension from *Granton Trawler*. The trawler is working its gear in a storm. The tension elements are built up with emphasis on the drag of the water, the heavy lurching of the ship, the fevered flashing of the birds, the fevered flashing of faces between waves, lurches and spray. The trawl is hauled aboard with strain of men and tackle and water. It is opened in a release which comprises equally the release of men, birds and fish. There is no pause in the flow of movement, but something of an effort as between two opposing forces, has been recorded. In a more ambitious and deeper description the tension might have included elements more intimately and more heavily descriptive of the clanging weight of the tackle, the strain on the ship, the operation of the gear under water and along the ground, the scuttering myriads of birds laying off in the gale. The fine fury of ship and heavy weather could have been brought through to touch the vitals of the men and the ship. In the hauling, the simple fact of a wave breaking over the men, subsiding and leaving them hanging on as though nothing had happened, would have brought the sequence to an appropriate peak. The release could have attached to itself images of, say, birds wheeling high, taking off from the ship, and of contemplative, i.e. more intimate, reaction on the faces of the men. The drama would have gone deeper by the greater insight into the energies and reactions involved.

Carry this analysis into a consideration of the first part of *Deserter*, which piles up from a sequence of deadly quiet to the strain and fury—and aftermath—of the strike, or of the strike sequence itself, which piles up from deadly quiet to the strain and fury—and aftermath —of the police attack, and you have indication of how the symphonic shape, still faithful to its own peculiar methods, comes to grip with dramatic issue.

The poetic approach is best represented by *Romance Sentimentale* and the last sequence of *Ekstase*. Here there is description without tension, but the moving description is lit up by attendant images. In *Ekstase* the notion of life renewed is conveyed by a rhythmic sequence of labour, but there are also essential images of a woman and child, a young man standing high over the scene, skyscapes and water. The description of the various moods of *Romance Sentimentale* is conveyed entirely by images: in one sequence of domestic interior, in another sequence of misty morning, placid water and dim sunlight. The creation of mood, an essential to the symphonic form, may be done in terms of tempo alone, but it is better done if poetic images colour it. In a description of night at sea, there are elements enough aboard a ship to build up a quiet and effective rhythm, but a deeper effect might come by reference to what is happening under water or by reference to the strange spectacle of the birds which, sometimes in ghostly flocks, move silently in and out of the ship's lights.

A sequence in a film by Rotha indicates the distinction between the three different treatments. He describes the loading of a steel furnace and builds a superb rhythm into the shovelling movements of the men. By creating behind them a sense of fire, by playing on the momentary shrinking from fire which comes into these shovelling movements, he would have brought in the elements of tension. He might have proceeded from this to an almost terrifying picture of what steel work involves. On the other hand, by overlaying the rhythm with, say, such posturing or contemplative symbolic figures, as Eisenstein brought into his *Thunder Over Mexico* material, he would have added the elements of poetic image. The distinction is between (*a*) a musical or non-literary method; (*b*) a dramatic method with clashing forces; and (*c*) a poetic, contemplative, and altogether literary method. These three methods may all appear in one film, but their proportion depends naturally on the character of the director—and his private hopes of salvation.

I do not suggest that one form is higher than the other. There are pleasures peculiar to the exercise of movement which in a sense are tougher—more classical—than the pleasures of poetic description, however attractive and however blessed by tradition these may be. The introduction of tension gives accent to a film, but only too easily gives popular appeal because of its primitive engagement with physical issues and struggles and fights. People like a fight, even when it is only a symphonic one, but it is not clear that a war with the elements is a braver subject than the opening of a flower or, for that matter, the opening of a cable. It refers us back to hunting instincts and fighting instincts, but these do not necessarily represent the more civilized fields of appreciation.

It is commonly believed that moral grandeur in art can only be achieved, Greek or Shakespearian fashion, after a general laying out of the protagonists, and that no head is unbowed which is not bloody. This notion is a philosophic vulgarity. Of recent years it has been given the further blessing of Kant in his distinction between the aesthetic of pattern and the aesthetic of achievement, and beauty has been considered somewhat inferior to the sublime. The Kantian confusion comes from the fact that he personally had an active moral sense, but no active aesthetic one. He would not otherwise have drawn the distinction. So far as common taste is concerned, one has to see that we do not mix up the fulfilment of primitive desires and the vain dignities which attach to that fulfilment, with the dignities which attach to man as an imaginative being. The dramatic application of the symphonic form is not, *ipso facto*, the deepest or most important. Consideration of forms neither dramatic nor symphonic, but dialectic, will reveal this more plainly.

4 Creative Use of Sound

The best way to start theorizing about sound is to start off, as we used to do in silent theory, by considering first principles. Here we said, beginning at the beginning, is an oblong patch of white, a *tabula rasa*. Here is a camera. What can we put on the *tabula rasa*, what art can we develop within the limits of the screen? By examination of our instruments, by examination of the camera and the cutting-bench, it soon became evident that we were not limited to the example of the stage. The perspectives of a new world and a new silent art opened out before us.

If only to formulate the method more clearly I shall run over some of these old arguments. The camera clearly can do much more than reproduce an action staged before it. It is a creative instrument, if properly directed, and not just a reproductive instrument.

It is light. It can get about in the world. Your screen accordingly is no longer the proscenium of a staged theatrical action. It can be a window on reality.

By the addition of close-up you give your camera power of intimacy. By the addition of one lens or another, you have a telephoto command of detail and intimacy. You have a microscopic power over reality.

By bringing in the element of angle you add new viewpoints which, if properly used, can add to the dramatic, that is to say, to the creative power of your description. Put your camera high, you get one power; put it low you get another.

These were elementary powers which immediately indicated a direction for the silent film. When we considered the possibilities of the cutting-bench, the possibilities of montage, still further powers opened up before us.

We could create rhythms and tempos, crescendos and diminuendos of energy to help our exposition.

We could bring detail together in mass formation. We could cross-section a street or a factory or a city.

We could work in images to add atmosphere to our action, or poetry to our description.

157

A Movement is Founded

We could, by the juxtaposition of shots, explode ideas in the heads of our audience. We could arrange the juxtaposition of our detail for particular dramatic effect.

Out of such *a priori* considerations was created a theory which gradnally took cinema from the example of the stage into a world of its own.

Films like *Potemkin*, even the Wild West films, had very little to do with stage example. They represented a new art which depended for its effects on powers peculiar to itself.

With sound film we must go through the same process. It is obviously not enough to seize on its power of reproducing synchronistically the spoken words of actors. At first it was a sufficient novelty to hear our shadows speak and sing, and hear their ham and eggs sizzle in the frying-pan, but if you look into the matter you will see that the microphone, like the camera, can do better things than merely reproduce, and that at the cutting-bench and the re-recording bench as many new possibilities open out before sound film as once opened out before the cutting-bench of silence.

The microphone, too, can get about in the world. By doing so, it has the same power over reality as the camera had before it. It has the power to bring to the hands of the creative artist a thousand and one vernacular elements, and the million and one sounds which ordinarily attend the working of the world. Regarded simply as a collector of raw material, the microphone, like the camera before it, has still to be released from the bondage of the studios.

The raw material, of course, means nothing in itself. It is only as it is used that it becomes the material of art. The final question is how we are to use sound creatively rather than reproductively.

Here perhaps it is useful to remember the example set us by the B.B.C. This great organization has been in possession of microphones for years. It has had an unparalleled freedom in the handling of sound effects, yet it is still content with an almost exclusive use of the microphone for reproductive purposes. It reproduces speech, it reproduces music, it brings the experts of one sound medium or another to our ears, but in the process it has added nothing. For it, the microphone is simply a reproductive mechanism.

Its only contribution is in its dramatic department. There it attempts to build up effects drawn from a dozen different locations. Some Napoleon at centre presses a button to bring in studio A and the piece starts with some music. At the proper point he mixes in studio B and overlays some conversation. At another point a button brings in a wind mechanism or the sound of a door banging.

Creative Use of Sound

Now, sound film permits all this to be done with greater certainty, greater exactitude, and much greater subtlety and complexity. If your sounds are on film you can with a pair of scissors and a pot of paste join any single sound to any other. You can orchestrate bits and pieces of sound as you please. You can also, by re-recording, put any single sound on top of another sound. A simple case is music in the background and a voice in the foreground, but, theoretically at least, you can have a dozen sounds all with their different reference sounding together. Add to these two possibilities the fact that the image is on one strip of film, and the sound on another strip of film. You can obviously put any sound or sounds you select alongside any given picture.

I take it one is ready to admit the principle that we must make our sound help the mute rather than reproduce it. Sometimes it is useful, of course, to hear what people are saying and see their lips move, but we may take it as a principal guide that wherever we can make the sound add to the general effect we should. Our rule should be to have the mute strip and the sound complementary to each other, helping each other along. That is what Pudovkin means when he talks about asynchronistic sound. He talks of the mute and the sound following each a separate rhythm, as instruments in an orchestra follow their separate parts to the end of creating together a larger result.

Sound can obviously bring a rich contribution to the manifold of the film—so rich a contribution in fact that the double art becomes a new art altogether. We have power of speech, power of music, power of natural sound, power of commentary, power of chorus, power even of manufacturing sound which has never been heard before. These different elements can all be used to give atmosphere, to give drama, to give poetic reference to the subject in hand. And when you remember that you can cut sound as you cut film and that you can, by re-recording, orchestrate any or all of these elements together in exact timing with the mute, the possibilities become enormous.

Some new uses of sound have been creeping into the studio pictures. There was a great critical noise when Hitchcock repeated the word 'knife', 'knife' in one of his early films. It represented a use of sound that described the subjective side of a situation. This use has been developed greatly since then. In the Hitchcock example this word, which stood out from the mumble of conversation, was simply a word which was drumming in the mind of one of the actors. In *Hell's Heroes* words subjectively spoken were cut similarly with words objectively spoken. In *Strange Interlude* almost the entire issue of the film was the

159

fact that the people said one thing to their neighbours and a different thing to themselves. On the stage, as I first saw this O'Neill technique developed, the actors had to use masks. They spoke with masks for the objective words and spoke without them for the subjective words, but the mechanics were of course clumsy. Here, in what you might call the world of monologue, sound film can do and do easily what is outside the power of the stage. It means of course that a new perspective can be brought to the personal drama, a perspective which if it is handled deeply might give the cinema some of the psychological power of the novel.

Another field in which sound technique is likely to develop greatly is in the use of chorus. I remember seeing in Paris before sound came, the Russian film *The Village of Sin*, and when the harvest scene came on, a chorus of *émigrés* concealed behind the screen broke into a Russian harvest song. This was very effective at the time. When Creighton synchronized *One Family* he used the same device for a Canadian prairie sequence, and was very much before his time. There is too the use of chorus in both René Clair and Lubitsch: not just as simple background chorus but as something taken up by different characters at different points of the action. You have a René Clair chorus used to cross-section a tenement building. The first line is sung by a man shaving on the second floor, the second line by a fat lady doing her hair on the ground floor and so on. So, by a chorus, characters are brought together and a single mood permeates a whole location. The Lubitsch use of chorus is similar. The characters begin it in a railway train, but it is taken up by the engine driver, by the guard, by the wheels playing rhythmically on the rails—even by the peasants in the passing fields. So too with Disney. A musical sequence is beaten out by the most various fantastic elements in the mute—or more rarely, though more excitingly, it is counter-pointed by the mute.

But the permeation of the silent images with a musical mood represents only an elementary use of chorus possibilities. In *Three-Cornered Moon* there was a quick cross-section of the American unemployed. The picture flashed from one desolate figure to another and the sound strip in complement picked up various bits of conversation revealing the lost hopes of the people in the bread queues. Call this the chorus of bits and pieces. With a sound strip into which you can cut any excerpt of sound you like, there is no limit to the cumulative selections of conversations you can build up. Conversational scraps from a street, from a factory, from any scene or situation, may very well help you to give colour and point to your description. There were glimpses of this in two G.P.O. films, *6.30 Collection* and in *Weather Forecast*.

There is another kind of chorus altogether. It might be called the recitative chorus. The very crudest form of it is in the commentary which you find ordinarily attached to 'interest' films. Imagine, however, that your commentary is spoken by a poet, or imagine that you are back with Greek chorus and that your poet is no longer describing the fact of the matter but delivering a recital which adds dramatic or poetic colour to the action. There was an example of this in a Hollywood melodrama, *Beast of the City*, which began with a survey of the Chicago underworld, in which the camera trucked from one dark sidewalk to another. The recital in this case was the monotonous rigmarole of the wireless messages going out from police headquarters. It went something like this: 'Calling Car 324 324 Calling Car 528 528 Calling Car 18 18', etc., etc.

There is nothing to prevent the further development of this recitative business. In *6.30 Collection* masses of letters were seen parading on the moving belt of a large sorting office. The sound was simple, for we contented ourselves in this film with a straight documentary account of the noises that were there. We could very easily have made the letters read themselves out in snatches, or for that matter we could have hired a poet to make *vers libres* of their contents. Or we could make the different senders come forward to say in snatches what their letters were seeking. I do not mean that these would have been good methods in this particular instance, for they would probably have overloaded the occasion. My point is that different choral possibilities are there to develop.

There is still another direction in which sound will develop very considerably, and that is in the direction of imagery. A great exponent of the silent film like Pudovkin could always be reckoned on to bring very beautiful images into his description. At the beginning of *The End of St. Petersburg* there is a sequence describing the birth of a child, and a small boy is sent off to pass the word to his father in the fields. As he runs, a single puffy cloud in the sky is cut into the sequence. In *Mother* the happiness of a woman is described in terms of waving trees and rushing water. In *Ekstase* and in *Romance Sentimentale* the moods of the central figure were similarly described by the introduction of appropriate attendant images. Sounds, of course, have not the same precise significance as visuals. Some of the sequences in *Weather Forecast* demonstrate how effective some seemingly irrational crossing

L   161

of sound can be: the sound of an aeroplane attached to a shot of a high mast, for example. The point is that once you start detaching sounds from their origins you can use them as images of those origins. It allows you to enrich your camera's observation. For example, the racketing of teleprinters in *Weather Forecast* is associated with a B.B.C. broadcast. In *6.30 Collection* the sound of a departing train is associated with the sweepers in the sorting office when the work is over and the mail bags have gone. In *Cable Ship* the sound of the cable itself is associated with a trucking shot of the International Telephone Exchange.

Another curious fact emerges once you start detaching sounds from their origins, and it is this. Your aeroplane noise may become not the image of an aeroplane but the image of distance or of height. Your steamer whistle may become not the image of a steamer but of isolation or darkness.

I cannot tell you how far this imagery will go because we are only beginning to become dramatically and poetically conscious of sound. The whole power of sound imagery will only come as, in the practice of sound film, more and more sounds are detached and matured into the special significance which I believe is latent in them.

But by discussing in this way chorus and imagery and monologue I only mean to give the broadest indication of the new possibilities. Practice has a habit of exploding all theories and generalizations. The main thing is that sound must help to fulfil the mute, and mute must help to fulfil the sound. This is not silent film with sound added. It is a new art—the art of sound-film.

In Cavalcanti's *Pett and Pott* the relation of sound to mute was so close that the film was regarded as of historic importance in the development of sound film. For certainly no sound film before depended so little on stage example. The music was written to create the mood of the theme. The sound strip invaded the silent strip and turned a woman's cry into an engine whistle. Recitative was used in the train scene instead of the usual sound of the wheels on the rail. The film illustrated how a commentator—a voice of God in the last instance—might be used effectively even in a story film. Other effects included the joining of a drum and fife band with a domestic quarrel, and the film showed the dramatic point that can be achieved by cutting from one sound sequence to another.

Sound film is glued to stage example, and however many the variations we see or hear, they do not represent any fundamental breakaway from the dialogue drama of the theatre. But that breakaway must

162

come. The documentary film will do pioneer work for cinema if it emancipates the microphone from the studio and demonstrates at the cutting and re-recording benches how many more dramatic uses can be made of sound than the studios realize.

5 The E.M.B. Film Unit

In official records you would find the E.M.B. Film Unit tucked away in a long and imposing list of E.M.B. Departments and Sub-Departments, forty-five all told. The Film Unit was number forty-five. 'Research and Development' interests accounted for the first twenty-four. There the major part of E.M.B. work was done. In one respect or another it helped to integrate or promote all the major researches across the world which affected the production or preservation or transport of the Empire's food supplies. Consideration of cinema was, properly, junior to the consideration of such matters as entomological, mycological, and low temperature investigation.

So, through considerations of Tea, Rice, Sugar, Tobacco, Tung Oil, and Forest Products, to 'Marketing Economic Investigation and Intelligence': Marketings of home agricultural produce, regional sales drives, marketing inquiries in general, and market intelligence services for fish, fruit, dairy produce, dried and canned fruits in particular, world surveys of production and trade, retail surveys, accounts of wastage in imported fruit, experimental consignments, and I know not what all. Then 'Publicity', banner-heading the departments of newspaper advertisement, posters, recipes, leaflets, lectures, broadcasts, exhibitions, shopping weeks, and trade meetings.

After the trade meetings, cinema. I give you its place not in humility, but for proportion. It was a department among other departments, and part of a very much larger scheme of educational and propaganda services. Whatever its pretentions in purely cinematic terms, it was dedicated and devoted to the usual cold-blooded ends of Government.

Of the fifteen hundred tyros who applied for jobs in the E.M.B. Film Unit, fifteen hundred exactly expressed their enthusiasm for cinema, for art, for self-expression, and the other beautiful what-nots of a youthful or simply vague existence. Not one considered this more practical relationship of commissions to be served, nor the fact that Treasury money, and opportunity to make any films at all, were entirely conditioned by these commissions to be served. The point is important. In Britain, as in any other country, there is little or no

164

money for free production. There is money for films which will make
box-office profits, and there is money for films which will create
propaganda results. These only. They are the strict limits within which
cinema has had to develop and will continue to develop.

The principal point of interest about the E.M.B. Film Unit is that,
within such necessary propaganda limits, it was permitted a unique
measure of freedom. The dogs of the commercial world are harried and
driven to quick box-office results. The dogs of the propaganda world
are more wisely driven to good results, for half the virtue of propaganda is in the prestige it commands. Another point: the commercials
are interested only in the first results of their films: that is to say, in
the amount of money a film takes in a twelvemonth. The long-range
propagandists are not. Quick takings are a guarantee of immediate
public interest and are therefore important, but the persistence of a
film's effect over a period of years is more important still. To command,
and cumulatively command, the mind of a generation is more important than by novelty or sensation to knock a Saturday night audience
cold; and the 'hang-over' effect of a film is everything. In this sense the
propaganda road to cinema has certain advantages. It allows its
directors time to develop; it waits with a certain patience on their
experiments; it permits them time to perfect their work. So by all
logic it should do, and so it did at the E.M.B. If the E.M.B. was an
exception in the degree of its patience and the extent of the freedom
which it permitted, it was because the E.M.B. at the time was the only
organization outside Russia that understood and had imagination
enough to practise the principles of long-range propaganda. It was not
unconscious of the example of Russia.

These more imaginative interpretations of the methods of propaganda were entirely due to Sir Stephen Tallents, whose book on the
Projection of England indicated only slimly the creative work he did
for the mobilization of the arts in the national service. The points of
contact of E.M.B. publicity, education, and propaganda were so many
and various that I doubt if even the war of 1914–18 produced so widely
ranged or so penetrating a system. The fact that it worked in a lower
key and without drawing attention to itself in easy species of ballyhoo
was the measure of its strength as a peacetime activity. The ballyhoo
method does for a pinch, but only so.

Its principal effect in six years (1928–33) was to change the connotation of the word 'Empire'. Our original command of peoples was
becoming slowly a co-operative effort in the tilling of soil, the reaping
of harvests, and the organization of a world economy. For the old

flags of exploitation it substituted the new flags of common labour; for the old frontiers of conquest it substituted the new frontiers of research and world-wide organization. Whatever one's politics, and however cynical one might be about the factors destructive of a world economy, this change of emphasis had an ultimate historical importance. History is determined by just such building of new sentiments. It was clear that we had to learn to make our building deliberate.

I give you this conception of the E.M.B. as a world force, without apology. I cannot speak for the various official intentions nor, for that matter, guarantee that they understood the implication of the E.M.B.'s growing proportions, but so it existed in some of our minds, and with consequent direction in most of the things we did.

In cinema we got the very brief commission 'to bring the Empire alive'. We were instructed, in effect, to use cinema, or alternatively to learn to use it, to bring alive the industries, the harvests, the researches, the productions, the forward-looking activities of all kinds; in short, to bring the day-to-day activities of the British Commonwealth and Empire at work into the common imagination. The only conditions laid down were that we should have the good sense to explore a few preliminary avenues, work for a period experimentally, and remember the sensitive nerves of Treasury officials: Mr. Hildred being the unhappy financial Atlas appointed to carry this new and incomprehensible infant on his shoulders. I cannot say we succeeded at first with this neurological aspect of our work. We were confused in Mr. Hildred's mind (and possibly very rightly) with the people who take snapshots at the seaside; and he was not sure that our results should cost any more than the customary five for a shilling. Whitehall, we discovered, was longer by a bittock than the road to Damascus, and sky splitting an even more valuable art than cinema. But we did, and for two long years, explore the avenues.

Before the E.M.B. Unit was formed for continuous production, Walter Creighton and I wandered about looking at things. I think we must have seen every propaganda film in existence between Moscow and Washington. We certainly prepared the first surveys of the propaganda and educational services of the principal Governments. We ran, too, a school of cinema where all the films we thought had a bearing on our problem were brought together and demonstrated in whole or part, for the instruction of Whitehall. *Berlin, The Covered Wagon, The Iron Horse*, the Russians; we had all the documentaries and epics worth a damn; though, in calculation of our audience, we had perforce to change a few endings and consider some of the close-ups among the less forceful arguments. In effect, we sold our idea of cinema sufficiently well to get cash in hand for our first experimental productions. Creighton plumped for fantasy and I for documentary: Creighton making *One Family*, a seven-reel theatrical, with B.I.F., and I *Drifters* with New Era.

The choice of documentary was made partly on personal grounds, and partly on grounds of common financial sense. A Government department cannot, like the commercial gamblers, take a rap: or at least its powers of resistance are keyed only to the very smallest raps. Alternatively, if the Civil Service or any other public service must have its illegitimate infants, it is best to see that they are small ones. Documentary is cheap: it is, on all considerations of public accountancy, safe. If it fails for the theatres it may, by manipulation, be accommodated non-theatrically in one of half a dozen ways. Moreover, by reason of its cheapness, it permits a maximum amount of production and a maximum amount of directorial training against the future, on a limited sum. It even permits the building of an entire production and distribution machine for the price of a single theatrical. These considerations are of some importance where new experiments in cinema are concerned. With one theatrical film you hit or miss; with a machine, if it is reasonably run, the preliminary results may not be immediately notable or important, but they tend to pile up. Piling up they create a freedom impossible on any other policy.

The fact that documentary was the genre most likely to bring method and imagination into such day-to-day subjects as we dealt with was, of course, a final argument.

On these high conceptions, the unit continued to operate. The problem was not so much to repeat the relative success of *Drifters* but to guarantee that, with time, we should turn out good documentaries as a matter of certainty. It was a case of learning the job, not on the basis of one director, one location, and one film at a time, but on the basis of half a dozen directors with complementary talents, and a hundred and one subjects along the line. And because the job was new and because it was too humble to appeal to studio directors, it was also a question of taking young people and giving them their heads.

That was in 1930. In the three years that followed we gathered together, and in a sense created, Basil Wright, Arthur Elton, Stuart Legg, and half a dozen others. Wright was the best lyrical documentary director in the country, Elton the best industrial, and Legg the best all-rounder. One or two others, it seemed, would presently be heard from.

A Movement is Founded

Their record at that date was not, of course, a huge one, and in the circumstances could not be. It comprised *Industrial Britain* (with Flaherty), *Big Timber, O'er Hill and Dale, Country Comes to Town, Shadow on the Mountain, Upstream, Voice of the World,* and *The New Generation.* Wright was working on three films from the West Indies (*Cargo from Jamaica, Windmill in Barbados, Liner Cruising South*), Elton a five-reel account of aeroplane engines (*Aero-Engine*), and Legg two films on the Post Office. Edgar Anstey made *Uncharted Waters,* a film of Labrador exploration. J. N. G. Davidson made *Hen Woman,* the unit's only story documentary. D. F. Taylor had a film on the stocks (for the Travel Association) dealing with the changing landscape of Lancashire (*Lancashire at Work and Play*). Evelyn Spice was working on a new series of films for schools, covering the English seasons and the economic areas of England. To these add two or three odd films for the Ministry of Agriculture, sundry experiments in abstract films by Rotha and Taylor, and non-theatrical makings or re-editings at the rate of about fifty a year. That was the production account, and it was fair enough for the period involved. Two years' apprenticeship, or even three, was a short time for the exploration of a new craft, and the maturing of new talent, and I doubt if we expected anything considerable or exciting in less than five.

What was important was that this was the only group of its kind outside Russia: that is to say, the only group devoted deliberately, continuously, and with hope, to the highest forms of documentary. And its policy was in this respect unique, that so long as the film's general aim was served, no consideration of a mere popular appeal was allowed to enter. The director, in other words, was free in his manner and method as no director outside the public service can hope to be. His only limits were the limits of his finance, the limits of his aesthetic conscience in dealing so exclusively with an art of persuasion, and the limits of his own ability. In the practical issue they might sometimes embarrass, but did not seem to prevent a reasonably good result.

6 Summary and Survey: 1935

An artist in this art of cinema may whistle for the means of production. A camera costs a thousand pounds, a sound-recording outfit three times as much, and the brute cost of every second of picture shot is sixpence. Add the cost of actors, of technicians, of the thousand-and-one technical processes which come between the conception and the finished film, and the price of production is already a matter of high finance. A poet may prosper on pennies. A film director, even a bad director, must deal in thousands. Six thousand or so will make a quickie to meet the English quota laws. With sixty thousand one is reaching to the *Chu Chin Chows*. The more garish efforts of the Napoleonic de Mille cost two hundred and more. *Ben Hur* at more than a million and *Hell's Angels* at nearly a million are exceptions, but they happened. The cost of a film ranges between the price of a hospital and the estimated cost of clearing the slums of Southwark.

The most interesting point about these huge production costs is that they can be recovered. *Ben Hur* made money. This fact must be realized, and, with it, the one consideration which controls the cinema and dictates its relation to the artist: that a film is capable of infinite reproduction and infinite exhibition. It can cross boundaries and hold an audience of millions. The world's cinema audience is 250 millions a week, each and all of these myriads paying his yen or rupee or shilling or quarter for the privilege. Chaplin's *City Lights* was seen by fifteen millions in Britain alone. Where the prize of popularity is so gigantic, considerations of art and public service must, of course, be secondary. The film people are businessmen and, by all law of commerce, their spiritual researches are confined to those common factors of human appeal which ensure the rattle of ten or twenty or fifty million sixpences across the world. In this respect they pursue the same principles as Woolworth and Ford. They have rationalized the hopes-and-dreams business: a more plainly dangerous development, if entered lightly into, than all other rationalization whatsoever.

There are, among the common factors of human appeal, higher factors like humour and religion. There are the lower common factors

169

of sentimentality and sensationalism. In the practical issue, nothing is quite so diffident as a million dollars. There is a certainty about the lower factors which the higher cannot pretend. Who—particularly a financier—can recognize the genuine prophet from the fake? Cinema has, on the whole, lost so much on its mistakes of prophecy that its simpler instinct is to avoid all prophecy together.

Humour it has held to, and faithfully. Epic—in twenty years or so—it has learned to distinguish from melodrama. These, in their blessed combination of simplicity and depth, have a sure record in commercial cinema: comedy in particular. They represent the two points at which wide human appeal may also have the quality of depth. And, so far from breaking through the economic law, it has been proved by Chaplins and Covered Wagons that they even more generously fulfil it. Simple inspiration, as priests and medicine men once discovered, was always a better box-office bet than simple entertainment.

But there, in comedy and epic, is the limit. Great cameramen contribute their superb craftsmanship, great story-tellers their invention, great art directors their splendour of décor, and the patience and skill which build even the average film are miracles to wonder over; but, at centre, in the heart and theme of the commercial film the financial consideration rules. It is a consideration of largest possible audiences and widest possible appeal. Sometimes, in comedy and epic, the result is in its simple way splendid. Nearly always the technical splendours of cinema loom gigantically over trivial and contemptible issues.

Only, therefore, in comedy, in epic, in occasional idyll does the commercial cinema touch the world of art, and is cinema possible for the artist. And epic and idyll being near to the problems of prophecy (note for example the difficulties of Robert Flaherty), comedy is of these the surest ground. Chaplin, Disney, Laurel and Hardy and the Marx Brothers are the only relatively footloose artists in cinema today. They are, in fact, free up to the point of satire. There, comedy merges with those deeper considerations of which finance must necessarily be sensitive. Footloose they are, these comedians, till in a moment of more considered fancy the Marx Brothers decide to play ducks and drakes with the banking system, Walt Disney with the American constitution, and Laurel and Hardy with the N.A.M.

Epic, too, can have its way if it is as rough-shod as *The Covered Wagon*, as sentimental for the *status quo* as *Cavalcade*, as heroic in the face of hunger as *Nanook*. Heaven defend it if, as once happened in

Griffith's *Isn't Life Wonderful?*, the hunger is not of Eskimos but of ourselves. Perhaps it is that people do not want to see the world in its more sordid aspects, and that the law of widest appeal does not permit consideration of either our follies or our sorrows. Certain it is that the magnates of cinema will deplore the deviation. Theirs the dream of shop-girl and counter-clerk, and exclusively they pursue it. The films of our modern society are set among braveries too detached for questioning. The surroundings vary, and they sometimes reach to the mills and factories and hospitals and telephone exchanges of common life. They even reach back to include the more solid pageantries of history. But seldom is it that a grave or present issue is struck. Industry and history might assuredly bring to dramatic point those matters which more nearly concern us. In film they do not, because the financiers dare not. These backgrounds are façades only for an article which—though in comedy and epic it may not be trifling—is invariably safe.

This is not to convict the film producers of a great wrong. Like other businessmen, they serve their creed and ensure their profit and, on the whole, they do it very well. In one sense even, the financier might regard himself as a public benefactor. In an age when the faiths, the loyalties and the purposes have been more than usually undermined, mental fatigue—or is it spiritual fatigue—represents a large factor in everyday experience. Our cinema magnate does no more than exploit the occasion. He also, more or less frankly, is a dope pedlar.

This, then, is the atmosphere in which the maker of films is held, however noble his purpose or deep his inspiration. He is in a closed circle from which he can only by a rare failure of the system escape. It is a threefold circle. The financier-producer will prevent him going deep lest he becomes either difficult or dangerous. But beyond the producer lies the renter who, skilled only in selling dope, is unfitted for stimulants. If the film deviates in any way he will either curse it as a changeling or, in an effort to translate it into his own salesman terms, deceive and disappoint exhibitor and public alike. In this way *Moana* was mis-sold as 'the Love Life of a South Sea Syren'. The exhibitor is the third circle. He is by nature and circumstance more nervous than either producer or renter. He could, of course, combine the capacities of teacher and showman. He could, by articulating unusual virtues in a film, introduce them to the public. He could thereby create a more discriminating and critical public. But the exhibitor follows, like his brothers, the line of least resistance. The more imaginative points of showmanship are not for him when the brazen methods of ballyhoo are so patently effective. He is, he will say in self-defence, 'in the entertainment business' or, sometimes, 'in the entertainment catering business'. Entertainment may be as rich as inspiration, but, being a complacent fellow in his world of sensational superlatives, it is difficult to convince him.

The wise director will accept these conditions from the beginning. Production money, renting facilities, theatre screens, with the qualifications I have noted, are held against any divergence from the common law. His stuff must be popular stuff and as popular as possible. It must also be immediately popular, for the film business does not allow of those long-term policies and belated recognitions so common to art. A film is out and away and in again in twelve months, and the publicity which is so necessary to wide and sensational success promotes a sally rather than a circulation. The system does not allow of that slow penetration which is the safeguard of the painter and poet.

In spite of all this, the system does sometimes fail and unexpected things come through. The fit of scepticism which overtook Germany after 1918 had the effect of encouraging a seriousness of outlook which was altogether novel in the commercial world. Theatres and studios combined in the contemplation of Fate, and the cinema had its only period of tragedy. *Caligari, Destiny, The Joyless Street, The Grey House*, were the great films of this period. They were humourless and sombre but they were imaginatively done. They added power to cinema and celebrity to directors. Hollywood almost immediately acquired the celebrity. Murnau, Pommer, Jannings, Pola Negri, Lubitsch went over but, subjected to the brighter air of Hollywood and the wider insistence of its international market, their skill was quickly chained to the normal round. The system, as it continuously does with able aliens, absorbed them or broke them. After a struggle Pommer returned to Europe, but could not rebuild the tradition he had deserted. Murnau also struggled and in a last attempt at escape produced, with Flaherty, *Tabu*: too late, perhaps, for the expensive and shallow outlook of the studios had caught him. Lubitsch discovered a genius for comedy and was whole-heartedly absorbed. The rule obtains whether it is the artist or only his story that passes to the commercial atmosphere. Like the Celtic warriors, 'when they go into the West they seldom come back'.

The other exceptions are individual ones. Occasionally a director has money enough to back his own venture. Distribution may be lacking: but he can in the meantime have his fling. Occasionally a director is able to convince or deceive a producer into doing something more solid than usual. Occasionally, the publicity value attaching to a great reputation may overcome commercial scruples. In these categories come certain deviations of Fairbanks, King Vidor, D. W. Griffith, von Sternberg and Jean Renoir and responsible versions of H. G. Wells and Eugene O'Neill and Bernard Shaw. Sometimes, again, the personal toughery or insistence of a director has managed a deeper result than was contemplated or wanted. In this category are some of the films of von Stroheim, the best films of von Sternberg, Flaherty's *Moana*, Dreyer's *Joan of Arc* and some of the best of King Vidor and D. W. Griffith. But even the toughs do not last long. These men have done much for cinema and Griffith is the greatest master cinema has produced, but only Sternberg seems to have any assurance of continuity. He is the golden producer of the golden Dietrich. As a parting shot from his retirement Griffith has announced that one line of Shakespeare's poetry is worth all that the cinema ever produced.

To be absorbed or eliminated is the only choice in the commercial cinema, for it has the virtue of singleness of purpose. It has no ambition to specialize for specialized audiences. It has no reason to exploit the artist for the individual or creative quality of his inspiration. It is a big racket, they say, and you must play it big: which is to say that you must play it good and wide and common to the exclusion of all height and handsomeness. Within its lights and limits the commercial cinema is right. The artist is an economic fool who confuses financial dealings with patronage and exploitation with understanding.

Commercial cinema, being the monstrous undisciplined force it is, has done a great deal of harm. It has also done a great deal of simple good. Even in the world of sentimentality and sensationalism its narrative is racy, its wit is keen, and its types have more honest human gusto than their brothers and sisters of the stage and popular novel. The vast array of thwarted talent so expresses itself. If cinema has not debunked the greater evils of society it has very successfully debunked some of the lesser ones. It has given many salutary lessons in critical citizenship, for it has taught people to question authority, realize the trickeries that may parade in the name of Justice, and recognize that graft may sit in the highest places. It has taught the common people to take account of themselves in their common manners, if not in their common rights. It has taught the world to dress better, look better, and, to some extent, behave better. It may not have added to the wisdom of the world but it has at least de-yokelized it. These are only some of the gifts of the commercial cinema. There is also the gift of beautiful women, of the fresh air of the Westerns, of much fine setting and brilliant décor. The skill and polish of its presentation, though only the professional may judge them properly, are a continuing delight. They may even exercise a continuing discipline.

The stars are not so easily included in the benefits of cinema. They are our version of the mythological figures who have at all times expressed the desires of primitive peoples. Here, as always, the figures of the imagination maintain the will. But to say so is to discover that other side of the picture which is not so beautiful. For loss and lack of other mythology, the millions are very deeply bound to their stars: not only in the matter of their dress and bearing but also in the ends they seek. On this criterion the stars are a queer lot. The inquiries of the Payne Trust in America discovered some interesting analyses in this connection, and I take the following excerpts more or less solidly from H. J. Forman's summing up of their findings. Thirty-three per cent of the heroines, 34 per cent of the villains, 63 per cent of the villainesses in one hundred and fifteen pictures—all these eminent protagonists—are either wealthy or ultra-wealthy. The 'poor' run only to 5 per cent. The largest classification for all characters combined is *no occupation. Commercial* comes next with ninety characters. *Occupation unknown* comes next with eighty. The gangsters, bootleggers, smugglers, thieves, bandits, blackmailers and prostitutes follow, also with eighty. *Theatrical, servants, high society*, the luxury trades in fact, follow, as one might imagine, the gangsters, the thieves and the bandits. These together account for six hundred and forty of a total character list of eight hundred and eighty-three. The remaining quarter of this crazily assorted population is scattered among many callings, notable in that common labour is not included in them at all. A few agricultural labourers exist, but only to decorate the Westerns. Mr. Forman adds: 'Were the population of the United States the population of the world itself, so arranged and distributed, there would be no farming, no manufacturing, almost no industry, no vital statistics (except murders), no economic problems and no economics.'

Dr. Dale contributes an even more entertaining analysis of *goals*. In his hundred and fifteen pictures, the heroes are responsible for thirteen good sound murders, the villains and villainesses for thirty. Heroines have only one to their credit. Altogether fifty-four murders are committed, to say nothing of fifty-nine cases of mere assault and battery. Thirty-six hold-ups are staged and twenty-one kidnappings, numerous other crimes scattering. The total score is remarkable. Forty-three crimes are attempted; four hundred and six are actually committed. And taking an analysis of forty pictures in which fifty-seven criminals are responsible for sixty-two crimes, it appears that of the fifty-seven only three were arrested and held, four were arrested and released, four others were arrested but escaped, seven were arrested and the punishment implied, twenty-four were punished by extra-legal methods. Fifteen criminals went wholly unpunished.

'The goals in the lives of these baseless ruthless people', says Mr. Forman, 'are often as tawdry as themselves. Of the social goals, the higher goals of mankind, the numbers are very small.' They are indeed, when one realizes that 75 to 80 per cent of the films deal more or less exclusively with sex and crime. Of the sixteen 'goals' figuring most frequently, *performance of duty* comes a miserable eighth in the order of merit. All the others are strictly personal. *Love* in its various forms is first, second, fourth, fifth, sixth, with *illicit love* quietly solid at tenth. 'Shoddy goals', says Mr. Forman, 'pursued frequently by highly objectionable human beings.' It is difficult not to agree, though economic estimate is, on the whole, more fruitful than moral indignation.

Out of this welter of influences for good and evil it is possible occasionally to isolate a dramatic film which is just a good honest film in itself—with spirit enough to dodge sociological criticism. The gangster films *Quick Millions* and *Beast of a City* were well done. So were the newspaper stories *Hi! Nellie, Five Star Final* and *The Front Page*. So were the convict films *I am a Fugitive* and *Twenty Thousand Years in Sing Sing*. So was the back-stage story *Forty-Second Street*. They have invention and gusto in the high degree we generally associate with Edgar Wallace. And this is as much as a wise critic will expect of the dramatic film. One film of the line did break through to subtler qualities. This was *Three-Cornered Moon*. It appeared humbly as a second feature and its deviation was plainly mistrusted, but it made a fine affair of family affection and said something quietly of the American depression. Among the sentimental romances there was *Ekstase*, not a film of the line but a freak of quality from Czechoslovakia. The commercial cinemas refused it. Sentimental romance does, however, vary a little. By dint of great directorial ambition (or is 'artistic' the word?) the sad, sad saccharine of *Seventh Heaven* becomes the sad, sad saccharine of *The Constant Nymph*. Here the object of the affection is no longer the rich young man next door: he is the poor young artist in the garret over the way. So the mind of the movies moves laboriously to higher things.

The creative reputations built on such foundations are, to say the least, slimly based. In great generosity the critics have made names for Milestone, Roland Brown, Mamoulian and others. They are great and skilled craftsmen certainly, but nothing of them remains at the midriff after a twelvemonth. Here perhaps the critics, finding no depth of theme for their consideration, have made a grave and continuing mistake. They have equated a mere skill of presentation with the creative will itself. So doing they have perverted criticism and misled at least one generation of willing youths into false appreciation. The only critic in Britain who has taken the proper measure of the movies is St. John Ervine. By blasting it for its shallowness he, by implication, defends a cinema which may yet—who knows—be measured to the adult mind. But it is the cinema-conscious and the cinema-critical who rise howling at his word. Our body of criticism is largely to blame. It is consciously or subconsciously influenced by the paid advertisement and the flattering hospitality of the trade. It is, consciously or subconsciously, affected by the continuing dearth of critical subject matter. The observation of technical skill is the only decent gambit available to a disheartening, sychophantic, and largely contemptible pursuit.

Outside the world of drama there are, of course, better things. There are the idylls, the epics and the comedies. Each has its own particular problems and troubles: financial in the case of idylls, as one might expect in a genre so near to poetry, technical in the cases of comedy and epic, because of the complications of sound. The great idyll of the period has been *Man of Aran*, and I precise its story for its bearings on the economic arguments I have laid. Flaherty came to Britain at the invitation of the old E.M.B. Film Unit, not of the cinema trade at all. He had done nothing in cinema since his co-operation with Murnau on *Tabu*: a film which was financed and made outside the commercial circle. Through the persistent efforts of Cedric Belfrage and Angus McPhail he passed to Gaumont-British, to be given *carte blanche* on the Aran Islands. This was altogether a freak happening in commercial cinema and entirely due to the supporting courage of Michael Balcon and McPhail at G.-B.

After two years the film came along. It was not altogether the film some of us expected. It made sensation of the sea, it restored shark-hunting to the Arans to give the film a high-spot, and Flaherty's genius for the observation of simple people in their simple manners was not, we felt, exercised to the full. But as a simple account of human dignity and bravery through the years, the film was a fine affair. There remained only the selling of it in a world inclined to be alien. Flaherty himself had to take up the necessary barn-storming tactics. He went through the country making personal appearances.

We Live in Two Worlds (British, 1937)
  Produced by G.P.O. Film Unit: directed by Alberto Cavalcanti

North Sea (British, 1938)
  Produced by G.P.O. Film Unit: directed by Harry Watt

Rain (Dutch, 1929)
   Produced and directed by Joris Ivens and Mannus Franken

Zuiderzee (Dutch, 1930)
   Produced by Capi: directed by Joris Ivens

Aran Islanders in home-spun and tam-o'-shanters attended with him and spoke at luncheons given to local Mayors. Flaherty's life story appeared in a Sunday newspaper and copies of it were handed out by cinema attendants dressed in fisherman's jerseys marked 'Man of Aran'. The champagne flowed and the critics raved. In the Edgware Road a now excited crowd tried to cut locks of hair from Tiger King the hero, and Maggie Durrane the heroine—a lovely creature—went on tour of Selfridge's under the *Daily Express,* to discuss silk stockings and the modern woman. So far as Britain was concerned the method worked. Salesman and exhibitor alike were driven into acquiescence and the British commercial cinema's only work of art was ballyhooed into appreciation. Without Flaherty behind it storming, raging, praying and publicizing, heaven knows what would have happened. The fate of the film in Paris is a fair guide. There the pessimism or inertia or stupidity of the commercial agent made all the difference. In a country more instructed than England in documentary, where *Nanook* and *Moana,* the other great films of Flaherty, had been running for twelve and eight years respectively, the commercial people cut down the film and billed it below the line as a subsidiary feature.

The cinema magnates, as I have noted, have been good to comedy, and so has the medium. It was, from the beginning, kind to the masks of clowns; its space and its movement gave the stage tumblers a more generous outlet; editing and trick work, from precising the throwing of pies, came to encourage a new ingenuity of comic event. The coming of sound was something of a disaster for the silent comedians like Chaplin, Keaton, Langdon, Griffith and Lloyd. The realism of the spoken word destroyed the more distant atmosphere in which the silent art created them, and none of them has had the ingenuity to develop a use of sound which would preserve the ancient quality of their mask and ballet. Cavalcanti's film *Pett and Pott* shows how this could effectively be done by formalizing the sound and making it contribute to the mute (*a*) in comedy of music, (*b*) in comedy of sound image, and (*c*) in comedy of asynchronism; but the studios have failed to experiment. Intoxicated by the novelty and ease of the spoken word they have not perhaps thought the old comedy of mask worth saving, and the mummers have not known how to save themselves. Their art is, for the moment, declining. The palm is passing to a new band of wisecrack comedians who, like the Marx Brothers, W. C. Fields, Schnozzle Durante, Burns and Allen, make as great a preciosity of talking as their predecessors did of silence. Laurel and Hardy do not depend quite so much on talk and the peculiar style of their comedy

M   177

has allowed them to make a more effective use of sound. They are clumsy, they are destructive, they are in essence noisy people; the world of sound is theirs to crash and tumble over. By making sound an integral factor in their mumming, they have tumbled on a first creative use of sound.

Out of the possibilities of sound synchronization a world of sound must be created, as refined in abstraction as the old silent art, if great figures like Chaplin are to come again. It is no accident that of all the comedy workers of the new régime the most attractive, by far, is the cartoonist Disney. The nature of his material forced upon him something like the right solution. Making his sound strip first and working his animated figures in distortion and counterpoint to the beat of the sound, he has begun to discover those ingenious combinations which will carry on the true tradition of film comedy.

Epic, too, has had its setback since the coming of sound. There has been *Cimarron* to succeed *The Iron Horse* and *The Covered Wagon*, but nothing like the same continuity of great outdoor themes, in which continents were crossed, jungles penetrated and cities and nations built. There has been the technical difficulty that outdoor sound with its manifold of background noise has been difficult to register, but apart from this there has not been the same will to create in outdoor worlds as in silent days. The commercial cinema has come more than ever indoors to imitate in dialogue and confinement the charade of the theatre. The personal human story is more easily told in sound than it was in silence. Silence drove it inevitably to wider horizons, to issues of storm and flood, to large physical happenings. Silence could hardly avoid epic and sound can. Just as silence created its own tempo'd form and its own sense of distance, the new medium might present a deeply counterpointed consideration of great event. The voices of crowds and nations could be cross-sectioned; complex happenings could be dramatized by the montage of sound and voice, and by the many possibilities there are of combining, by sound, present fact with distant bearings. Experimenting in *Song of Ceylon*, Basil Wright crossed a chorus of market cries and a rigmarole of international commerce with a scene of Buddhist ceremonial. Lost in the ease of dialogue, the studios will have none of this.

Man of Aran, if we accept it as near to epic, is a silent, not a sound film: a silent film to which a background ribbon of sound has added nothing but atmosphere. Its story is a visual story. Its effects are achieved by the tempo'd technique built up by the Russian silent films. The sound script does not jump into the narrative to play the part it might easily do in building up the issue. In *Man of Aran* perhaps it was not necessary. In films of wider range it is plainly foolish to avoid the powers which lie ready to hand. Where a film combines in significance the highlights of a nation's history there is much which an imaginative use of sound cutting and sound orchestration might do. Of *Cimarron* one can remember only the rumble of wagons, the chatter of crowds, the beat of horses' hoofs, and some dialogue of personal story: unimportant, uncreative noises all of them, which did nothing to build the body of cinema epic. Whatever horizons were crossed cinema itself stayed halting at home. This neglect of the creative element of the new cinema proves, if proof were necessary, that if the deeper purpose were not there it is not likely that the medium will be deeply discovered.

Outside these fields of popular cinema—of which this all too qualified result can be expected—there has grown up another more independent cinema. I do not mean here the *avant garde* cinema which for a while flourished in France and has raised its head wherever family fortune and youthful enthusiasm have allowed it. The French *avant garde* with René Clair (the early René Clair of *The Italian Straw Hat*), Cavalcanti, Epstein and Jean Renoir, made its dash for liberty by exploiting its friends. Working on a shoestring it created its own little distribution and theatre system. It built its own faithful audience at the Ursulines and the Vieux Colombier. All the requisites of an independent cinema were there except principle, and the loyalty which goes with principle. In fact, the moment the businessmen of the group made money they invested it in popular films and abandoned art and audience alike. The *avant garde* movement blew up because its directors were economic innocents and, until they go to Hollywood, film directors only too often are. It blew up because the tie which bound the director and his agents was not the creative one they imagined. In a dilettante sense it may have been, but it had no social basis which could withstand commercial temptation.

Something more solidly founded than the *avant garde* cinema there has been, and that is the propagandist cinema. With the failure of the French movement, it became evident in at least one quarter that, if an independent cinema were to become possible, some other economic basis than the entertainment world and other than private philanthropy had to be discovered. Education was first considered but, being the poor, neglected, unimaginative world it is, was quickly discarded. The choice of propaganda was inevitable. It has been responsible for odd periodic excursions into cinema in a hundred centres. The Canadian Government has a film bureau which produces films for its departments. Government departments in the United States, France, Germany and Italy have their annual issue of films on agriculture, health and industrial process. The vaults of great industrial houses are packed with the more or less pathetic efforts of commercial film companies (shooting at so much a foot) to make their processes and products exciting. But only in Britain—I except Russia—was propaganda deliberately exploited for the greater opportunity it presented to cinematic art, and made the basis for a school of cinema. This was at the Empire Marketing Board, under Sir Stephen Tallents, who is possibly the most imaginative and far-seeing of the masters of propaganda in Britain: certainly the only one who has considered how, and how deeply, propaganda may serve the State. He has maintained with John Stuart Mill that 'it is the artist alone in whose hands truth becomes impressive and a living principle of action'.

If you are to bring alive—this was the E.M.B. phrase—the material of commerce and industry, the new bewildering world of invention and science and the modern complex of human relationship; if you are to make citizenship in our vast new world imaginative and, therefore, possible, cinema is, on the face of it, a powerful weapon. But when the material of event has not yet been brought to imaginative form, research into new cinematic method is necessary. The example of the studios was not good enough, for it demonstrated little respect for common fact and less for common achievement. Its cameras and its technique had not prowled into this world of worker, organizer and discoverer. What was wanted was a cinema capable of building its art from subject matter essentially alien to the studio mind. On the bare evidence of Ruttmann's *Berlin*, Cavalcanti's *Rien que les Heures*, and with a side-glance at the Russians, the E.M.B. dived into what it called 'Documentary': giving a freedom to its directors never recorded before in cinema. Indeed it is a curious comment on our art that the only freedom given to directors since has also been by propagandist groups: by Shell, the B.B.C., the Ministry of Labour, the Ceylon Government, the Gas Light and Coke Co., and by certain shipping, creosoting and radio firms in Europe. It is, of course, a relative freedom only, for state propaganda has its own ideological limits. This, however, can be said for it: the freshness and even the difficulty of its material drive the director to new forms and rich perspectives.

Out of this world has come the work of Walter Ruttmann, Joris Ivens, Jean Lods, Basil Wright, Paul Rotha, Arthur Elton, Stuart Legg and Evelyn Spice. Save Ruttmann, they are all young people. They are all masters of camera and, more importantly, masters of *montage*. They have all learned how to make ordinary things stand up with a new interest, and make fine sequence of what, on the face of it, was plain event. They have begun to bring their observation of the world under their nose to an issue. Their documentary is not the idyllic documentary of Flaherty with its emphasis of man against the sky, but a documentary of industrial and social function, where man is more likely to be in the bowels of the earth.

Whatever the difference of their still developing styles—symphonic in Ruttmann, Ivens, Wright and Rotha, analytic in Elton and Legg and dialectical as yet in none of them—they have one achievement in common. They have taken the discursive cinema of the news reels, the scenics and the 'interests', and given it shape; and they have done it with material which the commercial cinema has avoided. They have not yet learned how to combine the lucid—and even academic— estimate of event in the body of imaginative work, but they are coming slowly nearer to the growing points of their social material.

The relationship between the artist and the themes of the community, so far from binding the artist, has opened new horizons for it. The documentary of work and workers has found endless possibilities stretching out before it: reaching not perhaps as its forebears did to halcyon horizons but by the nearest hole in the road to engineering master-works, and by the nearest vegetable store to the epics of scientific agriculture. And where there is so much occasion for observing the qualities of mankind, the human factor must be increasingly commanded. As though to demonstrate how in this seemingly sober world the mainspring of creation lies, it is remarkable how much quicker in the uptake this relatively small group has been in the exploitation of the new sound medium. The G.P.O. Film Unit, which succeeded the E.M.B. Film Unit, is the only experimental centre in Europe. Where the artist is not pursuing entertainment but purpose, not art but theme, the technique is energized inevitably by the size and scope of the occasion. How much further it reaches and will reach than the studio leap-frog of impotent and self-conscious art!

The near relationship to purpose and theme is even more plainly evidenced by the great Russian directors. They too were begun in propaganda and were made by it: in the size of their story and the power of their style. One cannot do less when recording a world revolution than develop a tempo to take it. But the most interesting story of the Russian film does not begin until after *Potemkin* and *The End of St. Petersburg*. These early films with their tales of war and

181

sudden death provided relatively easy material, and did not diverge greatly in melodrama from the example of D. W. Griffith. There was the brighter cinematic style; there was the important creation of crowd character; but the whole effect was hectic and, in the last resort, romantic. In the first period of revolution the artists had not yet got down, like their neighbours, to themes of honest work; and it is remarkable how, after the first flush of exciting cinema, the Russian talent faded. Relating cinema to the less melodramatic problems of reconstruction was plainly a different matter.

Eisenstein set himself to tell the story of the Russian peasants, and had to discover wicked poisoning kulaks to make a case for co-operatives. He took three years to make a mull of *The General Line*. The truth was that he came to his subject from the outside and did not sufficiently appreciate either the peasants or their problems. Victor Turin, more luckily, had the shooting of the Turkestan-Siberian railway: where the specious and romantic appeal of drought and desert storm could give colour to his story. *Turksib* gave every impression of building a railway but the approach was again too detached to appreciate just how precisely or humanly it was built. H. G. Wells very properly remarked that its epileptic way of doing things was too much for him. Dovjenko missed his footing in the same way as Eisenstein. He only incidentally and crudely treated the question of peasant organization in *Earth*, by melodramatically associating it with the personal villainies of an individual kulak. And, as Flaherty might have done, he ran the film into a song of the seasons: so beautifully that only the dialecticians noticed his avoidance. Vertov, coming nearer to the problem, used every camera exhibitionism to tell in *Enthusiasm* how wonderful the worker's life was. But the heroic angle of his vision of workmen always failed to observe what the men were doing. Altogether, the Russian directors have been slow in coming to earth. Great artists they are, but alien for the most part to the material they are set. Only in Ermler's first crude *Fragment of an Empire*: in his more mature *Counterplan*: and in *Men and Jobs*—where the central issue in Russia of giving industrial skill to a peasant community is the dramatic issue of the film—does the future seem assured. Eisenstein, after Parisian adventuring in *Romance Sentimentale* (a description of the moods of a female pianist) and further wanderings in the exotic atmospheres of Hollywood and Mexico, is still planning a successor to *October*. Pudovkin's *Deserter* has not yet, like *Men and Jobs*, found those common issues in which alone the work of that great artist can develop.

182

Summary and Survey: 1935

Pudovkin reveals more than any of the Russian directors the trouble which has faced them. Lacking a strong political head, he has blundered into the most curious and revealing mess which Russia has ever sent us—a film called *A Simple Case*. It was clearly Pudovkin's intention to demonstrate how the reactionary mind had faltered as it came to grips with the life of reconstruction. But this theme is based on a trivial personal story in which a Soviet soldier runs off with a vamp. The story, in other words, is not nearly large enough for the issue and, with heavy weather over nothing, the film fails. Not all Pudovkin's beautiful symbolic images of death and resurrection can save it. *Deserter* followed *A Simple Case*. It is also a personal story: of a German worker who deserted the class war in Hamburg for the ease of workers' emancipation in Russia. He finds in Russia, as one might expect, that the real thing is back on his own home front. The film is greatly spread; there are marchings and counter marchings, riots and revolutions in the grand manner; there is a scene in a Russian factory where the deadline for the completion of a giant generator is frantically kept. Indeed, one may only observe of Pudovkin at this stage that it is the foulest folly in industrial practice to keep any such deadline frantically. And his own recourse to Hamburg and the pyrotechnics of sudden death, when accurate industrial observation was open to him on his own doorstep, is the very desertion he is describing.

It is a commonplace of modern teaching that even with revolution, revolution has only begun. The Russian film directors do not seem to have appreciated the significance of this, for it would lead them to subject matter which, for the moment, they appear to avoid: to the common problems of everyday life and to the common—even instructional—solutions of them. But Russian directors are too bound up—too aesthetically vain—in what they call their 'play films' to contribute to Russia's instructional cinema. They have, indeed, suffered greatly from the freedom given to artists in a first uncritical moment of revolutionary enthusiasm, for they have tended to isolate themselves more and more in private impression and private performance. As much as any bourgeois counterpart, they have given themselves the airs and ribbons of art. This has been possible because the first five-year plan and the second have been too busy with essential services to get round to cinema. For the future, one may leave them safely to the consideration of the Central Committee. One's impression is that when some of the art and all of the bohemian self-indulgence have been knocked out of them, the Russian cinema will fulfil its high promise of the late twenties. It is bound to, for only its present romantic per-

183

spective prevents it coming to grips with the swift and deeply detailed issues around it. The revolutionary will must certainly 'liquidate', as they put it, this romantic perspective.

Of our own future there are two things to say, and the first has to do with sound. The habit is to consider sound-film as in some sense a progress on the silent form. What has happened of course is that the cheaper and easier uses of the silent film have been succeeded by the cheaper and easier uses of the sound-film. There has been as yet no succession to the mature use of silent cinema which slowly developed in Griffith, Sennett, Eisenstein, Pudovkin, in the great German school, in the French *avant garde*, and in the documentaries of Flaherty and Ruttmann. We have added sound and, in the process, have lost a great deal of our sense of visual form. We use sound to mouth a story from one more or less insignificant situation to another. We use music for atmosphere and sometimes to give tempo to our event. Our crowds roar and our carriages rumble. The shadows of our screen make noises now, and it is true that, at their best, they might be Shakespearean noises; but that is not to say we are thinking sound-film and properly using it. For sound-film is not simply an opportunity of doing what straight plays and magic lantern lectures have already done: it is, in its own right, an opportunity for something individual and different, and imaginatively so. A brief consideration of its physical nature will indicate this. The sound, like the mute, is visually registered on a strip of film. Like the images of the mute, the different stretches of sound can be cut up with scissors and joined by paste in any order one pleases. Any sound stretch can be laid over another and added to it. So natural sound, music, recital, dialogue can be orchestrated to the will of the artist; and his orchestrations may be in any relation he selects to the images which run alongside. A statue of the Buddha may be associated with religious music or with the sound of wireless signals relating to tea and international markets, or with some word spoken from a Buddhist gospel. An orator's speech can be variously associated with (*a*) its own noise, (*b*) a jazz band playing 'I Can't Give You Anything But Love, Baby', (*c*) the dictation of the secretary who determined its rhetoric, (*d*) a heavenly choir of female voices, (*e*) the applause or execration of a fifty-thousand crowd rolling up in carefully shaped waves, (*f*) any sound the artist cares to draw on the side of the film. A succession of Gs or Ks, for example, might make a remarkable and revealing accompaniment. The point is that one may add almost anything one chooses to an image or to a sequence of images; for there is, in sound-film, a power of selection which is denied the stage.

Summary and Survey: 1935

With these immense powers available, it is fairly clear that the synchronized dialogue with which we are universally afflicted represents a crude use of the new medium, hardly better than the B.B.C.'s reproductive use of the microphone. What must come is a conception of the sound-film as a new and distinct art with a genius of its own; to be slowly discovered as the silent art of cinema had begun to be discovered. The fine abstraction of that art we have lost among the chattering voices. In the weird perspectives of sound-film we shall find it again.

And regarding the future, there is this second point to make: that the cinema will divide and specialize and the more ambitious parts of it will break—as much as may be—from the stranglehold of commercial interests. Cinema is neither an art nor an entertainment: it is a form of publication, and may publish in a hundred different ways for a hundred different audiences. There is education to serve; there is the new civic education which is emerging from the world of publicity and propaganda; there is the new critical audience of the film circles, the film societies and the specialized theatres. All these fields are outside the commercial cinema.

Of these, the most important field by far is propaganda. The circles devoted to the art of cinema mean well and they will help to articulate the development of technique, but the conscious pursuit of art carries with it, in periods of public difficulty, a certain shallowness of outlook. The surface values are not appreciated in relation to the material they serve, for there is avoidance of the central issues involved in the material. We need not look to the film societies for fundamentals. They will continue to be bright about trivialities of tempo and other technique, and their pleasant Sunday afternoons will continue to be innocuous. The 'grim and desperate education' of propaganda is another matter. It comes more and more to grips with the questions of public life and public importance, and cinema, serving it, reflects a certain solidity of approach. The facts are simple enough. In a world too complex for the educational methods of public speech and public writing, there is a growing need for more imaginative and widespread media of public address. Cinema has begun to serve propaganda and will increasingly do so. It will be in demand. It will be asked to create appreciation of public services and public purposes. It will be asked from a hundred quarters to create a more imaginative and considered citizenship. It will be asked, too, inevitably, to serve the narrower viewpoints of political or other party propaganda. But where there are wide fields, the participation of the artist can be various.

185

A Movement is Founded

As I see it, the future of the cinema may not be in the cinema at all. It may even come humbly in the guise of propaganda and shamelessly in the guise of uplift and education. It may creep in quietly by way of the Y.M.C.A.s, the church halls and other citadels of suburban improvement. This is the future for the art of cinema, for in the commercial cinema there is no future worth serving. It represents the only economic basis on which the artist may expect to perform. Two possibilities there are which qualify this conclusion. The theatres, now so abandoned in their commercial anarchy, would, under any measure of national or international direction, be forced to larger considerations than they at present entertain. And the coming of television will bring a consideration of cinema as liberal at least as the B.B.C.'s present consideration of music. In these respects, the future is bright enough. But even under a controlled cinema and a televised cinema, it will be wise for the artist to organize his independence: going direct to public service for his material and his economy. There lies his best opportunity—and therefore his freedom.

Part III

DOCUMENTARY ACHIEVEMENT

A steadily expanding movement reached out to help the schools and the churches and the film was enlisted in the service of the community. Grierson wrote and lectured tirelessly on these related subjects during this period and began to expound the theories on education he developed later in Canada. With a characteristic discussion on films and the community is a comprehensive survey of the realist film which brings out clearly the intensified social reference. Grierson writes feelingly of his work for the Films of Scotland Committee. *Battle for Authenticity* reflects the bitterness of the struggle to record and export an honest film picture of Britain.

F. H.

1 Films and the Community

The use of radio and film in the classroom is a teacher's job. By radio and film in the classroom I mean all those various uses to which they are being put in illustrating lessons. Of course, they can illustrate lessons and help them. The only problem is to find out where and how they can help best; and that is for teachers to determine, not for the people who produce films and whose interests are best served by supplying the schools with as many films as possible.

One thing I can make clear from the beginning. I have no patience with those enthusiasts for radio and film who imagine that they are going to revolutionize the present method of teaching geography and physics and other routine subjects. They say with consummate naïveté that with their London pictures and London commentators they are going to do a better job than the teachers are doing in their local communities. They say that by seeing pictures the children will soon know, by a sort of miraculous process, what teachers so laboriously din into their tough little heads—forgetting that instruction is not a matter of impressions, but a hard detailed business of instilling disciplined observation and disciplined understanding.

In this matter of helping the teacher in the classroom I think we can lay down some very simple rules and be done with the subject. The curriculum, as it already universally operates, is a very delicate business and the average teacher is a very efficient craftsman; and there is nothing really very revolutionary that film or radio can do. Sometimes they can help him out with illustrations that cannot be done by the map or the blackboard or the epidiascope. Good: then let us have simple little illustrative films to do this simple job—and just those illustrations that are wanted and no more.

Sometimes, too, and inevitably, there is a limit to the teacher's powers of description. He may want, for example, to set the atmosphere for a lesson on England's Black Country. He may want to show the Black Country as not just a matter of imports and exports, towns and rivers and canals, but as a living community of workers and factories. Good: then let film or radio supplement his teaching in the appropriate period. But again let us have just those supplementary lessons which are really required and really valuable in a regulated course of study.

What I fear, and what teachers who have considered the subject must fear even more than I do, is the unbalancing of a curriculum which has taken a long time to build. I fear this unregulated invasion of the classroom. I fear that films may give too many impressions and bewilder the child mind. I fear that radio and film may not be so supplementary as they claim. You have to be very careful in talking about these supplementary powers of radio and film that you are not doing the local teacher an injustice and even an impertinence.

This classroom stuff is the teachers' job and they must work it out for themselves on pedagogic principles. There is, however, a problem which I believe to be a great deal more serious. I am disturbed, as I think many teachers are becoming disturbed, at the lack of contact between the educational system and the life of the community outside.

Good as it is, the curriculum is not the whole of education. And the way the world is moving, it is slowly losing its claim to be even the growing point of education. It is losing its relation to the community. Properly equipped and active citizens are not being made in the schools. And there is some suspicion that they are not being made at all.

This problem has been bandied back and forward and is to some extent associated with the deviations of Montessori and Dalton. It came first in the feeling that children were not being allowed to develop richly enough under the routine system. We have as a result the deliberate cultivation of freedom and the frantic pursuit of personality.

But the reaction has set in. It has been difficult to see how the creation of highly decorative individuals will bridge the gap between the school and the life outside. Do we fit children for the apprehension of the modern community life by detaching them from the discipline of corporate work? That at any rate is the doubt and it is all the stronger as one realizes how more corporate every day the operation of the modern community becomes. The cultivation of sensibility on purely personal lines may, in fact, be the very worst training for a world where only the corporate and the co-operative will matter.

I have myself come to this issue from another direction and, as I do not pretend to pedagogic theory, I shall follow my own line. Some years ago I came to study the problem of public opinion—how it is created or crystallized under modern conditions. Many have worked in this field from Machiavelli to Lippmann—some academically like Machiavelli and Lippmann, some more practically like Lenin. And the

190

upshot of recent study is a sense of the impossibility of pursuing the old liberal individualist and rational theory on which so much of our educational planning is based, and by which individuals were expected to know and understand all the issues of public life.

You cannot know everything about everything all the time. And even if teachers had the power of every cane on the banks of the Nile, they could not instil all the information which the liberal theory of education asked of the citizen.

The plain fact of the matter is that life has become too complex for extended apprehension by the individual citizen. Communications have spread and speeded up; and horizons have widened. Invention has made work more complex and the viewpoint of the individual more specialized. The nerve fibres of the community life stretch as far as China and Abyssinia, and the stimuli to behaviour come no longer from local pulpits and platforms, but from the west coast of America.

Much of the unrest of today is, I think, a mental one and arises out of the feeling of incapacity to apprehend the perspectives of our complex existence. The individual mind has lost its bearings and the educational system is not equipping the mind to take its bearings in a fast-moving world.

One could, I suppose, give a thousand instances of the plague of impotence which affects us. There was the tragic example in our failure to make the will to peace operative. There is another example in our failure to make the will to good housing operative. The problems are sensed but because of the criss-cross of economic and moral values the average mind falters at decision. There is no apprehension to the point of organized action, i.e. belief and participation. So with a hundred and one problems of both local and national citizenship. There is an inhibition in the air and at the root of it is this failure of our educational forces both at school and afterwards to give the citizen his bearings.

The failure, I believe, is not as some have imagined a failure in our informational services. In recent years we have had campaigns for a press which will give us all the news and nothing but the news—all the news without fear or favour. But, of course, that is impossible as lack of prejudice is impossible. All the news sounds very like an encyclopædia and would in fact be unmanageable for the citizen. In school terms this movement for more fact finds its expression in the movement for more general knowledge. But general knowledge is like 'all the news'. It has to be directive if it is to be manageable. It has to be keyed to specific ends or purposes if it is to be articulate.

191

We have, then, this situation. The way of personal culture is too personal—too much out of relation to our workaday world and to the living facts of the community. The way of information and general knowledge is too discursive, and unless it interprets, as well as reports, it, too, is out of relation to the living facts of the community.

The educational system has, of course, realized this for some time. We have had a great movement towards technical training: the attempt to fit the child more specifically for its work outside. We have had in many towns a courageous effort made to show the children something of the world in which they are going to play their part. In some places films have been used; in others radio talks have been brought into the schools. Excursions to local factories have been organized. All are evidence of an attempt to cross the desperate gap between the school and the community.

But these efforts have been inadequate. Technical training may help a boy to be a good craftsman, but does it help him to be a more active and participating citizen? These excursions to the local factory—are they giving a great deal for the time they take? And on what lines is instruction being given? Are the children being told processes or are they being given some indication of economic perspectives? I think the answer is they are just being taken round the factory without any clear conception of what it is best to teach them. As for the film and radio, are they really giving the living contact which the educationalists are seeking? Sometimes they are, but are they doing it very much and are they doing it enough?

Consider for a moment this boy who is going out into the world. He is going to work at a job, live in a town, raise his voice, mark his vote, and wave his flag in the government of his union, his city, his country. He is going to read the papers and go to the movies. He is going to discuss public affairs for good or evil in his pub and his union. He is going to help in one way or another to represent public opinion and the public will. In his millions he *is* society—its will is his will—and he is the only hope of peace on earth we have.

But do we teach him his way about journalism as we try sometimes preposterously to teach him his way about literature? Do we tell him his way about the movies as we tell him his way about Shakespearian drama? Do we make him realize the role he has to play in government and the active day-to-day dependence of governments on him? Do we give him an active responsible sense of his day-to-day role in government? Do we teach him the living presences of his civic life, as we teach its forms and hierarchies? Do we dramatize to him his role at the

Man of Aran (British, 1933–4)
Produced by Gaumont-British: directed by Robert Flaherty

Housing Problems (British, 1935)
Produced for the British Commercial Gas Association: directed by Edgar Anstey with Arthur Elton and John Taylor

Land of Promise (British, 1946)
Produced by Films of Fact: directed by Paul Rotha

factory, his role in the union, his role in the household, his role in relation to every public issue under discussion, as the movies already so brilliantly dramatize to him the role of gangster and racketeer?

Does education dramatize to the citizen the real ends of citizenship as Hollywood so successfully dramatizes the unreal ends? Here, surely, is the very heart of civics. All that we can claim is that we tell him the shape of the constitution and the plan of local administration. It seems to me that we give him just as much as we can write down on a blackboard and just as much as we can fit into the question and answer technique of an examination paper. The life of the thing is missed. It has not been made to enter for good and all into his imagination.

I know I am calling a high hand, but I am going to suggest that we are really facing something like a Copernican revolution. The mind—and that is to say the system of education—has been failing to take in the information necessary to organized and harmonious living. The old and well-tried principles of approach have been falling down on us. And we are, more or less urgently, seeking new approaches.

For three hundred years we have had our focus on the individual. We have distinguished him from the objective world as the Middle Ages did not think of doing. We have given him the world and the universe as a playground for exploration and discovery. We have built our State on the freedom of personal adventure. But discoveries have involved organization, greater and more complex organization. Individual adventure becomes less important than co-operation. In fact, the individual outlook becomes less and less valuable and more and more harmful unless it is transmuted into the corporate outlook.

If we are to bring the community duty alive to our children or ourselves we must realize it in a new way. We shall have to learn and speak a new language. As I have suggested, the way of information will not serve; it is too discursive. And the way of rational explanation will not serve, because it misses the corporate life we are dealing with. The new language of apprehension which must communicate the corporate nature of the community life must in fact be something more in the nature of a dramatic language than a rational one. The process will be one of interpretation rather than one of record. The quintessence will be more important than the aggregate. The artist will have to come into the educational system as representing the type which can provide the interpretative factor.

I see radio and film as essential instruments in this process, but they are not, of course, the only instruments. An analysis of the ways of modern art in painting and in writing shows the great changes in form which are taking place—changes of outlook which are as violent as those changes which swept over European art after the Copernican discovery. Novels have been trying to cross-section the individual life in its more complex modern bearings. Painting has reversed the tendency of the sixteenth century and has lost the individual in his perspectives. The sleek contour of the person is denied and discarded as no longer real. The arts, in fact, are sharing this problem and doing their best to find ways of expression more in keeping with modern necessity.

And when you consider that other great art, the art of journalism, please do not be too hard on the growth of yellow newspapers and the development of so-called sensationalism. If you look into the matter you may realize that here, too, is a manifestation of the great change in mental outlook which is taking place. When all the information cannot be given and no one has leisure to master all the facts, how can we give the news except by some shorthand method of dramatization? It may be that the wrong things are being dramatized, but that is another issue.

In film, however (now that we have television I include radio as simply an aspect of film), we have an instrument much more suited to the specific purposes of education than any other of the arts. It really can bring the outside world alive to the growing citizen. It really can extend his experience. It really can serve an interpretative function. Working as it does from the living fact it can, if it is mastered and organized, provide this necessary umbilical to the community outside. The main thing is to put the use of film into this other civic setting and take it out of the less important setting of the regular curriculum. The B.B.C. in its school activities, the film people in their educational film activities, are almost exclusively concerned with the question of the curriculum. It is not very important whether they break into it or not. What is really important is that film and radio should be used to prepare the children for citizenship.

I would say this to teachers: If there is any reality in the situation I have described, then they will have to do something about it, even if they have to blow up the curriculum. If they do not undertake this new teaching of citizenship it is more than possible that they will have Fascism—or Communism—doing it for them. Time will not wait for them.

*   *   *

As a pendant to this discussion of education, the film and the community, I should refer to the cinema in the service of religion. The subject is always cropping up but no one seems to do anything about it. The trouble may be that in making the word flesh there is nothing left to blether about.

The churches obviously prefer blethering for they have been on this particular gambit as long as I remember. When we started talking of films in the service of education and citizenship they were already next rostrum to us on the Hyde Park Corner of film notions. The first film book written in England was written from the churches. I forget the name of the book but it was fat and pale blue and said more than twenty years ago everything the British Film Institute and the morality councillors and the Payne Trust have been writing parish magazines about since. I remember with what tenderness the Reverend George Atkinson lent me his copy. I kept it and learned from it, for it was good stuff in that day and age.

The only consideration that makes it silly now is that we who were talking simultaneously about films in the public service proceeded to do something about it. We found money somehow; we built the documentary and educational film movements; we founded the Empire Film Library and other libraries; we grew a school of film-makers; we made hundreds of films; we out-wrote, out-spoke, out-manœuvred our oppositions, and drove our way to the screens of the country.

I say this impatiently and for good reason. In our struggle to vary the synthetic diet of the cinemas and find another depth or two in our bright and lovely art, I have, heaven forgive my innocence, expected a lot from the churches. They have the halls in thousands and the audiences in hundreds of thousands; people to be talked to, waiting to be talked to with bright and lovely arts. They have, even if they have gone lazy and lost their sense of the privilege, a basic contact with the life of Britain. Back of them is the commission to tell where the spirit gets off at, and speak of the deepest things that men may know. Just think of it from a film point of view. No fancifying, or doping with synthetics, or gearing the stuff down, but a full-blown commission with the church bells ringing and the choirs in full blast. And there isn't anyone, anywhere, but is waiting for the word that will vitalize, release, heroicize, and tell him where he gets off at. It is a terrific set-up, and when artists before now had the privilege of it they build cathedrals and painted pictures that are still the most inspiring things in civilization.

But with so great an opportunity for patronage the churches are still blethering. They have plenty of money, have the easiest access in the country to plenty of money. They know that for lack of imagination or something or other they are failing in their job of inspiration. Their emptying churches tell them so; the increasing disrespect for the personnel of the church tells them so. But that commission of theirs is not thereby altered and how could it be? The deep things have still to be spoken in the name of religion, if men are not to go empty in their bellies. And here is an art that could speak them. It is not the only art, but it is the one that could speak them simply and widely and that is the most important thing for religion. You would think that the job was easy and it is. They have only, at worst, to waste a million or two finding and building the people who will use the film to inspire people, and they waste that much now, and more aridly. Would the people of our bright and lovely art come through? There never has been a sponsorship of the cinema that asked for inspiration, and the art is panting for it. It would be a miracle releasing with a single blast every good power in medium and maker alike.

But here we had better stop dreaming. That is the logic of it but so far from the likely reality that we need not bother much. These good church people are inert and nearly only talkers and the little that they do is terrible. The Methodists take a wonderful story like Tolstoy's 'Where Love Is God Is' and add the sludge of utter commonness to their interpretation. It was not the producers' fault. I know, because I attended uncomfortably on the script and saw them debauch the theme; and in front of them was a fine and beautiful script from Cavalcanti which kept the spirit of the thing, but was turned down. Ironically, it was the film men who tried to put beauty and spirit into the thing; it was the churchmen who talked synthetics and the box-office.

On that example there isn't a Wardour Street producer I wouldn't sooner trust near the springs of inspiration than some of the churchmen who have been fiddling about with films. If the religious conservatives—and I am one—say 'Well, there are others who will see higher', I give you an utterance of the Hon. Eleanor Plumer in the *Church Times*. Miss Plumer is a great public servant and a good churchwoman and close enough to the film industry to speak of it with diffidence. But does she ask them to do the job of inspiration? Not on your life.

Listen: 'The most satisfactory method is a committee working with the trade. The committee can decide what it wants, but the trade is the expert who knows what can and what cannot be filmed. A final scenario is chosen, shooting begins, and *all the while the committee*

196

keeps a close eye on the work.' Is that, do you think, the road to anywhere? Why, it sounds like another damned panel of the Film Institute.

The mistake is a simple one and not only the mistake of thinking a group of matter-of-fact non-artists equals one feat of imagination. It is the mistake of thinking that the inspirational bit of the job will come from the church side and the technical bit from the artist. It is the old and common mistake of treating the artist as a chauffeur. You tell him where to go and he, knowing his motors, takes you. But the fun of the fallacy is that, in asking for chauffeurs, you get them. Set so glibly on determining the road, your committee only arrives, as ever, at its own composite little nowhere.

To me Miss Plumer, good woman though she is, is as hopeless as her predecessors. If the churches want the greatest service from this art, it is not just the cameras and the pictures that it wants, but the power that makes pictures light up and talk. That is the artist's power and no back-seat driving is any equivalent. Unfortunately for the good people, the artist or the inspirer tends to come in strange guises, and how many churchmen would be likely to know him if they met him? He will not seem to profess very much faith; it is highly doubtful if he will appear in the wings of a Sunday schoolteacher; but the measure will not be on these lower parrotwise levels of the spirit. It will be in the deep profession of faith and the arduous act of service which are implicit in every work of art whatsoever. Your artist will not for a certainty take a theme like 'Where Love Is God Is' and forget to put in the faith and the beauty that made Tolstoy great. Every commandment he may break, but not that.

Another thing. He will do his job with themes even less explicitly related to religion than the Tolstoy one. I do not know why it is that the church people, like the advertising people, should make so much of the brand mark on their product. They don't need to. Inspire people in those values on which religion properly insists and you do religion's job. Teach the fear of God, humility, and loving one's neighbour as oneself, and you do the church's teaching. But no. The church people go on insisting on the dumbly explicit. Hear Miss Plumer again. 'We need the screening of the parables in modern dress, the Prodigal Son, The Sower, The Great Supper, the Marriage of the King's Son, the Good Samaritan. We should try to approximate the incidents in the parables to the incidents of modern life *so that they may drive their lesson home.* We want films of the parish church, how it was first built; what the different parts mean. There should be films of our cathedrals, films of the religious houses, films showing our great inheritance from the Fathers and the Saints.' It sounds all very boring already.

I don't think that the churches will do much with films. They are still a long mile away from the right idea. You and I and the millions of others will take our *Good Earth* and *Pasteur* and *Man of Aran* and *Song of Ceylon* happily and know they are the real thing. We will curse the fact that they are so few. We will curse the churches in particular for not making it possible to have more of them, though they have the commission from society to give us more. The film-makers among us will see the deeper possibilities of an O. Henry story or a Tchekov or a play by Bridie or a fairy tale of Hans Andersen. We will know it is what the churches are really seeking but are too blind—too irreligious —to see. We will go on fighting our way through the commercial cinema and, occasionally, someone fantastically out of the argument like old Arthur Dent will permit some excited young director to add to the great exceptions. But the churches, you may be sure, will not know anything of that long and bitter war to make films a medium of inspiration and do their work for them. They will know no more and help no more than they have done in the fight of the documentary people to do their social work for them. They will still be talking and, in the enthusiasm of their talking, the deed will be satisfied and be dead.

2 The Course of Realism

Here is an art based on photographs, in which one factor is always, or nearly always, a thing observed. Yet a realist tradition in cinema has emerged only slowly. When Lumière turned his first historic strip of film, he did so with the fine careless rapture which attends the amateur effort today. The new moving camera was still, for him, a camera and an instrument to focus on the life about him. He shot his own workmen filing out of the factory and this first film was a 'documentary'. He went on as naturally to shoot the Lumière family, child complete. The cinema, it seemed for a moment, was about to fulfil its natural destiny of discovering mankind. It had everything for the task. It could get about, it could view reality with a new intimacy; and what more natural than that the recording of the real world should become its principal inspiration?

I remember how easily we accepted this in the tender years of the century when our local lady brought to our Scottish village the sensation of the first movies; and I imagine now it was long before the big towns like Edinburgh and Glasgow knew anything about them. These, too, were documentaries, and the first film I saw was none other than Opus 2 in the history of cinema—the Lumière boy eating his apple. Infant wonder may exaggerate the recollection, but I will swear there was in it the close-up which was to be invented so many years later by D. W. Griffith. The significant thing to me now is that our elders accepted this cinema as essentially different from the theatre. Sin still, somehow, attached to play-acting, but, in this fresh new art of observation and reality, they saw no evil. I was confirmed in cinema at six because it had nothing to do with the theatre, and I have remained so confirmed. But the cinema has not. It was not quite so innocent as our Calvinist elders supposed. Hardly were the workmen out of the factory and the apple digested than it was taking a trip to the moon and, only a year or two later, a trip in full colour to the devil. The scarlet women were in, and the high falsehood of trickwork and artifice was in, and reality and the first fine careless rapture were out.

Documentary Achievement

Thinking back over the years of development, fresh air and real people do appear for periods at a time. Obviously the economics of production in the early days were more cheaply served by the natural exterior. Till we learned to create our own sunlight, the heavenly variety was cheaper; until we mastered the art of miniature and dunning and back projection, it was cheaper to take the story to a natural location than the other way round. And the effect was to give not only naturalism to the setting but naturalism to the theme. One remembers the early Danish school which exported so many films before 1914; later the Swedish school with its noble exploitation in photography and drama of the Swedish light; the early English school of *Coming Thro' the Rye*, and the early American school of *The Great Train Robbery*, slapstick, and the Westerns. There was fresh air in all of them, but, more importantly, there was some reflection of ordinary life in the drama. In *The Great Train Robbery* the engineers and telegraph men were contacts with the real thing, and unimportant as they now seem, it was a long time before they cropped up again. Once inside the studio the tendency of the cinema was to make the most of its powers of artifice, graduating from the painted backcloths and wobbly colonnades to the synthetic and more or less permanent near-realism of three-ply, plaster, and painted glass. The supers like *Dante's Inferno*, and the highly expansive struggles for expression in a new medium which characterized the silent epics—those sweeping movements, those cosmic gestures—struck the keynote of the new art.

Cinema, I am inclined to think, has been from the first not the guttersnipe we all suppose, but something of a prig. It was not Zukor, clever little man as he may be, who first thought of attaching famous players to famous plays. The grand people of the French and British theatres had been gesturing to the studio roof for years before, and always in the grandest of causes: dealing with the destinies of Julius Caesar twice, King Lear thrice, and Hamlet six times before poor Zukor had begun to think about the cinema at all. Those early days produced forty versions of Shakespeare—Dante, Napoleon, and Marie Antoinette scattering—with a gusto for celebrity to which even silence proved no obstacle. So far from the latter-day Copperfields and Romeos representing a special advance of the cinema into cultural grounds, they merely show us back at the old and original stand. We may have whored in our time, but we have always been snobs at heart. Here, the higher economics. Big names and celebrated subjects brought attention, and attention brought money. They were easier to sell, for salesmen had not yet learned the art of giving cosmic importance to nonsense and nonentities. But, driven by economics into artifice, the cinema has stayed there for other equally effective reasons. It has never been quite sure of itself, never quite believed in its separate and original destiny. This, no doubt, is the price we have paid for being a new art, but the fact that we have been so largely in the hands of international traders and salesmen may have operated too. Great qualities they have brought out: fervour and excitement to the salesmanship of cinema and a certain extravagance to our spectacle. But social confidence and an easy acceptance of the right to social observation could hardly be claimed for many of those otherwise brilliant men who have built up the cinema. *Esprit* they have had, but hardly spirit.

Looking down the history of the actuality films, of what has seemed on the surface most natural and most real, there was, until the late thirties, a lack of fibre. From the beginning we have had newsreels, but dim records they seem now of only the evanescent and the essentially unreal, reflecting hardly anything worth preserving of the times they recorded. In curiosity one might wish to see again the Queen's Jubilees and the Delhi Durbars—with coloured coats that floated in air a full yard behind the line of march—the Kaiser at manœuvres and the Czar at play. Once Lenin spoke, here and there early aeroplanes made historic landings and war cameras recorded, till war cameras record again, the vast futility of the dead. Exceptional occasions, yes, and the greatest shot I ever saw came out of it with the *Blücher* heeling over and the thousand men running, sliding, jumping over the lurching side to their death—like flies. A fearful and quiet shot. But among the foundation stones, the pompous parades, the politicians on pavements, and even among the smoking ruins of mine disasters and the broken backs of distressed ships, it is difficult to think that any real picture of our troubled day has been recorded. The newsreel has gone dithering on, mistaking the phenomenon for the thing in itself, and ignoring everything that gave it the trouble of conscience and penetration and thought.

But something more intelligent arrived. It crashed through from the America that succeeded the slump and learned with Roosevelt the simple braveries of the public forum. It was called the *March of Time* and so strong is the need it fulfils that it will soon be called by a dozen names—Window on the World, World Eye, Brave New World, and what not. *March of Time* does what the other news records have failed to do. It gets behind the news, observes the factors of influence, and gives a perspective to events. Not the parade of armies so much as the race in armaments; not the ceremonial opening of a dam but the full story of Roosevelt's experiment in the Tennessee Valley; not the launching of the *Queen Mary* but the post-1918 record of British shipping. All penetrating and, because penetrating, dramatic.

Only three years old (in 1937), it has swept through the country, answering the thin glitter of the newsreels with nothing on the face of it more dramatic than the story of cancer research, the organization of peace, the state of Britain's health, the tithe war in the English shires, the rural economy of Ireland, with here and there a bright and ironic excursion into Texas centennials and the lunatic fringe of politics. In no deep sense conscious of the higher cinematic qualities, it has yet carried over from journalism into cinema, after thirty-eight years, something of that bright and easy tradition of free-born comment which the newspaper has won and the cinema has been too abject even to ask for. There are proper limits, it is true, to freedom of speech which the cinema must regard. Its power is too great for irresponsible comment, when circulations like the *March of Time*'s may run to nine thousand theatres across an explosive world. But it seems sensible for the moment that the *March of Time* has won the field for the elementary principles of public discussion. The world, our world, appears suddenly and brightly as an oyster for the opening: for film people—how strangely—worth living in, fighting in and making drama about. And more important still is the thought of a revitalized citizenship and of a democracy at long last in contact with itself.

In easier fields the actuality film has found a larger career, and the easier the more brilliant. Whenever observation has been so detached from the social theme as to raise no inhibition, its place on the screen has been assured. Films disclosing scenery and the more innocuous habits of mankind have come by the thousand, beautiful in photography, idyllic in atmosphere, though never till latterly exciting in substance, each with its Farewell to So-and-So raising a pleasant ripple on the art's nostalgia. Finer still, more skilled in observation, because further from wretched mankind, there has been the long and brilliant line of nature films. Studies of bird life, life under the sea, microscopic, slow-motioned, and speeded-up adventures in plant life: how beautiful they have been, with Bruce Woolfe, Mary Field, and Percy Smith staking a claim for England better than any: more continuous in their work, less dramatic at all costs than either the Americans or the Germans, more patient, analytic, and in the best sense observant. Here, if anywhere, beauty has come to inhabit the edifice of truth. Nor could there be any obstacle to the highly efficient analysis in slow-motion of what happens to bullets, golfers' swings, and labourers at work. In these matters of utilitarian observation cinema has built up a wide field of service, helping the research man, as it brilliantly did in the film observations on cancer research by Dr. Canti at Bart's, helping equally the industrialist and the salesman.

But the devil of reality has even then not been content. Ruttmann for Germany, Flaherty for America, Eisenstein and Pudovkin for Russia, Cavalcanti for France, and myself, shall I say, for Britain, we have taken our cameras to the more difficult territory. We have set up our tripods among the Yahoos themselves, and schools have gathered round us. Our realist showing, if secondary to the main growth of cinema, has assumed a certain bravery.

Flaherty adopted one gambit with *Nanook of the North*. By profession an explorer with a long and deep knowledge of the Eskimos, he had the idea of making a story about people he knew—not foisting, studio fashion, a preconceived story on a background for the decorative quality it added, but taking his story from within. *Nanook of the North* took the theme of hunger and the fight for food and built its drama from the actual event, and, as it turned out, from actual hunger. The blizzards were real and the gestures of human exhaustion came from the life. Many years before, Ponting had made his famous picture of the Scott expedition to the South Pole, with just such material; but here the sketch came to life and the journalistic survey turned to drama. Flaherty's theory that the camera has an affection for the spontaneous and the traditional, and all that time has worn smooth, stands the test of more than twenty years, and *Nanook*, of all the films that I have seen—I wish I could say the same for my own—is least dated today. The bubble is in it and it is, plain to see, a true bubble. This film, which had to find its finance from a fur company and was turned down by every renter on Broadway, has outlived them all.

Moana, which Flaherty made afterwards, added the same thought to Samoa. *White Shadows of the South Seas, Tabu, Man of Aran*, and *Elephant Boy* succeeded. But it was no wonder that Hollywood doubted his outlook. In *White Shadows* and *Tabu* they saw to it that a director of the other and approved species accompanied him. *White Shadows* and *Tabu* were, therefore, not quite Flaherty and were none the deeper for it. Poor Hollywood. No stars to draw the crowd, no love story, not much to whet an appetite ballyhoo'd into a vicious selectivity—only the fight against hunger, only the bravery of the tattoo, only—in Aran—the timeless story of man against the sky. They have been all too novel for a showmanship built on garish spectacle and a red-hot presentation of the latest curves. Flaherty might well call for a new and maturer language of salesmanship which can articulate the wider and deeper ambitions of the cinema, for the old salesmanship has served him and all of us pretty badly. He might well, with such high authorities as Ned Depinet and Sam Goldwyn, demand a segregation of the audience, for this insane cluttering of all species of audiences, taste and mood together, has completed the evil. The sales machine is mentally geared to take us everywhere, or not at all.

The position of the Flaherty species of realism is best evidenced in *Elephant Boy*, a film made from Kipling's *Toomai of the Elephants* and done in conjunction with the studio-minded Zoltan Korda of London Films. *Elephant Boy* begins magnificently. Toomai is set on the back of the highest elephant of all Mysore: in his youth and innocence giving a dignity to the Indian people one has never seen before on the screen. One is prepared for anything. The great herd of wild elephants is signalled. There are expectations of a jungle more exciting than the jungle of *Chang*, and of a relationship between man and nature as deep again as *Nanook*. But the synthetic spectacle of studio camp scenes and West End voices brings the film at every turn to an artificial, different plane. It comes between the boy and the jungle, and the full perspective of reality is not realized. They say an elephant will go mad on the death of his master and that he will go more mysteriously mad *just before* the death of his master. Nothing of this. Synthesis steps in, and an actor, in a fake beard, lashes the elephant to give a more Occidental motive for madness. The jungle might have been with its thousand eyes the image of all young and ardent Odysseys. Nothing of this either. The film drives on under the lash of the synthesists to the mere circus excitements of an elephant hunt.

The studio people insist on a species of drama more familiar and more dear to them than the fate of a native in the jungle and the limitation of their scale of values is going to be difficult to overcome, unless a producer comes along who can wed studio and natural observation in a new and vital formula. The salesmen have learned brilliantly to sell what is already important or may easily be associated with the excitements of sex and sudden death. They show no great signs of equipping themselves for the special task which the quality of Flaherty's themes demands.

We have been luckier in the field of realism which Cavalcanti initiated with *Rien que les Heures*, Ruttmann continued with *Berlin*, and some of us have developed on more deliberate sociological lines in the British documentary. The basis of this other realism is different from Flaherty's. We neither attempted so large a scale in our film-making, nor did we go so far for our themes. Limiting our costs, we did not have to struggle so wearily with sales organizations; and, from the first, we created a large part of our circulation outside the theatres altogether.

Rien que les Heures came later than *Nanook* by five years and was the first film to see a city through the turn of the clock. Paris was cross-sectioned in its contrasts—ugliness and beauty, wealth and poverty, hopes and fears. For the first time the word 'symphony' was used, rather than story. Cavalcanti went on to the more ambitious *En Rade*, like Flaherty taking his 'story from within' on the dockside at Marseilles, but the symphony approach had a lasting influence. Ruttmann carried on the idea in a still more whirling round of day and night in *Berlin*. No film has been more influential, more imitated. Symphonies of cities have been sprouting ever since, each with its crescendo of dawn and coming-awake and workers' processions, its morning traffic and machinery, its lunchtime contrasts of rich and poor, its afternoon lull, its evening denouement in sky-sign and night club. The model makes good, if similar, movie. It had at least the effect of turning the tide of abstraction in the German cinema and bringing it back to earth. It initiated the tradition of realism which produced such admirable films as *Mutter Krausen* and *Kameradschaft*, and it set a mark for amateurs the world over.

The British effort, while it owes everything to Flaherty and Cavalcanti initiative—latterly joining forces with Flaherty and Cavalcanti themselves—has been less aesthetic and more social in its approach. The shape of *Drifters*, the first of the British documentaries, was, for all its difference of subject, closer to Eisenstein than to Cavalcanti or Ruttmann. Though each chapter was a deliberate study in movement, the film took care to lead up to and stage an event. More important still, as I have come to consider, it had a theme in social observation— the ardour and bravery of common labour—and simple themes of the same sociological bearing have served us ever since, giving each new slice of raw material a perspective and a life, leading us in each new adventure of observation to a wider and more powerful command of medium and material alike. *Drifters* seems simple and easy now, though I remember the effort it took to convince showmen of the time that an industrialized fishing fleet might be as brave to the sight as the brown sails of sentiment and that the rigours of work were worth the emphasis of detail. This, after all, was before machinery had become 'beautiful' and the workaday life was 'fit' material for the screen. Behind us were hundreds of industrial films which industrialists had sponsored in pride and film companies had made in contempt, more often than not without script or direction, on the dismal basis of so much a foot. Work and workers were so dull by repute that, I remember bitterly, two hundred feet in the pictorials was the dead limit which showmen would offer for anything of the kind. Any director worth his salt was so busy trying to make the limelight of studio publicities that there was none so poor as to do reverence to the working theme.

This may explain why *Drifters*, simple film as it was, was so much of a *succès d'estime*, and why it so quickly became more of a myth than a film. It had the rarity value of opening, for Britain, a new vista of film reference. It may explain, too, why the workers' portraits of *Industrial Britain* were cheered in the West End of London. The strange fact was that the West End had never seen workmen's portraits before—certainly not on the screen. *Industrial Britain*, significantly, was hailed as a patriotic picture and has been widely circulated to this day for British prestige abroad. In the films that followed, from the idyllic pictures of Scottish shepherds to the complex and more difficult cross-sections of shipyards, airlines, radio services, weather forecasts, night mails, international economics, etc., etc., we relied similarly, beyond renter and exhibitor alike, on the people, and their superior taste in realism. In the seven or eight years following *Drifters* we put together some two hundred films of the documentary type and at the end of that time it was no longer so difficult to get into the theatres. The working theme and the civic reference contained in all of them were widely recognized for the aesthetic as well as for the national character they brought to the British cinema.

But the welcome, as might have been expected, was not unanimous. When the posters of the Buy British Campaign carried for the first time the figure of a working man as a national symbol, we were astonished at the Empire Marketing Board to hear from half a hundred Blimps that we were 'going Bolshevik'. The thought of making work an honoured theme, and a workman, of whatever kind, an honourable figure, is still liable to the charge of subversion. The documentary group has learned freely from Russian film technique; the nature of the material has forced it to what, from an inexpert point of view, may seem violent technical developments. These factors have encouraged this reactionary criticism; but, fundamentally, the sin has been to make the cinema face life. This must inevitably be unwelcome to the complacent elements in society.

Documentary, like all branches of realism, has suffered from the inhibitions of the trade, and the inhibitions have in due course been exploited by the more irresponsible and reactionary representatives of the political world. All the documentary directors have at one time or another felt the pressure of this criticism from outside. We have not only had to fight our material—new and therefore difficult as it was—but time and again there has been an attempt to apply that narrow and false yardstick of party-political value referred to by Paul Valery[1] which is the death of art and the death of all true national education.

It is worth recalling that the British documentary group began not so much in affection for film *per se* as in affection for national education. If I am to be counted as the founder and leader of the movement, its origins certainly lay in sociological rather than aesthetic aims. Many of us after 1918 (and particularly in the United States) were impressed by the pessimism that had settled on Liberal theory. We noted the conclusion of such men as Walter Lippmann, that because the citizen, under modern conditions, could not know everything about everything all the time, democratic citizenship was therefore impossible. We set to thinking how a dramatic apprehension of the modern scene might solve the problem, and we turned to the new wide-reaching instruments of radio and cinema as necessary instruments in both the practice of government and the enjoyment of citizenship. It was no wonder, looking back on it, that we found our first sponsorship outside the trade and in a Government department, for the Empire Marketing Board had, from a governmental point of view, come to realize the same issue. Set to bring the Empire alive in contemporary terms, as a commonwealth of nations and as an international combine of industrial, commercial, and scientific forces, it, too, was finding a need for dramatic methods. For the imaginative mind of Sir Stephen Tallents, head of that department, it was a quick step to the documentary cinema.

Sir Stephen Tallents referred to Henry the Navigator and the School of Navigation by which he opened up the New World, and pointed to film, radio, poster, and exhibition as the sextant and compass which would manœuvre citizenship over the new distances. He inspired a freedom of treatment which has rarely been the lot of documentary film-makers. We brought in Flaherty from America and Cavalcanti from France to strengthen our hands; the Russian films were run at the E.M.B. before they even reached the Film Society, and Cabinet

---

[1] 'Political conflicts distort and disturb the people's sense of distinction between matters of importance and matters of urgency. What is vital is disguised by what is merely a matter of well being; the ulterior is disguised by the imminent; the badly needed by what is readily felt.'

ministers argued our theories. We were encouraged in every experiment
which would help us to develop the new art. But the E.M.B. passed,
and only the film section carried on its belief in the new instruments
of civic enlightenment. The parochial voices of immediate departmental needs could at last be heard, and were. Later the inspiration
was strong at the Post Office, but much less strong where nationally it
could have been more useful: in Agriculture, Health, Transport, and
Labour. The flame lit at the Empire Marketing Board dimmed, and
the documentary film looked more and more outside the Government
departments—to the vast operations of oil, gas, electricity, steel, and
chemicals, to the municipal and social organizations, and to the
journalistic treatment of public problems on *March of Time* lines.

It seemed at the time a pity that others should reap the full benefits
of a medium which the Government service discovered but which it
was not quite inspired enough to mature. Names like Basil Wright
Paul Rotha, Arthur Elton, Stuart Legg, Harry Watt, Evelyn Spice,
John Taylor and Alexander Shaw came out of it, and they represented
together an outlook which, uniquely in the world of cinema, was as
deeply based in public as aesthetic effort. Personally I regretted the
Government retreat, for, as I know after many years, no service is so
great or inspiring, and particularly for film-makers, as a service which
detaches itself from personal profit. It frees one's feet for those
maturing experiments which are vital to the new art. It makes a daily
bravery of what, under British commercial film conditions, is a dull
little muddle of private interests and all too personal vanities.

If I emphasize this British documentary overmuch it is because I
know it best; and it serves as well as any school to indicate a social
approach to the cinema which, in the late thirties, was springing up
universally. The young men were taking command and, conscious of
the problems of the day, were coming closer to the world without and
to realism, resolved to give to cinema that commanding position in
public description so well within its grasp.

The Russians, after a brilliant period in which the Revolution was
starkly relived and all its triumphs registered, found it more difficult to
come to grips with Peace. The realistic powers of *Potemkin*, *The End
of St. Petersburg*, *Ten Days that Shook the World*, and *Storm Over Asia*
were barely matched in *The General Line* and *A Simple Case*. Conscious of the weakness, the Russians showed for a time a tendency to
slip back to the old victories, and *Thunder Over Mexico*, *The Deserter*,
Chapayev, and *We from Kronstadt* were all, in this sense, epics of
nostalgia. Conviction was lacking in the themes of peace. *Earth* was

beautiful, but only managed to melodramatize the issue between peasant and kulak. *The Road to Life,* with its story of reformed strays, was in a Y.M.C.A. tradition of patronage. It seemed, in the middle thirties, that the technique of mass energies and significant symbols, suitable for the stress of revolution, only embarrassed the quieter issues of a peacetime life, which was of necessity more domesticated and personal.

Nevertheless the technique has been changing in younger hands. Films like *Men and Jobs* seem ordinary against the old fireworks and are deplored widely as representing an abject surrender to Hollywood. But Russia, like every other country, has been coming closer to the common life and, unspectacular as its new films may seem in comparison with the old days, they are nearer the mark. With the United States, the Soviet Union remains during this period the most exciting of film countries. For America has been changing front with a vengeance. It may not understand the realism of Flaherty, but it is building up another realism, of a power and quality affecting film production everywhere. The tradition of the epics, of *The Covered Wagon, The Iron Horse, Pony Express, North of '36,* in one line, and of *The Birth of a Nation* and *Isn't Life Wonderful?,* in another, has flowered again in the national renaissance which succeeded the slump.

It is difficult to know why this epic tradition failed for a time. One may blame equally the complacency of the golden years which preceded 1929 and the alien invasion which succeeded the success of *Vaudeville.* There was certainly a sudden end to the epics and to those small town comedies of Cruze and Langdon which kept Hollywood so close to America, and only the desolate sophistication of Lubitsch and his American imitators succeeded them. But now, in 1937, there are new and remarkable developments. Most significant of these is the rise of the small-part player to a degree of vitality and importance which he does not enjoy in any other country, save Russia. Call-boys and typists, garage hands and lorrymen are mobilized behind the star and there is a new contact with the ordinary. With every year from 1930 the films have become braver and more real, as though the old men were out and the young men in. In films like *42nd Street* the element of realism appears as only a more detailed and observant treatment of the old romantic set-up, but there has also been an eager absorption of contemporary problems and materials in the American scene. However diffidently the more difficult problems may be handled, they are not altogether avoided. Prison life, the plague of gangsterdom, the new police, unemployment, lynching and the secret societies, the

New Deal, finance, and Hollywood itself are inspiring writer and director alike. Stories of medicine and research, aviation and labour, are added in good measure. This is the period which has produced *The Good Earth*, with its long vista'd story of Chinese peasantry, its trial by wind and drought and plague of the commonest and most persisting loyalty of mankind, its deep-laid sympathy for what is ordinary yet so spectacular because it is linked with the elements.

In comparison with such work from America, the outlook of the British film is blank enough. We stretch back into things that were and forward into things to come; we have musicals and farces galore; but there is all too little of the real thing. There is Flaherty, as of old, freed from the shackles of the studio and bringing back his jungle realities, but just as surely shackled again on his return with studio sahibs and Oxford-accented head-men. There is Gracie Fields doing her Saturday night turn in a Lancashire parlour, and George Formby following, and the East End of Max Miller debunking propriety in a check suit and grey bowler. The English music hall, at least, is in the line of direct observation—and not least when it breaks through and takes charge of the higher history of Henry the Eighth. There is the documentary, that too in the real line, but tight, tidy and removed in its own separate finances, and too wisely mistrustful of the commercial scramble to join hands with it. There is John Baxter with films sentimental to the point of embarrassment; but at least about real people's sentimentalities.

These are all we have to set at this time against the American wave of realism. Such flags of vitality as are flown over the British cinemas, in spite of quotas, city millions, and alien adventurers, are still, even increasingly, American flags. One reason lies with the foreigners. There are too many of them, cosmopolites of the world's cities, to whom Lancashire is only Gracie Fields's hundred-thousand a year and the men of the Clyde not even a whisper in consciousness. How could it be otherwise? If they had been artists, they might have sensed the *condition humaine* across the distance of nationality, but they are only promoters. Yet I do not blame the foreigners altogether. They are only abetted in their unrealities by their English allies. The West End stage, for all the presence of Bridie and O'Casey, has lost the accent of the people. As for the literary men, half a dozen have power together to blow the unreality to smithereens, but they are not so much in love with reality as to think the explosion worth their effort. Fantastic fees and flattering attentions are no irritant.

Even these factors are consequents rather than causes. At the back of the scene is a weakness in contemporary English life which those who, like myself, came to it from the outside, have never ceased to feel. The social and aesthetic leadership, as perhaps befits an old and, in itself, brilliant tradition, has long lost that proud contact with simple labour which characterizes the younger countries, and particularly America. The Labour movement, from which great aesthetic influence might have been expected, has only contrived to join forces with the old leadership. Artists who, by destiny, are the solvents of such detachment, remain, on the whole, a peculiar people in England. Following social rather than aesthetic distinctions, they reflect only a distance from the reality they should serve. The significant dramatists of this period, when they are not Americans, are, not strangely, Irishmen, Scotsmen, and far Northern provincials, deriving from traditions in which contact with the ordinary life has always been closer and less ashamed.

But I do not despair. All over Britain critics and leaders of opinion are conscious of the lack I have indicated and are hammering away at the forces governing our films. The championship by members of the Moyne Committee of a cinema closer to the national life is particularly significant. With such support, and in spite of all the artifices, inhibitions, inferiorities, snobberies, censorships, alien controls, and misguided party-political interventions, the British cinema may yet come, in realism, alive.

3 A Scottish Experiment

When the Scottish Development Council, in consultation with the Secretary of State for Scotland, set up its Films of Scotland Committee early in 1938, the news was given unusual prominence in the Scottish press, and not without reason, for both the Committee and the funds placed at its disposal were largely the result of newspaper initiative. For two years there had been something of a national campaign for Scottish films. The reason given was that we Scots wished to see the fair face of our country projected on the screens of the world and particularly so in the year of the Empire Exhibition; but as the newspapermen were (and are) also the mainstay of Scotland's little renaissance in writing and drama, and one of the constructive forces in Scotland, the reason lay probably deeper. It is as one aspect of the creative drive going on in the north that the movement for Scottish Films is most interesting.

In spite of the native fear of mistaking the shadow for the substance, Scotland is not without its little record in film affairs. We have had our Lloyds and Torrences and Finlaysons on Hollywood's frontiers from the beginning. The most considerable figure in British production and exhibition for some fifteen years was John Maxwell, a solicitor out of Glasgow. The education authorities of Edinburgh and Glasgow have been first in experiment in relating the cinema to the school curriculum. *Cinema Quarterly*, in its day the most independent film journal in the English-speaking world, was published in Edinburgh. Several of the young directors responsible for the success of the British documentary film have been Scots; and there may even be some odd relation between the Knoxist background and a theory of cinema which throws overboard the meretricious trappings of the studio. But, in general, we have not been satisfied with Scotland's place in the projection beam.

Here, we say, is a powerful medium which can give a country an imaginative sense of itself and bring world-wide recognition and honour to the nation which serves it well; and there is hardly a picture of Scotland but comes by grace of the alien and is false. There have been Rob Roys galore and Queens of Scots and Annie Lauries and half a hundred sentimental records, in broad American, of the Bonnie Banks of Loch Lomond. The music-hall tradition of kilties and comics has been all too eagerly served. It was pleasant to recognize for once the genuine accent of the north in James Bridie's and Ian Dalrymple's *Storm in a Teacup*, but we have always been more likely to get a *Ghost Goes West*, written by an American, produced by a Hungarian, and directed by a Frenchman. It has been pleasant too—by influence—to have as many documentary occasions as possible turned to Scotland's advantage and see the Englishman very kindly allow it, but these pictures of Scotland that also suited the London purpose—*Drifters, Night Mail, O'er Hill and Dale*, and the rest of them—have been at best indirect in their service to Scottish expression. The local accent has been lacking and the substance of it.

Remembering all the things that Scotsmen have been and done in the world, there is especial reason for dissatisfaction with the screen's picture of ourselves. For most of our record is sheer movie and, as the world's soldiers of fortune, we have been fore-ordained film actors. The synthetic picture of kilties and comics hurts when a nation remembers that it has been in its time both Robinson Crusoe and Paul Jones, conquered large slabs of Russia for the Czars, been so eager to fight out the fate of Canada that it provided warriors for both armies at Quebec, emancipated a couple of South American countries, developed steam and steam-hammers and bridge-building and shipbuilding and Macadam road-building and modern surgery, founded logarithms and the Bank of England, and travelled first down the big rivers of Africa and across Canada and Australia and, as the map will testify, many other places as well.

The problem seemed especially important to the Scot in 1938. Never before had he so needed to summon up his strength of character and remember his traditions. No country was more badly hit by the economic changes between the wars. In the nineteenth century the Scot was a pauper finding a gold mine in his back yard; and, developing his sudden claim with unparalleled ferocity, he found himself in the thirties paying for his concentration on the heavy industries. His exports slipped, and it was poor satisfaction to know that Scottish Carnegies across the sea had contributed to his undoing. The mess left after his coal rush had to be liquidated whether he like it or no, and if, as in the rush to the West, frontier towns like Dundee had become tragic Cheyennes, so much the worse for him. Worst feature of all, the export in men had gone. Scotland was still doing a driving trade in medical and scientific workers, but it was no compensation for the loads

213

shipped for hundreds of years to Europe and the Empire. The shipping of men was our speciality, and for the first time probably in Scotland's history the younger generation had of necessity to look at its own country and see what could be done about it.

It was into this wider movement of the Scottish spirit that we came with our films. Whatever general vision there might be of a Scottish film industry on Denham lines, we were called to more specific national service. The first handsome contribution to the Committee's funds was made by Sir John McTaggart, but a powerful contributor was, significantly enough, the Commissioner for the Special Areas; and it was not without interest that Walter Elliot thought it worth his time to sit in actively on the making of scripts and bring his dashing imagination to the service of the producer. Against so purposive a background it was easy to see how the Scottish film movement had to develop over the first two or three years. A first duty was the articulation of Scottish problems to the Scot and the firing of his mind and heart to the need of his generation.

In the first phase of development seven films were planned. Their aim was to interpret, and, where possible, dramatize the growing points in Scottish life. *The Face of Scotland* said something of what Scotsmen had done in the world and led the series. *Wealth of a Nation* followed the course of Scotland's coal rush and articulated the movement in time presented by Scotland's new industries and rural developments. *They Made the Land* described how Scotland in the eighteenth century peeled the peat off its central valley, drained Ayrshire and the south, how the nineteenth century built its breeds, and how in more modern times, it helped to lead agricultural practice the world over. *The Children's Story* was an account of Scottish education and what it was doing to maintain one of the finest traditions in the national life. *Sea Food* described Scotland's fisheries and there were two brief films on sport.

Founded in a deliberate attempt to use the film for national purposes, the Films of Scotland Committee was, for Britain, unique. Nowhere as in Scotland was there a public body using the cinema to maintain the national will and benefit the national economy. After twelve years spent in preaching and teaching the power of the cinema to national authorities, I found it very satisfactory that my own country should set this example.

214

4 Battle for Authenticity

With its insistence on authenticity and the drama that resides in the living fact, the documentary film has always been in the wars. As the forces of propaganda closed round it at the end of 1938, the battle for authenticity became more arduous than ever.

Not so long ago, the materials of steel and smoke were not considered 'romantic' enough for pictures, and the documentary film was supposed to be engaged on a sleeveless errand. Today, people find industry and the skills that reside within it, magical and exciting. But it was relatively easy to find the beauty in the lives of fishermen and steel workers. Their dramatic atmosphere was ready-made. Documentary moved on to more difficult work when it proceeded to dramatize the daily activities of great organizations (*B.B.C.—The Voice of Britain, 6.30 Collection, Weather Forecast, A Job in a Million, Night Mail*, etc.). It was a unique achievement when, in *Big Money*, it made a fine, exciting story of the Accountant-General's Department of the Post Office—surely, on the face of it, one of the dullest subjects no earth.

Behind the three or four hundred documentaries made in Britain up to the end of 1938, there was this constant drive to attack new materials and bring them into visual focus on the screen. Clerks and other suburban figures were more difficult to present than fishermen and steel workers, till the documentary men got the hang of the work they did and began to understand how to attach the importance of the great public organizations they operated to the seeming dullness of their daily darg. All this meant time, research, and getting accustomed to human materials which had never been creatively treated before.

Yet, I think the greatest advance of all came with two little films which, except among the far-seeing, went almost unnoticed. One was called *Housing Problems* and the other *Workers and Jobs*. I think I am right in saying that the credit of the first goes to John Taylor whose first film it was. The second was Arthur Elton's. They took the documentary film into the field of social problems, and keyed it to the task of describing not only industrial and commercial spectacle but social truth as well.

215

Documentary Achievement

These simple films went deeper than earlier films like *Drifters* and later films like *Night Mail* and *North Sea*. They showed the common man, not in the romance of his calling, but in the more complex and intimate drama of his citizenship. See *Industrial Britain, Night Mail, Shipyard* and *North Sea* alongside *Housing Problems*. There is a precious difference. *Housing Problems* is not so well made nor so brilliant in technical excitements, but something speaks within it that touches the conscience. These other films 'uplift'. *Housing Problems* 'transforms' and will not let you forget.

I have watched the various documentary men come to this point of distinction. They know that a thousand easy excitements lie right to their hand. A dozen I could name could possibly out-Bolshevik the Bolsheviks and out-Nazi the Nazis in highfalutin parades against the skyline. But they do not do it. Shunning the meretricious attractions of the easy excitements, they have kept to the line which *Housing Problems* first defined.

The powerful sequence of films which appeared during the late thirties about nutrition and housing and health and education were the measure of their achievement. Significantly enough, the big films of 1938 hardly deviated into the 'epic' of industry at all. They were *The Londoners*, a film describing London's fifty years of local government; the G.P.O. film on national health; *New Worlds for Old*, Rotha's discussion of the public utility of the fuel resources; and the films of economic reconstruction, education, and agriculture, made in Scotland.

These films of social reconstruction and the growing points thereof became a powerful force for the public good. They found their place in the cinemas; they had a vast audience outside the cinemas; they were attracting more and more attention and prestige abroad. Other countries made documentaries, but no documentary movement anywhere was so deliberately constructive in public affairs, or had so many powerful national allies as ours. Above all, its continuous and unremitting description of Britain's democratic ideals and work within those ideals, had a special pertinence at the time.

This policy was not popular in all quarters. Though the Minister of Health expressed publicly his gratitude for the Nutrition film, it is wise to remember that, when that film was first made, it was branded by political busybodies as 'subversive'. Silly enough it sounds, but obstacle after obstacle was put in the way of the documentary film whenever it set itself to the adult task of performing a public service. Sometimes it came in the cry of the Censor that the screen was to be kept free of what was called 'controversy'. More often it was in the whispered obstruction emanating from Conservative Party politicians.

For the documentary men, whose vision has sought to go beyond party politics to a deeper sort of national story altogether, the path has not been comfortable. It has taken a good deal of persistence to maintain that a full and true story of British life is more likely to describe our virtues as a democracy, and that the richest picture to present in Britain and other countries lies in the actual bone and substance of British life.

In many of the documentary films, the country is shown tearing down slums and building anew, or facing up to unemployment and reorganizing economically: in general, passing from the negative to the positive. It is in this, precisely, that most of us have felt that the strength of democratic Britain is made manifest.

In the time of which I write I feared one thing. The unofficial censorships had sought to embarrass this honest picture of Britain which we had then partially achieved, and had been anxious to substitute for the heartfelt interpretation of responsible artists the synthetic lie of partisan interests. There was always, however, the graver danger that they would seek, in presenting Britain abroad, to show only the superficial and bombastic elements in the British scene. No country is greater in tradition and ceremonial than Britain, and we may well be proud of it. Fine pictures might be made of it, and there is no documentary man who would not wish to join in making them. It was another matter, however, to have the ceremonial of Britain made the be-all and end-all of Britain's picture abroad. It could only be an unsubstantial and silly meal for intelligent foreigners. The monotony of Soviet propaganda at one period, and the monotony of Nazi and Fascist propaganda in the immediate pre-war years, were ample of evidence of that.

If we are to describe the panoply of power and forget the living, working, everyday Britisher in the process of projection, our picture will be both false and, from the point of view of international relations, foolish. People of goodwill, and the wiser heads of the State, will, I am sure, keep that truth before them, and resist distortion. As for the documentary men, they have been fighting synthetic nonsense all their lives. By their very principles, they cannot be a party to false witness.

5 Metropolitan

For four months past I have been writing, re-writing, throwing out the window and into the waste can, pages of the same identical problem that Ralph Steiner and Willard Van Dyke struggled with in *The City*. In England we too have been concerning ourselves with this question of community planning. In my absence from England, Basil Wright is producing and John Taylor directing the film. To indicate the slant we are taking we have been calling it *The World Beyond War*. So I am happier than anyone to see *The City*. It is ideal for a producer to have someone pioneer the job. The beauties—and there are many—set a mark for the oncomer. As for the weaknesses—and a few there are—one can only express all gratitude to Steiner and Van Dyke for taking a chance in chaos.

I shall say first what I get out of *The City* and then get down to the sort of analysis one producer expects of another. I remember much. I remember a lot of lyrical up-bubbling life in those children playing dangerously on New York sidewalks. I remember, too, the domestic vitality of people going out in the chaos of holiday traffic to the country. I remember the zingo of the switch from the—rather anæmic —scenes of rustic bliss to the industrial world.

I think they prove a point. In documentary you do not shoot with your head only but also with your stomach muscles. Steiner and Van Dyke, under suasion no doubt, try to tell us they are all against metropolitan madness, that they are sick of its nervousness, its wasted energies, its dangers, its damnations. They describe what they say is their road to heaven. It is, first of all, the rural paradise we have lost; and it is true enough that the rustic swinging with the seasons produced a harmonious art of life. But there is something wrong about the Steiner-Van Dyke paradise. There are fine shapes but no applejack. Van Dyke, as an old villager himself, might at least have remembered the smells that go with it.

The road to heaven twists. What is it now but a Washington suburb —neat and clean and tidy and utterly aseptic, with all the citizens practising to be acrobats? No smells here either. Youth—how blessed a rhythm to the camera is youth—lit up in bronze nakedness—gardens —sports—the old swimming hole—community centres. But what do they ever do in community centres? Is it only ring-o'roses?

What I am getting at is that I do not believe Steiner and Van Dyke believe a word of it any more than I do: and I have the proof of it the moment they shoot these children on the sidewalk, those domestic jalopies on the metropolitan road, the clamour of the industrial scene, or the open sesame of the automat. Like myself, they are metropolitans. Their cameras get an edge on and defeat their theories.

This, curiously, has a lot to do with community planning. We were bothered in this regard with our own script. Everywhere the architects were drawing up pictures of things we did not like, and it came to a head one day when a fine young bunch of architects were showing us an ideal town they had planned. There were all sorts of good things in it. Your little mother did not have to risk her infants across main roads, the shops were just around the corner from the school, the factories were nicely detached, the town was sectioned into groups, and the decorative trees could have bred enough fruit-bugs to devastate a district.

I was polite as befitted the occasion. But young John Taylor—who is often the honest conscience of us all—had had about enough. 'Christ,' he said, 'don't you have any fish-and-chip shops?' The effect was to blow our previous script—so like in some ways to *The City*—to smithereens. We found ourselves drifting back from the halcyon anæmics of the architects to a messier world that pleased us more. When I left the film we were trying to say something a little different from *The City*. We were saying: Here is this metropolitan world and a pretty mess of spiritual dislocation it is. *But how to make an art of life from what we have, and out of the rich vitalities that people actually have, that is the problem of community planning.*

It is not, I believe, a question of withdrawing from the metropolitan scene as *The City* suggests, but a question of shaping it. But who's to do it? One arrives at a point where one is apt to goddam all superior people—aesthetes and otherwise—who would foist their slim perfections on others. Why don't we develop an art of *living* architecture, in which the builder is only one of a team in which the magistrate, the doctor, the teacher, and the common or garden citizen—with, one hopes his sense of humour—are all integral partners?

There is another point about this community planning business which *The City* did not solve for me. I am one who likes the blueprint to be forgotten, as I like the script to be forgotten, once the living

219

flesh is on it. Community machinery there must certainly be, but I like to think of the democratic life as a very various business, with initiative and ideas cropping up all over the place. The vitality of the village life is not in the sweet scenes at the smithy door or along the country lanes. It is in a world of discourse in which people are all genuinely and co-operatively interested in the same things—in people, children, births, funerals, weather, soil, fields, crops, and the latest daft fancies of the local council and research station. That world of discourse is important. It represents the flowing life, the purposiveness without purpose, the permanence and the intimacy.

Practising to be acrobats does not mean enough, and why I do not like these plans and pictures of ideal suburbia is that I gravely doubt whether these bronze bodies represent anything more than a very thin world of discourse indeed. Babbitt was never quite as dim as he was— and is—painted. I mention it as one who during the prohibition days enjoyed his discourse in railroad trains and his hospitality in the basements of mid-western towns that seemed on their surface life the death of God. There must have been something else in that Washington suburb, and a better lead to community living than the bodies in the sunlight. I wish Steiner and Van Dyke had found it.

I don't know the answers any better than they do—but I am grateful to both of them. To Steiner for a visual sense of things that must be one of the greatest influences in our observation today. To Van Dyke for the great practical good sense with which he has been content with a partial solution of a problem none of us could pretend to solve wholly. This is an important film. It is one of the first directive social documentaries done in the United States. It is one step forward and, because of it, I hope we in England will be enabled to take the issue one step forward again.

Part IV

DEVELOPMENT IN CANADA

The outbreak of war in 1939 presented documentary with new opportunities, and laid new responsibilities on the movement. To Grierson these opportunities and responsibilities came when he was already in charge of film activities in Canada. He built up the National Film Board which, before the end of the war, was outstripping in enterprise and achievement its equivalent organizations in Britain and the United States. The articles grouped in this part are devoted to the Canadian development and the broadening scope Grierson was visualizing for documentary.

F. H.

1 The Film at War

The day war with Germany broke out, I was in Hollywood. I suppose everyone will remember that day in minute personal detail. It was the same on 4th August 1914. We all sensed, like a cloud on the mind, that here was the end of one epoch, the beginning of another, and all our personal worlds might never be the same again.

On 4th August 1914 I was on the coast of the Scottish Hebrides and the war was very near. I spent the whole day watching the trawlers and the drifters breasting the tide, puffing their way back in hundreds to become minesweepers and anti-submarine patrols. But on 3rd September 1939 I was in Hollywood, 6,000 miles away from the Scottish coast, and the seat of war. No minesweepers or anti-submarine patrols. Only white yachts, gliding along on a smooth blue Pacific. California was sunning itself on the beaches and Hollywood was behind me, the city of unreality, stardust, and people's dreams.

Yet instead of feeling a world away from the war, I felt no distance at all. I knew very well that there beside me in Hollywood was one of the greatest potential munition factories on earth. There, in the vast machinery of film production, of theatres spread across the earth with an audience of a hundred million a week, was one of the great new instruments of war propaganda. It could make people love each other or hate each other. It could keep people to the sticking point of purpose.

And that is how it is in our modern world. Like the radio and the newspaper, the film is one of the keys to men's will, and information is as necessary a line of defence as the army, the navy, and the air force. The leaders responsible for the conduct of war have to ask new kinds of questions. Which nation puts its case insistently and well and makes converts and allies? Who arouses the national loyalty? Who makes purpose commanding? Who mobilizes the patrol ships of the human mind? These are vital considerations among statesmen today. In the thirties European politics seemed to turn on the effect of propaganda and every nation was fighting for command of the international ether. Even the issue of the war may turn on the skill and imagination with which we formulate our aims and maintain our spirit.

In the early months of the war the film was mobilized like the newspaper and the radio alongside the fighting forces of the nations. Even Hollywood, far from the battlefront, was immediately affected. I never saw so great a scurry in my life as in that first week of war in the chambers of Hollywood's magnates. A third of their world market had vanished overnight or become completely uncertain. Who knew when the bombs would be raining from the sky and making theatres in the European cities untenable? The black-outs had driven people from the screen romance to sit waiting by their radios for the latest war news.

Hollywood was so nervous that it had a new idea every day. The first reaction was to draw in its economic horns, make cheaper pictures, intensify its American market. There was some talk of forgetting its international role and going all American. The result of that policy was seen in more pictures of North American history, more pictures of South America. Hollywood even began, in a sudden burst of light, to remember that Canada was a North American country.

There was another school of thought in Hollywood which remembered the war of 1914–18 and how the frothier kinds of entertainment had prospered. A great deal was heard in these first days about stopping serious pictures and giving people nothing but light-hearted ones —to permit them to forget their worries. 'Give them more fluff' was the way Hollywood described it. But not for long. The more modern school of production, the younger men, argued vehemently in every studio. They said, I think wisely, that people would be asking more questions in this war, and that this policy of froth and fluff would be an insult to the intelligence of the people. I confess I was greatly interested to hear how seriously these younger producers talked—the men like Walter Wanger. There was no question of avoiding world responsibility, no desire whatever to forget the war and make a false paradise of neutrality. In Wanger's office we installed a ticker service from the United Press and daily we sat around it, reading the war news, considering how best the film might serve mankind in this new situation. Everyone in this particular group was for going into propaganda of some kind, but everyone I noticed was for avoiding hatred. No *Beast of Berlin* and other childish exaggerations this time, they said. And through all their thoughts I noticed there ran the theme: 'Let us do something to keep the decent human values alive. Let us so

224

The Song of Ceylon (British, 1934–5)
  Produced by John Grierson with the Ceylon Tea Propaganda Board: directed by Basil Wright

Night Mail (British, 1936)
   Produced by John Grierson: directed by Harry Watt and Basil Wright

Coalface (British, 1936)
   Produced by John Grierson: directed by Alberto Cavalcanti

maintain men's sanity that when it comes to peace, we shall know how to make it stable.'

The warring nations had to be much more direct. They reached out, at once, to make the film their recruiting sergeant. In the newsreels they made the film an instrument of international information by which they could tell the world about their efficiency, their power, their confidence, and their will to win.

That new mood was apparent in two of the first films to come from Britain. There was not much peace in *The Warning*. It was a picture of England preparing for death and disaster; and you saw the old England made grotesque by war as in a distorting mirror. There was no peace in *The Lion Has Wings*. That work of film documentation was Britain actually at war, zooming and roaring above the clouds. It was also the film at war. There would be more and more as the days went on. And they would be far more real, far more documentary, these films of war, than any seen before from British studios.

I have been for a long time interested in propaganda and it is as a propagandist I have been from the first interested in films. I remember coming away from the last war with the very simple notion in my head that somehow we had to make peace exciting, if we were to prevent wars. Simple notion as it is, that has been my propaganda ever since— to make peace exciting. In one form or another I have produced or initiated hundreds of films; yet I think behind every one of them has been that one idea, that the ordinary affairs of people's lives are more dramatic and more vital than all the false excitements you can muster. That has seemed to me something worth spending one's life over.

I should have been an unhappy person if I had thought all this vanished with the war. Strangely enough the war seemed only to accentuate people's hunger for reality. It was proper that the film should take its place in the line of defence, as in duty bound. It was proper that it should use its powers to mobilize the full effort of the nation. But—so it seemed in these early months—one way, too, in which we could maintain our defences and keep our spirit for the struggle ahead was to remember that the aims of our society lie beyond war and in the love of peace. It would be a poor information service, it seemed, which kept harping on war to the exclusion of everything, making our minds narrow and anæmic. It would be a poor propaganda which taught hatred, till it violated the sense of decency which ten thousand years of civilization have established. It would be an inefficient national information which did not keep the home fires of national activity burning, while the men were off to the war. In war

P

as in peace, strength lies in hope, and it is the wisest propaganda which keeps men rich in hope.

The war would have achieved its final feat of destructiveness, and we should have been brought to the very brink of spiritual suicide, if we had lost the sense of what we were defending.

On this serious question of the relation of peace thoughts and war thoughts, I am going to quote from the great French writer, Giraudoux. Addressing the children of France, as Director of the French Ministry of Information, at the opening of their school year, he said:

'Thirty-eight thousand of your teachers have had to take machine-gun, bomb, and grenade and all the abhorred tools of destruction to form a rampart behind which you will be sheltered this winter—to learn from the masters left to you—and from your school books—your country's inviolable love of peace. . . . Young sentinels, learn a true history, a true geography, a moral without hatred, lessons in things which have nothing to do with gunpowder and bayonets.'

So there you have it. There are two sides to propaganda, and two sides to the film at war. The film can be mobilized to give the news and the story of a great historical event. In that sense our aim was to use it for all its worth to secure the present. But my hope has been that the film would also be used more and more to secure the future and serve the still wider needs of the people of Canada. War films, yes, but more films, too, about the everyday things of life, the values, the ideals which make life worth living. I hoped that we could use the film to give visual significance to the words of the Canadian Prime Minister when he said that the spirit of mutual tolerance and the respect for fundamental rights are the foundation of the national unity of Canada.

In that way I have thought to rescue from these barren days of trouble something we could hand on to the future.

2 Searchlight on Democracy

I write this in Canada and Canada is a good country in which to study the terms of democracy. Here you have a people strung out along three thousand miles of railroad. In the middle, between Winnipeg and Ottawa, there is a sort of no-man's-land. It is not like the States. It has no Middle West, no meeting place between peoples of the west and east.

The physical distances are so great that they place a heavy burden on the processes of democracy. People cannot come very easily together to discuss things. National committees can meet only rarely. If a committee decision is to be carried out, the gap between the decision and the action is accentuated by the sheer difficulty of mileage.

I cite this case of Canada, because it demonstrates how much the democratic way of discussing things and doing things depends on a quick and living system of communications. In Canada the difficult problem of yesterday is being liquidated to some extent under one's eyes. The new factor which has come into the situation is the airplane and airplanes are meaning more to Canada than to any country I can think of. This country of many days' journeys is being concertina'd dramatically. People are getting together more quickly. National discussion is becoming easier to arrange. Understanding between isolated localities and centres of opinion is becoming a simpler matter than it was yesterday. The tempo of consequent action which is the bugbear of the democratic method must inevitably become faster.

In one way or another this problem of communications is vital to every democratic society. Getting together is important. Getting our ideas together is important. Once good feelings and good ideas move like wildfire across the democratic sky, we are half-way towards building a community worth living in.

In this respect we depend more deeply on our system of communications than do the authoritarian states. It is true that the dictator needs his radio. The word from on high must be heard by all. The rhetorical moment must be enjoyed *en masse*. The band must beat out its rhythm across the entire domain. But the subtler and richer forms of communication are less necessary. It is not so vital to spread ideas or to spread initiative. It is not so vital to put upon the individual citizen the responsibility of taste and good feeling and judgment. In a democracy it *is* vital, and this responsibility for spreading good feelings and taste and judgment is the whole responsibility of a democratic education.

Your dictator with a wave of the hand can clear a slum or rebuild a town—and this is always an attractive prospect to people who want slums cleared and towns rebuilt. But the communication of dictatorship is of orders given and of organization set in motion. Our democratic interest in communications is very different. It is integral to the democratic idea that constructive action shall bubble up all over the place. Initiative must be not only central but local. By the mere acceptance of democracy we have taken upon ourselves the privilege and the duty of individual creative citizenship and we must organize all communications which will serve to maintain it.

I know the waving hand of the dictator can more spectacularly clear the slums, if—and who can ensure it?—it is disposed to clear the slums. I know that efficiency is attractive and the beat of feet marching in unison is a remarkable source of persuasion. I know, too, that when, in the democratic way, we leave so much initiative to the individual and the locality, the result is sometimes only too local. Local taste may be terrible to the metropolitan æsthete. The perfectly sound scientist will be challenged by rustic pigheadedness. But what we lose perhaps in efficiency and taste—and it is just possible that the dictator may be a man of taste—what we lose with our shabby local methods, we gain in spirit. It may be poor but it is our own.

The moment we accept this decision a great obligation is laid upon education in a democracy. It must perfect its system of communication so that individuals and localities may draw from the deepest source of inspiration. It must create a flow of initiative and ideas which, while maintaining the vitality of democracy, will help it to challenge authoritarian standards in quality and efficiency. This is a tall order but I can see no way out of it. In the first place it means reorientation of our education policy and a conception of education as an active constructive system in the maintenance of democracy. The detached view will no longer serve. Either education is for democracy and against authoritarianism, or it is for authoritarianism. The day of standing aside is over because the issue has become too vital. It is from now on an instrument of state with a part to play in fulfilling the democratic idea. It has the job of relating the individual to the responsibilities of that idea.

Searchlight on Democracy

I think all of us realize that we have in the past laid too much emphasis on a narrow view of individualism. We have geared our educational processes to the person in private rather than to the person in public. Haunting our minds and our policies has been the concept of a leisure-time education and not of a working-citizen education. Our ideal has been the cultured individual, the gentlemen in a library. We have made much of accurate information and the somewhat questionable efficacy of deductive logic. We have held before us the ideal of rational citizenship, where the individual, like a lone ranger on a detached horizon—which he never is—makes a cold judgment on the facts. We have pictured our educated man as someone with a knowledge of the classics and capable of polite conversation on literature and the arts. Inspired by these thoughts, we have proudly introduced our working man to Plato and the philosophies. I have seen some of that myself. I have gone through the farce of teaching *A Midsummer Night's Dream* to evening-school brush workers, and Plato to tired labourers. It was a pretty conceit: but we have, I think, all come to appreciate how detached from reality such an outlook on education is. This education is like a rose without a smell. It misses the essence of common thinking and common doing. It lacks integral contact with the living processes of citizenship. It approaches the labourer—and I can only think of it as a highly insulting approach—with the intention of improving him and of shaping him in an image which could never be his reality. He may be a fine labourer and a fine man: he will at best be but a poor gent in a library—and who wants to be that anyway? It is an anæmic conception. It lacks what seems to me respect for the labourer as such and for the man that is in him, and for the part he can play in his own community. It does not create an image in his mind of what he, himself, on his own doorstep, and out of his own rich human character, could do and enjoy within the community. It is education with its roots in the air.

On the other hand, if education is to be an active instrument of the democratic idea, it must first be socialized. By that I mean that it must at every turn take hold of its role as a social instrument. It is one of the remarkable revolutions of our time how all branches of human thought and activity are coming to appreciate their active relation to social forces. The scientist has come out of his cell. Each branch of science is losing the atmosphere of mere scholastic inquiry and academic discipline. It has become just one other aspect of the pursuit of human well-being. You see, particularly, how science is lending its aid to housing and health and establishing new measurements of

229

well-being by which the individual must live. You see the same revolution in medicine, in the overnight change from curative to preventative health service.

You see it in the new conception of living architecture, in which architecture is no longer a matter of mere building but a creative process of community planning in which the scientist, the doctor, the builder, the transport expert, the psychologist, the teacher, the public administrator and the citizenry are partners in a joint enterprise.

Education has been as conscious as any other field of the need for a new social outlook. But it has tended to be borne down by its own traditional emphasis on knowledge and books. Out in Kent, where I practised some part of my citizenship, we spent a vast sum (I think it was £50,000) running books out from Maidstone to our hamlets. But certainly, in my own village, it was not books we talked about and not books we wanted. We were all farmers and that was our principal world of discourse. We were interested in the things of the land and in every species of new magic which affected the land. What we most wanted to know was what they were doing at East Malling and Wye and other research stations. We wanted a more living discourse than books. We wanted, for example, a picture service through the winter nights which would show us what others were doing and what the scientists had to tell us, and so give us an opportunity for discussion and argument. But somehow or other that would not quite be education, and there was no £50,000 for the information we needed. Even in Kent where we were educationally progressive, the burden of the books was still upon us.

How then are we to twist the outlook of education so that it will become a more real power in the maintenance of democracy? I was discussing this with my friend, George Ferguson, the editor of the *Winnipeg Free Press* and one of Canada's most stalwart champions of the democratic idea. He said that the only thing you have to set against the spectacular appeal of the totalitarian state is the spectacle of liberty. I think the idea is worth examining. Looking back on our own documentary films, I know I have tried to do something of this sort in every film with which I have been concerned. I have asked the directors to call down a cinematic blessing on the fact that people in our world are so natively out of step. I have asked them to express the beauty that goes with the tatterdemalion good humour of a London bank holiday. We have in our own fashion and in a hundred ways described those manifestations of the human spirit which are not mobilized, not regimented, not dictated from without. We like, in our group, to quote the story of the fine housing estate which the beautiful æsthete of an architect designed, for it shows much of what we in our documentary films have tried to say. This architect had his design so sweetly planned that it was already decided in the blueprint which tenants were to have brown curtains, and which blue. One thing came unstuck and that was the tenants. They said, Hell, they would submit to having baths and one thing and another but curtains were private and they would do what they pleased with them. The architect said all right, but no lace. And the tenants said Hell again, if we like lace we will have lace. And that's the way it turned out. When the curtains went up they were every colour of the rainbow and a good few were lace. And the pleasure of the event was that the moment they did go up, the beautiful design of the architect got what it most needed. It came alive.

One would expect the democratic educational system to preach just such liberty and keep the æsthetes and other superior people in their places. I hope that as we blueprint for the community life, we will realize, the specialists among us, that we are specialists for and on behalf of people and not specialists from without. I hope that we, at all costs, see to it that people have the full freedom of their initiative and judgment and have the power to invest whatever is done with their own rich notion of life. In that sense, education has a great deal to do with the expression and maintenance of liberty.

It is the same thing when your educational system gives voice to the notion of fraternity or equality. In the democratic definition of these things, nothing very definite or spectacular can be said about either. Our conceptions of fraternity and equality are essentially undemonstrative. When you think of it, the dictator states did a magnificent job in presenting their own brand of fraternity. They had their comrade-in-arms gambit. They had the spectacle of men joining together in the religious brotherhood of the blood. Their fraternity was expressed in exciting forms like parades, flags and mutual salutes. One does not wonder for a moment if it seems to fill a gap and meet a need for recognizable comradeship which our own system lacks. It seems to me, however, that the democratic idea must shrink a little from the outstretched hand, the hearty backslap, or any such form of mania. I like to think that in our presentation of the democratic idea we will know how to present fraternity and a common feeling for one's neighbour with a degree of diffidence. But it puts a heavy burden on democratic statement when the very essence of it is that it should not be melodramatic and should not be spectacular.

231

Development in Canada

We are faced indeed with a very difficult problem. It means that people must be taught to appreciate that being together, talking together, living together and working together in common undemonstrative harmony is the whole fraternity. It means that we must praise and encourage every little grouping of common spirits who ride their bicycles out into the country, or hike across the downs, or meet in the local to organize a cricket team or hoist a pint. It means that we are concerned with a multitude of ordinary things and that the very secret of them is their ordinariness. We are led inevitably to the conclusion that if such simple human elements are to be made the basis of loyalty, then we must learn to make a drama and a poetry from the simple.

As in the case of liberty and fraternity, so with equality. One drives on inevitably to the conception that we cannot present a rich interpretation of dramatic virtues except we produce a poetry and a drama of ordinary things. The spectacular appeal, the organized uplifting emotion which the totalitarian system provided in its education could, I believe, be matched and could be matched tomorrow if the writers and the poets and the picture men among us would seize upon the more intimate and human terms of our society.

Our searchlight on democracy will in the end turn out to be a quiet soft light under which little things are rounded in velvet and look big.

As I review the special problems of education, I find myself involuntarily altering many of the literary measurements which I was taught. I find myself laying less emphasis on the Renaissance and on the great expression of the human spirit which it fired. I find myself drawing a distinction which is not in the copy-books, between the court traditions of English literature and the common or garden expression which is at all times bound up with villages and music halls. I find myself less interested at the moment in Milton and Shakespeare than in Crabbe and Burns. To use Gogarty's word, the *graffiti* of the people were never more important than now. It seems to me that the emotional and spiritual maintenance of democracy depends on an absolute acceptance of the idea that a man is a man for a' that, and that the most important poetry or beauty in the end is that which bubbles traditionally—and not always academically—out of ordinary people. It will mean a widening of our educational view in half a dozen classes of curriculum. It will mean that the pictures of Jimmy Cagney will jostle for attention in the presence of Shakespeare himself, and that when Cézanne is being discussed, the beauties of public house art will not be forgotten. If any complain of the vulgarity of the project I can only answer that the vulgarization of education is in the logic

232

of our time and that it will bring with it—this outlook on the actual—a deep inspiration that we need.

I began by saying that democratic education needed its own vital system of communications—its own system of wildfire across the sky. I have tried to suggest that the wildfire we need will not, by the very nature of democracy, be that spectacular answer to the authoritarian challenge which people today are asking for. Our searchlight on democracy, I have suggested, will be a quiet and intimate light as befits the idea we serve, though it will make up in its width of sympathy and in the far-reaching subtlety of its detail what it lacks in emphasis.

But how is our system of education to bring this art of democracy into being? It calls obviously for a change of outlook and of heart, involving the newspaper story, the poster, the radio, and the terms of instruction as well as the more permanent arts of poetry, drama and picture. How can we establish this change of outlook and of heart which will give a true and moving picture of our democracy?

You cannot go out in cold blood to create such a new appreciation of the ordinary. Art does not happen like that. It is not taken by assault. It is a better rule to say that art comes as a by-product of the more pedestrian task. I think that the way and the means become apparent when you look closely into the more specific problems of democratic education. In solving each problem as it comes up, I think that you will find that you are involved willy nilly in the creation of an art and that the solution of each problem will be a contribution to the spectacle you are asking.

Let me distinguish the principal problems of education in a democracy. Firstly, you must inspire interest in the community life. Secondly, by creating such warm sentiments in regard to one or other aspect of the community life, you will inspire that initiative which is the heart and soul of the democratic idea. Thirdly, you must help in creating common standards of community thinking and community doing, if democracy is to be not only spirited but fine. Firstly: *Interest*. Secondly: *The participation which emanates from interest*. Thirdly: *Standards of judgment*.

Look at what they involve. If you are to create interest in the community life, you are face to face with the Herculean task of articulating this monstrous new metropolitan world which we have built for ourselves. You must bring it alive, so that people will live intimately in it and will make an art of life from it. And you cannot do it by information alone or analysis alone, for the life escapes. You can only do it in those dramatic terms which present the life of the

233

thing and the purpose of the thing and make intimacy possible. The radio, the picture, the poster, and the story are the more obvious instruments in your hands and art has become inevitably half of your teaching.

Let me be specific. You will not succeed in bringing things alive in a general spate of new enthusiasm. Things do not happen that way either: vague enthusiasms are not the best of guides. As educationalists, you are concerned at every point with specific areas of interest. The child has to be prepared for citizenship in field or town. The world which has to be brought alive to him will, if you are wise, have a good deal to do with that field or that town, and only later with those wider perspectives of citizenship which reach out from it. The citizen, similarly, has his factory, his union, his family, his neighbours, his traditions, his news, his hobbies, his specialized world of discourse, his movies, his pub, his relationship with taxes and votes, and other aspects of local or national government. Perhaps he even has his church. These are the terms of his life and in each and every aspect of it his understanding is not so great that it cannot be greater or his harmony so assured that it cannot be brighter. At a hundred points education can touch the quick of his life and light the way for him. It may excite him a bit more about his neighbourhood. It may encourage him in his skill—as I kept asking the Kent County Council to encourage me in my strawberry-growing. It may, in general, make his world a more exciting place than it seems.

But again and again you will find yourself concerned with a dramatic or living process rather than a pedagogic or merely informational one. And I am thinking not only of the power of the movie and the newspaper. I am thinking of arts as separate as private discussion and child welfare: gardening and sport and music hall. These and a thousand more represent openings for your imagination as educationists, for they are the opportunity and the substance of the work you must finally do. All are media of communication and a way to the art and spectacle of democracy.

In my own field of documentary film-making, this is the inspiration on which we operate and I am not sure we may not have done just enough (since 1929) to prove its truth. We have been concerned with those very problems of bringing specific fields of modern activity alive to the citizen. We have worked in a dozen very different areas, and made a first tentative shot at picturing the worlds of communication and science, public administration and social welfare. We have followed along the perspective of modern life and sought to find themes which gave a new significance to the terms of ordinary living. Sometimes we have approached the task on a journalistic level or poetic level or analytical level or more dramatic level, but always we have been concerned to find a degree of beauty in the process and make our own contribution to the spectacle of democracy at work. It can be done and it can be done more widely. And all the thousand arts of human discussion and intercourse have their own special contribution to make.

I shall dismiss the creation of initiative by simply repeating that if you crystallize sentiments, you establish will power: if you create interest, you inevitably inspire initiative.

It is in the third field, the communication of *standards*, that education can find its other great opportunities for presenting a living expression of democracy.

When we were considering the creation of interest, we were involved at every point in bridging gaps between the citizen and his community. This is a general process. All of us need in general to know and feel intimately how the world we live in gets along.

But it is also a specialized process, for all of us have specialized interests. We need to equip ourselves better in terms of our agriculture, our care of children, our educational activity and so forth. There are, in fact, a thousand other gaps to bridge between, shall we say, the farmer and the research station, between the citizen and better practice. Our system of communications must provide for a rich flow of living records from which each of us, in our own separate interest, learns what the other fellow is doing and is thereby enabled to pull up our own standards. Leeds, they tell me, is away ahead in certain aspects of housing, with special arrangements for old people and for people disposed to tuberculosis. Leeds, in that case, is an important growing point of housing initiative. And it would be good for every municipality to have the sight of it in their eyes. Kensal House in London represents a vital experiment and achievement in community living. Here again, a living record of it will brace the spirit of similar experimenters elsewhere.

We arrive inevitably at the thought that propaganda or education in a democracy must operate on a large number of specialized levels and should be deliberately organized on a large number of levels. There must, of course, be a general spate of information and uplift, affecting the minds of general audiences: and you have the film and radio organized for that purpose. But I like to think that those of us who are interested in special aspects of the community life will develop our own systems of communications and that film and radio and other media of vital communication will do much for us.

When you see this from the international viewpoint, you will realize how much these specialized services could mean to international understanding and to the expression of the democratic idea. Wandering about the world, one finds that while countries differ in their expression and in their local idioms, they are in one respect identical. We are all divided into groups of specialized interests and we are all, at bottom, interested in the same things. There are the same essential groups everywhere. Here is a group interested in town planning, or in agriculture, or in safety in mines or in stamp collecting. Whatever the different language they speak, they speak the common language of town planning, agriculture, safety in mines, and stamp collecting. In that sense, one never thinks of Geneva as representing the real internationalism. The real internationalism is in the manias we share with each other.

How great is the opportunity this provides for the creation of the democratic picture! Several years ago Basil Wright and I suggested a scheme to the International Labour Office. We said, in effect: 'Why do you not create a great international interflow of living documents by which specialized groups will speak to their brethren in the fifty countries that operate within your system? You are anxious to raise the common standard of industrial welfare. Why do you not use the film to do it? If France has the best system of safety in mines, let other countries have the benefit of this example. If New Zealand is a great pioneer of ante-natal care, let other countries see the record of its achievement.'

I hope the I.L.O. will do something about that, but I would not simply leave it to the I.L.O. Britain is now engaged in far-reaching efforts of education and propaganda. There has been a lot of talk about the projection of Britain. I say frankly that I do not think anyone in high quarters has seriously thought about how it should be performed in a truly democratic way, or has seen the enormous advantage in international communication which the democratic idea gives us. In Whitehall there is no philosophy of propaganda and certainly none that is recognizably democratic as distinct from authoritarian. There is the same exhausting effort to look spectacular. There is the same noise. I am sorry to say there is the same tendency towards the synthetic and unreal. Yet I believe that democratic education and democratic propaganda are an easy matter and indeed far easier than the authoritarian type, if these principles I have laid down are grasped.

It will be done not by searchlight but in the quiet light of ordinary humanism. Speaking intimately and quietly about real things and real people will be more spectacular in the end than spectacle itself. And, in the process of creating our democratic system of communications, in bridging the gaps between citizen and community, citizen and specialist, specialist and specialist, we shall find that we have in the ordinary course of honest endeavour made the picture of democracy we are seeking. And we shall have made it not only national, but international too.

3 The Nature of Propaganda

Long before the war started, those who had studied the development of propaganda were constantly warning the British Government that a highly organized Information Service, national and international, equipped with all modern instruments, was as necessary as any other line of defence. I am thinking back to 1930 and even before Hitler came to power. Over the dog days of the thirties they preached and they pleaded, with only the most partial success; and in the meantime the greatest master of scientific propaganda in our time came up. I don't mean Goebbels: I mean Hitler himself. In this particular line of defence called propaganda, we were caught bending as in so many other spheres, because peace was so much in peoples' hearts that they would not prepare the desperate weapons of war.

The Germans attached first importance to propaganda. They didn't think of it as just an auxiliary in political management, and military strategy. They regarded it as the very first and most vital weapon in political management and military achievement—the very first. All of us now appreciate how the strategy of position—the war of trenches—was blown to smithereens by the development of the internal combustion engine. Fast-moving tanks and fast troop carriers could get behind the lines. Aeroplanes and flying artillery could get behind the lines. War, in one of its essentials, has become a matter of getting behind the lines and confusing and dividing the enemy.

But the chief way of getting behind the lines and confusing and dividing the enemy has been the psychological way. Hitler was cocksure that France would fall and forecast it in 1934, almost exactly as it happened. The forecast was based on psychological not on military reasons. 'France,' he said, 'in spite of her magnificent army could, by the provocation of unrest and disunity in public opinion, easily be brought to the point when she would only be able to use her army too late or not at all.'

The theory behind all this is very simple. Men today, by reason of the great spread of education, are, in part at least, thinking beings. They have been encouraged in individual judgment by a liberal era.

They have their own sentiments, loyalties, ideas and ideals; and these, for better or worse, determine their actions. They cannot be considered automata. If their mental and emotional loyalties are not engaged in the cause you present, if they are not lifted up and carried forward, they will fall down on you sooner or later when it comes to total war. The usual way of expressing it is to say that their morale will break.

That is why Hitler said: 'It is not arms that decide, but the men behind them—always'; or again, 'Why should I demoralize the enemy by military means, if I can do so better or more cheaply in other ways?'; or again, 'The place of artillery preparation and frontal attack by the infantry in trench warfare will in future be taken by propaganda; to break down the enemy psychologically before the armies begin to function at all . . . mental confusion, contradiction of feeling, indecisiveness, panic; these are our weapons. When the enemy is demoralized from within, when he stands on the brink of revolution, when social unrest threatens, that is the right moment. A single blow will destroy him.'

Just before they entered Norway, the Germans arranged for the State dignitaries in Oslo a special showing of their film of the Polish campaign. A portion of that film was included at the end of the American film *The Ramparts We Watch*. Even a portion of the film gave some idea of the effect such a demonstration was likely to have on the peace-loving Norwegians. It showed the mass mechanical efficiency of German warfare with brutal candour. The roaring aeroplanes, the bursting bombs, the flame-throwers, the swift unending passage of mechanized might all constituted an image of the inevitable.

That is how the strategy of terror works. It worked with us in Britain at the time of Munich. I won't say the men had the wind up— in fact I should describe the male reaction as one of vast disappointment and even shame—but the women were weeping all over the place. The picture of inevitable death and destruction Germany wished to present had been successfully presented; and it is one of the best evidences of British stamina that the new united courage of the British people was welded so soon out of these disturbed and doubtful beginnings.

Terror is only one aspect of propaganda on the offensive. The thing works much more subtly than that. Here is a quotation from someone in Hitler's entourage to show how deadly the approach can be: 'Every state can, by suitable methods, be so split from within that little strength is required to break it down. Everywhere there are groups that desire independence, whether national or economic or merely

239

political. The scramble for personal advantage and distorted ambition : these are the unfailing means to a revolutionary weapon by which the enemy is struck from the rear. Finally, there are the business men, whose profits are their all in all. There is no patriotism that can hold out against all temptations. It is not difficult to find patriotic slogans that can cover all such enterprises.'

We saw in France how groups of men could, in the name of their country, give in to Hitler. Perhaps, in the name of France, they wished to crush the popular front and keep out socialism but they gave in to Hitler. Perhaps, in the name of France, they wanted to crush capitalism in the name of socialism, but they gave in to Hitler. Perhaps, in the name of France, they sighed for some neo-medieval religious authoritarianism but they gave in to Hitler.

In the United States the German inspired organizations did not trade as such. They were always to be found under the slogan 'America first' and other banners of patriotism.

The principal point to take is that, when the Germans put propaganda on the offensive in war, their psychological opportunities were rich and widespread. They appealed to men's thwarted ambitions; they offered salvation to disappointed and disheartened minorities; they preyed on the fears of capitalist groups regarding socialism; they preached controlled capitalism and a socialist state to the socialist minded. They harped on those weaknesses of democracy of which democratic citizens are only too well aware; the verbiage of its parliamentary debates, the everlasting delays of its committees, the petty bourgeois ineffectiveness of its bureaucracy. They probed the doubts in the mind of democracy and inflamed them to scepticism. Everything was grist to their mill, so long as they divided the enemy and weakened his belief in himself. No one will say that German propaganda did not do that job brilliantly and well, as it marched its way across Europe. It found the population divided against itself and ready for the knife, and Lavals and Quislings everywhere drilled and rehearsed perfectly in the act of capitulation.

The Germans believed that Democracy had no genuine convictions for which people would be willing to stake their lives. They proceeded cynically on that assumption, marched on that assumption and their entire military plan depended on that assumption. Hanfstaengel actually declared at one time that this lack of conviction within democracy was Hitler's fundamental discovery—'the discovery which formed the starting point for his great and daring policies'.

It is perhaps as well that we know where the heart of the matter

Pett and Pott (British, 1934)
 Produced by G.P.O. Film Unit: directed by Alberto Cavalcanti

Industrial Britain (British, 1933)
 Produced by E.M.B. Film Unit: directed by Robert Flaherty and John Grierson

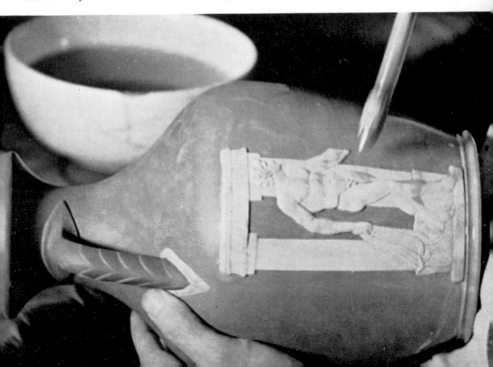

The Islanders (British, 1938–9)
  Produced by G.P.O. Film Unit: directed by Maurice Harvey

London Wakes Up (British, 1938)
  Produced by Strand Films: directed by Ruby Grierson

lies, for if lack of conviction, as they say, always results in defeatism and defeat, the challenge is plain enough. It behoves us to match conviction with greater conviction and make the psychological strength of the fighting democracies shine before the world. It behoves us to match faith with greater faith and, with every scientific knowledge and device, secure our own psychological lines. If propaganda shows a way by which we can strengthen our conviction and affirm it more aggressively against the threat of an inferior concept of life, we must use it to the full, or we shall be robbing the forces of democracy of a vital weapon for its own security and survival. This is not just an idea: it is a practical issue of modern scientific warfare.

Propaganda on the offensive is, like every weapon of war, a cold-blooded one. Its only moral is that the confusion and defeat of the enemy are the supreme good. In that sense it is a black art and in the hands of the Germans was a diabolical one. But, objectively speaking, you will appreciate that it depends for its success on a deep study of the psychological and political divisions of the enemy and is therefore based on close and scientific analysis. Catch-as-catch-can methods in propaganda can no longer serve against an enemy so thorough.

The more pleasant side of international propaganda is the positive side, where you ingratiate yourself with other countries; where you state your cause, establish alliance in spirit and create world confidence that the issue and the outcome are with you. That was Britain's great task, particularly after the fall of France and particularly in regard to the Americas.

Britain's method derives from her great liberal tradition. She is not, I am afraid, very scientific; but she does believe, out of her liberal tradition, that telling the truth must command goodwill everywhere and, in the long run, defeat the distortions and boastings and blatancies of the enemy. The Germans believe that men are essentially weak; they believe that the mainsprings of action are primarily economic and selfish; they believe that men are more interested in the *élan vitale* than the *élan morale*; and they derive the principles of their propaganda accordingly. The British still believe in the *élan morale* and hope that an appeal to the Platonic principle of justice will triumph.

I won't say Britain tells the whole truth but I think that most detached observers agree that she tells as much of it as she reasonably can. The accent of honesty and forthrightness is her principal suit. You would never find the B.B.C.—you certainly would never find Winston Churchill—under-rating the dangers and difficulties which beset the country. Germany could not get out of her make-up an

Q   241

element of boasting; and Mussolini, for many years, was the image of braggadocio. The British quality, and it has the mark of a national talent, is under-statement; and in the long run—if there is a long run—it is strangely penetrating and effective.

If Britain has a fault, it is that she is still the proud old nation, so sure of her cause and of her good spirit that she takes it too much for granted that other nations will immediately recognize them. You remember what we used to say about English salesmanship. The English said in effect: 'Our articles are articles of quality; they have the best craftsmanship in the world behind them and, word of an Englishman, you can take our word for it.' It was all very true, but down in South America and elsewhere there were other habits of mind and other habits of buying and the Englishman never quite got round to studying the other fellow's point of view and the special require-ments of the market. He certainly never quite got round to saying 'The client is always right'.

Propaganda, some of us believe, is like selling or showmanship, a study in relativity. I don't mean that it must always, like the chameleon, take its colour from the country or the community in which it is operating. It was the German style to be, cynically, all things to all men, and that was the essence of the German doctrine; but it is not the British. At the same time, a study of the other fellow's point of view is essential.

We used to argue a good deal in pre-war England about the policy of the British Council for Cultural Relations Abroad. There were two schools of thought. One school had not yet got away from the idea that the one way to present Britain abroad was to show the Horse Guards Parade and the ceremonies of old England, Oxford and the law courts, Ascot and Canterbury, the green lawns of the cathedral towns and the lovely rustic quiet of the shires. It was difficult to quarrel with things so fine; but others said plainly: 'No, there is a world without, which wants to know more than that. You have a responsibility before the world, in terms of modern leadership, modern ideas and modern achievements. The world wants to know how up-to-date and forward looking you are. It wants to see the light of the future in your eyes as well as the strength and dignity of your past. It wants to know what you are doing to deserve your privileged posi-tion in the world; and God keep you if you do not answer them.'

If you examine British propaganda today, you will find that there are still the two schools of thought, but I am glad to say that, the younger school has been winning hands down. Never, in a sense, was

Britain a more modern, revitalized, forward-looking country than she is today.

Britain is beginning to see that accents and styles count in propaganda and that every country has its own way of thinking and its own special focus of interest. 'Other nations', says Wickham Steed, 'are not interested to hear what good people we are or how excellent our intentions may be. They are interested in what is going to happen to themselves and it should be the business of our propaganda to make this clear to them.'

On this question of international differences, I received a letter from England from someone who had seen our Canadian films. He said, was it possible that Canadians thought faster than Englishmen. I replied that when it is a problem of thinking in a straight line, Canadians think much faster; but that when it comes to thinking in five concentric circles, the Englishmen are undoubtedly the better. Our policy, however, when we send Canadian films abroad is to invite the countries receiving them to remake them in their own style and use their own editorial comment. It sounds curious but there are really vast differences of mental approach as between Canada and England. There is even a vast difference of approach as between New Zealand and Australia. He is a very optimistic propagandist who thinks he can easily pen a message or strike a style which can be called international.

London Can Take It was a beautiful film but it raises a very special issue of relativity in propaganda. That is the difference between primary effects and secondary effects. You might call it the difference between conscious and subconscious effects. *London Can Take It* created enormous sympathy for England and so far so good. The question is whether creating sympathy necessarily creates confidence. I cite that psychological problem only to indicate that in the art of propaganda many deep considerations have to be taken into account. Short-range results are not necessarily long-range successes. Conscious effects may not necessarily engage the deeper loyalties of the subconscious. In propaganda you may all too easily be here today and gone tomorrow.

All in all, however, one may be proud of many things in Britain's Information Service. It has followed its own native light and no one will say it has not been a noble light. It has not been scientific, but neither has it been cynical. To its scientific critics it has said with Sir Philip Sidney 'If you will only look in thy heart and write, all will be well'. I am of the scientific school myself and would leave less to chance in a hard and highly mobilized world. But no one will deny that at least half the art of propaganda lies in the ultimate truth that truth will ultimately conquer.

For myself, I watched the German procedure and wished a little sometimes that we could, without running over into harshness and blatancy, say a little more about ourselves and put our propaganda more plainly on the offensive. They flooded the world with pictures of action, of their young troops on the march and going places, of deeds done. In their pictures to America, they laid a special emphasis on youth and efficiency and, to people starved of belief in the future, they drummed away with their idea of a new world order. They most subtly showed great respect in their presentation of their French and English prisoners of war and emphasized the model discipline of their troops in occupied territories. They most carefully presented the Führer as a gentle and simple soul, weeping over his wounded soldiers, kind to children, humble in his triumphs. It was a calculated, impressive and positive picture as they presented it.

The Germans' careful study of the requirements of particular countries must have had particular effect in South America. They appreciated the South American objection to being exploited by alien capital and posed carefully as the outside friend who wished nothing so much as to help them be themselves and develop themselves. They knew how to pump in free news services to countries which appreciated them—by radio from Berlin, translated and typed out and put pronto on the editorial desk by local German agents. On the special national days of these countries to the south they knew how to shoot flattering broadcasts from Berlin, in the language of the country and with the fullest knowledge of the local vanities to be flattered.

The Germans knew better than to say, as a certain well-known American said of cultural relations with South America, that 'the idea was to spread the American idea to the South American Republics'. I have no doubt he thought the American idea God's own blessing to mankind, but it is worth remembering that not a few South Americans, allied to a more aristocratic and courtly tradition, still regard the American idea as the ultimate in barbarism—or as a French jester has put it, an idea 'which has passed from barbarism to degeneracy without any intervening period of civilization'. The Germans certainly knew better than to define their interest in South America with the *naïveté* of an advertisement in *Time*. 'Southward,' it declared, in a phrase calculated to raise every hackle south of the Rio Grande, 'Southward, lies the course of Empire.'

Where the Germans failed was in the fact that their cold-blooded

The Nature of Propaganda

cynicism spilled over and was spotted. You can impress other countries with your might and your will. You may even impress them with your new world order. But you can't start blatantly talking of conscience as a chimera; morals as an old wives' tale; the Christian religion as a dream of weaklings; and the pursuit of truth as *bourgeois* fiddle-faddle, without raising a few doubts in the heart of mankind.

Finally, there is propaganda within our gates. I suggested earlier that faith must be met with greater faith and that our first line of defence is in the unity of our purpose in these ideological struggles which are now upon us.

A democracy by its very nature and by its very virtues lies wide open to division and uncertainty. It encourages discussion; it permits free criticism; it opens its arms wide to the preaching of any and every doctrine. It guards jealously this liberty of the individual, for it is of the essence of democracy and, in the long run, makes for justice and civilization. But in times of stress it is difficult to see the wood for the trees. Whilst we are consulting this freedom and that, we may lose that discipline, that centralized power and dynamic, by which the principle of liberty itself is safeguarded from those who are less punctilious. When we are challenged in our philosophy and our way of life, the beginning is not in the word but in the act.

The Nazi viewpoint was that we had not found within our democratic way of life a sufficient dynamic of action to meet their challenge —that it was not in our nature to find it—and that we should not find it. 'The opposition', said Hitler, 'is dismally helpless, incapable of acting, because it has lost every vestige of an inner law of action.'

In the long run they found that was not true but it would be folly to dismiss this criticism without thinking about it. The self-respect of free men provides the only *lasting* dynamic in human society; and the most powerful and vivid statement of this proposition is to be found in Walt Whitman's preface to his *Leaves of Grass*. But we also know that free men are relatively slow in the uptake in the first days of crisis. We know that much that has become precious to free men in a liberal régime must be forsworn in days of difficulty—the luxury of private possession and private security—the luxury of private deviation in thought and action—the supreme luxury of arguing the toss. Moreover, your individual trained in a liberal régime demands automatically that he be *persuaded* to his sacrifice. It may sound exasperating but he demands as of right—of human right—that he come in only of his own free will.

All this points to the fact that instead of propaganda being less necessary in a democracy, it is more necessary. In the authoritarian state you have powers of compulsion and powers of repression, physical and mental, which in part at least take the place of persuasion. Not so in a democracy. It is your democrat who most needs and demands guidance from his leaders. It is the democratic leader who most must give it. If only for the sake of quick decision and common action, it is democracy for which propaganda is the more urgent necessity.

There is another deep reason for the development of propaganda in a democracy. The educational beliefs of democracy have been criticized. 'Universal education', said the Nazis, 'is the most corroding and disintegrating poison that liberalism ever invented for its own destruction.' This, of course, is another distortion, but there is again a grain of truth. With universal education, democracy has set itself an enormous and an enormously difficult task. We have had it for two or three generations only; and it would be crazy to think that in that short experience we have worked out a perfect technique or discovered all the principles by which it should be guided. Our system of universal education has made vast mistakes and has today grotesque weaknesses. Every progressive educationist knows that. This does not mean that we must throw the essential machinery of democracy into the discard, but rather that we must correct its mistakes and strengthen it where it is now weak.

There are some of us who believe that propaganda is the part of democratic education which the educators forgot; and that is what first attracted us to study its possibilities. Education has always seemed to us to ask too much from people. It has seemed to expect every citizen to know everything about everything all the time—a patent impossibility in a world which grows wider and more complicated every day. We believe that education has concentrated so much on people knowing things that it has not sufficiently taught them to feel things. It has given them facts but has not sufficiently given them faith. It has given them the three R's but has not sufficiently given them that fourth R which is Rooted Belief. We believe that education in this essential has left men out in the bush without an emotional map to guide them; and when men are starved of belief they are only too prone to believe anything.

If you recall the origin of the word propaganda, you will remember that it was first associated with the defence of a faith and a concept of civilization. Propaganda first appeared in the description of the Catholic office—Congregatio de Propaganda Fide—which was to

246

preach and maintain the faith. It may be just as easily today the means by which we preach and maintain our own democratic faith. Man does not live by bread alone, nor the citizen by mind alone. He is a man with vanities to be appealed to, a native pride to be encouraged. He has a gambler's heart to be allowed a flutter and a fighting instinct which can be associated with fighting for the right. One part of him at least asks to live not safely but adventurously.

So we may usefully add a new dramatic factor to public education— an uplifting factor which associates knowledge with pride and private effort with a sense of public purpose. We can, by propaganda, widen the horizons of the schoolroom and give to every individual, each in his place and work, a living conception of the community which he has the privilege to serve. We can take his imagination beyond the boundaries of his community to discover the destiny of his country. We can light up his life with a sense of active citizenship. We can give him a sense of greater reality in the present and a vision of the future. And, so doing, we can make the life of the citizen more ardent and satisfactory to himself.

We can, in short, give him a leadership of the imagination which our democratic education has so far lacked. We can do it by radio and film and a half a dozen other imaginative media; but mostly, I hope, we shall do it by encouraging men to work and fight and serve in common for the public good. To have men participate in action is the best of all propagandas; and radio and films and the rest of them are only auxiliary to that.

Canada is a young nation which has not yet found herself but is today in the exciting process of doing so. I like to think that the breathless reception given to the King and Queen was due not so much to their presence, brilliant as it was, but to the fact that Canada found for the first time a ceremonial opportunity of raising her young national face to the sunlight. I like to think that subconscious Canada is even more important than conscious Canada and that there is growing up swiftly in this country, under the surface, the sense of a great future and of a great separate destiny—as Canada.

In other words, I believe the country is ripe, if its imagination is given true leadership, for a new burst of energy and a new expression of Canada's faith in herself. In these circumstances, I don't think it would be difficult to create a powerful sense of spiritual unity, whatever the threat may be.

4 The Documentary Idea: 1942

The first part of our work in Canada was finished early in 1942. It produced a film organization which suggested it could do great things for the country if it was looked after in good faith till the young people developed. Much of it was pulled off the sky. On the other hand, there are special reasons why the national use of films should have fitted so quickly and progressively into the Canadian scene. The need to achieve unity in a country of many geographical and psychological distances is only one of them and not the most important. More vital, I think, is the fact that Canada is waking up to her place in the world and is conscious, as few English-speaking countries seem to be, that it is a new sort of place in the world. A medium which tries to explain the shape of events and create loyalties in relation to the developing scene is welcome. I cannot otherwise explain the measure of support we have been given, nor the long-range hopes that have been placed in this school of projection we have set up.

Stuart Legg has been such a worker as you never saw: with one film a month in the theatre series for a couple of years, and stepping up later to two. It will be easier as the research staff grows, for the key to that sort of thing is in the first place academic. There is first-rate support in the fields of economics and international affairs. This is a characteristic of Canada and will have considerable influence on the development of the group.

The *World in Action* series says more of what is going on in our minds. The films in this series develop in authority and command good critical attention both in Canada and in the States. We are concerned in these films primarily with the relation of local strategies to larger world ones. This is partly in reaction to what some of us regard as a dangerous parochialism in English-speaking propaganda: but also because Canada is moving as swiftly towards a world viewpoint as England in recent years has been moving away from it. The style comes out of the job. Since it is a question of giving people a pattern of thought and feeling about highly complex and urgent events, we give it as well as we know, with a minimum of dawdling over how some

248

poor darling happens to react to something or other. This is one time, we say, when history doesn't give a good goddam who is being the manly little fellow in adversity and is only concerned with the designs for living and dying that will actually and in fact shape the future. If our stuff pretends to be certain, it's because people need certainty. If our maps look upside down, it's because it's time people saw things in relativity. If we bang them out one a fortnight and no misses, instead of sitting six months on our fannies cuddling them to sweet smotheroo, it's because a lot of bravos in Russia and Japan and Germany are banging out things too and we'd maybe better learn how, in time. If the manner is objective and hard, it's because we believe the next phase of human development needs that kind of mental approach. After all, there is no danger of the humanitarian tradition perishing while the old are left alive to feel sorry for themselves and make 'beautiful' pictures about it. Sad to say, the beating heart of the Stuarts was all they had left and so it is with vanishing politicos.

The penalty of realism is that it is about reality and has to bother for ever not about being 'beautiful' but about being right. It means a stalwart effort these days: one has to chill the mind to so many emotional defences of the decadent and so many smooth rationalizations of the ineffective. One has even to chill the mind to what, in the vacuum of daydreams, one might normally admire. In our world it is specially necessary these days to guard against the æsthetic argument. It is plausible and apt to get under the defences of any maker in any medium. But, of course, it is the dear bright-eyed old enemy and by this time we know it very well. Documentary was from the beginning— when we first separated our public purpose theories from those of Flaherty—an 'anti-æsthetic' movement. We have all, I suppose, sacrificed some personal capacity in 'art' and the pleasant vanity that goes with it.

What confuses the history is that we had always the good sense to use the æsthetes. We did so because we liked them and because we needed them. It was, paradoxically, with the first-rate æsthetic help of people like Flaherty and Cavalcanti—our 'fellow travellers' so to speak —that we mastered the techniques necessary for our quite unæsthetic purpose. That purpose was plain and was written about often enough. Rotha spent a lot of time on it. We were concerned not with the category of 'purposiveness without purpose' but with that other category beyond which used to be called teleological. We were reformers open and avowed: concerned—to use the old jargon—with 'bringing alive the new materials of citizenship', 'crystallizing sentiments' and creating those 'new loyalties from which a progressive civic will might derive'. Take that away and I'd be hard put to it to say what I have been working for these past fifteen years. What, of course, made documentary successful as a movement was that in a decade of spiritual weariness it reached out, almost alone among the media, towards the future. Obviously it was the public purpose within it which commanded government and other backing, the progressive social intention within it which secured the regard of the newspapers and people of goodwill everywhere, and the sense of a public cause to be served which kept its own people together.

These facts should have made it clear that the documentary idea was not basically a film idea at all, and the film treatment it inspired only an incidental aspect of it. The medium happened to be the most convenient and most exciting available to us. The idea itself, on the other hand, was a new idea for public education : its underlying concept that the world was in a phase of drastic change affecting every manner of thought and practice, and the public comprehension of the nature of that change vital. There it is, exploratory, experimental and stumbling, in the films themselves : from the dramatization of the workman and his daily work to the dramatization of modern organization and the new corporate elements in society to the dramatization of social problems : each a step in the attempt to understand the stubborn raw material of our modern citizenship and wake the heart and the will to their mastery. Where we stopped short was that, with equal deliberation, we refused to specify what political agency should carry out that will or associate ourselves with any one of them. Our job specifically was to wake the heart and the will: it was for the political parties to make before the people their own case for leadership.

I would not restate these principles merely out of historical interest. The important point is that they have not changed at all and they are not going to change, nor be changed. The materials of citizenship today are different and the perspectives wider and more difficult; but we have, as ever, the duty of exploring them and of waking the heart and will in regard to them. That duty is what documentary is about. It is, moreover, documentary's primary service to the state: to be persisted in, whatever deviation may be urged upon it, or whatever confusion of thought, or easiness of mind, success may bring. Let no one say that a few brighteyed films or a couple of Academy awards— from Hollywood of all places!—mean anything more than that a bit of a job was done yesterday. Tomorrow it is the same grind with ever new material—some easy, some not so easy—to be brought into design; and no percentage in it for anyone except doing the rightest job of education and inspiration we know how for the people. Considering the large audiences we now reach and the historical stakes that depend on rightness of approach, it is a privilege worth a measure of personal effort and sacrifice. If there is common agreement in the 'strategy' I have indicated, differences in daily 'tactic' will not seriously affect unity.

We should see equally straight regarding the social factor in our work over the thirties. It was a powerful inspiration and very important for that period. Without *Housing Problems* and the whole movement of social understanding such films helped to articulate, I think history would have found another and bloodier solution when the bombs first rained on the cities of Britain. But that Indian summer of decent social intention was not just due to the persistence of people like ourselves and to the humanitarian interests of our governmental and industrial colleagues. It may also have marked a serious limiting of horizons. It may have been an oblique sign that England, to her peril, was becoming interested only in herself. Some of us sensed it as we reached out in every way we knew for an opportunity of wider international statement. We did not, I am afraid, sense it half enough and we share the guilt of that sultry decade with all the other inadequate guides of public opinion. The job we did was perhaps a good enough job so far as it went, but our materials were not chosen widely enough.

Nothing seems now more significant of the period than that, at a time so crucial, there was no eager sponsorship for world thinking in a country which still pretended to world leadership. Russia had its third International and Germany had that geopolitical brain trust which, centred in Hausofer, spread its influence through Hess to Hitler and to every department of the Reich. In the light of events, how much on the right lines Tallents was and how blind were the people who defeated his great concept! For documentary the effect was important. The E.M.B., which might have done so much for positive international thinking, died seven years too early; and it was hardly, as we comically discovered, the job for the G.P.O. There was the brief, bright excursion to Geneva: there was that magnificent scheme for the I.L.O. which Winant liked but which the Rockefeller Foundation turned down: there was my own continuous and fruitless pursuit of the bluebird we miscalled the 'Empire' and the momentary hopeful stirring in the Colonial Office under Malcolm MacDonald: there was the Imperial Relations Trust, five years too late, and affected from the first by the weight of impending events. The international factor, so necessary to a realist statement of even national affairs, was not in the deal.

It is, of course, more vital than ever to a documentary policy. We, the leaders of the people and of the instruments of public opinion, have been out-thought by Russia, Germany and Japan because we have been out-thought in modern international terms. Because documentary is concerned with affecting the vital terms of public thinking towards a realistic comprehension of events and their mastery, its duty is plain. To use the phrase of these present days, you can't win the war, neither 'outside' nor 'inside'—without a revision of the public mind regarding Britain's place in the world and the larger morale that goes with a sense of being on the bandwagon of history. Thumbing a ride to the future is not nearly good enough.

I look back on Munich as representing a milestone in my own outlook on documentary. From that time on the social work in which we had been engaged seemed to me relatively beside the point. Munich was the last necessary evidence of how utterly out-of-category our political thinking was and how literally our political leaders did not know what it was all about. From that point it seemed clear that we had, willy-nilly, to relate the interests of the British people to new world forces of the most dynamic sort—physical, economic and ideological. It was inevitable that our first instinct should be to put our head in the sand and in a last frantic gesture try to avoid the implications of the future; but the significance of our indecision in regard to both Germany and the Soviet Union was plain to see. World revolution had broken out on the biggest possible scale, and to the point of having people like Churchill recognize it as such. Win or lose, the economy of Britain and her place in the world were under threat of serious alteration and, however we might presently hide our eyes, people's minds had to be prepared and made fit for them if what was great and good in Britain was to survive. It was not much use concentrating on changes in a *status* whose *quo* was being challenged from every active corner of the world and apt to be blown to historical smithereens. Internal social issues were no longer enough when the deeper political issues had become the whole of realism.

This was one person's reaction. I knew it meant the exploration of a wider basis for the public instruction which documentary represented than the reactionary régime at that time allowed. But I was altogether doubtful of where the journey would lead. I hoped, vaguely I must admit, that youth and the viewpoints their world position imposed upon them would bring a measure of progressive strength from the

252

Dominions. I did not know how that strength could ever be articulated in time to save documentary from its greatest setback: the official sponsorship of the old, the obstinate and the inept. That period, thank heaven, is over and, in the combined force which documentary has so hardly won, it should be possible to create a new strength of thought and purpose.

In spite of many difficulties and confusions in the public scene, I see no reason why documentary should not do an increasingly useful job within the limits of official sponsorship. Some of the difficulties are constantly quoted to me and particularly from England. We are, it is emphasized, far from articulating our war aims. We still insist on tolerations and freedoms which often, some say, merely disguise the 'freedom' to go back to Britain's *status quo ante* and the 'tolerance' of past stupidities. We have not yet learned to state the new creative terms which will give reality to 'freedom' and 'tolerance' in an actual future. We denounce fanaticism in others because we have not ourselves discovered a shape of things-to-come to be fanatical about. We still stand bravely but vaguely between two worlds and talk the language of indecision: resting our case on hopes of Russia and the U.S., the bravery of our youth, and our capacity to stand up to other people's offensives. As usual, I take the position that while I believe political issues are the whole of realism, the 'agency' of correct political change is not my concern. It may come in any colour of the rainbow, and call itself the British Council or the Society of St. George for England Canterbury Inc. so long as it is the midwife of correct political change. *Die tat ist alles.* To put it in its simplest and naïvest form— which is still good to remember and maintain—correct political change will be that alignment of political principles and loyalties which, given the circumstances of the world today, will best serve the interests of peoples of all lands, and the British people in proportion, and actively mobilize the *native* heart and mind to these ends. It will be that alignment which actively eliminates the evil forces, wherever they may be, which are against such interests and all decadent forces, wherever they may be, which are not competent to control the developing scene. That is something on which all healthy elements must agree, and the unhealthy elements present events are sufficiently taking care of. War has this grim compensation that only the successful generals are considered good ones; and there is a daily measuring-stick for leaders in that most powerful quarter of public appraisal, the stomach muscles of the people.

It is also fairly plain what areas of chaos have to be reduced to order, whatever political alignment develops. The armies of the world are carving out new geographical concepts and shapes. The processes of total war are developing new economic concepts, and more modern methods of administrative control. First things are miraculously coming first, including the food and faith of the people. Though minor social changes are not major political ones and the radish may be one colour outside and another in, the present flow of social decency must lubricate the development of state planning, corporate thinking and co-operative citizenship. The most important of the British films have, of course, been those which have seized on one or other of these changes, and it is of first-rate significance that Jack Beddington should have sponsored them. Their importance is that in explaining the shape of these developments they are exploring the inevitable shapes of the future, rough and jerry-built as they may now appear. It does not matter if the films are at first not so good. The history of documentary is the history of exploring new fields of material, always with difficulty first, then easier and better. Its chief temptation has been to abandon exploration and, doing better what has been done before, pursue the comfort of technical excellence. It will be remembered that this also was one of the reasons for Russia's attack on the 'formal arts'.

The new fields of positive material are wide and we have, all of us, only scratched the surface. The field of social changes, is not, *per se*, the most important of them. Kindness in a queue at Plymouth which means so much to the B.B.C. overseas broadcasts, does nothing about India. The important shapes are obviously those more directly related to the national and international management of industrial, economic and human forces. They are important in winning the war without. They also represent, on a longer term view, a new way of thought which may be the deepest need of our generation. In so far as documentary is primarily concerned with attitudes of mind, this aspect of the matter is worth a great deal of attention. 'Total War' is said to require 'total effort' but this has not been easily come by in nations which still have a hang-over of nineteenth-century thinking and *laisser-faire*. At a hundred points today wrong attitudes are still being taught: some in innocence of the dynamic change which total effort involves: some in conscious defence of the sectional and selfish interests which total effort must necessarily eliminate. This psychological fifth column is more deeply entrenched than any other and all of us have some unconscious affiliation with it as a heritage from our out-of-date education. Rotted in the old 'untotal' ways and in the personal pleasures we enjoyed under them, we have to examine every day anew what in

254

our words and sentiments we are really saying. A critique of sentiments is a necessary preliminary to propaganda and to documentary as its critical instrument.

It will certainly take continuous teaching of the public mind before the new relationship between the individual and the state, which total effort involves, becomes a familiar and automatic one. A beginning has been made, but only a beginning. The capacity of the individual for sacrifice has already been well described and honoured. So has team work, particularly in the fighting services. So has the mastery of some of the new technical worlds which the war has opened up. So far so good, but it is the habit of thought which drives on towards the integration of all national forces for the public good, which goes to the root of things. Here we come face to face with the possibility of integrating these forces in a thousand new ways: in particular in the release of co-operative and corporate energies on a scale never dreamt of before. To consider this simply as a temporary device of war is to mistake its significance and by so doing to dishearten the people; for it is what people in their hearts have been harking for and represents the fulfilment of an era. Total war may yet appear as the dreadful period of forced apprenticeship in which we learned what we had hitherto refused to learn, how to order the vast new forces of human and material energies to decent human ends. In any case, there it is, a growing habit of thought for documentary to watch and describe and instil at a hundred points: serving at once the present need of Britain and the shape of the future.

Total effort needs, in the last resort, a background of faith and a sense of destiny; but this concept of integrating all resources to an active end gives the principal pattern for a documentary approach. It will force documentary more intimately into a consideration of active ends and of the patterns of integration which best achieve them. It will also force it into a study of the larger phases of public management which may not have seemed necessary before. To take a simple example, we have an excellent film from Anstey on how to put out incendiary bombs and handle the local aspects of fire-watching; but we have had no film covering the basic revolution of strategy in anti-blitz activities which the experience of blitz inspired. Britain's discovery of the intimate relationship between the social structure and defence provides an excellent example of 'total pattern' and indicates the revolution in public viewpoint required by total effort. Consider, at the other end of the field of war, *Time*'s report from Burma. 'The Japanese fought total war, backed by political theory and strengthened by powerful propaganda. They made this total war feasible by cornering economic life in conquered areas, utilizing labour power and seizing raw materials to supply continuing war from war itself. It is a type of war thoroughly understood by the Russians and the Germans, half adopted by the Chinese, and little understood by Britain and America.' If it is 'little understood' it only means that in this aspect of activity, as in so many others, effectiveness depends on a new way of thought which we have not mastered deeply enough to practise in new circumstances. The result of peace as well as war lies in the hands of those who understand it and can teach it.

One phrase, sticking out like a sore thumb from the reports of the Eastern war, reveals a further perspective. Referring to the loss of native Burmese support we were accused of 'lacking sound political theory'. Britain's failure to understand other points of view may again be the heritage of a period in which we were powerful enough and rich enough not to have to bother about them; but that day has gone. Again new attitudes have to be created in which Britain sees her interest in relation to others. You may call it, if you like, the way of relativity. It involves an attitude of mind which can be quickly acquired, rather than a vast knowledge of what those interests are. It will mature more easily from a consideration of the patterns of real and logical relations with other countries (geopolitical and ideological) than from exchange of 'cultural' vacua. The latter have never stood the test of events; yet Britain makes no films of the former. In this field, documentary might do much to deparochialize some of our common ways of thought. There are many opportunities. Let me take an oblique example in Anstey's *Naval Operations*. Here was a neat, tight little film with that cool technical treatment which has always been the distinction of the Shell Film Unit. But there are other fleets beside the British, including the Russian, Dutch, Australian and Canadian. They also have 'relative' importance in a total view of naval operations. So has the German. So have the American and the Japanese, for even if the film was made before Pearl Harbour, the fleet in being is also a factor in naval operations. In this film, good as it was, the relative viewpoint was not taken because the total viewpoint was not taken, and the design of it, on the theory I am urging, belonged to the past. I am not complaining of a film I like very much. I am merely indicating how various are the opportunities for the relativity approach.

Once consider that Britain is only important as it is related to other nations and its problems and developments only important as they are recognized as part of wider problems and developments, and many subjects will reach out into healthier and more exciting perspectives of description than are presently being utilized. The past lack of a sense of relativity in Britain has been responsible for a good deal that seems trivial and even maudlin to other peoples. However stern and manly the voice that speaks it, it is still the unrelative thing it is and in my view does not give an account of the reality of the people of Britain. The falsity of the impression comes from the falsity of the approach. It will not be easily cured for it derives from historical factors of the deepest sort, and even documentary is bound to reflect them, however objective it may try to be. The fact that it is being presently cured at good speed represents indeed a triumph of clear thinking in difficult circumstances. A deliberate attempt to relate British perspectives to others would help the process. It may be the key to it. Incidentally, this relativity approach, apart from being one of the guides to a logical and sure internationalism, is a necessary guide to retaining allies. It is worth noting that there is a difference between making a film of the Polish forces to flatter Poland, or making a film of a Dominion to show what that Dominion 'is doing for England', and making a film in which Britain takes her due place in a 'total' pattern.

So much for new materials and new approaches. Styles are more difficult to talk about for they must inevitably vary with countries. I think, however, that it is possible to make certain generalizations. Since events move speedily, and opportunities pass just as speedily, the tempo of production must change accordingly. A lot has to be done and done quickly if the public mind is to be tuned in time to what, amid these swift moving changes of public organization, is required of it. It is not the technical perfection of the film that matters, nor even the vanity of its maker, but what happens to the public mind. Never before has there been such a call for the creation of new loyalties or bringing people to new kinds of sticking points. Times press and so must production; and with it must go a harder and more direct style. A dozen reasons make this inevitable. There is the need of striking while irons are hot, and this is particularly true of front-line reporting and has its excellent examples in the German films of Poland, the West Front and Crete, and in *London Can Take It*, the Commando raids and *War Clouds in the Pacific*. There is also the need to create a sense of urgency in the public mind, and gear it in its everyday processes to the hardness and directness which make for action and decision. If there is one thing that good propaganda must not do these days

R   257

it is to give people catharsis. This again, not just because 'the war has to be won', but because as far as the eye can see, we are entering an era of action, in which only the givers of order and the doers generally will be permitted to survive. Someone winced when I suggested in England that in times of great change the only songs worth writing were marching songs. This makes the same point, except that the term must be read widely to include everything that makes people think and fight and organize for the creation of order. One doesn't have to associate oneself with the German definition of order to see that their insistence on activism is an all too successful recognition of the same need. So with a spectacular flourish, is Goering's 'when anyone mentions the word culture, I reach for my gun'. It is not peculiarly or specially a German sentiment. In the name of the inaction they call culture they have permitted a wilderness, and it will certainly not be in the name of culture that it will blossom again. In its basic meaning, culture is surely the giving of law to what is without it. That hard but truer way of culture will not go by default if we search out the design in the seeming chaos of present events and, out of the experiments in total effort now, create the co-operative and more profoundly 'demo-cratic' ways of the future. To go back once again to Tallents's Mill quotation, the pattern of the artist in this relationship will indicate the living principle of action.

So the long, windy openings are out and the cathartic finishes in which a good, brave, tearful, self-congratulatory and useless time has been had by all. The box-office—pander to what is lazy, weak, reactionary, sentimental and essentially defeatist in all of us—will, of course, instinctively howl for them. It will want to make 'relaxation', if you please, even out of war. But that way leads nowhere. Deep down, the people want to be fired to tougher ways of thought and feeling. In that habit they will win more than a war.

Part V

EDUCATION: A NEW CONCEPT

While in Canada Grierson developed the theories on education he had begun to formulate before leaving Britain. His belief is that education is the key to the mobilization of men's minds to right ends or wrong ends and urges that the times call for a great change in our thinking and in our values. The old individualist and nationalist viewpoints, he suggests, are incapable of mastering the problems of today. The essays grouped in this part give challenging expression to this new concept of education.

F. H.

1 Education and the New Order

I don't think we have done very well in education. The world has been changing about us—drastically changing—and we have not kept up with it. I suspect we have held on to concepts of education fit for the last century but no longer for this and have therefore failed to create the mental qualities and capacities our generation has needed. We face one of the deepest crises in the history of human organization. There is no question of that, with the whole world at war. This in itself represents the failure of the human mind to order human affairs in our time; and this in turn represents a failure in understanding and capacity for ordering human affairs.

I hardly think education can be absolved from its part in that failure. Talk as you will of pursuing the highest ends of man and the service of God, the base of the pyramid is in deeds done and in results achieved. In that sense, education is surely never anything other than the process by which men are fitted to serve their generation and bring it into the terms of order. It is the process by which the minds of men are keyed to the tasks of good citizenship, by which they are geared to the privilege of making a constructive contribution, however humble, to the highest purposes of the community.

Grant that in so doing education does, in man's high fancy, tune the human spirit to the music of the spheres, none the less its function is the immediate and practical one of being a deliberate social instrument—not dreaming in an ivory tower, but outside on the barricades of social construction, holding citizens to the common purpose their generation has set for them.

Education is activist or it is nothing.

If that is so, the utter disorder of society in this our time does not represent a very brilliant achievement for that instrument on which society depends for understanding and guidance. We have loosed the inventions and armed the human race with brilliant physical weapons for creating a rich civilization. But we have not known how to solve the simplest problems of economic integration—either nationally or internationally. Power has been a synonym for selfishness and posses-

261

sion has been a synonym for greed. I do not mean that education should be blamed for this and for the wars that have resulted as night from day. I merely mean that education is the key to the mobilization of men's minds to right ends or wrong ends, to order or chaos; and that is what education is. If men's minds have not been mobilized aright, the educational process has not been good enough. If, on the other hand, men's minds are in the future to be mobilized aright, it means an increase in the wisdom and power of the educational process. So, looking beyond the immediate, the greatest task of our time is not one for the soldiers but one for the educators and, because of the nature of the problem, it is certainly the hardest task they have ever been set.

These changing times of ours do not represent ordinary changes. There are periods in history when the whole basis of truth is re-examined and when the operative philosophies are revolutionized and renewed. This is one of them. We had such a period before when the Middle Ages passed into the Renaissance. The key to that change was not in the rediscovery of Greece as the text-books say, but in something much deeper. It was in the discovery and development of the laws of quantitative measurement. Out of it came the philosophy of pioneering and personal acquisition—the philosophy of individualism and individual rights—which has ruled our minds to this day.

No period of history has been more spectacular. But I wonder if we have not for a long time been seeing the last phases of it. Everyone today talks of the war not as a war but as a world revolution. And I wonder if the world revolution does not lie in this: that the great days of unmitigated individualism and governmental *laisser-faire* are over, and the day of common unified planning has arrived.

If that is so, it means an enormous change in all our thinking and all our values. It means nothing less than a drastic spring cleaning of the concepts we teach and the sentiments by which we govern our action. At the time of the Renaissance the bases of religion and philosophy and government were altered to accommodate and articulate the deep change in human affairs. You will remember, for example, how into painting came the study of perspective and the placing of the individual in space; and into literature came the study of personal character. Personal measurement became, in varying degrees, a principle of philosophy in Berkeley, Locke, Rousseau, Bentham and the rest of them. In religion, came the Reformation with a new emphasis on conscience and individual relationship with God. The arts and the philosophies changed to give men a working vision and a working faith under the new conditions of society. They followed public necessity. The same obligation may be upon us now and I think it is.

This is not a sudden development. All the years I have been watching the educational process, it has been difficult not to be conscious of it. The only difference is that the picture which was dim twenty-five years ago is today rushing into focus.

Perhaps an illustration from that earlier period may be of some interest. It goes back to the small Scots village in which I was brought up and where my father was a schoolmaster. He was a good dominie of the old school. He called himself a Conservative, but his operative philosophy in education was a good sample of what a liberal Scottish education meant. He believed in the democratic process as Burns and all Scotsmen naturally and natively do. A man was a man for a' that. We were partly agriculture, partly coal mining, and it didn't matter where the boys came from. If they were lads of parts, he felt it his God-given mission to put them on their way. At 8 o'clock in the morning before school and at 5 o'clock after school, he was at work intensifying on the bright ones, so that they could win scholarships and go to high school and on to the university. Learning was power and he was taking his job seriously. It is still pleasant to think how he would trudge off miles into the country to prevail on stubborn ploughmen, who needed the extra money coming in, to give their boys a chance and not put them to work at fourteen.

The basis of his educational philosophy was certainly according to the eternal verities. It was deeply rooted in Carlyle and Ruskin and the natural rights of man. The wind of the French revolution still blew behind it. But it was strictly individualist. Education gave men a chance in the world. It put them in good competitive standing in a grim competitive world. It fitted them to open the doors of spiritual satisfaction in literature and philosophy. But it was in the name of a highly personal satisfaction. Behind it all was the dream of the nineteenth century—the false dream—that if only everyone had the individualist ideals that education taught, free men in a free society—each in independent and educated judgment—would create a civilization such as the world had never seen before.

Even when that kind of education was conscious of social relationships, the approach was on an individualist basis. Conservative as he was, this village schoolmaster of whom I write was something of a pioneer in the teaching of the social amenities. He pioneered school gardens and domestic science for girls at the beginning of the century. With a sense of bringing a wider horizon into the classroom, he

263

brought to that obscure village school, more than thirty years ago, the first film show ever seen in educational circles in Scotland. He helped to build a village institute, so that his fellow citizens would have more literary papers on this and that, and particularly more papers on Carlyle and Ruskin. But the prevailing idea was as always that the individual might be more enlightened. One suspected that the end of it all was to make every workman a gentleman in a library—perhaps without too much leisure to be a gentleman and not too much of a library, but still as good as any man alive in the deep pursuit of truth and beauty.

The smashing of that idyllic viewpoint has been probably the greatest educational fact of our time; and I saw it smashed right there in my village and I saw the deep doubt creep into the mind of that school-master that everything he stood for and strove for was somewhere wrong. That was many years ago, long before the events of today made the dim things so much plainer.

As I have noted, one half of that village consisted of coal miners. The every effect of the education they were given, conservative as it might be in intention, was to make men think; and, thinking, they became less and less satisfied with the miserable pays they received. The life of the village became more and more affected by strikes and lock-outs. As amalgamations were developed, the employers stood ever further and further away and the battle for wages and safeties and securities became the fiercer as the fight became more abstract—as decisions came to depend on massed unions and massed corporations.

Somehow or other the educational process got to be beside the point. What were the delights of literature when a distant judgment by a distant corporation could throw a man into six months of economic misery? What were the pleasures of Shakespeare and *A Midsummer Night's Dream* in the evening schools, when industrial conditions were tiring the boys to death? What was the use of saying that a man was a man for a' that, when you were dealing day in day out with a war of economic forces in which only armies counted and where the motivating powers were abstract and unseen? In his local way this schoolmaster did a great deal. He started soup kitchens and got the soup kitchen principle so well established that the miners actually in one great strike organized the feeding of their whole community. Perhaps the soup kitchen idea was the one great educational achievement of his life. But before he finished I think the true leadership in education had passed to other shoulders. It had in fact passed to the miners themselves and the economists among them. They read their Blatchford and Keir Hardie and Bob Smillie; they attended their trade union meetings; and the day came when they elected their first Labour member of parliament, and, with so many other villages in Scotland, joined in the great drive for a socialist Britain.

At the time, I drew two conclusions from that village story. The first is that education can only, at its peril, detach itself from the economic processes and what is happening in the world. In that sense, if official education does not give realistic leadership in terms of what is happening and what is most deeply needed in the world, be assured the people will find other more realistic leadership. The second lesson was that the individualist dream in education is over and done with in a world which operates in terms of large integrated forces. There is nothing I can think of so cynical today as to teach a boy that the world is his personal oyster for the opening or talk, as Lord Birkenhead did, of the glittering prizes that fall to a flashing sword.

There is, and of course must be, a place for individual talents, but it becomes ever clearer that the heart of the matter today lies in teamwork and in unity. Individualism, that dream of so many centuries, has given us one of the golden ages. But what was so great a force in a simple world has become a nuisance in one more complicated. By its own bright energies, individualism has in fact created its Frankenstein. It has loosed energies and forces which it is, of all philosophies, least fitted to co-ordinate and control. We have arrived at an ironical situation. The spirit of competition which was so great a breeder of initiative yesterday has become only a disturber of the peace today. Rugged Individualism, so honourable yesterday, is only rugged irresponsibility today. A philosophy in which nobody is his brother's keeper has become impossible when a decision by a board of directors hundreds of miles away will wipe out a town overnight and doom the inhabitants of a rich country to desolation and despair for years. We have seen just that, no less, in Scotland, Wales and Northern England, time and again. I need not emphasize how, in international affairs, the philosophy of irresponsible competition, governmental *laisser-faire*, *laisser-aller*, and failure to plan has landed not towns but nations and continents in the deepest disaster in the history of mankind.

I want to make it eminently clear that this is not a question of blaming any particular forces. My simple point is that the values and virtues of yesterday may not be the right values or the right virtues today. My point is that in maintaining so stubbornly the old individualist, sectional, free competitive and nationalist viewpoints, we have been holding to concepts which may have, in their day, been great and

265

Education: A New Concept

glorious concepts capable of motivating men to great achievements, but which are incapable of mastering the problems of today. I regard it as foolish and unnecessary to say that financial and industrial forces have been selfish or that labour has been blind. It is similarly foolish to blame the United States for not entering the League, Britain for not supporting the Weimar Republic enough, Ottawa for making the international economic struggle inevitable in the Imperial Conference of 1932. The only real conclusion worth making is that all these events followed inevitably from the fact—as always happens in history—that we were into the new world of facts before we were out of the old world of attitudes. I am concerned to suggest that the inevitable historical process has found our operative philosophy and educative attitudes inadequate to cope with events.

To make my argument still clearer, let me say that I am not talking of the passage from Capitalism to Socialism. Like Professor Burnham, I do not believe that Socialism as we have thought of it will come at all. That surely was plain when the Workers' Soviets with all their Socialist dreams of workers' control in a classless society were driven out of industrial managership in Russia and Republican Spain, and by their own leaders. They were driven out not because Socialism did not represent a high ideal, but because, given the conditions of modern technocracy, workers' self-management represents an unpractical and inefficient one. My view, if any, would be that we are entering upon a new and interim society which is neither capitalist nor socialist, but in which we can achieve central planning without loss of individual initiative, by the mere process of absorbing initiative in the function of planning. I think we are entering upon a society in which public unity and discipline can be achieved without forgetting the humanitarian virtues. As one watches the implications of the New Deal and of what is happening today in the development of centralized planning at Ottawa, one sees that hope not only on a national scale but on an international one too.

But I emphasize the first and main point which is that we grasp the historical process and not bother about recriminations or moral strictures. Men are all the fools of history, even the greatest and best of them. A man or a nation that is historically wrong may not be evil. A man or a nation that is historically right may not be good. But when we come to consider the philosophy of education we have no alternative. As educators we must go the way with history and men's needs, or others will come to take the privilege of education away from us.

Education and the New Order

All this carries with it the suggestion of a drastic change in educational outlook. I do not expect it to be popular. It is no more popular with me than with you, for like everyone of my generation I am imbued—I should more accurately say rotted through—with the old individualist ideals and cannot for the life of me be rid of them. I am still as soft as anyone to those emotional appeals that are based on concepts of personal initiative and personal right. I still find the greatest image in rhetoric is the single man against his horizon, seeking his destiny. But simply because we are so deeply imbued with these concepts and images, our effort must be the harder to change them. If they are not the key to the social future it is our duty as educators and scientists to forget our personal predilections of the past and build the concepts and images that are the key to the future.

We have no alternative, though we shall at least have the comfort that certain familiar concepts must forever remain, because they do represent the eternal verities. We may forget nationalism but still need the cohesion and spur of national tradition. Always there will be the concept of the people and the native pride in one's own people. Humanity will remain one of the essential dramatic concepts of human thought and endeavour. So will Justice; so will Freedom; though Justice may lose its contact with the maintenance of private property rights, and Freedom may return to the Platonic notion of freedom only to serve the community.

As I see it, the really hard and disagreeable task of education to-morrow is that it will have, willy-nilly, to re-examine its attitude to such fundamental concepts as Property and Wealth, Natural Rights and Freedom of Contract. It will have to think more cautiously when it comes to the word Opportunity and the phrase Free Enterprise. The concepts themselves will not be obliterated. They are simply due for a sea change which will leave them somewhat different from what they were before.

On the positive side, we shall find new concepts coming more power-fully into our lives; and we shall find ourselves dramatizing them so that they become loyalties and take leadership of the Will. We shall talk less of the world as everyone's oyster and more about Work and Jobs. We shall talk less about free enterprise and competition and more about the State as a partner in initiative. There will be less about Liberty and more about Duties: less about the pursuit of Happiness and more about the pursuit of Sacrifice. Above all, there will be less about words and more about action and less about the past and more about the future. Already you hear the new words in the air: Discipline, Unity, Co-ordination, Total Effort, Planning. They are the first swallows over the horizon; and there are going to be more of them.

In another field, education is going to see equally drastic change. The entire basis of comprehension and therefore of educational method may change: in fact it is now changing. When we talk of bridging the gap between the citizen and the community and between the classroom and the world without, we are asking for a kind of educational short-hand which will somehow give people quick and immediate compre-hension of the highly complex forces which motivate our complicated society. We are seeking a method of articulating society which will communicate a sense of the corporate and a sense of growth. No one, I hope, imagines that the new society with its wide horizons and complex perspectives can be taught in the old ways, and in fact we are discovering that the only methods which will convey the nature of the new society are dramatic methods. That is why the documentary film has achieved unique importance in the new world of education. It does not teach the new world by analysing it. Uniquely and for the first time it *communicates* the new world by showing it in its corporate and living nature.

But if you add the new words together—Work, Unity, Discipline, Activism, Sacrifice, Total Effort, Central Planning and so forth—I think you will realize where the greatest change of all is likely to happen. Education will come out of the schoolroom and the library, the literary circle and the undergraduate conference, into the light of day. At least it will come out a great deal more than it has ever thought of doing in the past. It will go into the factory and the field, into the co-operatives of production and distribution. It will express itself not as thought or debate but as the positive action within the community of organized youth groups, women's groups and men's groups. One half of education, the stronger half, will lie in the organization of active citizenship; for there can be no concept of Planning without the concept of Participation.

In particular we need to guard against the danger of making public guidance a matter of one-way traffic. The government has as much information and guidance to get from the people as the people from the government. The government can gain as much from local inspira-tion as the people from central inspiration. We should, therefore, insist that information work both ways and we should insist that new local organizations of every kind have constant and active representa-tion at centre. It will be our fundamental safeguard against discipline and unity turning into something else.

Education and the New Order

When you deal with alterations that challenge the accepted and honoured attitudes of society, the path is always dangerous. I am not going to pretend that I do not realize how 'totalitarian' some of my conclusions seem, without the qualification I have just noted. You can be 'totalitarian' for evil and you can also be 'totalitarian' for good. Some of us came out of a highly disciplined religion and see no reason to fear discipline and self-denial. Some of us learned in a school of philosophy which taught that all was for the common good and nothing for oneself and have never, in any case, regarded the pursuit of happiness as anything other than an aberration of the human spirit. We were taught, for example, that he who would gain his life must lose it. Even Rousseau talked of transporting *le moi dans l'unité commune*, and Calvin of establishing the holy communion of the citizens. So, the kind of 'totalitarianism' I am thinking of, while it may apply to the new conditions of society, has as deep a root as any in human tradition. I would call the philosophy of individualism Romantic and say we have been on a spectacular romantic spree for four hundred years. I would maintain that this other, 'totalitarian', viewpoint is classical.

There is a further point I want to make: a simple dynamic change which I foresee in educational approach. In times of crisis—particularly in times of crisis—men crave a moral imperative: and I greatly doubt if education will mean a thing or will be listened to, unless it acquires a moral imperative.

The reason is plain and I hope that we shall not be so short-sighted as to miss a fundamental psychological factor in the world situation today. Down under the surface, men have lost their faith. As the war raged across Europe and absorbed one country after another, no fact was more patent, and not least to the German propagandists. Much of their technique was built on it, and successfully so.

We all know why men have lost their faith. They have seen the world going into disorder; they have had a sense of things going from bad to worse; and nowhere have they found that leadership, mental and religious, which seemed to be taking hold of essentials and clearing the way—positively clearing the way—to the future.

Now faith is a simple matter: at least simple of analysis. It is the complex of loyalties and attitudes by which men's needs are first appreciated and then fulfilled. So, if we are to help in re-creating this essential path to action and true victory, it behoves us to bind ourselves to the recognition and fulfilment of men's needs, with an unswerving loyalty which may well be called religious. For, you will remember, religion itself comes from a word which means 'a bond'. Many have recently deplored the separation of education from religion. I am making the same point, but I am also saying that religious power in education will only come if its recognition of men's needs is simple, fundamental, definite, activist and unswerving. If the religious reference is merely a return to the pie-in-the-sky motif, or if it is merely a return to rhetorical play with the word of God, I believe it will avail you nothing, for you will neither be talking religion nor giving the benefit of it.

Men's needs were never in our generation hard to see. They have to do with such simple matters as food and shelter and the good life for everyone and, more particularly, as a *sine qua non*, they have to do with the mobilization of men's will to these essential ends without any deviation whatsoever. These ends may have been forgotten in sectional selfishness and private privilege; and the privileged ones may have allowed every kind of complacent, urbane, cynical and indifferent attitude to hide from them the primitive fact that their neighbours, national and international, have been starving and dying in their midst. Or it may be that the leadership has been depressed by the progressive difficulties of a complex world and has lost its will-power and has wearily given up the task of leadership without abandoning its privilege. Whatever the analysis, if education is to find its moral imperative, it must get back to the forgotten fundamentals of men's need and take upon itself the courage and the will to realize them. It will have to clear itself, in the process, of a lot of bric-à-brac so often called culture. For example, it will hardly get away with anything so easy as telling people that they are fighting for the old way of life, even if people are reminded of its unquestionable beauties and benefits. Education will not get away with it, because too many people believe in their hearts that the old way of life is the mother of chaos; and they will settle for something short of its beauties and benefits. We will have to give a plain demonstration that we have willed a new way of life and mean it. The details, even the plan, will not matter so long as the will is patent and the demonstration real; for of all men's needs the first and most principal is hope, and it is of the essence of belief that the fact must follow.

The solution is straight and simple; and in an educational world which has come perversely to worship indecision and feel honoured in unbelief, I hope I shall be forgiven my certainty. I suggest simply this, and it is the moral imperative for education as I see it.

Go out and ask men to mobilize themselves for the destruction of greed and selfishness. And mean it. Ask them to forget their personal dreams and pleasures and deny themselves for the obliteration of economic anarchy and disorder all over the world. And mean it. Mean it so much that men will know that no power on earth will stop you in your tracks. Tell them that in desperate unity and before God they will give the world a greater leadership—a more humanitarian new order—than the thwarted and vengeful people of Germany can be capable of. Say with the Prime Minister of Canada that 'never again in our own land or in any other land will the gods of material power, of worldly possession and of special privilege be permitted to exercise their sway'. Mean it, and mean it so much that the people will know that, as far as human fallibility allows, the age of selfish interest is over and done with. Say it and mean it and think it and act on it. Make it your religion; which is to say, make it your bond with the people. I haven't a doubt that they will accept the new loyalties and the new attitudes of sacrifice and effort without a qualm or a question. And I haven't a doubt whatever that they will march with you till the skies open and the future is born.

2 Education and Total Effort

It may seem at first sight somewhat beside the point to be talking about education when there are so many more grandiose things, like Total Effort and Getting on With the Job, to talk about. But some of us think that education has a great deal to do with total effort and getting on with the job. We even think that it was just because he solved his educational problem that Hitler achieved total effort among his Teutons. In other words, I am thinking of the educational problem involved in mobilizing the will-power of the nation. I am going to suggest that we have only begun to scratch the possibilities in this direction, and that the world events we are passing through will force us to revolutionize our educational outlook and methods on a scale we have not known for a hundred and fifty years.

This is not altogether a new story. Some of us have been criticizing democratic educational theory for the past twenty years; and, in fact, I would not be doing films now if I had not taken my criticism seriously a long time ago. The basis of our criticism has been simple but fundamental. We have seen, on the one hand, the world of citizenship becoming more and more complex. We have seen communications grow swifter and economic horizons widen. We have seen the growth of corporate entities, national and international. We have seen local considerations reach out in perspective to embrace the widest geopolitical considerations. We have seen the growth of complex intelligence services and centralized controls; measuring and determining almost every aspect of the ordinary citizen's life. We have seen strange new languages growing up, attempting to give verbal and conceptual form to these changes: languages financial and fiscal, and economic and administrative, and technocratic, and even propagandist. One or two perhaps we understand well because they are our native professional languages; others we may half learn as an intellectual courtesy to our friends, others the best of us do not pretend to understand at all. We have seen the growth of many specialized fields of interest which, because they are new and have to be pioneered intellectually

Wealth of a Nation (British, 1938)
   Produced by Strand Films: directed by Donald Alexander

Shipyard (British, 1934–5)
   Produced by Gaumont-British Instructional: directed by Paul Rotha

The Heart of Scotland (British, 1961)
 Produced by Templar (Glasgow) for Films of Scotland: directed by Laurence Henson

and actively, so much command the attention of the specialist, that he has little time for any other consideration.

We have seen problems—difficult problems—arise in all these fields. There are international problems, federal problems, provincial problems, and problems more local; corporate and inter-provincial problems; agricultural and rural problems; social problems and labour problems; there are co-ordination problems and co-ordination of co-ordination problems.

We have this changing, somewhat bewildering, world on the one hand. We do not object to it. We have it, and that is the way it is, and it is probably as exciting a circus of human effort and mutability as men have ever been asked to live and perish in. What we find curious is that our outlook on education has not only not kept pace with these great changes in the social process, but has lagged seriously behind. Nor is it just a question of lag. We think the theory of education itself is wrong, and that, in fact, it proceeds on an altogether false assumption.

That false assumption is the mystical democratic assumption that the citizen can be so taught to understand what is going on about him that he and his fellows in the mass can, through the electoral and parliamentary process, give an educated and rational guidance to the conduct of the state. In its extreme form, it is the false assumption that a man can know everything about everything all the time. This assumption, we say, has led education woefully astray and is continuing to do so. We say quite precisely that education has set itself an impossible task and therefore a wrong task; and we add that, by so doing, it has blinded itself to what is possible and therefore right. We even add that, by bringing democracy to a state of disappointment, discouragement, impotence and frustration, it has put the survival of democracy itself in jeopardy.

If the so-called voice of the people—for all the efforts of education—does not know what it is talking about, what is the citizens' actual state in the welter of events that surround him? Let me quote Walter Lippmann:

'While he, the citizen, is watching one thing, a thousand others undergo great changes. Unless he has discovered some rational ground for fixing his attention where it will do the most good and in a way that suits his essentially amateurish equipment, he will be as bewildered as a puppy trying to lick three bones at once. . . . The orthodox view of education can bring only disappointment. The problems of the modern world appear and change faster than any set of teachers can grasp them, much faster than they can convey their substance to a population of children. If the schools attempt to teach children to solve the problems of the day, they are bound always to be in arrears. . . . And so . . . the citizen finds that public affairs are in no convincing way his affairs. They are for the most part invisible, managed, if they are managed at all, at distant centres, from behind the scenes, by unnamed powers. As a private citizen he does not know for certain what is going on or who is doing it or where he is being carried. . . . Contemplating himself and his actual accomplishment in public affairs, contrasting the influence he exerts with the influence he is supposed according to democratic theory to exert, he must say of his sovereignty what Bismarck said of Napoleon. . . . "At a distance it is something, but close to it is nothing at all. . . ." In consequence . . . there is not the least reason for thinking, as mystical democracies have thought, that the compounding of individual ignorances in masses of people can produce a continuous directing force in public affairs.'

The suggestion made by our criticism is not that education is no good at all or that the expression of public opinion is of no use at all. On the other hand, what we are saying is that the educational system is wasteful and wrong, only because it sets itself an impossible task. What we are saying is that the belief in the voice of the people is wasteful and wrong only because it expects from the citizenry an impossible, because rational, judgment. In other words, we are not throwing Democracy out, like the baby with the bath water. What we are trying to arrive at is the point where we abandon that purely mystical concept of Democracy which encourages the illusion that ten million amateur thinkers talking themselves incompetently to death sound like the music of the spheres. We want to arrive at the point where the democratic ideal can be brought down to the realm of practical consideration and achievement.

We need not necessarily arrive at a Fascist conception. You can exercise what Austin calls the power of the militia, and a gun in the ribs is a most powerful means of persuasion. You can develop a single dictatorial party, carried along by a faith and a doctrine and giving mental and active leadership to all elements of society. This is a ready solution of the problem. As a method it has behind it the historical example of the Roman Catholic Church in earlier times, and the philosophical authority of Dostoievsky's Grand Inquisitor. But some of us believe that there are advantages to be got in the encouragement of a rich measure of mental independence, on the simple ground that, in the long run, it makes for a more civilized world of discourse.

Education and Total Effort

Our problem then has been to think of educational methods which, while suited to the complexity of the modern world, still fit this democratic conception. We do not want people to know everything about everything all the time, because it is impossible. We do not want the people to make up their minds on specialized problems, because that is asking too much. We do not want to see them given, as individuals, a false notion of their freedom in society, and have them paralyse action with the infinite din of their amateur judgments. In particular, we do not want to see encouraged a din in which the people's own best interest cannot be heard. On the other hand, we do want to see them given what they are not getting now: a service of information on the immediate needs and services of the state. We do want to see them given what they are not given now: a living sense of what is going on. If we do not want to see their rational minds set impossible tasks, we do want to see their sentiments and loyalties crystallized in forms which are useful to the people and to the State alike. Above all, we want to see our society emancipated from its confusion and bewilderment, and given some imaginative leadership in the articulation of a faith.

All this, I am afraid, is very general. These conclusions, as I said, are old ones and have been the stock-in-trade of our educational criticism for a long time. The war, however, has given them very special significance. Vast changes in the structure of the State have been wrought during the war and particularly since April 1940. Before the war we lived in what was brightly called a free society. Freedom of contract, freedom of production, freedom of investment, freedom of choice, freedom of price and freedom of the devil to take the hindmost. Perhaps it was not quite as free as that. We policed the mines and the factories to prevent the exploitation of children. We policed the grocer and the milkman, to keep the sand out of the sugar and the water out of the milk. The State had stepped in on essential matters of education, housing and public health, and it was doing so on a growing, if tentative scale. But the dream still held that the two greatest statesmen a country could have were those abstract gentlemen, Supply and Demand. It is true they could not keep the people employed, and they could not save the wheat farmer; and, in fact, they looked like causing bloody revolution all over the place; but, by and large, the dream of a free society still held.

When one thinks of the speed with which we discarded this dream, and how prepared and ready our statesmen and specialists were to discard it, we are bound to conclude that the desire for discipline and

275

total effort, and the willingness to accept price, profit, wage and other controls, were there all the time, and not only for war but also for peace. It is only my opinion, but it seems unlikely that the very dramatic and revolutionary centralization of financial, economic and even technocratic initiative in the State will be altogether undone after the war. We may, indeed, have given ourselves just that measure of social control which social justice and the complexity of the modern world demand, and on which there can be no substantial argument as between political parties.

But I notice one persistent thought in the pronouncements of these social revolutionaries of ours. When it is a question of telling the people what they shall eat and drink, what soups they shall make, what clothes they shall wear, what nail polish they shall or shall not have, they glide happily along, knowing all the answers. But I notice too a certain respect for the original sin of the people and their imaginative capacity for bootlegging and black markets. Every now and again a doubt besets them. You cannot really control without having the militia behind you; and the problem of control, viewed realistically, involves sacrificial alterations in the personal habits of a generation that was brought up in an almost anarchical conception of freedom. Our social revolutionaries very reasonably shy at the prospect of a vast police force and, most importantly for us, they fall back on the concept of persuasion. Indeed, what the statesmen have failed to discover, the economists have, of sheer necessity, discovered, and that is the need for a vast new system of education by which the people will be made aware of the living processes and needs of the State and of their duties as citizens.

With an interesting, if academic, bow to the old democratic principle, Mr. MacIntosh of Canada's Department of Finance puts this very precisely: 'The problems of co-ordination extend very far beyond the circles of the Government Services. The achievement of a successful war effort will require not merely co-ordination within Government Services but an effective co-ordination between the public at large and the Government agencies. Such a co-ordination can be realized in part through control, but in the wider sense can be attained only through a broad policy of public education.'

Mr. Taylor of the Prices Board complements this pronouncement: 'In a democracy we need something more than technical knowledge and experience at the top; we need the understanding of a whole people—East and West—city and country—producer and consumer—labour and management.'

276

Education and Total Effort

I don't think anyone of us believes that the present educational system is geared to this special task. There are certain things, it is true, which the orthodox pedagogical system does very well. It teaches the elements of literacy. It teaches certain fundamental aspects of co-operation and public behaviour. In its upper brackets, it sometimes quite brilliantly teaches special skills and specialized fields of intellectual interest. The breakdown or gap lies in the teaching of citizenship: that is to say, in the gap between the citizen and the community, between the individual mind and the highly complex processes and purposes in which the State is contemporaneously involved.

There have been many clumsy efforts to bridge this gap. Once upon a time they used to teach the nature of the constitution and the State on a sort of anatomical basis, as though their forms were everlasting and permanent. We have got away from this and have at least introduced the idea of the community life as evolutionary: that is to say, as a matter of change and development. But in most of the schemes for teaching citizenship, the rational fallacy which I mentioned at the outset persists. We think we can teach the public on a vast scale to give a rational judgment on what is going on; and, trying to teach them too much, we have only succeeded in teaching them too little. We keep harping away at the idea that the only kind of judgment that matters is the rational judgment and, in that respect, there is hardly a teacher who is not, by training and tradition, an intellectual snob. But in so doing we fail to crystallize the emotions and direct men's loyalties. Whence these dreadful Cook's tours of all the world's problems which pass for courses in citizenship: like Cook's tours and Baedeckers, giving surface information only and completely out of touch with the life of the thing. Whence the derelict result that most people give up the task of trying to understand what it is all about, stick to the headlines and the funnies and the pictures on the back page, and, in their dereliction, follow anyone who has the wit to fill the vacuum of their minds with hearsay and sensation.

The adult education movement, with the best intention in the world, has fallen only too often into the same error. It, too, has insisted on being very serious and very rational. How often have the causes of the last war been analysed, how often has the structure of the League of Nations been examined, how often has the concept of Democracy been praised in a nice general philosophic way—when, all the time, the very people who were analysing and debating and arguing were moving blindfold, in mass, and at speed, to war and the breakdown of the League, and to measures of authoritarianism which, the moment a

277

country is driven to a common and total effort, prove completely logical and completely necessary.

The educational effort is not, of course, confined to the orthodox pedagogues. The newspapers and radio convey an infinite amount of information, and commentary on events. Specialized clubs hear various problems discussed. Popular magazines and specialized magazines and pamphlets and books swell the tide of information and interpretation from a hundred and one angles of special pleading. There is no lack of blue books, no lack of public relations services, no lack of material for thought thrown at the head of the benighted citizen. If the mystical ideal would only work, if the citizen could only catch it all in his head, and pick and choose, and snap off his judgments as Buffalo Bill snapped off his pigeons—one-two-three-four-five-six—just like that!! —it would be wonderful.

But what, of course, we have failed to do, and it is the most important thing of all, is to give the citizen *a pattern of thought and feeling* which will enable him to approach this flood of material in some nseful fashion. For except the citizen's mind be so predisposed and shaped in its essentials, he will find himself, as he finds himself today, utterly at sea. In this I follow Lippmann and say:

This is not an educational matter at all: it is a political matter. In other words, the key to education in the modern complex world no longer lies in what we have known as education but in what we have known as propaganda. By the same token, propaganda, so far from being the denial of the democratic principle of education, becomes the necessary instrument for its practical fulfilment. Everything else is incidental.

The State is the machinery by which the best interests of the people are secured. Since the needs of the State come first, understanding of these needs comes first in education. If the operation of controls is necessary for war or peace, understanding of these controls is a necessary part of education. Since co-operative and active citizenship have become more important to the State then amateur judgments on matters beyond the general citizen's sphere of understanding, education must in part abandon the classroom and debating society and operate in terms of co-operative and active citizenship. So the argument reaches out to wider and wider, and not unexciting, prospects. The implication of it from the first is that in determining these patterns of thought and feeling which will guide the citizen in his citizenship, education has to give far more direct leadership and far less opportunity for the promiscuous exercise of mental and emotional interests.

Education and Total Effort

The needs of the State in this great period of revolutionary change are urgent; and the citizen has neither the leisure nor the equipment for the promiscuous exercise of his mental and emotional interests.

There is another point of, I think, deep and essential importance. We cannot long keep men in a sense of mental and emotional confusion. They will go in on themselves. They will feel frustrated in their work if they do not see its end and importance. Without understanding or faith in the whole, they will exaggerate the local issues they do appreciate to the damage of the whole. Lacking faith, they will look for it desperately wherever they may find it: at the expense, if need be, of every equilibrium our civilized world has learned to hold precious. It becomes, therefore, an essential function of the State in these times of revolutionary change to give men a pattern of faith. One of the lessons we have learned in these last twenty years is that the State is in a perilous position which fails to do so.

I arrive, therefore, at certain conclusions. The first is that the State is bound to take a more direct hand in the terms and shapes of education. The second is that much of what we now know as education will become what we now know as propaganda. The third is that a dramatic approach, as distinct from an intellectualist approach, to education must increasingly develop. The fourth is that the machinery of what is called public information must inevitably be extended far beyond its present scale and purpose.

3 Propaganda and Education

Catholics remember that the Church long ago started the idea of propaganda, and they know that it was associated with the defence and propagation of a faith. Those who remember the last war remember something about propaganda, too. It was in those days what we now, a trifle deviously, call 'political' or 'psychological' warfare. It stood for the attempt of the Allies to preach the doctrine of parliamentary democracy to the Germans. It also stood for those stories in which we painted the Hun as a monster and ourselves as the exclusive children of sweetness and light. It was the instrument by which we sorted out simply and roughly the moral issues of the war and built up the morale of our fighting forces. Perhaps that is why we gave propaganda a bad name after the last war. We thought it put the world's issues in too strong a contrast of black and white. Like decent people, we wanted to understand; and we knew that there are shades of right and wrong in every individual and every nation. We knew that great issues are not exclusively moral issues, but also involve economics and national pride and race instincts and class instincts too. We revolted from the bottom of our hearts against any attempt to batter our minds into an over-simplified mould. We resisted what we thought to be an assault on human freedom.

The irony is that, in spite of all our protests, we have had an even greater development of propaganda since that time. We have seen Soviet Russia rise into world power, and one of the tremendous forces of the war, not without a great and deliberate use of propaganda. We have seen Germany emerge from the sackcloth and ashes of a defeated nation and become an even more destructive force than before, again through the instruments of propaganda. We have today reached the point where there is no longer anything particularly gruesome in the thought that Britain and the United States are as deeply involved in the war for men's minds as other countries.

We have, of course, discovered some marvellous new propaganda weapons since the last war, and particularly the radio and the film. The Nazis saw their propaganda possibilities at once and began to use

280

them on a Napoleonic scale, both at home and abroad. But, obviously, the instruments were not themselves responsible for the development which urged their use. The urge to propaganda is the important thing, and we are only now beginning to realize that this urge is somehow deeply associated with the nature of the modern state. Whether we like it or not, everywhere the new dramatic methods of appeal are being used on a colossal scale to crystallize men's sentiments and so affect their will. The relatively innocent days are over when propaganda's principal concern was whether we bought this or bought that. Today propaganda's concern is that we should feel this and not that, think this and not that, do this and not that. The scale ranges from the community which is served by a local radio station or newspaper, to the national and international hook-ups of the radio, the news services and the film. Whatever we say about propaganda, to justify or disparage it, the reality of it is with us today in every proceeding of our lives.

So it is high time we were clear what is essential or unessential about it and where it relates to those other 'old-fashioned' forces of society that are supposed to look after men's minds. I mean, of course, education and art and the free expression of opinion which the newspapers dubiously stand for in the name of a 'free press'.

One guide to the place of propaganda in modern society is its association with the idea of total effort. Wherever nations have tried to plan their society to an end, the full forces of propaganda have been unleashed. In the case of Russia there was the direction of a nation to a specific social doctrine. This involved not only the liquidation of the opponents of that doctrine, but, as Lenin put it, 'a persistent struggle, sanguinary and bloodless, violent and peaceful, military and economic, educational and administrative against the forces and traditions of society. The force of habit of millions and tens of millions is a most terrible force'. By their 'ordinary, everyday, imperceptible, elusive and demoralizing activity' they can effectively destroy the most cherished plans for the socialist-democratic state.

Lenin justified his case by arguing that particular groups of individuals in a reactionary society were so bound to false ways of thinking that they were either conscious or unconscious enemies of the good life. He urged that their enlightenment should be continuous and unremitting. He held out the dream of a society of free individuals in which the process of enlightenment had, in course of a couple of generations or so, succeeded. He reserved, however, to the leadership of one particular creed, the direction of the curriculum. In the case of Hitler's Germany there was the same mobilization of the nation to a particular plan of society, but there was a different and, all democrats will say, abominable tenet: that the ordinary man did not want to exercise his free judgment or, alternatively, that he was better without it. Differences apart, both make the argument that if and when total effort is vital to society the unity of men's minds is as important as the unity of their energies, and the democracies are today accepting this principle readily as a measure of war. They, too, have discovered— or rediscovered, the churches will say—that where there is a dynamic and common faith, manpower acquires the extra mystic virtue of workpower and fighting power.

On the face of it, this use of the instruments of persuasion and inspiration is of precious value to the state and society. Under stress of war we articulate the terms of our faith in progressive democracy. We learn to integrate the loyalties and forces of the community in the name of positive and highly constructive ideals. We beat out a rhythm for our time: a hard, tough and exacting rhythm which takes the head higher and the shoulders a little further back. We bring the airplane into our imagination and blow the old map to pieces with new proximities and new neighbours. We dismiss the old frontiers of achievement as sentimental and excite our imagination on the new frontiers of communal achievement represented by medicine, science and administration. We begin to think internationally, to think not of markets but of needs. To sustain this rhythm, to crystallize these images, many have a feeling that propaganda is a positive and necessary force, providing the patterns of thought and feeling which make for an active and imaginative citizenship in the particular circumstances of our time.

In spite of this argument, the case for propaganda is by no means generally allowed, even now. Who are for it and who against? The churches are for it because the enlivenment of the spirit is their business. The people who remember the unemployment and vast dislocations of the thirties are for it. Today, they say, we begin to discover the secret of full employment and the secret of adding to the common wealth on a scale never dreamt of before. The churches were always for the mobilization of men's minds to what was right and good, and the people are progressively for it as they see in it one of the keys to their economic future. Shall we not, they say, mobilize as greatly for the achievement of the Four Freedoms as for the destruction of Nazi Germany? Shall we disregard what we have learned about co-operation on a national and international scale?

But the right of the state to use propaganda as an instrument of

282

creative change is still deeply denied, and particularly in the United States. The heart of the matter lies in the fact that we are passing from one conception of society to another. On the one hand, we have the old conception of a society of free institutions in which the executive authority of the state is, at best, a necessary evil, to be watched over and kept from separate ambition by the Supreme Court or the Parliamentary institution. It has excellent ancestry. It derives from the Puritan sects of the seventeenth century with ideals of 'freedom of prophesying'. It suited an agricultural community in which the horizons were free institutions lived consciously on a religious and moral basis. It did not envisage a day when the community would have to act as a whole in discipline and total effort to definite ends. It did not envisage a day, after the industrial revolution and the growth of corporations, when free institutions ceased to operate on a religious and moral basis. But for many Americans this freedom *from* the state is still the most deliberate and deeply instilled pattern of political thought. It is so, although a large proportion of the population came in relatively recent generations from Europe and from far different patterns of thought about the state and democracy. The French Revolution was willing to follow the founding fathers on the equality of men and the rights of property, but it had a bigger job for the state to do than the simple police work of a widespread agricultural community. The state had a decadent old régime to liquidate and a new one to defend.

For Europe, the state has from the first represented the positive and creative force of the community, operating as a whole to positive ends. This, of course, provides a very different basic pattern of political thought, whether we are dealing with Russia or Germany or the liberal movements of Italy and France. At every turn the American pattern is challenged as belonging to the special circumstances of a new nation and as now out of date. It is challenged on the grounds that the problems of a modern highly developed industrial economy involve the creative action of the community operating as a single, integrated and unified force.

This challenge comes not least in the land of 'new deals', and Wendell Willkie distinctions between 'private enterprise' for the public good and 'private property' for selfish enjoyment. It comes not least in a country whose war effort is a model to the world of the colossal results of mass planning and mass execution, under what Henry Wallace calls the co-operation of industry and business and the 'leadership of the government'. The Wallace description is the North American rendering of a change of attitude in this matter of the state. If it

Education: A New Concept

does not allow the European conception of the state in full, it does allow the state a new and active part in America's political pattern of thought. It does not represent a special view. In spite of the sacred doctrine of 'free institutions'—free from the state—Walter Lippmann bears witness that as between Democrats and Republicans 'there is no issue of fundamental principle as to the responsibility of the modern state for the modern economy'.

My local paper speaks similarly. 'The truth is, it is a long, long time since enterprise has been free or since business has really wanted to be free. They didn't want it to be free when they asked for tariffs, with government agents collecting duties on their goods or giving them assistance to market their goods. They didn't want it to be free when they asked for government subsidies and grants. Nor did they want it to be free when they asked the state to provide them with low freight-rates and heaven only knows what else. Free enterprise! Scores of laws and regulations on the statute books, some of which have been there for a long time, tell how through the years government has been interfering and controlling business increasingly and nearly always because business wanted it. In a modern state and with the world getting smaller and smaller it is hard to see how it could be otherwise. In the good old days—or should it be daze?—of the stagecoach, *laisser-faire* was good enough, but no one could be so simple as to imagine that it could be good enough today. When a man says that business must be "free", that "free enterprise" must go on without government interference, he is talking nonsense. Free enterprise isn't free, and the world being what it is there isn't a chance of it being free.' My local paper is the *Ottawa Journal*. It is 'conservative'.

What we are seeing in the attack on propaganda today as a power in the hands of the state is a last reminder of the old point of view. It derives from the time when men regarded the state as only a necessary evil. Like the advocacy of free enterprise in its naïve form, it is no longer realistic. Let me add that the use of propaganda by the democratic state is exactly on a parallel with the 'government leadership' of Mr. Wallace and Mr. Lippmann's 'responsibility of the modern state' and my local paper's 'necessary government interference'. It is no closer to the totalitarian use of propaganda than subsidies, grants, low freight-rates and 'heaven knows what else' are to the Nazi system. It is, in fact, the concomitant of these departures into government leadership, for it represents the information system by which the government explains its directives and gives an account of the new stewardship which has, by democratic process, been thrust upon it.

Propaganda and Education

Of course, there are dangers in the government use of propaganda or information. There is the danger of a political head creating a public myth about himself, and the danger of a department concealing its incompetence, and the danger of a political party using the power of information to perpetuate its existence and thus thwart the democratic process. But these dangers can, by ordinary democratic watchfulness in press and parliament or congress, be avoided. They should not be used to blind people to the real nature of information as a necessary concomitant of government leadership. The possibility of abuse does not mean that proper uses cannot be allowed. In fact, they have for a long time been allowed and with the agreement of democratic institutions, simply because directives have had to be explained if they were to be effective and stewardship has had to be accounted for if it was to be understood and sanctioned.

The use of propaganda in time of war is spectacular and appears to many as a new aspect of government activity, and therefore possibly a passing one. This is not true. Government propaganda has never been challenged when it has been a question of propaganda for foreign markets or propaganda in support of a country's diplomacy. Even more importantly, it has never been seriously challenged when there was a true understanding of what propaganda should be. When it has proceeded on lines of explanation and elucidation and understanding, and when it has had the good sense to strike beyond party differences to the deeper loyalties of civic understanding and civic co-operation, parliaments and congresses have not failed to vote its funds and accept it for what it is: education in a world where the state is the instrument of the public's enterprise. Realistic observers of the nature and necessity of propaganda in the democratic state will find its constitutional authority tucked away in the files of tourist and children's and health bureaus, of trade and agriculture and labour departments, and of embassies and consulates the world over.

There is nothing new about it. It has developed hand in hand with the responsibilities of the state and has grown in direct proportion to the use of the state as a creative instrument of the community, operating as a whole to definite purposes. And it has tended, as it has found its democratic bearings, to become less and less the propaganda of legend and, more and more, part of that process of persuasion or education which is the tap-root of the democratic idea.

The chief problem of propaganda in a democracy does not lie, therefore, in proving its necessity, but rather in developing its wise and democratic use along the path of education. This, obviously, is of the utmost significance for the educational system. Government information has to deal with a wide range of materials which at every turn affect the terms of active citizenship. The educational system receives materials which are necessary to it and has, as an inevitable partner in the process, a great chance to mould the character, not only of the citizenry at large, but of the government's approach to them. By representing at many points local understanding and local participation, it has the power to affect the relationship between people and government in the profoundest and most democratic way.

Educators cannot, however, fill this role without a measure of self-examination. So far they have not fully realized the significance for themselves of the development of the state as the creative instrument of the community, nor seen that the development of government information must drastically affect them. Governments have raced ahead informing and explaining, exhorting and enlightening, in a thousand-and-one fields without the direct help or guidance of those whose native function in the state is to do these very things.

If I may say so, the educators have failed to realize their duty and their opportunity. One reason for this failure is that education is too little conceived as related to an active and participant citizenship. It is, some may think, 'away in the mind' and too much out of gear with the realities of today and tomorrow. But, I believe, the principal reason for failure is that education has not known how to absorb the vast and complex materials of civic observation and action today. Its analytic technique has been inadequate. I do not think education can assume the partnership in national information which I have outlined for it until its technique is revolutionized and fitted for the task not only of demonstrating the living terms of a living community, but of *realizing* them in action and by action. The secret of the relationship between propaganda and education in the future lies ultimately in this matter of technique, and it involves, I believe, a new consideration of the dramatic or interpretative factor in education. One cannot see propaganda become education, except it translate the materials of citizenship into terms which are capable of being grasped and which are inducive of action. On the other hand, one cannot see education conveying the duties of citizenship in a wide and complex world, except in terms of living patterns and on the level of the imagination.

Education might well have learned from its own experience. By tradition it has frowned on dramatic and interpretative methods and on the brilliant new instruments of dramatization and enlightenment which the generation has produced. It has stuck to its rational guns, and in its way it has been right. No one can disagree that the pursuit of truth is a prerequisite of understanding. No one can disagree about the need to emphasize mental disciplines in which the citizen contributes his own effort and character to the pattern of thought. Where the goodness has come unstuck is that the educational system has forgotten—in the name of these good things—to equip the citizen for the social realities in which the poor devil has had to participate. And it has avoided the imaginative and inspirational methods that would give the citizen a grip on reality, only to abandon them to the hands of others. It has as a result lost control of the real educational process and it has lost this control to the men who govern the newspapers films, radio, advertising and public information, few of whom have a licence to teach.

Not all of these men have been conscious propagandists, but all have had a propagandist effect by reason of the fact that they have used dramatic or inspirational methods. They have formulated story or pictorial or dramatic shapes. They have evaluated the good and the bad, the heroic and the unheroic, the exciting and unexciting, the desirable and undesirable. They have observed the things that interested people; they have researched into the patterns of report that commanded men's understanding, attention and desire. They have done so in the name of entertainment, news reporting, salesmanship and public instruction and, except in the case of public information, they have done it for profit. They have not always gone deep or sought to choose the most imaginative and socially valuable patterns, but they have, in fact, provided a system of evaluation for men's daily experience where such a system was lacking. They have consequently created loyalties and formed the pattern of men's thought and action. The headline has been as important in this matter as the editorial; the advertisement and the comic strip as important as the Hollywood epic. They have, to a large extent, taken charge of men's minds. The 'ordinary, everyday, imperceptible, elusive habit of millions', which Lenin called such a 'terrible force', is largely in their hands. It is, by contrast, not in the hands of educators.

The more progressive forces in education have long been aware of this situation. There has been increasing use of radio and the film for both juvenile and adult education; there has been much improvement in school-book techniques and in the use of illustrative material on school walls. The growth of contacts between school and community has been sought by bringing postmen and firemen and other representatives of community action to tell their stories to the children, and submit to their examination. The children themselves have been sent to explore their community and they have been encouraged in free discussion and civic debate. On the higher levels much has been done to pursue academic inquiry on location. But these developments are still piecemeal and somehow only 'progressive' and 'experimental'.

Back in the early twenties, Walter Lippmann presented a clear picture of the limitation of the educational approach which was based on 'knowing'. He pointed to the growing complexity of the modern world, its speeding communications and the national and international horizons of every economic and social problem. He drew the sad portrait of John Citizen, tired after the day's work, being asked to express his free and rational judgment on matters he could not possibly be equipped to judge. He charged that education was on the wrong lines if it thought to produce the all-knowing and rational John Citizen of the old-time liberal dream. He suggested that in barking up the tree of knowledge, education was barking up the wrong tree.

Others—A. D. Lindsay, for example—were concerned with the same criticism. But they confirmed John Citizen, however tired he might be, in his valuable role as judge of public events. They said a man might be a great expert but not have John Citizen's 'sense of smell'—meaning that John would know best where government regulations hurt him, know best how far a government could go which was to get his sanction and support. Moreover, the expert was not so good when it came to experience and common sense, and John Citizen had the role of providing that extra measure of essential wisdom to the community's judgment. There has been in consequence, in adult educational circles in the past generation, a valuable drive for public discussion involving as many John Citizens as possible. It has provided innumerable forums, locally and on the air, and they have been a useful supplement to the natural forums provided by village pubs and country stores, and to the functional forums provided by trade unions, chambers of commerce and service clubs.

Some of us thought at an early date that these forums did not themselves provide the material on which discussion could most usefully be based. We were afraid of Mr. Lindsay's discussion becoming discussion in a vacuum. We were conscious that discussion might not in itself lead to action, but might fall off into the dreary impotence of discussion for discussion's sake. In sad fact we saw discussion in the twenties—and it was to continue in the thirties—hide from men's eyes that essential picture of the time in which the great economic and political forces were climbing into place on the horizon.

Granton Trawler (British, 1934)
Produced by E.M.B. Film Unit: directed by John Grierson with Edgar Anstey

Windmill in Barbados (British, 1933)
Produced by E.M.B. Film Unit: directed by Basil Wright

Look to the North (Canadian, 1944)
  Directed by James Beveridge

   Both films produced by the National Film Board of Canada

Handle with Care (Canadian, 1943)
  Directed by Graham McInnes

Propaganda and Education

We thought that we could reveal that picture and would meet Mr. Lippmann's criticism by providing a shorthand method for world observation. There are, we said, basic dramatic patterns in the terms of civic relationship since all social problems are bound to involve a relationship between people and forces. Revelation of these dramatic patterns is a first essential in the process of modern education. For young people and adults alike require a broad and lively picture of their society to stir their imaginations and instil the loyalties necessary if they are to face up to its problems. In short, we felt that the dramatic pattern could convey a sense of growth and movement and opposition, provide a grip on reality and secure a sense of action regarding it.

I have myself been most closely associated with this theory of education. I can at least say that I have put it into successful practice; for it was out of these considerations and this theory that the documentary film movement arose. If I recall its origin and development, it is merely to illustrate with concrete example that the educational impasse can, in fact, be broken through.

The documentary film movement has been widely noted as representing a development in film technique and it has perhaps been too much thought of as a contribution to the art of the motion picture. Certainly some fine films have come from this business of observing reality and making beautiful or dramatic patterns from everyday observations, and some people are acquainted with Flaherty's *Moana*, Lorenz's *The River*, Basil Wright's *Song of Ceylon*, and with the deep drama based on actual observation in films like *Stalingrad* and *Desert Victory*. But the 'art' of documentary is, as always with art, only the by-product of an interpretation well and deeply done. Behind the documentary film from the first was a purpose, and it was the educational purpose with which we have been dealing. It was developed as a movement, and deliberately, to 'bring alive' to the citizen the world in which his citizenship lay, to 'bridge the gap' between the citizen and his community. These are, in fact, the phrases we first used about it in the late twenties. As events have turned out, the documentary film has succeeded in meeting the need of citizens in the school and elsewhere for a living description of their community; and this is the secret of its economy and of its importance.

The idea of documentary in its present form came originally not from the film people at all, but from the Political Science school in Chicago University round about the early twenties. It came because some of us noted Mr. Lippmann's argument closely and set ourselves to study what, constructively, we could do to fill the gap in educational

T

practice which he demonstrated. At first, I must confess, we did not think so much about film or about the radio. We were concerned with the influence of modern newspapers, and were highly admiring of the dramatic approach implicit in the journalism of William Randolph Hearst. Behind the sensationalizing of news we thought we recognized a deeper principle, and I think Henry Luce at very much the same time was recognizing it too. We thought, indeed, that even so complex a world as ours could be patterned for all to appreciate if we only got away from the servile accumulation of fact and struck for the story which held the facts in living organic relationship together.

It was Mr. Lippmann himself who turned this educational research in the direction of film. I talked to him one day of the labour involved in following the development of the yellow press through the evanescent drama of local politics. He mentioned that we would do better to follow the dramatic patterns of the film through the changing character of our time, and that the box-office records of success and failure were on file.

I took his advice and a young man called Walter Wanger opened the necessary files. A theory purely educational became thereby a theory involving the directive use of films. That directive use was based on two essential factors: the observation of the ordinary or the actual, and the discovery within the actual of the patterns which gave it significance for civic education.

I may say that we soon joined forces with men like Flaherty and Cavalcanti. They had been separately interested in this observation of the actual. They were concerned with the film patterns which went deeper than the newsreel and the scenic, and arrived perhaps at the idyll and the epic. The educators have never from that day altogether strait-jacketed the æsthetes in documentary, and it would be a loss if they ever succeeded; but it is the educators who have at all times held the economic secret of documentary film and have therefore been its masters as a 'movement' and as a developing force.

The battles within the documentary movement are all illustrative of this. They have lain between the politicians and the educators and between the æsthetes and the educators; but neither the politicians nor the æsthetes have succeeded or survived for long and they have tended to scatter to the wide winds of local and opportunist activity. It was the old economic story. It was in its educational interpretation and not in its political or æsthetic interpretation that the documentary film 'met a felt want' and was therefore financeable. The point is of great importance in presenting the documentary film as a fundamental contribution to government information and to educational theory alike. It was financeable because on the one hand it met the felt want of government for a colourful and dramatic medium which would interpret the information of state; and on the other hand it met the felt want among educators for a colourful and dramatic medium which would interpret the nature of the community. One provided the audience, the other the sponsorship; and the economic circle was complete from the beginning.

For fifteen years the validity of our educational analysis has had this important proof, that the documentary film, which was one of its results, has grown to the point where democratic governments are involved in the production of hundreds of documentary films a year, and the democratic educational systems are providing an audience of progressive millions for them. The scale and nature of this development are not to be estimated by the circulation of these films in theatres, though they have done very well in the theatres, and not least in the case of the *March of Time*, the *World in Action* and the films from Britain. Civic education certainly has been possible in theatres wherever the education has been made sufficiently entertaining. It has been helped by the fact that, in these troubled times, men have had problems of citizenship on their conscience even in their moments of relaxation. It has been helped by the fact that the film industry has come closer and closer to realizing its duty as not only an entertainment industry but also as a public utility. But in the theatres there are limits. The degree of civic conscience varies with classes and theatre types and with the sense of duty on the part of exhibitors. An industry based on mass entertainment has to be cautious. The most sensible have allowed twenty minutes of civic seriousness and let it go at that. They have observed that it takes a victory like North Africa, a star like Montgomery and the spectacle of immediate battle to impose further on the mood of relaxation.

This gives the theatre only a limited place in the educational picture. It is not the best proving-ground for those patterns of exposition which must of necessity be sometimes experimental. When we bring under observation new and stubborn materials—the seemingly desolate problems of housing and unemployment and health, for example—it is difficult at first to make them entertaining and to qualify them theatrically on the ground of either entertainment or inspiration. Happily there is more seating capacity outside theatres than there is inside them. Also happily, men are creatures of mood. The very people who are united in relaxation inside the theatres are otherwise united in

291

terms of their professional and specialized interest outside the theatres. It is in this latter field that the educational picture is filled out: in schools and colleges, in civic social services, trade unions and professional groups of all kinds. The access to the public thereby obtained is today colossal and growing at great speed in every country where governmental need for exposition is matched by the citizens' demand for it. The Canadian Government, to take an example from a country of eleven and a half million people, today maintains upwards of a hundred travelling theatres, moving from village to village and from factory to factory. Voluntary projection groups, trained by the Government, maintain services in the community halls of the cities. Repositories all across the country serve the schools and groups which have provided themselves with technical equipment.

But the scale of development is only interesting as proving the double argument: that what we once feared as 'propaganda' will no longer be feared if it is necessary education in the circumstances of our time; and that the educational system itself is reaching out and must inevitably reach further in the use of the dramatic media if it is to secure for the citizenry a true sense of their living relationship to events. What is true for films can also be true for radio and travelling exhibitions and for all the bright addenda to school walls, village halls, shop windows and factory notice-boards. They, too, are important media of the new education and waiting instruments of an enlivened democracy.

As to the nature of the service progressively provided by Government information and progressively welcomed by education, let me offer this guide. I take my illustration from what I have seen done in films, but it should be understood that the same sort of thing has happened wherever the radio, the pamphlet, the poster, the newspaper, the magazine and the exhibition have gone to the heart of the matter. We have all, without knowing it, been working progressively together, and have something to show for our labours. I knew the day when it was revolutionary to think of making 'peace as exciting as war', and I think I was among the first to hear an audience applaud the film appearance of industrial workers as though they were applauding the national flag. For there was a time when the ordinary was rejected as boring and when we were told firmly that people wanted to escape from the contemplation of their own lives and their own problems.

That obstacle was overcome. We put glistening patterns of vigour and skill and mass industrial achievement against the sky and men today accept them as part and parcel of the testament of beauty. We did so because governments wished to celebrate the essential terms of modern citizenship and because industrial corporations wished to celebrate their public utility. Behind agriculture we dramatized the desolation that comes with wasteful methods and with ignorance, and projected a new agriculture based on an affection for the soil and an understanding of its conservation and care. We did so because the soil was blowing away under the eyes of men, and governments had to do something to stop it and so had to make people understand its dreadful significance. I have seen a film on weather forecasting made which demonstrated, I always think miraculously, that men spatially distant and unknown to each other combine each day in great and co-operative dramas. The immediate reason for it was that a government wanted to prove the importance of a public service and hearten the men who operated it as a daily and pedestrian task.

Such efforts represent only the bare beginning of the educational activity of government as I have seen it develop. We have delved into social problems and tried to articulate the nature and the duty of citizens in regard to them. With the help of the ancillary information services of the public utilities, we are wise today about the problems of health and housing, nutrition and child welfare. We know more about economics because we have dramatized the dangers of inflation; and more about the place of the scientist because we have dramatized his contribution to medicine and agriculture and even to household economy. We know more about our international duty because we have all, at least imaginatively, flown in airplanes, crossed frontiers and seen our neighbours as ourselves.

Not all of this, of course, has happened out of the initiative of the governments' own information services. The free operation of the press, the radio and the film has also played a tremendous part. I am content to say that governments have not been able to avoid a vast and directive contribution to the educational process. They have not been able to avoid it because an imaginative participation of the people in the designs of the state has been progressively necessary to the successful execution of these designs.

Today, in a drive for an even greater degree of national unity and co-operation, we move into interesting new fields. The approach as ever is functional. Active participation is the end purpose. But we are less and less concerned with mere departmental information and more and more concerned with national information in the truest sense. As we face, let us say, the problem of absenteeism in industry, we find ourselves in a world of information which includes the conditions of

293

housing and health and transportation and infant welfare under which industrial workers operate. We see these things in a new light and together, not as matters to be merely sympathetic about, but as matters essential in an organized democratic economy. What was perhaps only a departmental worry becomes a matter of deeper concern, related clearly, for everyone to see, to the life of the nation.

So with any programme of information on conservation or reconstruction or, for that matter, of national unity or national morale. These easy concepts and easy words, when they are once broken down, bring us in full view of the social and political reality of our time, with all its problems and all its perspectives and all its hopes. We do not achieve an understanding of any one of them by splashing romantically, Hollywood fashion, through the braveries of battle or by dwelling in great self-righteousness on abstract issues of might and right, evil and good. One might successfully do it in a totalitarian state, though I doubt it; we certainly cannot do it in a democracy in which we still allow to a man the right to inquire where exactly his own particular local citizenship relates to the whole, the right of every man from Missouri 'to be shown'. If we are to persuade, we have to reveal; and we have to reveal in terms of reality. Recognizing this responsibility to the local and particular, recognizing the deeper levels of understanding and exposition into which information in a democracy must inevitably reach, it is possible to appreciate that even the once-haunted concept of propaganda may have a democratic interpretation, and that its democratic interpretation makes propaganda and education one.

4 The Library in an International World

The idea of every man a gentleman in a library, enjoying in a world of quiet and genteel leisure the grace notes of human thought was, of course, an attractive notion and it is easy to see why it should have caught the human imagination. With the new world of universal and equal opportunity opening before the people, why, indeed, should not everyone have the privilege of the *seigneur* and the squire, with access to the best the human mind could offer in poetry and art? So men dreamed. All that has been wrong with the dream is that so many things the idealists did not think of have come to disturb it. We have broken illiteracy over great areas of the world. We have published books without end, we have built universities by the thousands, and we have established libraries more universally than we could have hoped. But we have also somehow managed to develop bigger and more terrible wars.

Our passion for human enlightenment has been at least equalled by our passion for killing by the million the very people we enlightened.

Far be it from me to deny the old ideal which the libraries once set before us. It is proper that all men should have access to the best thought of the ages and be encouraged to know it. It is proper that men should have, if they can, the higher understanding of man and his nature, which only the great philosophers, prophets and poets can convey. 'The languages are necessary to the understanding of the writings of the ancients,' said Descartes in his *Discourse on Method.* 'The grace of fable stirs the mind and the memorable deeds of history elevate it. Eloquence has an incomparable force and beauty. Poesy has its ravishing graces and delights and Theology points the path to heaven. The perusal of all excellent books is, as it were, to interview with the noblest men of past ages who have written them and even a studied interview in which are discovered to us only their choicest thoughts.'

This is the strength of the old conception of enlightenment. The weakness of it I can best illustrate by referring to the village I come from. We were in part a mining village and in the years before World

295

War One and on until today, we were continuously involved in the economic dislocations of our time.

It seemed to some of us that even to press these larger matters of goodness, truth and beauty had an air of cynicism under the conditions which actually prevailed; and, while I would not deny the pursuit of goodness, truth and beauty, I have thought ever since that education in a vacuum and without reference to the immediate urgency of men's lives and men's problems can only be unreal and ineffective. If the people of my village can now look forward to better lives and better conditions of work, it is certainly not because of the ideals which education set before them. It is because they thought out their economic problems for themselves and because they organized and struck and fought and finally voted the conditions of their own future. If in this process, the school and the library were valuable to my fellow-citizens, and indeed they were, it was not on the high level of Platonic discussions, but on the simple, practical levels on which human hope was encouraged, human aspirations were confirmed and the nature of the modern world was taught. It was on the levels where men and women were equipped for the business of actually achieving their hopes and their aspirations.

I cannot apologize for mentioning this now far-away village of mine, because today its striving and its strife have spread to the whole wide world. The same active dissatisfaction with slums and conditions of labour and a dollar a day are the common possession of millions in the underprivileged parts of the earth. The same liability to economic dislocations and the same sense of gnawing insecurity have spread further still, for, as we have painfully discovered, the privileged, as well as the underprivileged, are liable to both.

All over the world we are faced today with the same old disturbing questions. Why is it that our educational methods seem so far away from the realities of the human struggle? Why is it that our educational ideals do not quite seem to fit in with the actual problems which engage men's minds? Whence the dreadful gap between our peaceful intentions and the warring conditions which actually prevail? Is the way of the books—or at least the way of the books alone—outdone and outdated? Is the ideal of a literary education now inadequate? And, finally, what must we do to add to our tools of education if we are to do the job which society expects of us?

The anxiety I have expressed about the educational problem is, of course, no special reaction of mine. In every responsible circle today of politics and education, the same note is being sounded. Only the

other day, the President of the United States put the matter as con-
cisely as anyone. Speaking at Fordham University, Mr. Truman used
these words:

'The new age of atomic energy presses upon us. Mark that well,'
he said. 'What might have been essential yesterday in international
understanding, is not sufficient today. New and terrible urgencies, new
and terrible responsibilities have been placed on education. Civilization
cannot survive an atomic war, for nothing would be left but a world
reduced to rubble. Gone would be man's hope for decency. Gone
would be our hope for the greatest age in the history of mankind—an
age which I know can harness atomic energy for the welfare of man
and not for his destruction.

'And so we must look to education to wipe out that ignorance which
threatens catastrophe.'

At this point the President quoted one of the last exhortations of
Mr. Roosevelt, part of a speech which he did not live to make. 'We
are faced with the pre-eminent fact that if civilization is to survive we
must cultivate a science of human relationships—the ability of all
people of all kinds to live and work together in the same world at
peace.'

'There is at least one defence against the atomic bomb,' Mr. Truman
added. 'It lies in our mastery of this science of human relationships
all over the world. It is the defence of tolerance, of understanding, of
intelligence and thoughtfulness. It is not an easy task. It is one which
places burdens without precedent both upon those who teach and
those who come to be taught. There must be new inspiration, new
meaning, new energies. There must be a rebirth of education if this
new and urgent task is to be met. All of our educational resources—
all, note you—must be pledged to this end.'

Certainly nothing ever before has brought home to us in so stagger-
ing a manner as the atomic bomb this deep relationship between the
urgency of events and the processes of public enlightenment. One is
of the other. If only for that reason, we may yet live to forgive the
dreadful revelation of Hiroshima. The atomic bomb is the writing on
the wall in letters of fire, warning us at once and for all to see, of both
our infinite strength and our infinite weakness as thinking beings.

By our ingenuity on the one hand we have been able to discover
and unleash a power of untold potential benefit to the human race.
One scientist says: 'We can now make anything out of anything or
nothing anywhere in the world in any amount, almost without
measurable cost.' Chancellor Hutchins calls up the bright picture of

a future under atomic energy in which 'distances and scarcity of fuel will cease to influence the location of industry and communities', a picture of new industries and new smokeless communities which can be created anywhere 'because the cost of transferring the material from which atomic energy is drawn is negligible'. As for the benefits to medicine and health, the scientists say that 'this discovery is for the biologist and the doctor as important as the invention of the micro-scope' and that 'we need never worry about the scarcity of radium again'.

Thus our ingenuity and strength as thinking beings, but what in this case have we done with them? Let me again quote Chancellor Hutchins: 'In this case, we elected to drop on the women and children of Japan, without warning, a new explosive against which they were utterly defenceless and which was utterly indiscriminate in its destructive power. A quarter of a million people were killed or injured by one bomb in one minute. Twenty-seven out of thirty-three fire stations were destroyed. Three-quarters of the firemen were casualties. The medical chief was killed, and his assistant was killed, and the assistant's assistant was killed. The Commanding General was killed and his *aide* was killed and his *aide's aide* was killed and his entire staff. Out of 298 doctors, only 30 were able to care for the wounded. Out of 2,400 nurses, only 600 could work. Only one hospital remained.'

There, in high relief, is our paradox, our strength and our weakness as thinking beings. It is also basically the problem which besets all of us in education today.

I shall attempt to analyse the nature of that problem and try to indicate where, as writers, artists, teachers and librarians we should go from here, if we are to meet President Roosevelt's challenge and mobilize all our educational resources, so that we can live and work together in the same world at peace. Complex and difficult as the task may be, I do not think we need despair of the ultimate result. As writers, artists, teachers, librarians, lecturers and leaders of discussion, we have a great power in the land, and, in the last resort, the greatest power on earth. It is we, in the long run, who can indicate and reveal the obsolescent ways of thought and combat them. It is we, in the last resort, who can point the way to the new patterns of thought and feeling which will make it possible to shape our strange new world in the moulds of harmonious action which are required of us.

What we are really seeing behind our problem of education today is the biggest burst of technological progress in the history of the world: a burst of technological progress which inevitably brings greater difficulties in mental accommodation than ever before. Aristotle said the natural community was the community which could gather within the range of a man's voice. But what is that today in a world of radio and films, in which all men are brought within each other's sight and hearing? Transport and communications have, indeed, made us all members of a single body politic; world trade has made us all members of a single body economic; and not only peace, but human welfare itself, is indivisible. But not least important is the fact that, by very reason of the new immediacy of communication and contact, all men everywhere of all colours and creeds expect today to share in the great wealth which machinery and mass production have unleashed, and to share, in a measure of equality, the social benefits which science and medicine have brought. This is not the least important development, for it is the root and basis of the troubles we see. Back of them all are eager hands of all colours and creeds reaching out for the benefits of man's ingenuity and skill; and it is no wonder at all that these hands are sometimes violent hands, that the new hopes clash with the old established interests and that ancient prejudices come between all of us and the appreciation of these new and inevitable stirrings across the world.

The solution for educators like ourselves will only unfold itself in action. We have, in the first place, to realize that the world will not right itself, that we have an *active* and *positive* role to play as educators, artists, writers and librarians. We must, indeed, absent us from felicity awhile and get out from behind our desks and institutions and make our various powers of enlightenment a dynamic force in our communities everywhere.

I hardly think that any one of us would wish to escape from the educational crusade to which we are called, in which the end is the internationalization of men's minds and the raw materials of our task are the common interests of humanity. These common interests are in themselves good to the spirit and lively to the imagination. All of us remember the flashing power of President Roosevelt's oration on Freedom of Speech, Freedom of Religion, Freedom from Want and Freedom from Fear. And all of us remember with what unanimity the peoples of the world hailed it as though together they were seeing a common vision. In the inspiration of such a vision we are the more ready and willing to face the daily job and hammer away at the local tasks which in solid and determinable fact lead to the achievement of Freedom of Speech and Religion and lead to an economic and spiritual security for all.

A further blessing is that we shall find good will everywhere. Whatever the pessimist may say, there are people everywhere eagerly reaching out for the books and the films and the radio programmes and the discussions and the mental leadership generally which will inspiringly direct their thought to the duties of citizenship in an international world at peace. As Albert Guerard reminded us the other day, the masses may be confused in their minds, but they are not confused in their feelings. They hate war and they hate oppression and they hate injustice. It is on this we can count and it is on this we can work.

We can work, too, on the fact that all men everywhere of every colour and creed are alike in the essentials of their interest. If we educators would only get off the sky and down to earth, we would realize that the people everywhere are not full of differences, but full of similarities, and, in fact, have the same basic wants and desires: to eat, to have shelter, to have homes and families and health and the friendly association of neighbours. The first charge to us all is to become more active about our educational tasks in the community; the second charge is to become more simple and more elemental about the interests which hold man together, for it is only in that way we can discover a common international language and speak across the prejudices and the distrusts which now separate peoples, nations and races.

I say this in spite of all the ideologies which now clamour for the attention and the loyalty of the millions. I am all for systems of ideals and I am all for systems of doctrine. They do help in their stolid, strait-jacketed, clumsy and slightly illiterate way to satisfy man's hunger for belief and for the spirit of confidence which attends an illusion of certainty. I like to think of Descartes's definition of philosophy, and he was no mean philosopher himself, as 'the art which affords the means of discoursing on all matters with an appearance of truth and commands the admiration of the more simple'. The admiration of the more simple is a necessary instrument of education, but when the philosophies and ideologies become actually dangerous—and they sometimes do—I withdraw my loyalty. I say a plague on ideologies, all of them, if they obscure the common nature of man's interests in food and shelter and homes and families and the good life and drive man on in hatred to mutual destruction. If they serve these common interests, they are good; and that is the measure of them and that is the only measure of them.

At all costs, let us not be bewildered by the madmen who say that this way of life or that is so exclusively noble that none other may be allowed. In an atomic war, it will be no great comfort—except in such few lunatic asylums as may remain—to say that because we wanted to save civilization we, therefore, enthusiastically destroyed it. Let us, in fact, add the conception of universal tolerance as not merely a visionary virtue, but as a necessary law and a necessary discipline for every moment of our lives.

There is, of course, one principal issue on which we shall be continuously tested in our attempt to teach and maintain tolerance; and that is the apparent clash between the ideological force of liberal democracy emanating from the United States and the ideological force of international socialism emanating now principally from the Soviet Union, but increasingly from other countries, too.

It is true that Russia has political views which many millions in the world, and particularly on this continent, do not share. Nevertheless, we must find what meeting ground we can and there is more than many people, in the first burst of prejudice, suppose. Russia is dedicated in its own way, just as the Catholic Church is, just as the liberal democracy of North America is, to the higher interests of mankind. It is as fervent as America in the exploitation of the earth's resources and of science for the betterment of the conditions of life. Its theory and its practice in the matter of inter-racial relations are of a kind which everyone amongst us who believes in the basic equality of men must warmly welcome.

It is true that in the discussion of ways and means we differ greatly. The Russians say that political freedom is an illusion if men starve. We, on the other hand, say that economic welfare is an illusion if men are not free. Ironically, both sides to the argument have a part of the truth and we are approaching the same ideal from different directions. There is no reason in philosophy why we cannot establish a common understanding in the conception that true freedom involves at once the right to seek men's highest ends and the economic capacity to do so.

What is intolerable is that each of us should deny the other's claim to truth, and, standing off from each other, create the no-man's-land of political discussion which now exists. The existence of this no-man's-land today is not only rotting our minds, but sending us off into thoughts and actions which are not only mentally stupid, but physically dangerous.

Mr. Roosevelt's words and Mr. Truman's words are spoken into the thin and futile air and there will be none of that science of human relationships which is to save mankind, if we frustrate and stifle the generous thoughts of our youth or by any action of Church or State bar them from the fullest knowledge of the ideas operating in the world today, whether they come from Russia, Rome or George Bernard Shaw.

The libraries all across the continent have an especially powerful position: they are rooted in the communities of the country. They are part and parcel of the life of the small towns and the cities and the universities. They are at the heart of the matter. In our film world we certainly command vast audiences and even the simplest film address we choose to make can look to an audience of scores of millions. But some of us have not been deceived by the illusion of power these great audiences bring. If I may cite the example of Canada in the film world, we have in these past years sought to relate our films ever more closely to the local interests of local people. We have attempted to develop the directness of approach to the educational problem which I have been urging. We have struggled, therefore, to bridge the gap between the child and the community and between the citizen and the world community, by beginning our explanations of national and world affairs on the doorstep of men's actual local interests.

Today the great drive is to make films which will help rural communities to solve their rural problems and see the actual relationship between their rural problems and the wider world without. And so similarly with the industrial communities we are trying to relate the immediate problems of labour management relationship, town planning and regional planning, nutrition, health and community living with the same issues as they present themselves in other parts of the globe.

In one matter, we are very particular: we do not believe in the general public quite so naïvely as the salesmen and the advertisers seem to do. We see the so-called general public as divided up into a thousand and one publics of specialized interests: people interested and active in rural libraries, rural community halls and rural planning; people interested in the active and actual achievement of higher standards of nutrition and child welfare and public health; people actually and actively interested in town planning and regional planning; people actually and actively interested in the elimination of prejudice and the development of inter-cultural relations. I mention these, but, of course, librarians, above all people, will best know how to fill out the list, for they are great specialists in specializations. What I stress is that we have tried to convert the problems of education into the terms of men's actual and active interests, that we have striven to take education out of the clouds and bring it to the groups from whom action and the propagation of ideas can be expected. These must inevitably be the growing points of an activist system of education.

In so doing, we have tended more and more to move out from the capital and the big cities to join hands with the community organizations. That is what the development of the non-theatrical film actually signifies. Progressively we have found that our main work of public enlightenment is in co-operation and alliance with the local schools and universities, the local women's groups, the local business groups, the local farmers' groups and the co-operatives and trade unions. Inevitably we have come face to face with the librarians across the country and have found them the natural community centres of enlightenment in a democratic society. But we have wondered sometimes why they were not with us as we decentralized our systems of information and built our local circulations and developed our forums of public discussion. I have wondered often why they are not in fact the heart and soul of the whole effort. And not just in the matter of the circulation of film, but also in the discussive development of radio, the circulation of prints and wall newspapers and all the other vital forces of enlightenment today. I cannot, in fact, think of any greater, more widespread, more penetrating or more co-ordinate and effective voice in the country today than the libraries of the country, active and mobilized, and in full possession of all the modern powers of illumination and enlightenment.

The old library outlook is over and done with. It served its day, and, indeed, the spread of popular education which the schools and the libraries have effected has been one of the initial forces making for the great upsurge of human effort which it has been our exciting privilege in this generation to witness. But the new problems involve new methods. I suggest that if libraries do not adopt these methods the essential job of popular education to which they once enthusiastically dedicated themselves will pass on to others; and it may well pass to people who have perhaps a less profound tradition of public service and a less unselfish conception of community interest. That today is one of the greatest dangers which confronts us. I do not say that the day of books is over, but the day of the books only is certainly over. It is not information that is needed today; in fact, it is not information that is sought. It is enlightenment, and that is a very different thing, involving, as it does, the dramatic process of sparking the mind and the heart into new hope, new vision, new realization and new efforts in citizenship.

From the beginning it was never the amount of it, but rather the manner of it that counted, and it is to the manner of it that we ought now to address ourselves. I shall put it shortly by saying that the complex of information today is so great that we have at all costs to present it in a form which can, in fact, be absorbed. Information in itself is cold stuff. Information of distant peoples and distant problems is particularly cold. It has to be brought alive and it has, in the last instance, to be brought home.

We ought today to be grateful for one especial gift which the technological revolution has brought us. It may have faced us with difficult issues in education, but it has also blessedly handed us the new tools for their solution. We have in radio, in film, in television and travelling exhibits and in the infinitely cheap reproduction of news-sheets, paintings, posters, pamphlets, books and wall newspapers, vital new media by which the world can be elucidated and brought to our understanding. Everywhere we are mastering new techniques of illustration, presentation and display. Everywhere we are discovering new ways of putting the issues of our complex world into the dramatic forms which people can quickly grasp. That is what 'bringing alive' means in the educational process. No longer think that the work is done if the information is made available or even conveyed. The work is not done until we spark the gap between the citizen and the world of his citizenship, bring into his imagination the great and beneficent struggle of men which we see today and finally secure his creative participation in that struggle.

To this end I would suggest six principles of educational policy.

The first is that we must internationalize the minds of men if we are to live in an international world and that we must dispose men to co-operation in a world where co-operation is the price of civilization and even of survival.

The second principle is that we cannot do this without an active and dynamic policy: that, indeed, we must all, writers, artists, teachers and librarians, get out into the hard but constructive business of directive leadership in the community.

The third principle is that we must strive for simplicity and an understanding of the elemental interests which unify all men and represent the only international language which is possible.

The fourth is that we must create a spirit of tolerance at all costs, even if we have to sacrifice the luxury of old loyalties and old beliefs.

The fifth principle is that we must bring education home and convert the complex issues of the world into the terms of local interest on the farm, in the factory, in the family, in the schools, in the universities, in the co-operatives, the trade unions, the women's groups, the service clubs and the churches.

And lastly, we must make of information and education a dramatic process of enlightenment and bring to the stubborn fact a measure of imagination and inspiration. We must, indeed, bring into our use all the bright new media and techniques which lie now in our hand in an ingenious and amazing world of new illuminations and new skills.

Part VI

FUTURE FOR DOCUMENTARY

During the decade and a half of documentary's growth, Grierson has been continually extending the scope of the movement and adding to its responsibilities. Latterly he has seen the film as a vital medium of international communication and his departure from the Canadian Film Board where, in the *World in Action* series, he had begun to realize this aim, gave him the wider freedom he sought in order to develop a world circulation of films on international affairs. The essays in this section set forth this conception of documentary's role in the post-war world. In particular Grierson argues that the International Labour Office should take a lead in developing the exchange between countries of documentary material describing their common interests.

F. H.

1 Films and the I.L.O.

It is important that the I.L.O., beginning to face hopefully towards the future, should consider this medium of mass education. If the interests, principles and causes for which the I.L.O. stands are to grow, it must inevitably concern itself with mass education. It must, in particular, be interested in the capacity of the film for exchanging living, visible records as between its member nations.

The I.L.O. is concerned with working standards and working relationships and we have all been learning over the years how wide and deep this interest goes. The war period, especially, has provided a revelation of how the quantitative achievements of industry are completely dependent on the conditions under which industry is carried on, how war efforts of every kind involve close consideration of the social structure which supports them. The war period has, not least, brought a revelation of this relationship to the people concerned with war information and industrial morale.

Not all of them, I am sorry to say, have appreciated the humanistic terms under which the work of men's hands is secured. In spite of the experience of the I.L.O. over the years, the worst mistakes were made from the beginning. First we had the 'patriotism is enough' period— the 'my country right or wrong' period. To integrate the workers' front with the soldiers' front, we thought it sufficient to call up the sacred images of the tribe and the nation. The flags flew, the bands blared. The lights of common sense were dimmed; spotlit, our national banners fluttered in an artificial breeze. Then we had the 'black and white' period. We built up the Nazis as the children of darkness and ourselves as the children of light. We asserted our way of life as the best in the best of all possible worlds. Forgetting the dark thirties, we assumed an affectionate and even fervent belief in the *status quo*. Then we had the 'finger of scorn' period when we bullied the workers from factory platforms, telling them how they were killing soldiers and sinking ships and letting down the war effort if they so much as cast a critical eye over wages and working conditions in time of war.

We had to come sooner or later to a more realistic conception of our information to industry. We discovered that absenteeism might have a great deal to do with local transport conditions or local health conditions or local housing conditions. We discovered that the employment of women involved a consideration of crèches and communal kitchens, and even a consideration of the opening hours of beauty parlours. We discovered that there was a basis in reason—local reason —yes, even for the attitudes and actions of the people. With any true sense of democracy we should have known it from the beginning.

That was not all. We discovered that the co-operation of the workers in any effort, national or otherwise, is dependent on the amenities which surround not only their lives inside the factory but their lives outside it. We discovered that the degree of their participation depends on the degree to which, as free men, they are allowed to participate in the understanding, direction and management of their own work and their own destiny. We discovered, finally, that all the patriotic ballyhoo, all the generalizations about black and white, all the exhortations, abuses and threats are not so important or so basic as a credible pledge, implemented in action, that the war is for the sake of the common people everywhere, and nothing if not that.

The fact that these big mistakes have been so deeply made everywhere in our approach to industry is in part due to the failure of the I.L.O. to tell the world what it knew. It acquired this knowledge laboriously and skilfully over the years, but, if I may say so, its system of conveying it on a world-wide scale was inadequate. In my view, that is a failure of the deepest significance which cannot be allowed to happen again. If the I.L.O. is pledged to the improvement of working standards and working conditions throughout the world, it is of necessity pledged to the duty of world education in the matter of standards and conditions. If the sociology of industry is simply the other and complementary aspect of its technology, it is pledged to the duty of securing a better and wider understanding of all that the sociology of industry implies.

I may say that I have some right to say this to I.L.O. representatives. Some years ago an American writer, Ernestine Evans, came to me in London with an idea. I have had the fortune to hear a lot of good ideas for the constructive and educational use of films in the public interest, but this seemed to me one of the very brightest. She said: 'The I.L.O. has some fifty member nations. They are interested in working conditions all over the globe: in health, housing, child welfare, nutrition, co-operatives, and all the amenities of the workers' leisure. Can't you see this is the first basis we have ever been offered for a world

Films and the I.L.O.

educational system dealing with the things that most deeply concern people everywhere in the world.

'It would be easy to organize,' she continued. 'If Britain represents, let us say, the highest standard of safety in mines, let us make a film record of it for all the mining nations to see and let it pass out to the world through the agency of the I.L.O. If Sweden has the best system of hospital service, or New Zealand the highest standard of pre-natal care, or France the best service of medical information to farmers, let the record of them go out to all the other countries for their consideration and benefit. It is only a question of using the I.L.O. as a world centre. Let it encourage the various countries to produce those film records which by their example will best contribute to the common interest. Let it plan, let it co-ordinate, let it make suggestions, let it circulate the records which the many nations under its inspiration contribute to the common pool.'

The possibilities of Miss Evans's suggestion seemed to me enormous. They seemed all the more enormous when I realized that no country worth its salt would want to hide its light under a bushel, that no country could afford to be out of a scheme like this, once it was initiated. With my colleague, Basil Wright, we worked out this scheme and took it to Geneva. I even crossed the Atlantic to bring it to the Rockefeller Foundation. It involves, as you can see, hardly any problem of finance when you are concerned with fifty partners, each with a native and national interest in demonstrating to the world his special contribution to the social wealth of nations.

I will say for both the I.L.O. and the Rockefeller Foundation that they took our scheme seriously. Mr. Butler did, Mr. Fosdick did; and only recently Mr. Winant was regretting to me the ill fortune which attended it. In all cases the answer was the same—and it had, of necessity, to be: the sands of peace are running out. Now that they man be running in again, I hope I may be pardoned for taking it from the old pigeonhole. This time, however, I pull it out not just hopefully, but with every confidence that it is of the logic of the I.L.O. and is therefore inevitable. Anyway, it is the I.L.O.'s for the taking and there isn't one of us concerned with documentary films or with film education in the various countries of the world who will not willingly stir our countries into participation.

If the I.L.O. is the international centre for the discussion and improvement of labour affairs, all its conferences, all those brilliant studies and publication of studies which it did between the wars, are not enough. Sooner or later its educational processes must come down

311

to earth, and it must be very local earth. I do not think this is a difficult matter. We have the instruments and we are slowly acquiring
the techniques of mass information and mass education, even when
they concern the difficult and complex fields of international relationship.

Basically, the ends we seek are simple ends, and they are identical
ends. In spite of all the talk of ethnical and cultural differences which
now beclouds the sky, the ends men seek are identical and simple and
concrete, whether they come black, white or yellow. They concern food
and health and housing and the other highly visible evidences of the
good life. I have no doubt that when these are fought for and secured,
the invisible aspects of the good life—whatever these may be—will
come to inhabit the edifice we have built. In the meantime, it is in the
fulfilment of actual and visible human needs that we shall find the
basis of a common philosophy and, if I may say so, the only one which
the peoples of the world will any longer trust. In this progressive
struggle for welfare which is actual, we all need the example of other
countries, the example of other peoples' genius, other peoples' ingenuity and other peoples' good fortune. This example of others is a
weapon in our hands, wherever we may be, with which to intensify
the educational effort in our own domain.

We have heard a good deal about the indivisibility of this and that,
but in nothing is the world so remarkably indivisible as in the actual
interests of the people who populate it. If I talk films and education,
I can meet my kind everywhere from China to Peru, and cease in that
regard to be an alien anywhere. One finds it easy to say, in the city of
Philadelphia, that the world public consists of so many societies of
friends. The bonds of human interest are international, on every level
from stamp collecting to learned societies. There is an internationale
of interest in medicine and town planning and agricultural research,
and in each of the thousand and one specialized fields of human effort.
From this point of view there is no such thing as a general public,
nationally or internationally. There are thousands of publics, all trying
to do something about something. The only time they all get together
and become 'general' is when they get tired of doing things, and lazy
and lackadaisical and want to get off the earth. The trouble is that
we have organized the people brilliantly in their moods of relaxation.
We have organized them in the movies and the dope sheets of the
sensational press and the dance halls of the nations. But we have not,
with anything like the same intensity or deliberation, organized the
people in their moods of resolution. We have not, with anything like

the same adequacy, sufficiently fed them in the terms of their constructive and creative interests.

As an example of what I have described as the internationales of interest, let me cite the case of a little film we once made on philately. The late Sir Kingsley Wood, when he was Postmaster-General, asked me to have it made in celebration of King George's coronation. I was not very interested, but just to give it some kind of lift I asked the director to go down to Buckingham Palace and shoot some pictures in colour of the Royal stamp collection, which they told me was one of the great collections of the world. After that, and to my astonishment, nothing could stop the circulation of the film. The philatelists of England were so eager to get at it that they practically tore my place apart. They ran a special issue of their philatelic journal to celebrate it. They hailed me as some kind of world benefactor, and this humble little film as a new high in the art of the motion picture. Then they took it to the International Congress of Philatelists in Boston, and from a national philatelic sensation it became an international one. We discovered for the first time that this strange breed spread to the ends of the earth; that there were stamp collectors in Siam and philatelists in Patagonia. For years we sent copies all over the globe, and for all I know they are running yet.

This example, simple as it is, demonstrates how widely the national examples in which the I.L.O. is interested can be spread throughout the world. One of the great discoveries in the history of film was the simple discovery that there is more seating capacity outside the film theatres than there is inside them. It is today exercising a revolutionary influence on film development. Those of us who are dealing seriously with films as an instrument of public education no longer think of the theatres as providing our principal platform. We are going out into the highways and the byways, not depending on people's interest in entertainment, but depending on their interest in their work and in their citizenship.

Speaking for Canada, we are today building this audience outside the theatres on an intensive and even scientific scale. Like the United States, we have libraries of films all over the country, available to every social, education, professional and service group which either wants them or can be persuaded to want them. We have voluntary projection services, organized in the big towns to provide projection. They are trained by the government and give their services as a private contribution to the community welfare. We have travelling theatres, maintained by federal and provincial authorities, trade unions, co-

313

operatives and national associations. They move from village to village and town to town, on schedule. Some of them play the rural schools and the village halls, and address rural audiences in terms of the special interests which rural audiences have. Others move from town to town, playing the factories, in and out of working hours. Presently, we hope to develop other such specialized services to women's groups and others, and we look forward to the building of community halls throughout the nation in which projection services are an essential part of the life of every community.

We find these audiences very practical in their demands. We do not get the picture of a public bent to the last button on entertainment and escape. On the other hand, the picture which comes to us is of a people who are hungry for a knowledge of the future, for a chance to understand what is in the making, and how they can best participate in it: not only as to its benefits, but as to its duties. Discussion clubs and forums have grown up spontaneously with our film showings, particularly among the rural people. They demand their own teaching notes, their own discussion notes and their own specialized journals of information. The people as we know them want film materials which will help them in their actual and present citizenship: films about farming and farming research, about housing and community halls, about credit unions and co-operatives, about a world which is organically related to their own interests and their own functions within the nation.

As this movement grows—and it is growing far faster than we can keep up with it—there will be room for all the educational materials which organizations like U.N.R.R.A. and the I.L.O. care to turn out. The people want, very especially, such materials. They are no longer interested in dreams of the future, but in all the news we can give them of how it is in fact being organized. I admit that in Canada we have the advantage of a liberal-spirited and imaginative régime—it is certainly the most imaginative I have had the fortune to serve—but what we are presently encouraged to pioneer and develop in Canada must, I think, inevitably be developed on very similar lines in other countries. The demand for the materials of an organic, civic understanding is in the nature of our time. It is only a question of organizing supply and organizing it from such institutions of vital interest as the I.L.O.

I shall conclude with a somewhat abrupt generalization. I shall not argue it but assert it for what it is worth. The source of vital education today is no longer the formal educational system. It resides rather in functional international organizations like U.N.R.R.A. and the I.L.O.,

Films and the I.L.O.

and in functional national organizations which are actively concerned in developing the welfare of the people. I doubt if the people any longer put their hope in formal education, and for the good reason that it is not associated with their actual needs. There are brave exceptions, I know; but, by and large, education has been so anxious to avoid political difficulty that it has steered away from those needs which produce political expression and therefore produce political difficulty. It has come to teach the techniques of understanding but not the substance of it. It gives technical skills but not the sense of a living and organic social participation.

Back of its weakness today lies the fact which our industrial and rural audiences have so illumined for us. However wide and deep the political strategies of the world may develop, they begin for a farmer or an industrial worker in *his* job and *his* community and *his* immediate sense of interest. The only system of education in which he is going to be interested is the one which associates itself directly with *his* job, *his* community and *his* sense of interest. If we ever again sit in our capitals and throw at him those old abstractions about international co-operation and the League of Nations which so pleased our intelligentsia in the twenties and thirties, we shall deserve all the isolationism we shall certainly get. The farmer or the industrial worker is not just being selfish or materialistic or parochial. He is being sensible. If international co-operation—if the war, even—does not, apparently and for all to see, mean anything to his destiny and to the destiny of all who are like him in the world, he has good reason to be sceptical. If his leaders have not enough sense to appreciate that he can only understand in the living terms of his actual and local understanding, he has the right to doubt the realism of their ideas and their capacity for representing his interests.

That is the danger which we are all running today with our U.N.R.R.A.'s and our I.L.O.'s and our more national dreams of progress. The dreams are complex and difficult to articulate and we all, somewhat naturally, get tied up with our colleagues in esoteric worlds of discourse. In the years between the wars we lost contact with the people; and the progressive forces lost contact as much as any. We forgot to relate our thoughts and endeavours to what the people were thinking and trying to secure. I am not sure that we did not finish up in our own ivory towers, not remembering the people at all.

Anyway, I am going to say that if we are to develop international co-operation we have got to develop education in internationalism, and that it begins on the local doorstep. What people want to know

315

today is where they get off. They want to know what the fancy notions mean in terms of the homes they will live in, the bread they will eat, and the families they will raise, and they are right. This represents an enormous opportunity for organizations like the I.L.O. because the I.L.O. has within its field of interest the practical materials for the education the people want. It presents an enormous opportunity to governments also. Because they are interested in political pressures, they are interested in the actual needs which these pressures represent. For my part, I prefer to follow Aristotle. I would sooner trust a system of education that derives from political authority, because it derives from human needs, than a system of education which comes off the sky. Education has no more claim to operate by divine right than any other social institution.

To complete my abrupt generalization I shall say that if the education of the next generation does not come from functional international organizations like the I.L.O. and U.N.R.R.A., and from functional organizations like our various government departments of health and welfare, reconstruction, labour and agriculture, it is not coming from anywhere; and that twenty years from now we shall be back in Philadelphia setting up the I.L.O. all over again.

2 The Challenge of Peace

I do not think there is much use discussing what to do with a medium unless we are talking about it in terms of access to the means of production. I think it vain to write unless there is power of publication. I think it vain to talk about films unless there is power of production and distribution. I think it vain to paint unless the presentation of painting is at the same time organized and secured. I dismiss as out-of-date and ridiculous a position in which the creative worker lives in the hope that the blue eyes of his personal talent will serve him; and I think it possible to suggest that there is hardly a body of workers today so poorly organized for the modern world or so impotent in securing the right to work, and particularly the right to give of their best to society, as the creative workers of the western democracies.

The key to the creative worker's position and strength is of course that he should first and foremost understand the nature of the problem which society at this specific moment imposes upon him and that he should not only align himself with the forces that are shaping tomorrow but himself add his measure of creative leadership to them.

Certainly your creative worker has an astounding world to look out upon. We have just finished a brutal war and are entering upon a phase of rehabilitation and reconstruction involving not only our own country but every country in the world. This new phase calls for the very highest order of heart and mind and the workers in every medium have at this moment a crucial contribution to make to the progress of mankind. In my own lifetime and experience I have seen little else but war, and I think that by this time we know the basic nature of its perverse continuity. The wars of 1914 and of 1939 are only vicious episodes in a much longer struggle in which under-privileged nations and under-privileged races and classes have fought desperately for a share of the world's goods and the decencies of life. They have fought wisely and fought disastrously, followed good leaders and bad, but we do not see the reality of our time unless we see the class wars and the race wars and the national wars—China, India, Spain, Germany, Russia, Italy and Greece, all those dramatic images of our own ex-

317

perience—as manifestations, varying and various, of the single basic struggle for a more equitable distribution of the good life.

The irony of it is that the struggle has intensified and become more horrifying in direct proportion to the advance of technical knowledge and our capacity to provide a good life for all mankind. Today the situation is temporarily lightened by the defeat of Germany and Japan. We have eliminated a powerful but false leadership of the world's revolutionary forces: false, because it sought to make the world's goods exclusive. But we have still to prove that we can substitute a true leadership for that false one, and until we do so peace will have no reality. This is of all moments in our generation the most testing one. The issue was not so sharply drawn after the last war, for the peoples then had not so widely revolted and the challenge to new ways of thinking was not so desperate. But then, too, we had an opportunity to give a new deal to common people the world over. We of the rich and powerful and so-called enlightened western democracies did not do it, and the chaos of today is the measure of our failure.

It is against that picture and that problem, I believe, that all creative workers must operate and I should add that the occasion is too urgent and too concrete for the sweet abstractions on which man has founded his faith in the years gone by. Freedom is only a word till you make men free, democracy only a word till men have actual enjoyment of rights. Goodness, truth and beauty are no longer just abstractions but actualities which today men demand with guns in their hands, and actualities they properly translate into the terms of food and houses and a right to live.

I am afraid that my interest in films is limited to what they can do in and for this particular situation. If I have any complaint against the film industry, it is that it has done less than it might. It did much at a crucial juncture to mobilize the anti-fascist forces in America but, on the whole, it has not devoted the time and energy to international observation or even to national observation, which its vast international market and its great power in its own nation would seem to warrant. For a medium not given to diffidence it has been unusually diffident in assuming the great public responsibility which is its to command. Its newsreels could have been more influential and so too could have been all those short films which in one way or another observe and comment on the passing scene. As for the big films, the last thing in the world I would ask of them is that they should all be socially significant. They would be a colossal bore if they were. One can, however, reasonably ask that they should, in the patterns of their drama, reflect something of the reality of our time. I leave it to the psychological experts to say if they do. I shall only say, for my part, that I doubt if the individual destiny is quite so important and the public destiny quite so unimportant as Hollywood would make them appear. I would say, just to be simple about it, that a technological society is necessarily an inter-dependent and co-operative society, and that the patterns of its drama must inevitably become patterns of inter-dependence and co-operation.

I am not going to pretend that I know better than anyone else what the documentary future is going to be and I am certainly not going to announce the horoscope of the various producers and distributors who are today concerned with this branch of film work. On the other hand it may be valuable to indicate the principles which are bound to govern the development of documentary in the future.

The documentary film has made great strides during the past fifteen years as an art form and as a public service. In Britain today upwards of thirty production units are concerned with this kind of production. Their films are in great and growing demand by the government and also by provincial and civic authorities as well as by the more important public utilities and corporations.

I emphasize the sponsors of documentary films first, because it is of first importance to see where the economy of documentary lies. In the case of governments, there has been a growing realization that the complexities of modern administration involve necessarily a new understanding by the people. Any medium which can help government to give an account of its stewardship, elucidate its legislation or otherwise help to provide a background of civic understanding is very precious to governments today. It will be more and more precious as governments are called upon for more initiative. This is not a matter in which the political viewpoint makes any difference. By the very nature of the growth of our technological society, all governments alike are involved in problems of co-ordination and management involving not only national but also international relationships.

It is in the logic of the situation that you cannot ask governments to co-ordinate or manage without giving them the right to explain or otherwise seek and secure the co-operation of the citizen whence, as we have seen, in every country, the growth of government information services of one kind or another. It is true that these services of information are frequently challenged and particularly in the United States. But they appear to be challenged only when there is suspicion of the administration seeking partisan advantage. These information services are not challenged when they are associated with, say, progressive agriculture or when they are associated with the promotion of international trade and the support of international diplomacy. So far from being challenged, the government information services are warmly applauded when and where they relate to the reporting and better understanding of civic duties associated with recognized public need.

It is not too early to conclude that government information services are natural and necessary to modern government, that they are bound to increase as governments learn to dissociate them from political partisanship and that they are bound to provide one of the most important sponsorships for all those arts which are interested in public observation and the education of the public.

It is worth noting that the documentary film has acquired in some countries a very special relationship to this development of government information. In both Britain and Canada more money possibly is devoted to this branch of information than to any other. It may be that the documentary people in both cases have been especially persuasive but there are good reasons for the relationship. From the very first the documentary people in these countries have taken the view that the first duty of their art was to the public service. They have constantly asserted that they were public workers first and creative workers not the less for that. They accordingly fitted into the public service to the point of becoming professionals, experts many of them in the forms and problems associated with government administration.

The nature of their medium has, of course, helped them greatly. It enjoys the possibility of mass circulation but also enjoys in 16-mm. size the possibility of highly specialized and highly scientific circulation. It has the special capacity of dramatizing the fact of the matter and having an air of authority. In particular, it has the power of putting in comprehensible pattern the complex inter-relationships of the public service.

Whether the governments produce their films directly or indirectly— and there is no reason whatsoever for direct production if suitable outside production units are available and a creative relationship can be struck up between government experts and production experts—I think it inevitable that governments will provide a large mass of documentary films in the future, covering every aspect of the government's interests and therefore very many aspects of the citizens' interest. We now see only the bare beginning of the government's approach to participation in the directive education of the citizenry in all matters of social and economic concern.

Wartime Housing (Canadian, 1944)
  Directed by Stanley Jackson

  Both films produced by the National Film Board of Canada

Hands for the Harvest (Canadian, 1944)
  Directed by Stanley Jackson

Trans-Canada Express (Canadian, 1944)
  Directed by Sydney Newman

    Both films produced by the National Film Board of Canada

Coal for Canada (Canadian, 1944)
  Directed by Leslie McFarland

The Challenge of Peace

I said it was best to begin with the sponsors because it is as well to know where the economy of documentary lies. Partly because of the early British example, we have got accustomed to think of governments as the most important sponsors but, although I am a government official and have spent most of my life developing government sponsorship of the documentary film, I doubt if public governments will be more important in the immediate future than those private governments which Beardsley Ruml talks about in *Tomorrow's Business*. I am thinking particularly of the documentary potential of the next ten years or so. I would guess that some of the best and most valuable sponsorship will come from city councils and state governments, from national and trade associations, from the trade unions, as well as from the big corporations and public utilities. It is the custom, particularly in the United States, to consider dangerous the educational materials emanating from corporate groups. Danger of course there is, but none that cannot be guarded against, at least in the field of technological description. Good film producers who have the concept of public service in their imaginations should always be able to direct the path of these films along constructive lines. The work of the British group with the Post Office, Gas, Shell, Anglo-Iranian, Imperial Airways and I.C.I. proves that it can be done by resolute men who serve ideals and know how to discover the creative relationship between business and the public welfare.

Doubts I know must arise in many minds and I am as conscious of them as anyone. It has been my business for many years to be conscious of these doubts. However, I suggest this for consideration. The first problem of education today is essentially one of understanding the technological world in which we live and every force which directs its development has something of importance to say. People will realize their worth all the better for knowing what railroads do for farmers, what telephones do for trade, what radio does for airlines and what automobiles do for both private amenity and public knowledge. The patterns of inter-relationship which lie at the root of modern citizenship and therefore challenge us to new ways of management have all a technological basis and I cannot think of a gas pipe or electric wire or road or ship or plane or factory that has not something to say.

The great problem of corporate sponsorship in this vital reference is, of course, that business groups are more imaginative in the matter of technological progress than they are on the human relationships which results from technical progress. In this connection much may be expected from government and much indeed has been done by governments. It is important to note, however, that nothing can be expected from governments beyond what I shall call the degree of general sanction. The degree of general sanction is not the degree of sanction by the party in power: it is the degree of sanction allowed by all the parties of Parliament or Congress. For example, in England, the degree of sanction was left of the Conservative Party in power and in Canada it is slightly right of the Radical Liberal Party which is now in power. I say, as an old public servant, that if the degree of general sanction is accurately gauged, maximum support is forthcoming for creative work. Where, however, advantage is taken and the degree of sanction is estimated on partisan lines, ineffectiveness and frustration result.

This, of course, imposes a clear limit on the creative artist working within the public service, for, obviously, the degree of general sanction does not easily allow of forthright discussions on such highly controversial problems as, say, America's record with the Negroes in the South, or Britain's record with the Indians in the East. The creative worker must not, however, simply denounce this limitation and dissociate himself from government service. If he is a practical operator and a practical reformer he will take the situation for what it is and do his utmost within the limitations set, and this is one of the disciplines which the creative artist must learn in this particular period of society.

If he wants to pursue the more difficult and controversial themes, I am afraid he must look elsewhere than to governments, and here I think it will be well to examine in future years the sponsorship potential of authorities and associations who are less ham-strung than governments necessarily are. In particular, one expects much from the trade unions and co-operative movements. One also expects much from the associations devoted to such matters as nutrition and town planning and public health. To take one example, why should Mayor LaGuardia, of the city of New York, have a radio station and not a film unit? I can imagine no more effective centre for films dealing with town planning, child welfare, public health, educational progress and inter-racial understanding than a film centre based on the social interests of the city of New York. I make this suggestion not only for New York but for every Mayor everywhere. City Councils, professional associations, trade unions, alike, are all directly concerned with the media of public observation and analysis and for the simple reason that they are all equally concerned with the growth of professional and civic understanding.

Here I am not altogether guessing. Even now there are many signs of a growing use of documentary films by these bodies. In my own experience hardly a week goes by that I am not asked for advice on how to make or circulate films by groups whose varying interest ranges all the way from physical research to stamp collecting. It is one of the phenomena of the time that there is hardly an organization that is not in, or about to be in, the documentary film business, and simply because it is an instrument by which knowledge of a functional nature can be exchanged and extended. There is one field of development which is of very special concern to all of us today. We hear a good deal about international competition in film production and the struggle for markets. We still seem to be talking the language of competition when we should be talking the language of conciliation and co-operation. So far as our documentary films are concerned, I, for one, do not care who makes them so long as they are a contribution to the understanding of today and the making of tomorrow. All creative work which promotes peace and goodwill is, like peace itself, indivisible. I look, therefore, for much greater concern than ever before with the international exchange of documentary films.

I hold that the I.L.O., which in the twenties and thirties did much good work at Geneva, could have done more if it had created a more living exchange between countries, of documentary material describing their common interests. I do not say that this or any other exchange would have prevented the war. What I do say is that now and in the future all international understanding must inevitably be based on a realization of the common interest of working people; their common interest in food and housing and children, and in the ordinary enjoyments that make for the good life. That realization can only be effected if the creative workers in all media see to it that it is effected. It was in our thought in the thirties that wherever a country showed a high example in, let us say, safety in mines or workers' health, the I.L.O. should have circulated that example to the whole world. In the social, economic, and educational instruments of the new international body we have, today, the same opportunity for exchange, and there will be no excuse whatever if this time we fluff it.

One thing that would result from the development of these agencies is that we would come closer to an international viewpoint in both the production and distribution of documentary films. One serious limitation in government support in the past has been the tendency to serve national interest to the exclusion of all others, and this is particularly so in the case of the United Kingdom and the United States. Whatever they may say in their diplomacy, they have not learned to come off

323

their blaring national band waggons when it comes to information. I suggest mildly, if I may, examination of the somewhat different policy of Canada. It has been one of the interesting things about Canadian policy in information that it has really, and from the first, conceived of itself as a United Nation, and has spoken most boldly when it has talked about its international relationships and its common interests with other peoples.

I have suggested that we can look for a great development of the documentary film because it is necessary to so many people. The nature of the development of government, the nature of the development of business, of trade unions and civic associations, alike suggest a greater use of visual aids to understanding. I add that the nature of the development of education itself gives a new authority to any medium which, like the documentary film, strikes out the living patterns of modern citizenship. This association with advances in educational theory is so important that I hope I shall be borne with, if I labour over a necessary distinction between the documentary film and the simple pedagogical film.

We ought to be clear from the first that in education we are not just concerned with mobilizing new techniques for the teaching of the same old thing. We have had exciting new media made available in our day to the process of instruction—the radio, the film, the exhibition, the dramatized newspaper story, and so on. If it were just a matter of teaching more quickly the known laws of medicine and science, I suppose we could sit around and plan the effective use of these new media right away. It would be no trouble at all. The armed services and the war industries have done exactly that for the past five years. They have made efficient sailors and soldiers and airmen and mechanics in half the time that it took by older methods of teaching. But let us not be led astray by these developments, however interesting they are. The problem of education today is not one of new techniques or of visual aids or aural aids or of any other aids. These represent specific improvements in the teaching of known areas of knowledge and very important they are, but they do not go to the heart of the matter. As a matter of fact, education has done not a bad job at all in the known areas of knowledge, with or without these new devices of instruction. The technological revolution which lies at the root of all our problems is itself the miraculous result of a superb education in scientific knowledge and technical skills. Nor is the matter of literacy in question. Again education has done a very presentable job. We can, most of us today, read a little, even if we only read the headlines, the sports columns, the comic strips and True Confessions. I will go further still and say that education's problem today is not even the conveying of knowledge. The spate of knowledge conveyed daily by the various forces of education, inside and outside the schools and universities— and, of course, I include the newspapers, the radio and the film—is nothing short of colossal, and, considering the mass of it and the complexity of it, it is astonishingly well conveyed by an army of observers, analysts and mechanics who have developed very difficult skills in the matter of world observation.

In my view, the basic problem of education lies not so much in the acquisition of literacy or of knowledge or of skills, as in the patterns of civic appreciation, civic faith and civic duty which go with them. They mean nothing—literacy, knowledge or skill, the whole lot of them—if they do not make for order in the world, and today they quite obviously do not. Where I think we have failed is that we have not sufficiently realized the implications of the change which the technological revolution has brought upon us. The objective nature of that new society we understand well enough but not its subjective implications. We know that the old self-contained, self-subsistent and relatively static community is dead and done with, and no more real in our conceptual life than the tattered friezes of the Parthenon. We have obliterated the obstacles of time and space and have made the world's riches of matter and of mind potentially available to everyone. We have become specialists, in the safe knowledge that we have the benefit of the specialization of others in a new and more complex system of creation and enjoyment. They used to ask in the school books if seven men took twenty-one days to build a house, how long does it take twenty-one men. We have discovered that the answer is not seven, but probably one. We have learned the two and two makes five of the corporate and the co-operative.

But, on the other hand, we have become more and more citizens of a community which we do not adequately see. The knob of a radio set switches in the voices and opinions and aspirations of men all over the globe, but not without the thought and work of thousands of people like ourselves, which we have not yet the habit of realizing. Under our feet go wires and pipes leading to complicated supply systems we blindly take for granted. Behind each counter of our modern buying lies a world system of manufacture, choice and conveyance. A simple weather forecast is a daily drama of complicated observation over a large part of the earth's surface, without which men could not safely fly or put to sea. We do not see it. Messages that roll easily from the local press may have come at six hundred words a minute from Moscow or may have been relayed south from London to Africa and by complicated steps north through the Americas again to overcome an atmospheric problem we know nothing about. It is a nickel buy, like an ice-cream cone or a packet of chewing-gum. Sleeping or walking, we are concerned each day in an inter-dependency, one with another, which in fact makes us each our brother's servant and our brother's keeper. This is the fact of modern society, whatever medieval theories of self-subsistence operating in the name of art or operating in the name of religion may try to tell us. This is the fact of modern society, yet we are slow to adopt the habits of thought which must necessarily go with interdependency if we are to control the forces which we ourselves have released. We operate in a new world, but are not yet possessed of it. We have given ourselves a new kind of society, but have not yet given ourselves the new kind of imagination or the new conception of citizenship which makes it tolerable. Like Tomlinson who gave up the ghost in his house in Gloucester Square, we stand betwixt and between, with the winds of the universe blowing through our empty spirits. We operate in a system of complex interdependency, but still like to think that we are simple souls face to face, and on the most personal basis, with our Maker. We have given away our capacity for self-sufficiency, but still want to be free individuals so-called—free to go our own gait and let the devil take the hindmost. Now, when we ought more than at any time in history to be talking most about responsibility and disciplines and duties, we are talking most about freedom from controls and freedom from restraints, even when they are only our own necessary self-controls and self-restraints. This is the most paradoxical fact of our time. I think it is no wonder that we are full of frustrations and neuroses of one kind or another, for we are, in fact, in the process of trying to eat our cake and have it too : enjoying the interdependence but still demand the privilege of independence.

This, of course, places a great burden and a great creative responsibility on education and on art, if we are dealing, as I think we are, with the intangibles that affect the imaginations of men and determine their will. It is no longer a problem of known areas of knowledge simply and directly communicated. It is a question of the images that direct men's vision and determine their loyalties, and we are concerned not only with the conscious processes of the mind but with the sub-conscious ones which insensibly govern the pattern of men's attention and the manner of their action.

The Challenge of Peace

I suggest, in fact, that the problems of education and art, and their inevitable interest today, lie in the realm of the imaginative training for modern citizenship and not anywhere else. We owe ourselves, as H. G. Wells once before observed, a thorough overhaul, not of the facts we teach, nor of the techniques with which we teach them, but of the images and patterns on belief in which these facts are framed. I am not going to suggest which images and patterns should be retained and which discarded and what new images and patterns are vital to our future. But let me say this about images and patterns. What are the images which we associate with our country? Are they the static images of forests, or the dynamic images of afforestation? Are they the static images of flat or rolling landscape, or the dynamic images of soil conservation and co-operative marketing? Do we really see beyond our personal circle to the circle of the community in such a manner that the community is the deeper reality? Must our stories and dramas inevitably follow the shape of personal fortunes, or are we learning to find new dramatic patterns in a life rooted in scientific discoveries and mass production and based on interdependence? Are we still concerned with the romantic horizons of the old-time pioneer, or are we beginning to find imaginative sustenance in the new horizons of the researcher and the organizer? Do we still see the world in a rectangle, up and down left and right, or do we really in our heart and mind see over the world and think over the world and feel over the world in the circles of common interest and actual interdependence? That, I think, is the style of question which education and art will presently be asking themselves. It involves inevitably a re-answering of Tolstoy's question as to what men live by and a re-answering which will not inevitably leave the classic conceptions in their old and honourable places. I hesitate to suggest it, but we may even have to revise our views on Plato, Milton, John Stuart Mill, and the hundred best books. It is possible that we need not take them quite so seriously as guides to the special and urgent problems of what may be, in the light of time and philosophy, a new dispensation of thought and habit —as new a dispensation as that which followed the development of measurement and perspective at the end of the Middle Ages. The key to this new dispensation may well be our use of the two words corporate and co-operative. They represent, it is possible, a new species of measurement and perspective and therefore a new species of power and thought and habit.

It is significant that the record of the educators in the imaginative training of citizenship over the past generation has been a very poor and tawdry one. They have tended to stick to the safer patterns of the known way, and the direction of the civil imagination has fallen in large part to the daring innovators of the other media—to the newspapers, the radio, the film, and the advertisements. It is significant that the leadership has fallen, in fact, to those who know how to use the new dramatic media and have had the sense to use them dramatically. Inevitably they have been driven by the very nature of their media into something approaching a living description of the new world that has grown up about us. I myself regard the dramatic pattern of the modern newspaper story as the greatest single contribution to civic education in our time, not because of the substance of it, but because of the form of it, which, it seems to me, is basically necessary to the comprehension of our time. Something does something to something. Something affects something. Someone is relative to someone. It has, more than any other single factor, turned men's thinking to the active or dynamic form without which it is difficult to conceive of any understanding of the nature of the modern world. Only less important is the influence of the radio, with the immediacy and personal nature of its contact with places and problems and people in far places.

I shall not say nearly so much for the film. The most powerful of all mass media, the mass medium most capable of bringing the disparate elements of the wide world into obvious juxtaposition and association, the medium of all media born to express the living nature of interdependency, it has stuck all too stubbornly to the drama of personal habits and personal achievements. It has, I am afraid, done all too little to impose the co-operative habit of thought. In a world holding almost with a sense of spiritual dereliction and agony to the lost cause of isolationism, it has been the naïve proponent of personal isolationism. On the other hand, it has done something to open a window on the wider world, and so widen the stretch of men's eyes, and, in the documentary film, it has, I believe, outlined the patterns of interdependency more distinctively and more deliberately than any other medium whatsoever.

3 Report from America

The other day at Princeton University Harold Laski, in one of his more downcast moments, informed us that 'The world faces a crisis of vaster proportion than any since the Reformation and despite the longing of the ordinary people everywhere for security from war it is not excessive to say that the major governments of the world stand in the position of gladiators one to another.' If I am not misreading *The New York Times* account, he went on to conclude, more or less, that there is no hope of peace in our time: that 'despite the insistence of statesmen on their passion for peace' he can see 'no prospect of its achievement in any future with which this generation is concerned'. If true, this is a somewhat melodramatic utterance when it comes from a professor of political science. It is a wholly unnatural one when it comes from an educator whose job it presumably is to accentuate the positive and lead the younger generation into the future. And I would not have brought the matter up at all except that it does present an opportunity to restate the directive duty of the educators, enlighteners and creative artists of all the media in this particular phase of Gulliver and his Travels.

We are all conscious of the crisis which Laski very properly emphasizes, though it represents no sudden melodramatic cloud upon the horizon, but rather a growing crisis that has been building up ever since the industrial revolution and in full critical view as long as one remembers. We are all conscious that the national and imperialist patterns of human development are under great strain as the necessity of a new and mutually co-operative international pattern is imposed upon them: that the paradox of our time derives from the fact that we are caught between the two: drawn to the international, yet unable for basic reasons, psychological, political and economic, to let go of the national patterns to which we are so deeply attuned. It would, moreover, be a wonder if the national concepts which have shaped our thoughts, our loyalties and actions, were to hand over suddenly and without a struggle and our minds, loyalties and actions were all in a bright miracle turned into the moulds of international co-operation.

329

Like all the revolutionary generations, we live in two worlds and, like all such generations, can only look forward to a considerable period of directive effort before the old is put off and the new assumed. It may therefore not be a very happy time for the traditionalists and formalists in any sphere of human action but it ought, by all order, to be a whale of a time for those who pretend to creative work. With the problem goes the privilege, as Mrs. Roosevelt more or less remarked when she saw Pare Lorentz's *Fight for Life*. Lorentz, if you remember, made a great to-do about his maternity ward and the pain and the travail were given the best dramatic outing since the 51st Psalm; but Mrs. Roosevelt thought, in her gentle way, that having babies had also 'something to do with happiness'. There, I imagine, even so high a matter as a crisis 'greater than any since the Reformation' can rest too. So far as the creative arts are concerned—and I mean all of them from teaching up, or down, which have the power to mould men's thought, feeling and action—the historical task of establishing a spirit of co-operation one to another which will fulfil our actual economic dependence one on another brings incentive and opportunity which should normally light up all our horizons.

In any case the various forces afoot will not leave us be, even if we so wanted. The technological revolution goes on apace, arming the peoples of the world with new powers but also, and in its farthest corners, with new expectations. The peoples, who, because of inadequate ways of thought and deficiencies of will, have been subject to the disasters of war and the injustices of peace are everywhere patently on the march and in increasingly good order, disturbing the equilibrium of every doctrine, faith and political formula which does not take them into most practical account. The reshuffling of the doctrines, faiths and political formulæ becomes, therefore, not altogether a matter of choice and certainly none of the world-leading doctrines—of liberal democracy, of the churches, of socialist democracy—can on this occasion hide itself away. Even for æsthetics, as we have recently noted in Brooks Atkinson's debate with the Russians, there is no coral strand these days in which to conceal its fair-haired, blue-eyed little noggin. This is perhaps what makes so much of the high intention of the gentlemen in the libraries only grimly deceptive and, for no reason at all, I think of Chancellor Hutchins of the University of Chicago and his *Hundred Best Books*. The essays that once broke men's minds out into the future from just such crises as ours appear now only in support of the formulæ and definitions that will not budge, piling up behind them all the influence and power which

330

a natural affection for the past or a frightened affection for it can all too easily create. Touchingly, we are invited to the lumber room of the human spirit, to go over the old snapshots and the old occasions when the world was young, with Plato to Milton to John Stuart Mill, matching the nostalgic baseball memory of Tinker to Evers to Chance. Against the express warnings of the Ancients themselves, the net effect is to confine the living terms of thought in the strait-jacket of other times and other conditions which were specialized, local and static in a way that has little bearing on the mastery of international forms in a swift-moving time.

An important example of this is the reiteration of the older definitions of democracy and freedom which do more at the moment to confuse the public mind and paralyse the public will and make international understanding impossible than any other educational influence whatsoever. Faith is found, says Michelangelo in one of his sonnets, only in the creative processes of time: which I take to mean where the actual forces of the future are shaping. It would seem on the face of it that this other world of technical and economic relationships, which is patently upon us, imposes, as it requires, other and relevant patterns of thought and sentiment if we are to bring it to order, and that is to say, if we are to live spiritually in it.

This suggests to me a certain drastic re-examination of all the media in the light of the very great new responsibilities placed upon them; and I mean a re-examination different in character and kind from the normal re-examinations which artists and critics at all times affect. For example, much of our æsthetic approach, and here was the indissoluble difference in the Atkinson debate, is still reflective rather than directive. If this analysis of the crisis is correct—and in spite of all the regard we owe to the courtly cultures and all the secret wishes we may stifle that they will in grace return again—there is no alternative at this time to throwing dear old Wordsworth and his 'recollections in tranquillity' out of the nearest metropolitan window.

In the field of enlightenment all the barriers break down between the media and all become one *in education* as the creative process becomes a directive one.

In actual fact we are nearer to this position, and in all the media, than many people realize. Not only are the policies and viewpoints in the theatre, in films, in the press and in education itself coming closer to an urgent sense of the public service and of their directive function within it, but larger, more co-ordinated, more activist forms of organization, reflect an appreciation of the magnitude of the task. There is a powerful image of this in the council room of the United Nations at Lake Success. The crescent-moon table faces the general public and the world's press with a new sort of directness and there is an altogether new scale and character in the facilities demanded by the various instruments of world communication and permitted to them: in the floodlights for the cameras and in the glass-fronted silence loges for the operation of both the radio people and the film people. One has only to pull a switch and here under the searchlight we have this new international democratic process under highly organized world review. The machinery of world observation has actually begun to exist. Perhaps it is not yet adequate enough. Melodramatic and immature forms of reporting distort some of the important issues and suppress all too many of the pedestrian but constructive achievements. The direct participation of the scholastic system as one of the mass media of equivalent power and influence is not yet sufficiently organized. Nor is the participation sufficiently organized of that even more powerful mass medium of enlightenment which is represented on the community level by the churches, youth organizations, women's groups, business and service clubs, trades unions and all those other organizations which provide direct and immediate leadership of functional civic interests. The participation of the arts is, as usual, not organized at all. None the less, the picture is already impressive and the more so as critical forces in all the media reach out for qualitative, as well as quantitative, improvement in the handling of public affairs.

In the field of books there are a hundred and one new experiments in cheap publication and quite remarkable developments in the attendant fields of visual illustration and presentation. Even the school books are becoming exciting and the range of their inquiry extending enormously. In the press services a new generation of international observers is coming along, matured in the complex deliberations which inevitably attend the complex relationships between peoples. The mass magazines are reaching out from the trivial into considered commentary on matters of public importance. As significant as anything of the general stir is the debate of great moment which is now ranging across the nations on the principles determining the freedom and the responsibility of the press. In radio the F.C.C. insists on higher standards of public service and one is not unaware of the general influence in the educational departments of the networks. N.B.C.'s strong support for the establishment of a U.N. world network in which an objective news coverage of international discussion will be made available everywhere, represents a maturer sense of responsibility and statesmanship.

The film, of all the media, has in the past concentrated most on entertainment and least on these deliberate processes of enlightenment with which we are now so progressively concerned. It had, it thought, no pressing reason to do so. It was from the first a simple and easy way to spread the popular drama and the romantic story to the small towns of the nations and this it has done with such enormous success that there has never been any pressing commercial incentive to reach out to larger considerations. Yet in spite of this, and for twenty years, there has been an increasing drive, both inside and outside Hollywood and the other studio centres of the world, to make the film a vehicle for ideas and a more deliberate instrument of the public service. Achievements have been scrappy to say the least, but they do include a considerable measure of experiment on the popular level by men like Warner, Wanger and Zanuck.

There is at this time an interesting debate going on, led by Louis de Rochemont of the *March of Time*, in which the influence of American films abroad has been brought seriously under review; and it is significant of a perturbation, if not of a new critical spirit, which is affecting in varying degree every level of film production and film organization, national and international. 'I wish to report', Mr. de Rochemont says, 'that the French, for instance, think that we Americans are somewhat off our rocker. Their impressions of the American Army remain those of force, effectiveness and swift purpose. They cannot understand how such military power grew out of the civilization which Hollywood depicts for them, a civilization in which the chief values are luxury, ostentation, opulence and frivolity, and in which constructive action and concern for the rest of the world and its problems have no place. To them it all adds up to complete irresponsibility. We are giving Europe an eyeful, to be sure, but an eyeful of what?

'In Europe the American way of life is under attack, and the attack goes to the very roots of our American existence. The extreme Left calls us imperialist and without conscience. Moderates fear we are unstable, easily swayed and planless. The renascent Fascists are convinced we will eventually be a soft touch. American films, our last best point of contact, lend themselves handily to the confirmation of these suggestions. . . . The European public is hungry for American films, and any reasonably good film can add millions of francs to its distributor's blocked balances. But beyond the European's willingness to convert his vanishing currency into an hour or two in the house of illusion there is something more profound. Europe is asking us for spiritual and emotional bread, and we are giving it a glittering cascade of rhinestones.'

This criticism, severe as it may sound, is matched by much that is being said in the Screen Writers' Guild, by the film critics both here and abroad, and by those who in the highest quarters are striving to develop those non-theatrical uses of the film which have been so largely ignored till now. It is true that Hollywood insists on staying close to the mass public in its fancies and its foibles, and I am one who agrees with this insistence, and for the good reason that the *realpolitik* of the human spirit demands it. Now, as at all times, one must go where the people are, and whatever creative work we seek to do must be done, not in superiority over them, but in co-operation with this our larger self. It would be not only a poor future but a fascist one, which did not take the people along with it. Apart from that, the film industry is becoming conscious, as never before, of the experimental films which are breaking through the meretricious formula of the studios. The greatest success of *Open City*, a film on the Italian resistance, has been in the professional circles of the industry, and nowhere are the realistic qualities of the British film style so much noted. I do not consider *Henry V* greatly contributive to the problem with which we are concerned, but it is at least remarkable that its special standards of quality have drawn from the salesmen an effort of distribution which has never been known before for a film of this kind.

Best signs of all are the plans of the major companies to develop the use of the film in education and create side systems of distribution outside the theatres. They have been a long time in coming to their decision, but I think it certain that they will progressively conceive of the medium as a medium capable of many other uses than the simple uses of amusement: as a medium, in fact, which will join with the schools and universities, the youth organizations and the churches, the women's organizations, the business clubs and workers' groups in a considered effort to support community leadership.

Some sign of the new attitude comes from the Eric Johnston office, which is already pledged to an experimental programme of films for schools and promises that this is only a beginning. The Independent Producers' Association under Donald Nelson has moved similarly to ally the facilities of the industry with the requirements of the teacher. All the films of general interest in education previously gathered in the Bell and Howell library were significantly bought up recently by one of the Hollywood majors as a basis for the thoroughgoing nationwide service of films of specialized interest. In fact, in spite of the industry's everlasting and weary defence of its old traditional position, there are happenings within it which contradict its complacent assertions. The cynics may hold that it realizes that a new market is opening up and that it is merely reacting to a new opportunity for profit. A simpler explanation is that the people of the motion picture industry, like every other section of the population, are becoming progressively concerned with the march of events and that the younger generation which came through the war is reaching out beyond the elders to wider worlds of public responsibility.

There is another factor of even greater importance. In film as in all the other media—of press, of radio, of education itself—it is not just the medium which decides what it will do. Governments everywhere are too deeply concerned in the state of opinion within their borders to avoid active consideration of the instruments which affect the minds of their people. Even if Hollywood would like to, it cannot avoid close examination as it crosses the borders of every state outside America. And even inside America, the forces of public opinion and of public demand are everywhere learning to require new services and new standards of performance. While Hollywood has been sticking to its formula of entertainment, a host of others have been exploring the documentary uses of the film to further the interests of agriculture and industry, to promote public health and child welfare, and perform a hundred and one educational duties which cannot be gainsaid by any force whatsoever in progressive communities.

This development which has been most scientifically matured in Britain has been responsible for the creation of very large audiences outside the theatres: in schools and universities and in the clubrooms of the various specialized interest groups. In Britain it is a common observation that there is more seating capacity outside the theatres than there is inside the theatres, and when people think of non-theatrical distribution they think of the specialized interests and activities of people in their local communities. As a result, the Film Service of the British Government plays to an audience of some 27,000,000 people composed of thousands of little groups, gathered together in the ordinary service of their communities and their professions. In Canada, the Government Film Service, operating on a similar approach, plays to an audience of over 12,000,000. This is the measure of the new development which is now emerging in the film industry of America. The potential here is an audience of something like 250,000,000 people a year. It will not be an audience mobilized by the film industry as such, but an audience mobilized by the educational community organizations themselves: and if these organizations show even a modicum of intelligence in regard to this development, they will be in a position to direct the whole force and character of the film services which are developed.

What now appears likely is the creation in every community of community visual councils, centred possibly in the public libraries. As I see it, the universities, schools, churches, youth organizations, business and service clubs, trade unions, women's groups and professional associations would be represented on these councils, and each council would maintain an information service by which all documentary and educational films, and from all over the world, which are of pertinent interest to any one of the contributing groups, would be described and routed to it. I imagine these visual councils of the communities as having, in turn, a National Council, through which producers would be told what films were most required. This pattern of development is already apparent in Britain and Canada, is under examination in other countries, and becomes more likely everywhere, as the United Nations reaches out for national and community instruments through which its overall international service can effectively operate.

I would be the last to say peace it's wonderful, but every medium, I suggest, is going through, as the film medium is going through, an important phase of self-examination and reconstruction. The fierce words of negative criticism are valuable but they are also deceptive. Whatever the noise of protest on the inadequacies of the past, all media are showing signs of extending their services on a dramatic scale: improving the spread of their communications, widening their coverage to the ends of the earth, and invading new fields of responsible public service. No one can say that the advances are adequate enough for the task in hand, and the best service that any critic can do is to hold all the media of understanding to still higher standards of achievement, but no one who has the duty of illumination upon him need lack in prospect.

Great Lakes (Canadian, 1945)
  Directed by James Beveridge

  Both films produced by the National Film Board of Canada

Battle of the Harvests (Canadian, 1944)
  Directed by James Beveridge

Highways North (Canadian, 1944)
Produced by the National Film Board of Canada: directed by James Beveridge

Part VII

INTERNATIONAL

Although heavily committed in production and administration, Grierson continued to find time to survey the achievement of the documentary movement. Annual visits to the Edinburgh Film Festival, which grew out of admiration for the documentary idea and which brought together films from the world's chief producing countries, gave him a regular opportunity for comment. During the fifties leadership in realist film-making passed from Britain and the articles in this final section examine some of the causes. Grierson, now working in television, describes what he learned from the new medium. He sums up this and other experiences in 'A Mind for the Future', an address delivered in Glasgow on St. Andrew's Day, 1962, and broadcast on the Scottish Home Service of the B.B.C.

F. H.

Part VII

INTERNATIONAL

1 Documentary: The Bright Example

A good deal of gloom surrounds the British documentary operation in this summer of 1947. I think the situation is urgent and warrants an immediate official inquiry if a great national asset is to be saved from damage, and most important needs of the state in the field of information are to be imaginatively fulfilled. But first let us see the problem in proportion.

The documentary film development in Britain is still the one bright example to a great many countries of how the film can be mobilized in the public service to give image and perspective to the national and international scene. Canada demonstrates possibly a more orderly use of the film but not yet a more extensive or more penetrating one. In the *A.C.T. Journal*, there is a register of thirty to forty companies which, in one way or another, are concerned with films of reportage, or instructional, or documentary qualities. This scale of the British operation is important because it means that the demand for production, of whatever sort, has been established.

Looking from the outside, I think also that we miss the point if we do not realize how deeply and uniquely bedded in the public service the British documentary film has become. I hear grumbles about the cold hand of bureaucracy, but show me please anything elsewhere like the acceptance of the documentary film's uses by all the branches of government. This represents a great step ahead, whatever the problems of growth, or of order in growth, or of quality in growth may appear to be.

The complaint takes various forms. Something—the best ones say—is going out of documentary, and in fact why are they so dull and why did we not make such a show at Brussels as we once did with *Song of Ceylon* and sundry other minor masterworks of the moment? Far too many units, it appears, are going into instructional work in plain avoidance of the difficulty of revealing in dramatic or poetic or other creative form the stubborn social material of the day.

The films are slack for lack of fire, and so are the boys who make them, runs the criticism. There are shocking stories of people of talent

339

doing nothing for a year and losing their competence. Production procedure lacks the tempo which is essential for creative work and there are endless dying delays as between the film-makers, the sponsors and the people of the Treasury. Committee production, I am told, has raised its ugly head to the point where films are killed in the script by bureaucratic indecision.

It is said that the economies and administrations of the units are not always as orderly as they might be, and that many of their efforts could be better co-ordinated. It is doubted in some quarters whether production by thirty to forty units with separate overheads and sometimes insufficient resources can represent an efficient system. One comment is made that pettifogging independences are turning the documentary business into a small shopkeeper's business and that failure to concentrate ideas and energies and plan their more intensive development is not in keeping with the times.

There is criticism on both sides. The units charge the sponsors, and particularly the Government sponsors, with a lack of decisiveness and a lack of imagination. They say they have lost the conception of a total driving plan for the use of the documentary film in the urgent service of the nation. The sponsors, on the other hand, say that the film-makers are too independent by half and cannot be relied on to deliver efficiently or even to deliver what they have undertaken to deliver, and finally that the boys are so full of small politics these days that nary a one of them has time to throw his cap over a steeple.

It is all a little like quarrelling with your wife, except that there are some sponsors and producers I know who should make honest women of each other, and vice versa.

That is the sort of criticism I hear. If I am to believe it, the great art of sponsorship which Tallents and Leslie and Jack Beddington and Wolcough have represented in the past is now progressively usurped by the little people playing for departmental exactitudes and personal safeties; and that we, on the other hand, have only created a regiment of directors capable of making competent pictures which, for all their technical adequacy, are dead in the eyes. I doubt if the problem is quite so simple. My notion is that it is a deeper one than people, be they sponsors or film-makers, and goes to the heart of the historical moment. If so, it is not to be solved by disappointment, or complaint, and certainly not by flurried excursions into denunciations one of another.

The documentary film was conceived and developed as an instrument of public use. It was conceived, moreover, as an instrument to be used systematically in all the fields of public instruction and enlightenment. It is true that we hoped that individual artists would have every opportunity within the framework of the public service; but the other half of our socialized or public conception of art was that we could only secure this larger hope by tying our effort to the organized forces of social growth under whatever form they came. No one ever said that the said forces would automatically love us for our blue eyes. Some of us have even insisted that the developing process was bound in its nature to be positively difficult, and this has always been the catch in our continuing argument.

The organized forces of social growth, be they the Departments of State, or the great corporations, or the trade unions, or Rank, or even the Boy Scouts and the Y.M.C.A., are not necessarily tutored in the arts nor even sensitive to what the arts might do to increase the national life. I myself have served many Ministers, yet some of the best of them were æsthetic yokels. I have lived most of my life among bureaucrats only to wonder why, in the name of planned economies and the increase of human welfare, so many of the unelect should come to inherit the earth. But this itself is the very condition of the planned economies which are of necessity being imposed upon us.

Inevitably, there has been a great and swift expansion of the public services, and with every expansion goes the need for systems of budget control, personnel control and all the other paraphernalia of large-scale administration. Inevitably, too, new bands of specialists arise, not all of whom have a classical education, nor even any width of education. It is to these new hosts, and they come often in uncomfortable form, that the artist working in the public service must expose himself today, and it is with these hosts that he must enter into understanding and collaboration.

The new patronage of the arts has to be worked for. Because, like all other socialized forms, it has to be built out of the new and rising social forces of our time, it cannot come either by miracle or in the simple innocence of expectation. There are still, it seems, remainders in the artist's mind of the days when he was the king's or the queen's player and a stroller generally, and waited for his betters to take notice of him. This has obviously no part in the democratic or socialized times in which the artist now operates.

We in the film world are in a specially difficult position, for we work in an expensive medium and make a larger claim than most on the public economy when we seek the freedom of art. It is, therefore, more important to us than to others that the socialized patronage of the arts

341

should be successful. We cannot, even if we would, turn away from it for, by the nature of our work, if it is conceived on any large and commanding scale, there is nowhere else to turn.

I agree when people say that, without imaginative support from the sponsors, imaginative films are impossible. I even sympathize a little when people talk of throwing up the government relationship altogether and re-discovering their freedom. But I still conclude that it is a suicidal attitude and not realistic, either socially or æsthetically. Our stuff is where the public process is and nowhere else. What we could spin out of our own little tails in a time like this would be little and not for long.

I therefore suggest that the solution does not lie outside the terms of public sponsorship but, on the other hand, lies in deliberately and patiently working to make that sponsorship an imaginative sponsorship. This is where the emphasis should now lie. Criticisms which do not recognize this task, and defections which are merely impatient, do not greatly help.

The situation calls for a new measure of mutual confidence and a new measure of leadership on both sides. As for the documentary people, I would have them count their blessings, even if they find their rations short. Where elsewhere has the documentary idea been so richly maintained even when a good deal of formless stuff which neither taught nor revealed was passed off in its good name? Where elsewhere have so many companies been maintained in such continuity of public work that they have come to expect it, no matter what administrative shapes they gave themselves?

As for the sponsors, they are fortunate at this time to have a school of film-makers at their disposition who, whatever their foibles, have made a profession of this realistic field of cinema and have remained faithful to it. With better organization, they represent an essential asset to Britain at this juncture, because there is much in these days of change on which the British public needs to clear its vision and strengthen its will for the job ahead.

Perhaps the documentary people are not at the moment so vigorous in new ideas as they might be, but who, pray, is? The new forms and the new fates were not educated for by the schools, the churches or the arts—not even by the schools, churches and arts of Whitehall—and the gap created is a spiritual one which is evident everywhere. The documentary people are part of a larger picture, and there is no great difference between the frustrations of the C.O.I. and the frustrations of the units who think they are afflicted by it. Neither are yet at the stage of seeing where the positive way of the public will lies, and who can blame them when the leaders themselves flounder in equal uncertainty?

There was recently at Cannes and Brussels a cynical and widespread comment as the films of the Western nations passed under review. The upshot of it was that if the great economic slump had not yet come, the great spiritual slump certainly had. The American vitality was considered as ever an empty vitality, but I caught the feeling that even the Henry V's and Hamlets and Nicholas Nicklebys were regarded in some critical quarters as representing no more than the genteel recollection, in anything but tranquillity, of another generation's creative strength. I would say that the so-called 'dullness of documentary' is not yet a disaster. Only its defection from the service of reality could be.

This contact with reality lies, as we know, in using the medium, with every disciplined effort possible, as intensively and imaginatively as possible, and on as wide a scale as possible, in both aiding the public enlightenment and, through the great images of creative action of which our medium is capable, firing the public will.

In this matter, the documentary people have, of necessity, to look to the brightness of their creative weapons and the methods by which they work. The situation calls for an examination of what they are doing on every level of talent to take the documentary film beyond the level of mere technical proficiency and into the world of imaginative interpretation. They cannot continue to live on the word 'documentary' itself, nor on its successful contribution to educational theory, nor on its reputation of practical achievement in the hard days of the war.

The whole idea was that we should make of this medium an instrument so sensitive to the needs of the public service that we would always be level with the problems of the time as they came along and, if possible, just a little ahead of the time. The idea was that we should so understand the problems of these sponsors of ours that we would be ahead of them in realizing their creative implications so far as the documentary film was concerned. Our freedom was to come, surely, from our demonstration that we were, in the practical issue, a necessary force for public understanding and public order, and not from any simpleton thought that, because of this and that in the way of acquired prestige, we were doing someone a favour. The condition of our freedom lay in fact in the capacity to be so expert in public issues that our need of Whitehall was matched, in normal human terms, by Whitehall's need of us.

343

International

We knew very well from the first that the day we did not command that expert sense of what was deeply required, the men of the camera were bound to return from whence they came, and that was from behind the camera, shooting to another's ideas and another's direction. I begin to suspect that this is what has begun to happen, and for the reason I state.

I do not want to push the point too far in a difficult situation, but I do not like the loss of direct and confident relationship between the artist and the government official; and I am bound to think that if something is going out of documentary, it is because something has gone from its essential underpinnings. Ground has to be made up. A notable understanding of the needs of the nation is the first condition of a positive, fresh and imaginative contribution towards their fulfilment.

The second condition may lie in recognizing the need to reorganize the documentary business, and radically, from an administrative point of view. The documentary people have lived a charmed life in some ways, though on the other hand it was also worked for. They came up before the full shock of Britain's new economic position in the world was felt, and they have disposed altogether of the largest sum given, in our time, to any band of creative workers.

They prospered because of the new Great Britain-Dominion relationship created by the Statute of Westminster. They prospered again as they, rightly enough, discovered images in the general will towards social reconstruction. Above all, they were equipped to serve most usefully, during the war, in the mobilization of the fighting front of democracy. They were politically correct; and they were politically correct because they were liberally correct. There was never a time when anyone could say of the documentary people that they took personal advantage from the work they did, or served their own comfort. I have been told a hundred times over that this was silly and that we could never hold a group together on such a basis. But the documentary people did so, and, even when my friend C. A. Lejeune speaks dividing words now, this she must allow.

Where Miss Lejeune has something, and where I must at this moment speak out, is in saying that now is not the time for complacency. I do not think the documentary people can afford the independent luxury of so many units. I do not think they can afford the present high cost of films. I do not think they can afford the present laboriousness in which a film is conceived, or the present tempo in which it is made. We cannot afford it for the simple reason that we are shooing our sponsors away.

344

Documentary: The Bright Example

It is not in films only that realism is wanted, but also in the manner of their making. The realism of that manner—and no matter what arguments are advanced for spiritual or æsthetic holidays with pay—is strictly related to the enormous amount of work to be done on the one hand, and, on the other, to the present situation in Britain and what the actual economic traffic will stand.

Here I had intended to bring forward the idea of the commission of inquiry, but I see with pleasure that others have already been talking along the same lines. Miss Lejeune's recent piece in which she says it would be a good idea to 'pause for a moment in the study of the "finest documentaries in the world", and consider what people are effectually doing to them', represents a sensible and helpful warning.

Short of a proper inquiry, I have myself no conclusions to offer. I simply want the documentary film in Britain to be even better in the public service than it has been before. I want the documentary group to be in the vanguard of the national effort and an example of good sense and discipline in the creation of the future. Above all, I do not want the documentary group to wait around for things to happen to it from the outside, when now, as it has always done, it can write its own brave ticket. It requires, however, a special effort; and I think now, and not later, is the time for it.

345

2 Edinburgh and the Documentary Idea

The Edinburgh show this month, (August 1948), is going to be a big show and an important one, and we will go into that later. To keep the decencies and the proportions, I should begin by saying that the Edinburgh show was always a big show anyway.

This year as last it is a Festival with pictures from everywhere and of all kinds, stretching all across and inside the denotation and connotation of the documentary thing. Twenty-seven countries are showing, they say, and the best is present. Bob Flaherty is there with his new one, *Louisiana Story*, and yet another brilliant evocation of the damn fool sense of innocence this wonderful old character pursues: his eye keener than ever, sensibility ever softer and so on, and Frances still around. Rossellini is there with his *Berlin Zero* and a turning camera on cat-feet which should interest the long shot-midshot-close-up boys in their technical vitals. Canada, bless the Chinook wind which thaws its winters, presents itself in the rough and tough European time with perhaps the best of all reportage items on European itself. It had no reason, except in its native and national generosity, to make it at all. France is there with the brilliant edition by Nicole Vedrès of the Edwardian years of Fallière: not so much nostalgic as witty and civilized. Norway is there with its big Nordic tale of Norwegian wartime bravery in *The Battle of Heavy Water*.

Documentary looks quite a thing in the Edinburgh programme, as though it really was an idea that had started something, in reportage and interpretation, inside countries and across boundaries, for the illumination of much.

But—and I have been holding the but on a now longish string—Edinburgh isn't an accident in all this. It might have been Geneva and wasn't, or New York and wasn't, or Paris and wasn't. It might have been Warsaw and wasn't; and that is an item all by itself of which more will be heard.

The point is that Edinburgh has served the documentary idea from its inception with more continuity, more common sense, more constructive effort in film societies, film clubs, cinema quarterlies and

346

whatnot, and more of the stuff that it takes when it comes to the critical punches than any other city. If there is a centre today which deserves more than any other to be regarded as the city where our wares can all-properly be shown and our accounts kept, it is surely this place in the north, with its rock behind it and its fuddy-duddy old sense that there might be sin itself in pursuing the shadow instead of the substance.

For all this we are indebted to a few unique characters who really believed it all from the first, and simply, and by sheer strength of their own sense of service, became the conscience of an idea which could all too easily have slipped without them.

Just to mark out the group and put it on this all too inadequate record, let us note down the central names of Norman Wilson, Forsyth Hardy and Charlie Oakley. Now that it is all a big, big show and everyone takes it for granted, let us note also that even in this latest stage of international coming together, documentary is still their local theirs.

It has been hard work for them over the years. They were not film men and had no reason, except in their faith in others, to give their time, energy and organizing capacity to the service of those of us who drew the dough and took the bows. I hope, in this year's Festival, they have the feeling that they have matured a personal work of great and unselfish order, worth a dozen and one sentimental and uncreative excursions into international necking.

For British documentary itself the occasion is especially important. It is easy to knock British documentary around at this moment and say that it looked a poor stick and a sad squirt at Brussels last year and that Roberto on the other hand is wonderful, which he certainly is. But it should be equally easy to remember, if the will is there and if the smartypants and the people we will always henceforth remember as our 'warm admirers' can think in proportion, that British documentary is still much the biggest operation in the whole international set-up.

In its very size it has its special problems which should at this stage be respected and worked on: of organization, of finding pattern within an extending field, of keeping its eye on an ever more difficult but more real æsthetic ball, of renewing and refreshing its political sense in the light of new circumstances, of maintaining its original fervour in the discovery of new talents and in the provision of experimental opportunity for them.

All this will appear in Edinburgh, or should as the stuff of the world goes across the Scottish screens. It will be simple for the side-liners to go ooh! aah! with Flaherty. It will be much more difficult to note that single swallows don't make a summer and that, whatever the present weather may be like, ours collectively is certainly a summer.

Therefore the meeting of the documentary people themselves, with the thrashing out of their problems, their needs and their short-comings, is going to be one of the more important occasions at Edinburgh and in the history of the documentary development. Wright on national documentary, Elton on international documentary, Pearson on colonial documentary, Alexander on second feature documentary, Rotha on documentary's influence on feature production, Manvell on the æsthetic of documentary, have together the opportunity of bringing the whole thing into new focus and fit for the size of the privilege which national needs and international implications have brought it.

They have a task of leadership to attempt more momentous than at any time before. They have the great new problems of peacetime to face up to and definition to make of what documentary has to give in illumination of the technological, scientific, colonial, international and, in general, economic changes which are upon us.

For presenting the documentary effort everywhere, for reminding us that documentary is not only an established medium of public service but a medium continually revealing new forces and requiring new efforts, all of us in its profession must be grateful for the screen and the platform which Edinburgh now so handsomely provides us. One suspects that it comes easily to the capital of a country which for six centuries has given so much encouragement to so many adventurers that it quite reasonably suffers the illusion of being the capital of the world.

3 Progress and Prospect

It is difficult to review the progress and prospect of documentary at this time (August 1949). Yet I do not feel to blame if I have not been able to see easily where the light now leads for the situation economic, affects us all and the inspirational side, for reasons economic and other, is dust in the throat.

Good things there are and we had better begin with them. The new establishments of documentary are holding and developing well. The last batch from Canada—collections they call them among the *couturières*—was very good; nothing stupendous but a standard of free-line drawing, so to speak, which meant good heart; and that is very much something these days. One weakness which I shall return to: a certain reaching for the metropolitan which may yet unstick the National Film Board from its roots in the great spaces and take the country shine from its notable complexion.

Similarly in New Zealand, with its one-a-week essentially local reel, representing an outstanding national service for a small unit. Australia keeps steadily on, and considering all the political difficulties of that toe-tramping continent, the Stanley Hawes epic in personal persistence is one for the book.

South Africa, moreover, has asked for a design for government film work and this will go ahead in the fall. The Government interest there and the willingness of the present established government film interests to stand down for a wider plan of development give promise of putting South Africa in line with Canada and Australia.

India it is too early to reckon on. There is much discussion of the use of films and many people have passed through over the year to look at the shape of our work in Britain: some to stay and learn, in spite of the incompetence of our present arrangements for overseas students. But it is too early in India. All the problems are huge and not least the problems of education and national planning which affect the film medium most. It would take a brave man to write a plan for India at the present time, and Nehru, who keeps returning to the film problem when he can, is right to hold his hand until the native genius

349

in the matter has sorted itself out. I add that a government film unit is grinding itself in in Rhodesia and that first flickers of interest begin to appear in Pakistan. Indeed, so far as the Dominions are concerned, all are more or less conscious of the value of the film and all, at different speeds, are seeing to the establishment of the film as an instrument of national policy.

Most encouraging too are the signs of life in the countries overrun by the war. One gets the warmest of impressions in Germany, although there is, and properly, a good deal of reserve. Most striking is the sense of latent power there. It was evident in the unit of young men working to the British Information Office in Hamburg. They were certainly feeling their way but they were at least feeling, which is more than even the fortunate people are doing today. The camera work was outstanding in sensibility, although perhaps there was a note of Wer-therism too. I remembered Dostoviesky's, 'when you are sorry for all the world, you are only sorry for yourself'. I still regret that we cut the Airlift film to a reel and did nothing much with the Refugee film. We murdered the Airlift film to get it a fast place among our one-reel theatre reports; and the Refugee film similarly did not connect with usability.

They set, as so many films do, the problem of either designing for established uses or so developing distribution that it provides organized presentation for all kinds and species. With the flow from different countries becoming ever greater and ever more various, our catch-as-catch-can system of distribution—founded some of it on amateurism and some of it in narrow purposes—appears ever more inadequate. It poses the major question perhaps in film organization today.

The other day in Paris I sat in at a show of films by the Brussels Pact Powers; and this Pact, incidentally, looks like having a film result in the next two or three years. The U.K. was represented by *Daybreak in Udi*. It went well enough. It is a good film but for sheer movie there was stuff from both France and Holland that returned the eye to the old excitement. Most interesting of all, if you please, was a Dutch picture of a Gas Works. I haven't seen better shooting for years, and that is the measure of what appears to be happening in the Western Union countries. While we are retiring from behind the camera and shooting from the deck chair or something, the directors there have got themselves excited, as in the first chapter, by the old bag of tricks itself. It is important, and not only as indicating technical fervour, but as representing too an energy of approach which un-doubtedly is reflected in the freshness of the films themselves.

As for France, you never know: for, in spite of the failure of the

Progress and Prospect

Government to plan and finance, and in spite of the notable chaos of its film operation as a whole, there always seems to be an individual or an individual group round the corner to take something exquisite from a pigmy or a peasant. Art spills out of the French like blood, although in what illicit adventure so unlikely a people got that kind of blood I have never been able to figure.

But, by and large, France, of all the great powers, is furthest behind in the ordered use of the film in its national process; and its exceptions, pleasant as they are for the film societies, are a false guide to the film's contribution to national momentum.

Holland is in better heart, much better, with Dr. Vroom of the Department of Education a powerful imaginative and far-seeing driving force. So too is Denmark. In both cases the idea of government planning, borrowed it may be from Britain and Canada, has taken firm hold. The Dutch governmental relation with the film industry has something to teach us all.

The British set-up in some ways is far and away the most developed, yet its present qualities in production are noticeably less spectacular than in Russia and Italy. Our films are for the most part technically adequate but not more technically adequate than the Canadians. We reach particular high points in, say, the *Cornish Engine* from Shell, *Daybreak in Udi* from Crown and *Atomic Energy* from G.B., but not more particular high points, for all our extra strength, than France and Holland. The reasons for this we had better analyse at this time, lest among the swings and roundabouts of the Edinburgh Festival the root of the matter is lost sight of.

Compared with the other countries—outside the Soviet group— Britain is certainly more strongly planned and more widely organized for documentary. In sponsored production it has approximately half a million from the C.O.I. alone, more from the Colonial Office and the Boards of Coal and Transport. Television disposes of an increasing amount of film money. So do Shell, I.C.I., B.O.A.C., the Travel Association and the odd sponsors. Adding the monies of the commercial operators, the total available for actuality and documentary must reach to a million a year.

When it comes to distribution we appear on the surface to be in a state of considerable disorder but I doubt if that is the correct analysis. It does not appear so much a state of disorder from countries overseas but rather a profusion of non-theatrical interests which require to be integrated, representing the rich initiative of a hundred and one interests. What has happened is that we have developed our non-

351

theatrical distribution out of all sorts of motivations and purposes and have not yet taken time to work out the total strategy for the development as a whole. Thus we have the film society movement developed from local groups interested in the art of the film, and the scientific film society movement deriving from academic and professional interests as well as the general interest in scientific progress. We have the education people, the agricultural people, the health people, the local government people, the Co-ops and the political parties, etc., similarly establishing, even if sketchily, film operations to enliven their services and their causes.

The Government, because of its various interest—save the political party side—and because of its own specific interests, has developed a central library and created a regional system of travelling units. In complement, G.B. and Pathé have established production and distribution services for a large variety of films from both national and international sources. The Government, moreover, has set up not only an organization (C.O.I.) to look after the film in national information, but also two organizations (British Film Institute and Educational Foundation for Visual Aids) to look after the film in its relationship with culture and education.

No country, in other words, is better served in local and professional zeal or in government support of the pretensions of the film as an instrument of specialized purpose.

The theatre may be another matter. Certainly we do not enjoy the dictates which, with Hitler and Mussolini, made the film a national must in the Fascist theatres; but there is a quota law which, by and large, gives theatre circulation for 200 films a year. I do not think it is more despite the wishful thinking of the producers and, even then, some of the 200 do not circulate widely, in a field which has double-feature programmes and does not want much in the way of information anyway. Yet 200 represents a helpful outlet for those who can gear documentary to the necessary fast-moving shapes of the theatre programme or, otherwise, in novelty and spectacle, command its curious attention.

What then is wrong that, with so much opportunity, we do hardly as well in film itself as we expected when the field was developing? Let me take distribution first, and for the reason that distribution makes not only the life of a film but the spirit of the film-maker. It requires sorting out from the film-makers' point of view and it calls, as I say, for integration. Sorting out it needs in the sense that we must make up our minds what precise relation we have to our audience, and

352

especially which audience we serve. At the beginning I deplored the
Canadian Film Board's ever reaching for the theatre audience. It
derives, I am sure, from a local need to show cause to the Treasury
and bring in an extra couple of dollars. I am sure too, that the illusion
rears again its ugly head that the odd spot among the theatre millions
is worth more in public information than the persistent influence of
the community groups that in every known way lead the opinion of
the community. What disturbs me, however, is the limiting and rotting
effect of a theatre distribution policy for documentary as a whole; and
it was ever so from the beginning.

It is true that theatre distribution can be improved for documentary.
The Government, by diktat, might, e.g. force a one-feature programme,
although I think there is not much chance of this as yet. Or it might
insist on one reel in every programme being devoted to national information or encouraging the national effort, although the time is hardly
ripe for it. Or the mobilization of the independent theatres in a third
circuit might nurture the supply of a third series of films outside
Pathé-A.B.C. and the G.B.-Rank group, although this will take the
time of local Wardour Street politics and it may be government diktat
again. Or the theatres might be 'educated' to documentary, although
this, after twenty years of it, gives no hope of sudden revelation. Or
a super theatre distribution effort, say at the C.O.I., might carve its
way publicity-wise through the catch-as-catch-can shorts booking
methods of the trade: although why dog should eat dog and a highly
financed operation should eliminate the independent units that are
trying to get along, it would be difficult to defend. Or the Government
might buy the best, from whatever source, and give them away to the
theatres, though the theatres do not necessarily want give-aways of
however high æsthetic an order. Many thoughts there are and many
a priori possibilities, but the fact of life would appear to be that there
is room in the theatres for 200 reels at most. Pathé is planned to supply
a minimum of sixty-eight; G.B. what with one thing and another,
thirty, and C.O.I. has a present guarantee of twelve and an inevitable
presentation of thirty plus. Altogether they occupy enough of the
available field to make you think. Against this consider the theatre
hopes of so many independent units today.

It isn't simply that the space available is limited. We ought, I think,
to make up our minds now that because of the special laws of the
popular theatre and because the exhibitors do not largely share our
special hopes of documentary, much of what we do and want to do
has no relation whatever to theatre distribution.

z   353

In fact, the biggest and silliest curse that has come over us is the thought that the success of documentary as an idea means any difference to its prospect in the theatre: save where the theatre laws—not the documentary ones—apply. These laws demand for the spot on the programme, which is not necessary anyway, a maximum in novelty, spectacle or journalistic urgency. Bugs Bunny is not accidentally the top theatre item in American shorts. *March of Time* does very well, with the Luce organization behind it, to stay where it does. But witness the struggle even in so large a market to make ends meet with the Disneys. The only certainty I know in Britain is an intimate study of Prince Charles. For the rest, given the costs involved and all the other circumstances, the opening is for fast journalistic types in the form of direct report or in the form of magazine specials.

But what all this has to do with documentary, except in its journalistic aspect, it would be difficult to say. The true secret lies, I am sure, with Shell's *Cornish Engine*. It is the film of the year, except for *Daybreak in Udi* which shows at least that the larger stuff of documentary is there for the finding. *Cornish Engine* is the film of the year for the good reason that it knew from the beginning what it wanted and has achieved it superbly. Somebody liked Cornish engines—probably Elton with Wolcough concurring—but realized from the beginning that the only people who could possibly share their regard were the engineers and engineering fans across the world. In setting themselves this audience they could accordingly lavish all their affection on the subject without twisting it here and sugaring it there to serve the Philistine. Even *Udi* has the curse of talking down upon it. It is so busy being simple for the ordinary—the last error of authenticity—that it misses time and again the poetic or other rich far-reaching note. The common sense of it is that the ordinary ordinarily expect the poet to be extraordinary and that we serve the ordinary with nothing less.

It is a simple proposition but I will let it stand: that the qualities will come again to our work if we will only define our projects in such a way that the affections are engaged and will be warmly supported. This means in the first place a *volte-face* from the theatres altogether to the non-theatrical audience of our original documentary persuasion. It means returning ourselves to the local bailiwicks of the film societies and other specialized audiences and serving them directly and fully without further wandering around in the fields which we neither command nor have interest—outside reportage—in commanding.

I do not know whether a post-mortem is worth while at this time because it seems to me so much error has to be undone that it would be better to have it undone than say why. To my mind there were two stages of illusion. The first one came with people like Harry Watt who wanted to reach out to what appeared to be the greener grass and larger life in the studios. With Watt it was all very well. He had a natural flair for theatre and a natural distaste, which his great father would have gorgeously approved, for the film society and the specialized audience. I can see him now reaching for the great liberal horizon of all mankind, as is his way. Very properly too, the war was his, for it gave him the perfect combination of dynamic event and serious intention and a public reaching for both.

But few enjoyed either the driving talents or the driving illusions of Watt. With Watt it was a question of storming the studio with documentary and nothing else and this he has done and will continue to do. Less must be said for his followers. The stormed citadel quietly and effectively absorbs them and God only knows what ignominy of melodrama and passable second feature awaits them.

The second stage of error in my view came in Britain with the wartime and somewhat wanton success of documentary. It was profusely financed and fanatically supported by Jack Beddington. Its success—again in a period of dynamic event and serious purpose—was superb. But one feels today that in the very urgency of the event there was no time to consider where the roots would very differently lie at the war's end; and the M.O.I. did not prepare for it. Nor did the film-makers. What was only a temporary command of the marquee was taken for granted as a sign of ultimate conquest. Read in these dimmer days the Hosannas surrounding the wartime achievement and take note. The trouble is that so many people believed it all; and off they were to the fun and the fair of the studios to take their shilling.

Even now the truth is only beginning to dawn on them: that in times of urgency, yes, documentary is a national asset which even the theatres will recognize, but in lesser times, no; it belongs to where the serious purpose is continuous; and that is where the community leadership of all kinds quietly and continuously lies. I wish the Canadian example was properly understood where, with urgency less pressing, the whole development was geared, as it could be geared, to a long term conception of documentary's relation to the national service. It will be a pity if, falsely interpreting its success, it too, but more gratuitously, falls into the error of following the wrong signpost.

As it is, we have three major fronts on which to work. Non-theatrical has to be built up with new thought and energy—a new overall

355

strategy I suggest—so that it will justify both the cost and energies of serving it. The non-theatrical audience is in and around twenty millions a year at present. We should aim at fifty millions in the next three years. To that end we have to organize specialized audiences as never before: in terms of their functional needs as well as in terms of general cultural interest. Essentially a supply of cheap projectors—under £150 —has to be established. Regional Film Councils and Film Locals have to be organized to see that each specialized interest in the community is organized and served. Here the B.F.I. has a lead to take, but there must be such support of it from all quarters that it has the real financial wherewithal to do its work.

Production must now free itself from false leads and forget any notions it may have had that documentary is God's gift to the exhibitor except where film journalism is concerned, and that success in it is a short cut through the looking-glass to the studios and the Screen Writers' Bar. A stop there must be on this utter confusion.

Documentary's freedom and quality lie where they always did lie— in the simple process of serving where service is wanted, however modest the prizes may seem to be. It is not by accident that the camera work is less fresh and moving today, the cutting less dynamic, the sound less exploratory and inventive than they were ten years ago, nor is it by accident that the writing in general is terrible and the habit of work less satisfactory to all concerned. In the confusion of ends there is neither concentration of energy nor the happy exercise of special *fortes*. In the organization of non-theatrical distribution and the sorting out of all the many talents in regard to it there is much hope. I could only wish that A.C.T., that haggard echo of the great illusion, would see it that way. Television, so to speak, is here with us, and no voice in the wilderness or wild honey about it. If it inherits, as it surely will, the great B.B.C. tradition, at least half of what we have wanted is secure. We have had to take it the hard way, finding sponsorship in government and elsewhere when the ways of commerce failed; and we have had the advantage of giving our work a real and practical consideration. But the television way with film must by its very nature be freer of foot. Good people and good things will be allowed for, if the Third Programme is any guide, but even at that it will not allow for all. There are deeper and fresher interests still which even now make the Third Programme sanctimonious, old-fashioned, right, long after the right time and stupid with academic humbug. That other interest we must surely guard and keep for ourselves. Many specialized groups and interests there are which will be served as the

Progress and Prospect

B.B.C. now in sound serves them; but again there are others which television on a general service cannot be expected to reach.

So the broad road forks out today. Some will be wise to take the path of television before the West End theatre boys get hold of it and frivol it for good. Others like myself must keep to sponsorship and not only out of the long habit of living with the hair shirts that go with it. Contact with government has its own special privilege, even creatively; not less in these days when governments begin to make definition of æsthetic. Where, however, the way of the artist lies it would be difficult to judge. It will be a hard way either way.

All I know is that a daffy civil servant—like Sir Stephen Tallents—is the nearest thing to the Medici the free artist is likely to find in these difficult times, and I am glad beyond words that he has been invited to open the Edinburgh Festival. It is the opportunity for the free artist that needs most to be emphasized today, when reorganization of so drastic an order has necessarily to occupy our minds so much.

4 The Malaise of Disillusionment

Norman Wilson, Chairman of the Edinburgh Film Festival, writes: 'It seems to me that documentary has fallen on evil days. Good enough expositional films still get made, but without a sense of urgency or belief. There is no fire, no guts. People are good enough at making films but not at using them to shape ideas, to dig out the heart of a matter. Whether this is so or not, there is a wide-spread feeling that it is. It may be the post-war malaise of disillusionment. But what are the portents? Is the spring recoiling? If a resurgence of the old spirit means a new advance, what direction is it likely to take, is already taking, or should take? Does it take the attack right into the feature field and do in the public cinemas what it once did in non-theatrical? These are the kind of questions that need answering. Everyone is bloody disgusted with the way the world has gone and, before long, the sulky pessimism will become septic. Faiths have become politics and people are sick with mistrust. I don't know how all this fits with the present set-up but what is the score as you see it?'

In a way, I wish Wilson had asked someone else, for it is a hard go for me to answer: at least answer objectively. I have been personally involved at so many points; and personal disappointments do not make for the coldest judgments. One thing I will not do this time, however, is to follow my common practice and begin with an account of all the good things I see. I have done that too often: and not least at the C.O.I. What was intended as an encouragement to further sight and effort has been used, to my chagrin, to support a goodly number of dull wits and fat backsides in complacent and now utterly ugly mediocrity.

By and large, the men who run documentary today—and I mean the people who sponsor its ultimate shapes and qualities—do not care a damn for the purposes it once professed and the ends which gave it its larger life. And how could they care any more for its æsthetic possibilities when, with rare exception, they don't know æsthetic form from a hole in the ground? No, I think the time has come to say plainly that documentary as an art, documentary as a power of persuasion, documentary as a valuable instrument of national projection, is being allowed to go by default and a generation of film-makers ruined and lost to the State by a fumbling régime of sponsors unworthy of their predecessors and their origins. Comfortable as they may be in their all too vulgarly sought bureaucratic security, they are stifling a great public asset and serving their country ill.

But all this negative stuff is not explanation. Let us say what we can of good for the sponsors—and it is the Government ones, of course, I mean. If they took the easy and frequently cowardly path, it was in a difficult situation. Any idea of a national programme—i.e. of films that took inspiration from the basic themes of national life and progress—was bust up when sponsorship was returned by law to the Departments. There was, for a moment, a brave little loophole. The C.O.I. had, in principle, a degree of latitude for other than departmental films. It could, with persistence, have had an 'own right' programme, i.e. a national one. But the Treasury was, of course, cagey lest an over-use of 'own rights' contravened the spirit of the order to return sponsorship to the Departments. The safe thing was to let 'own rights' go by default; and safety was certainly the watch-word of the P.R.O. tribe of Whitehall outsiders who so anxiously and unctuously sought its protective shelter.

Then again, the moment was the moment of socialism in its first flush of electoral victory. Heaven forgive an old radical for saying it, but we have had too many socialists in the P.R.O. system. Correct, as I am sure they all try to be, I never knew a group so uncritically quick to serve their masters. The only great friend documentary had, and the film industry for that matter, was Sir Stafford Cripps. The others, for many good reasons and some bad ones, could not allow their imaginations or their energies to reach that far. They had vast new political programmes and could only think of information services that were tied directly to these programmes. Whence the new emphasis on exposition: whence the bewildering boredom in these first years of exhortation on exhortation: whence above all the sensitivity to any atmosphere of criticism whatsoever.

In the issue, art went out because the relationship of art to the all too immediate purpose and the all too immediate measurement of results was not within the political mood. Add, too, that here was a party with long years of opposition behind it and a trades union foundation which in its grasp of cultural values had never seen beyond suburbia. The only arts it really understood and trusted were the art of the platform and the art of political management. You might think that the new school of university experts which they recruited would have supplied that little something else they didn't have. Not a bit of it. The even greater limitation of the London School of Economics offspring and their like was that they understood no arts at all. I once argued with one such that the socialist movement would never come near owning the country till it pinched the English spring from the Tories. He thought it was good fun for an idea but crazy. Of course there hasn't been a film of the spring or anything near the spring for years. For spring, read that so many many themes that could lift the heart again and documentary with it. I have proposed them by the dozen only to lose them, without support, to the mere two and two makes four of the new bureaucracy.

I think I know what has been lost, but it is not only people like myself who should worry about it. It is not the artists who have lost most but the ministers and the régime itself. I say no régime has ever been so profoundly let down in certain fundamentals by its advisers as the Socialist one. The alternative thought is that the disorder is integral to its nature and bound in time to destroy it. Some of my Tory friends say so and gladly as they realize my difficulty; and certainly, the happier early history of the documentary film is with them. I will not believe it; but, if I do not, it means a long row to hoe before that X factor is added. It means an attack inside the party and towards the ministers themselves. All too many of their servitors are a positive screen against a more deeply imaginative and more national service of information under socialism and, by that token, are positive enemies of the co-operative state itself.

Don't think, however, that the film people have not had a responsibility too for the present disorder. Again I shall be plain. I think a lot of people came into documentary who had no conception whatever of its larger reaches; and a great number still have no inkling of the difference between artist and technician. In fact, the standard of approach has progressively over a period been sadly lowered. For another factor, the unusual protection secured for documentary film-making over a period of years was shockingly exploited. In some cases, there was not even a bare modicum of responsibility towards costs and schedules; and the freedom of the artist, a vital principle in itself, if realistically urged, was made a cover for attitudes and actions which had only a nodding acquaintance with creative effort. When irresponsible, half-baked political slants were being sneaked into films, it meant of course that documentary films came to be watched. It did not greatly help, for the watchers were generally as dumb a lot as the people they were watching. In the event the whole thing suffered. The inevitable controls came and had to.

There was an implicit understanding that when reasonable disciplines were established and confidence restored, there would be expansion again. Perhaps we did not look closely enough into men's eyes. The undertaking was not implemented. The bureaucrats had at last got something they understood. Why undergo the daily embarrassment of not knowing when two and two makes five? There it presently rests.

Now another gambit. Forget the government boys and take the documentary movement itself. It rode in on a wave of the future; for, correctly, it understood and allied itself with up-and-coming social democracy. It had the success which comes to all movements that are just ahead of their time when it took as its basic themes the discovery of working people, the dramatization of modern technological society and the social revolution inevitably developing within it. It represented in fact the only art which social democracy has uniquely produced; and this will be true even if all Socialist ministers save Cripps have been sublimely unaware of it. But where, with the Socialist victory, did we go from there?

Already some of us feared the complacency which would set in. We went after the international aspects of the co-operative society and did so long before the United Nations got organized. We had foreseen the implications of W.H.O. and F.A.O. in early films. We had the dramatic implications of international trade and communications and of the humanist responsibilities which went with them before our minds since the days of the E.M.B. and the G.P.O. As we saw it, documentary could only keep really alive as it kept in the forefront of political and economic thought, realizing at every step the æsthetic implications. I have already said that a lot of people came in who had none of these larger considerations in mind. In fact, documentary came to be no longer a school of thought and of conscious continuing public effort, but a vast overexpanded rabble of individuals competing for jobs and vanities. Perhaps a core of co-ordinated thinking could have been maintained. All I know is that there came a time when a lot of characters got tired of the effort. Their psychiatrists, when they had psychiatrists, and their womenfolk, when they couldn't afford psychiatrists, told them that they were wasting their time, and that they were heaven-sent artists on their quite quite personal account and that the less they had to do with schools and their disciplines the better for their immortal souls. I wouldn't know about immortal souls but I am still waiting for the heaven-sent artists who didn't need the old give-and-take of co-operative effort to support their genius.

The truth is that the constant politico-social-æsthetic drive which British documentary presupposed is a tough show to maintain when detached from, say, an organized political discipline. One part of my head tells me it is, in fact, impossible; another still beguiles me with the thought that the persistence of a co-operative unit to liberal creative purposes is, in a co-operative world, infinitely more possible in the end than the persistence of an individual. Whence, incidentally, the most careful development, by documentary, of the word 'unit'.

Why does Norman Wilson talk of the lack of a sense of 'urgency or belief'? Why does he mention the 'post-war malaise of disillusionment'? Why is 'everyone bloody disgusted'? Wherefore this 'sulky pessimism which will become septic'? He is surely describing a world in which individuals thought to find their own little primrose paths, all bravely by their own little selves.

For my part I say that the reaching towards the manners, disciplines and æsthetic of co-operative man must take a long time; and this of course, Lenin said before me. And break down in a co-operative art like ours cannot be final so long as social democracy halts so tragically at its national frontiers, leaves the larger mass of mankind to its own troubled devices and challenges everyone daily to renew his faith in the brotherhood of mankind. The old themes are there to be seen afresh in the vital struggles of uprising peoples; new themes are there too, almost begging, in their international cross reference, that all the film's command of relationships in time and space be exercised to articulate and illumine the extraordinary new human shapings of our time. Since the making of films cannot be commanded by individuals, obviously a real co-operative effort must be made again if documentary is in the next phase to have authoritative significance.

But what are the immediate practicalities? Such suggestions as lie implicit in this argument will not of course immediately recommend themselves to normal film finance. On the other hand, films about the Colonies would. If based on a common humanism and in dramatic terms enough, I see no special bar to their emergence. Dramatic documentary at home? Well, the inquiry into the Knockshinnoch disaster was a great story in itself and, as I think, sure-fire from a theatre viewpoint. Putting it at its lowest, did you ever know a mining film that didn't make money? But why did no documentary unit register it? So also with the story of Poole the gunman, who, I am told, actually appeared in *Children on Trial*. For failure of a really organized, purposive documentary school, themes like these, with every practical possibility in them, have been almost childishly passed by, and will again.

I know how difficult it is. Our film financing is crazily anarchic, taken as a whole, and is only in the first infant stages of being brought to national order. But it does not excuse everyone looking to others to touch their genius on the shoulder, as many have been looking latterly to Group 3. The fact is that it has money for five films, without the guarantee of continuity which is necessary if it is to be a real factor in the situation. So far, it has at least had the wit to pick up Knockshinnoch: but in the name of story, not documentary. So far as the larger life of documentary in the theatre is concerned, it is at present only a spit in the dark. That, too, means further emphasis on the point I have noted that there must be a genuinely purposive central school of thought and effort which will develop all possible opportunities wherever they may appear.

Knockshinnoch and Poole represent a more or less traditional approach to the documentary uses of film. Paul Rotha's *No Resting Place* does not, but who will say that in this story of life in the rough among Irish tinkers he does not express in dramatic realism what is at the heart of the documentary approach? Not because it is a rough film about tinkers but because it comes close to the bone and muscle of actual human relationship, it cuts away under the surface from the world of make-believe in which we are presently, as Wilson puts it, so 'sick with mistrust'.

But given that new and purposive centre for documentary, given the new leadership which the younger generation has so often and so boldly said it would give, there are a dozen other fronts: some waiting for ideas, some ripe, for one reason or another, to be stormed. Television is still wide open and would, I am pretty sure, have taken a theme like Knockshinnoch. Both W.H.O. and F.A.O., short of direct money as they may be, are so functionally associated in purpose with so many forces all over the world that one must conclude *a priori* that the opportunities which reside in them are enormous. The disturbances in the Middle East and elsewhere have their implications in a new will on the part of government and industrial authorities alike to bring alive, and in dramatic form, their foreign relationships. And if I read aright, the Colonial Office is a great big sitter for a concerted authoritative attack. No, it won't come except from within the documentary movement itself, organizing itself anew to undertake it.

I say in the end that difficult as things have been, and thwarted by

political and economic circumstances as so many are, there is much
that a re-dedication to basic documentary terms and organization
along classical lines can in good measure effect. In infidelity to both
we have lost time and opportunity. It is a high moment for a few brave
spirits to separate the sheep from the goats and secure the concentrated
effort of an organized group willing, in loyalty and discipline, to give
documentary a purpose again and work and plan and fight for it. Our
deviations, personally comfortable as they may have proved for some,
have not recently produced a single film that does not make *Housing
Problems* look a master work of integrity. I repeat, not one.

5 Documentary: A World Perspective

Because of Britain's unique contribution to the development of the documentary film in the thirties, there is still a tendency in England to judge the documentary film today by the British example. That would be wrong. Documentary films of one kind or another are being produced all over the world. The total world production may be in the region of fifty thousand films a year or more. Britain produces two or three hundred only. Think of all the different categories of documentary production, e.g. public reporting, scientific films, technical films, instructional films, etc. Think of all the governments and government departments which in various countries have their own film programmes of public information and education. Remember all the hundreds of state and civic authorities, industries, laboratories, colleges, hospitals which make films for their own special purposes. The largest producers are bound to be those most concerned with intensive technical education (e.g. Russia and the U.S.A., possibly China). The most organized production countries are bound to be those with national planning systems for both education and uplift. I do not know the figures for Russia and cannot get at them. Poland, Czechoslovakia, Yugoslavia, East Germany and Hungary have each an annual production of some hundreds.

The original British documentary school made much of 'poetic' documentary and 'humanist' documentary. This type of film is very much in a minority today in contrast to the flood of documentary films in the above mentioned more practical categories. By and large the most distinguished documentary films æsthetically are to be found in Poland, Czechoslovakia, Canada, Germany, Holland, Italy, France and the United States. There are occasional good ones from odd countries like Brazil (Santos) and Bolivia (Jorge Ruiz). Australia is always on the edge of good documentary in this æsthetic category. The British contribution is not as relatively important as it once was.

There were two reasons for Britain's original importance in the documentary field.

One. It was the first country to use the documentary film in an

365

organized way to implement governmental and public purposes (E.M.B., G.P.O., health, slum clearance, town planning, popularization of scientific discovery, Commonwealth relations, international communications, colonial education, etc.). No one should think now that because of its success this was an easy and smooth development. The Treasury was always against the idea of the government participating directly in film production. In fact it got out of it after the war but not before presenting an example to the world of government sponsorship and, by its own example and teaching, encouraging the creating of good independent production units outside the government service. British documentary's most interesting period was in its early stages when individual ministers were directly and personally interested in the documentary film (Kingsley Wood, Walter Elliot, etc.). Its most powerful period was during the war when the Treasury guards were down (Crown Film Unit).

Two. The early British approach to documentary was from the beginning both complex and ambitious. The film-makers sought finance in the name of public information, public relations, technical instruction, etc., but at the same time sought to develop the æsthetic forms of the documentary film within the framework of public information. The first film in that category was *Drifters*. Other good examples were *Song of Ceylon, Night Mail* and *North Sea*. Others had made documentary films before the British school developed (Flaherty, Ruttmann, etc.). The unique British message to film-makers was that good documentary in its æsthetic forms could be achieved within the limits set by public information and with some prospect of a share in the vast financial support which public information offers. It was this possibility proved practical which lit up the film-makers across the world. In an important way the British documentary idea discovered for film-makers everywhere the prospect of making a living at it.

The official acceptance of the relationship between public information and the film-makers was, of course, limited in England. It depended very largely on personal persuasion at the higher levels (ministers and senior civil servants, i.e. people like Walter Elliot and Sir Stephen Tallents). The constant critical influence of *The Times* had also great effect. The writings of the documentary people (Paul Rotha and myself mostly) piled up and so enlarged documentary's public authority. It is notable that in other countries it has been relatively easy, following the British example, to secure government support for straightforward reportorial and instructional films and for straightforward propaganda documentary. But documentary as an art form has emerged in the public information field only where the same forces as in England operated, i.e. personal persuasion at the highest levels and the support of important newspapers and good critical writing generally. The best example overseas is Canada where the Prime Minister, Mackenzie King, gave me his personal backing and almost a blank cheque in support. Other examples today of government sponsorship at a high level are to be found in Poland, Czechoslovakia, Yugoslavia and Holland. The power to deliver has, of course, also to be taken into account. In every successful case there were the artists present to deliver on the æsthetic promise and within the framework of public information purposes.

The wartime achievement of the Crown Film Unit is not a true guide to the general line of development. The conditions then were favourable to effort of any dramatic order and, as I have noted, the Treasury guard was down. In the thirties we could only with care and persistent effort get over it. Around 1934 and 1935 there was a logical attempt to expand the range of documentary from communications (G.P.O.) to health, housing and labour relations—in fact an attempt to bring in the Ministries of Health and Labour. It failed. The effect was to drive us to such other sponsorship as would allow us the same relationship between public information purposes and documentary in its various forms—with informational forms as the mainstream, æsthetic forms if possible. It was for this development that Film Centre was set up and independent production units, based on the principles of the original documentary group, established (e.g. Realist, International Realist, Strand, Basic and Data). This was spectacularly successful. The Shell organization welcomed the idea and started on a documentary film career which has been as influential as any anywhere. The Gas Light and Coke Company for years did first-rate work in health and housing. The Films of Scotland was set up to organize independent sponsorship in Scotland and operates to this day. The example of these earlier leaders in the field has been followed by other industrial sponsors—B.O.A.C., I.C.I., The British Transport Commission, etc. But only in the case of British Transport has there been the same drive towards æsthetic result.

This acceptance by industrial sponsors of the British government's example involved an important development of their normal ideas in publicity and propaganda. It meant: (*a*) The acceptance of the idea of the long-term persuasive power of æsthetic forms as distinguished from the shorter-term effect of mere publicity and propaganda; (*b*) A study by industries of the wider implications of their public responsibilities and public image. This acceptance has had in time a considerable influence on both government and industrial film-making in the United States largely through the American film-makers who learnt directly or indirectly from our teaching and example. In Canada the industrial and other non-governmental sponsors had the present example of the work of the National Film Board to follow which, of course, was of our own founding. Here again the government film-makers became the leaders of a more imaginative sponsorship in the non-government world.

I don't think there is any question that British documentary's principal claim to importance in the history of the cinema is in what it taught about the wider and more organized uses of the film in the public service, and about the more various and deeper aspects, the documentary film might take in the public service. In these matters it went far ahead of anything before it and in fact was something different in kind. There is, of course, nothing comparable to the organization of the so-called documentary 'movement' in Britain and the missionary zeal with which it set out first to expand its range in Britain and then explain its doctrine to countries outside Britain.

The once so-called British Documentary School may not be important in Britain today nor are British documentary films as distinguished or distinguishable as they once were at the international festivals. But, I repeat, the limitation today means only that the British Documentary School did not stay at home but, because of its nature, spread abroad and particularly to those countries where the need for it was most deeply rooted (in young countries like Canada and in the underprivileged countries which like Malaya, Ghana, Egypt, Iran, Iraq, Venezuela and India, had much to do in building the future—and in those countries like Poland where the central planning and direction of the educational forces were most intensive). The real continuity of the original documentary idea lies in fact elsewhere and logically so.

Here are the influences which propagated the British documentary idea overseas.

One. The overseas film distribution service of the Foreign Office, Dominions Office and, at various times, of other government agencies —largely inspired by the early documentary movement—did much to show the British documentary example across the world.

Two. The critical attention given to British documentary films in Britain influenced critical attention elsewhere. Here the attachment of *The Times* to the documentary development was important. So were

Desert Victory (British 1942–3)
 Produced by the Army Film and Photographic Unit and the R.A.F. Film Unit

Fires Were Started (British, 1943)
 Produced by Crown Film Unit: directed by Humphrey Jennings

Crofters (British, 1944)
   Produced by Green Park Productions: directed by Ralph Keene

Children of the City (British, 1944)
   Produced by Paul Rotha Productions: directed by Budge Cooper

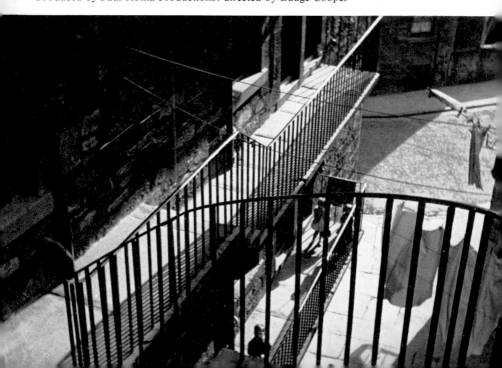

the critical notices of specialized film journals, e.g. *Cinema Quarterly, World Film News, Sight and Sound* and *Documentary Newsletter*. Our own documentary writings had world-wide circulation and translation, particularly those of Rotha and myself. To this add the influence in international film meetings of the British Film Institute and the Scientific Film Association.

Three. The Imperial Relations Trust had a lot to do originally with the setting up of the National Film Board in Canada, Australia and New Zealand and in turn the example of the National Film Board of Canada had a most powerful influence in setting up similar organizations to meet national needs in many countries. This participation of the Imperial Relations Trust (Lady Reading and Sir Stephen Tallents had a lot to do with it) which is almost totally forgotten today, is quite a fascinating incidental chapter in the total story. I personally owed it much for its co-operation at an important juncture in documentary development.

Four. The establishment of film units in the colonies by the Colonial Office, particularly in Malaya and Ghana and the sending of documentary teachers to India and the creation of non-theatrical distribution systems in many of the colonies should be taken into account for the examples they provided to other under-privileged countries.

Five. The world abroad of Film Centre working with Shell has been very important. Sir Arthur Elton was chiefly responsible. It involved the setting up of units and the training of native documentary groups in Iran, Iraq, Egypt, India, Singapore, Nigeria and Venezuela. It is a fascinating story of modern missionary work undertaken in the name of industrial public relations.

Certain incidental factors contributed to this development apart from the original international potential of the documentary idea itself. The first flush of documentary in Britain was sustained by such practical realities as the drive to a new conception of Commonwealth relations after the Statute of Westminster, the swift growth of modern international communications, the growth of international interdependence on scientific levels and of course by the wave of social reconstruction in Britain which in the thirties affected government policies no matter what party was in power.

Driving forces of this kind have either diminished or have not been mobilized as they once were for documentary purposes. Perhaps there has been a diminishing of the creative will. Certainly there has not been the same sense of relationship with government and other sponsors on high levels of public policy. Certainly there has not been the same wish on the part of new documentary film men to be part and parcel of the larger public purpose.

Note that the government after the intensity of the propaganda drive during the war most deliberately demobilized its propaganda forces. Government sponsorship passed to the bureaucratic committees of the various ministries working through the bureaucratic controls of the C.O.I. So far as documentary films are concerned there has been no first-rate imaginative approach to government sponsorship since the war. Oddly enough it was the Labour Party which carried out the demobilization. I think only one Labour minister really realized what was creatively involved. That was Sir Stafford Cripps.

This has not been the total disaster it might seem. It is true that the documentary films produced on the old sponsorship basis do not make the same impact today on the international scene and are outshone by films of many other countries, except in the case of the scientific films of the Shell Film Unit. On the other hand, much of what was best in the documentary movement has been taken over by the B.B.C. To get a fair picture of British documentary on its wider fronts you must take into account not only the international development noted above but the national development in the television field.

It is clear that in the straight reporting field and in the editorial field inherited from *March of Time* and *World in Action*, work is being done in British documentary television as good as any in any other country. On the reportorial level consider the excellence of the coverage on the Coronation, the crowning of Pope John, the Rome Olympics, the wedding of Princess Margaret, the return of Gagarin and the Moscow May Day Parade. On the editorial level consider the impact of the B.B.C. reporting of the Electrical Trade Union story. Remember the first-rate stuff on the American presidential elections and Anthony Lotbinière's 'The Candidate'. In other categories of documentary take into account 'The Magistrate's Court' (Ross-Atkins); 'Unmarried Mothers' and 'Prostitution' (Morris-Calder); Dennis Mitchell's 'Morning in the Streets', 'Night in the City', 'Strangeways Gaol', 'Chicago' and the trilogy from Africa. There is John Schlesinger with his 'Innocent Eye', Benjamin Britten and 'The Class'; Kenneth Russell's 'Prokofiev' and 'House in Bayswater'; Cawston's 'On Call to a Nation' and 'The Lawyers'. There is John Ormond at the B.B.C. in Wales with 'Borrowed Pasture' and 'Once There was a Time'. You would certainly have to include Philip Donellan's work in 'Joe the Chainsmith' and Robert Barr's in 'Medico' and find a special spot for many excellent documentary vignettes in 'Monitor', 'Panorama' and 'Tonight'.

Documentary in television makes, you see, quite a story. There are some first-rate documentary people at the B.B.C. on any level of criticism and don't forget the people behind the scenes like the editor behind 'Monitor' (Allen Tyrer) and that powerful woman on many fronts of production, Grace Wyndham Goldie.

You have still more to take account of in ITV with Granada's Report on the Pill and Homosexuality and A.R.'s 'Two Faces of Japan' and 'The Quiet War' by Peter Morley and 'Main Street, America' by James Breedon.

Here a note in parenthesis about the group which called itself Free Cinema. It is easy to dismiss it but in my point of view it will turn up again and in more powerful form. It was an attempt to fill the gap left by the after-war failure of government sponsorship but in fact it found no alternative source of finance for ambitious documentary films and perished like the French *avant garde* in the late twenties and for the same reasons. Its origins were mixed. It was partly influenced by the neo-realist movement in Italy and by the *Nouvelle Vague* in France. It reflected—oddly in Britain—something of the spiritual pessimism of a defeated France. It was conscious too of the neo-anarchism of the beatnik movement in America. In so far as it was English it was close to the lower middle-class protest against upper-class privilege of the so-called Angry Young Men. In so far as it adopted a working-class motif its affection was a little like the Jewish affection for the Negro cause in the United States. What was best in it, and most native, turned up in the theatre with two or three very considerable talents—John Osborne, Arnold Wesker, etc.—to give it reality and with an economic root that proved a practical one. I haven't a doubt that you will hear of it again as the group's success in the theatre emerges as a phenomenon of the commercial cinema.

In fact the story of the British documentary film is only weak if you look at its continuity under British government sponsorship which is pretty awful these days and under industrial sponsorship which is no longer as inspired as it was. This latter may be partly the fault of the film-makers who may have gone too commercial or just plain complacent.

Look at the British documentary overseas, look at it under B.B.C. television auspices, look at it as it is coming up via neo-realism in the theatre and you may have a very different picture.

371

6 Learning from Television

What had I learned in five years of television? Quite a bit I thought. Now I am not so sure. Reckoning it up, much of television is derivative, not to say parasitic, which is Sinatra's word. There is nothing necessarily wrong in the derivative. It is good, for example, that more people should see plays. What's wrong in being derivative is when you debase the original tradition. The great tradition of the theatre is not greatly served. The tradition of the cinema is quite shabbily served, except in the case of the newsreels, the sports reports and the actualities generally, which are done better. Yet even news and political and public commentary are more thoroughly done elsewhere. As for television as parasite, it is a continuously uncomfortable and ugly thing: invading privacy on what the victim, poor devil, has thought a privileged occasion, exploiting personal emotions and human weaknesses as nastily as the dirtiest of sideshows; the B.B.C. with even more unforgettable and unforgivable instances than its commercial competitor.

But then again there is much to put in the balance. I think immediately of the horses and the fights and Real Madrid and Cliff Michelmore: Michelmore and his like a phenomenon one only glimpsed at the *Deux Ânes* and the *Dix Heures* and patently one of the unique gifts of the new medium itself. I think too of the unexpectedness that goes with television. You never know what is going to turn up: something you never thought to see, or even thought seeable: someone precious you never thought to meet. Nor may one deny to television that with all its faults and failures, superficialities and vulgarities, it is widening the horizons of observation and of consideration, on a vast scale, and making people just a little more fit to be citizens of a modern society.

For the present I confine myself mainly to two points that interest me personally. The first is the visual tradition deriving from the cinema and what is now happening to it in television. The second is the nature of the television relationship with people. I carefully don't say the 'public' because I have a notion that television has other and more

372

intimate relationships than the word 'public' denotes. I will take the two points separately.

A recent article in the London *Times* made the announcement that 'pure cinema is dead'. 'There it is,' the article repeated, 'pure cinema has perished,' but pure radio, i.e. sound radio, has not. It was a thoughtful article, devoted to the proposition that television, like the talkies, is a bastard form so far as visuals are concerned, but that steam radio is a purer medium altogether, with 'therapeutic and restorative' powers to which television cannot aspire.

It is this notion that the cinema has been killed off along the way by the talkies and television, which fascinates as a point for argument. I won't take advantage of the fact that there never was a purely visual or silent cinema, for there was always attendant noise of some kind or another. Indeed the more the silent cinema came to take itself seriously the more seriously its exponents took their musical scores. Round they went to the theatres and, in many cases, it was a matter of compulsion to play them. What matters, however, is that we consider a little more carefully what really happened to this visual art of ours with the coming of synchronized sound, and what is happening to it now with television. It has been enormously affected, but is there something *sui generis* and precious which has actually and inevitably perished?

There has been from the beginning something special and, if you like, *sui generis*, in what the motion picture could do. The old simple arguments are still valid, e.g. the camera can get around and so provide new vistas of things observed. Not the least of these new vistas was in the comedy that got out and about and into the streets with Mack Sennett. Add the various kinds of lenses and there are other worlds again open to the cinema. Speed the action and slow it and you not only add to your possible effects, dramatic or other, but the range of human observation is extended still further. Develop the idea of the 'Kino-eye', consider the infinite possibilities of varying the viewpoint of the camera, develop the possibilities of the 'montage' and you finish up with an array of powers, all native to the cinema, capable of bringing it to the point of æsthetic measurement. These were the elementary principles on which we all in the early days operated. They are probably so obvious to everyone today that they have been lost sight of, by being taken for granted like Chesterton's postman. It may be that what was once exciting because it was a new kind of observation is so much part and parcel of our common observation in television that many no longer recognize it as cinema, not to say pure cinema.

International

Certainly there have been developments in the cinema which have affected movie as movie for better or for worse. For example, one influence of television on the film business has been to drive it to very large-scale films and diminish the production of 'B' films and 'C' films. Here is an observation on that by Norman Holland in the *Hudson Review*. 'Hollywood unfortunately has come to prefer the impure or un-film: the meticulous redaction of Broadway plays and best-selling novels. To some extent, of course, Hollywood has always drawn on the novel and often with consummate success (*Sierra Madre*, *No Down Payment*, and so on). But within the last four or five years, this kind of safe-A film has almost blotted out the B's and C's and X's that worked from less successful (therefore, less fulfilled and exhausted) novels and treated them more cinematically. It used to be idle—or scholarly—to compare films to the novels from which they were taken; now, one can scarcely avoid it. The index to the change is the difference between Stanley Kubrick's *The Killing* (1956) or *Paths of Glory* (1957) and his *Lolita* (1962). The earlier films were real films; *Lolita* is in the current style of the un-film.'

This would seem to make a point in our correspondent's favour but we have *The Times* in yet another moment of judgment noting with admiration—presumably cinematic admiration—the work of Bunuel, Bresson, Antonioni, Bergman, Godard, Truffaut and Fellini, with an accolade for Hitchcock that could only possibly go to his devotion to cinematic technique. And *The Times* might well have noted at the same time the work of the Polish, Czechoslovakian and Japanese film schools. On this balance it would seem the battle for movie as movie is taking a long time to get lost.

One thing must certainly have made our correspondent gloomy. It is the ponderous record—in the dramatic story field—of television with its cameras. It is, to say the least, a simple record and even at times a simpleton record. One reason, they say, is that the cheapness of television's methods—the sometimes appalling and appallingly unnecessary cheapness of television methods—drives it inevitably to what we can only in visual terms describe as amateur theatricals. But there are other factors involved. The medium itself is in some ways predisposed, and properly predisposed, to the amateur. Then again there is in England a far-reaching suburban preference for the uncomplicated in art; and this æsthetic laziness reaches even to the highest quarters of criticism: as when T. S. Eliot is preferred to O'Neill on one of the greatest theatrical occasions of our time; as when the Royal Academy declares itself on Picasso. Indeed the amateur and/or suburban is so much less challenged than it is say in France or America that many might claim that the predisposition to it is, in its shabby, proud sort of way, a national or Anglican characteristic.

This, of course, affects in the first place the choice of theme and subject matter and to that extent makes many people like myself restive in the presence of television programmes and of the dramatic programmes in particular. I simply do not share their sense of importance. On the other hand the picture is not altogether dark. There is an obvious challenge coming up from below in the choice of subject matter which, even if it is not critically articulate as yet, is making a rough impact of the suburban complacencies. One notes cheerfully the presence of 'foreigners' like Sydney Newman in our midst and the growing strength of talent with a more continental sense of dramatic value.

The same relative optimism does not however apply to the visual presentation in television. If there is one generalization one may make with something like certitude it is that in certain categories of production television is just not good-looking enough and, after any considered experience of the cinema, uncomfortable to look at. In fact our wonderful peripatetic cameras are not getting around any more, at least not enough. The special powers of expression resident in the multiple possibilities of the camera and the multiple possibilities of recorded sound (just as important and just as native to the cinema) are largely ignored. You might think sometimes that we have hardly gone a step forward from the days of *The Co-optimists* and *Rookery Nook*. That was over thirty years ago.

Yet here again the picture is not all dark. Dark it is in the dramatic field and deep dark it is in the matter of visual poetry, but there have been other visual developments in television which positively delight. For one thing Newman, who is after our old persuasion, is not likely to forget the number he first thought of and there has been sign of this; and I seem to remember in the comedies things from Charlie Drake and Arthur Haynes and Benny Hill and, on occasion, from Hancock, harking back to the more joyous technical days of cinema comedy. Michael Bentine is as movie as they come and so, they tell me, was Spike Milligan in his Australian programmes.

As for the visual record of television in the matter of actualities, it is positively first rate. Television's newsreels are better than we ever had from the cinema. Its sports reporting is in a different and higher class and not just because of television's immediacy: it is better and far more knowingly shot. Its 'editorial' reportage, deriving from the

375

March of Time and *World in Action*, covers a far wider and more penetrating front than we could pretend to, though the present proponents are not, I think, as visually conscious as we were. I am sure that must come.

In general, we can say that in England today the documentary film has in television its most powerful sponsor. I think British television *as producer* has largely failed documentary in its wider and more æsthetically important aspects; on the other hand, it has to be said that television is its most appreciative and powerful presenter and exhibitor. It may be that in television today there is a relative ignorance of what these other more æsthetically important aspects are. Some of the boys down below know very well and, given a chance, show it; but how little, relatively, are they given that chance. The very success of television with its reportage and actualities today—derived, note you, from a movie tradition—has it would seem blinded television somewhat to the larger reaches. When it comes to the poetics these bright young fellows in their new high places just don't want to know and say so openly. Much as one must admire their achievements, it represents a sort of blind ignoring of other possibilities which makes one shudder. Will it last? Of course it won't, and let this be a first cheerful shot across their bows to remind them that they are under observation. The issue is for me deeply important. I just hate to think that all the good things in the poetic line of documentary are coming from foreigners: the more so in that it was from England they first learned to follow it.

Summing up so far, I get a picture of television as a very mixed bag of tricks in a pioneer situation with a strong and positive challenge to mediocrity in all aspects of reportage and a fair prospect of better things even in drama; with visual developments in television far behind reasonable expectation in every field except actualities. I discount to some extent the excuse of budgetary limitations on the ground that others, before television, have done well with their visuals and on similar short rations; and here I cite early Chicago and early Hollywood, the French *avant garde*, early British documentary, early Russian cinema and the best of the American 'B' and 'C' pictures. As they say on the motto of that Girls' School in the Parliament Hill Fields 'It's the low aim that does it', not the nature of television as such. That anyway is my view and I propose therefore in a separate note to have a look at the television medium to see where possibly it may of its nature be limiting or enlarging to the larger creative ambitions.

Television involves a vast and various service and with much of that

I need not be concerned. It is altogether proper that it should provide a hundred and one diversities which may be thought to be superficial by some but are welcomed by many. As I have noted, television has a predisposition to the amateur in the sense that it provides a platform for people and for problems which we could never conceive of the theatre or the cinema accommodating. This I find excellent, for it means that we, devoted no doubt to the tittle-tattle of our own community, share the equally vital tittle-tattle of others. Without disrespect, let me cite the gardening programmes as representing that splendid category of television interest, at its best.

But even if we allow that television is correct in giving all these ordinary services to ordinary people and utterly right to see that nobody monkeys around with their blessed ordinariness, there are other fields in which television operates and must operate which of their own nature carry the implications of creative effort and public responsibility. It is at that point and only at that point that the low aim becomes important and the excuses, pointing to the 'inevitable' limitations of the medium and the 'inevitable' limitations represented by the TV audience, obnoxious. To begin with, I doubt if we know much about what the medium is greatly capable of, dramatically or in general æsthetically, for the simple reason that we have only superficially tried it out; and with first-rate creative visual artists only oddly, and in only one or two categories of effort.

Then, too, I doubt if we know very much about that so-called audience, for the equally simple reason that the television conception of audience is the most blindly derivative of all television derivatives. It comes directly from the mass approaches of the film business, not in its best aspect but in its worst. As I watch them count their heads, whether on ITV calculations or the B.B.C.'s, I find myself having the same doubts we once had in our early movie days, when we initiated the Film Societies, the specialized cinemas and the non-theatrical distribution of films. And now are added new and even more powerful doubts. I ponder the thought that heads in a movie emporium are not heads in a home, and far from it. I look at my own ratings and I am supposed to jump with joy if, as indeed has happened, the rating beats the Sunday Palladium in my own bailiwick. I don't, and for the simple reason that a programme like mine would be dead by the dyke-side if I worked on that sort of measurement. Whatever league it is in, it is just not in that one.

As for the greater visual development of the medium I am in some critical difficulty. Confining myself to the categories of drama, comedy, dramatic documentary and poetic documentary, and allowing even for the possibility of spectacle, I am bound to think the medium cannot be developed properly as a visual medium unless it uses the complete apparatus of film techniques in both image and sound: in other works, unless we put television into the business of film-making, either on celluloid or tape, when tape can be as subtly managed as celluloid. This is of course an expensive and frightening prospect if we are to take our measure from the present relatively parsimonious budgets of television. I can say—a little lamely—that the production values of the cinema were never altogether measured by expenditure. I can say with Leonardo, more or less, that you don't buy your golf or your cookery in the shop. But, however ingenious or brilliant the use of film techniques to give size and depth, expenditure is involved and on a scale not now thought practicable. This drives me however not to the thought that television cannot be less developed in practice but that television must inevitably become part and parcel of the film business and in its larger creative efforts in certain categories merely a means for the distribution of the art of the cinema. I have thought from the first that pay-as-you-go television is inevitable in our economic society; and I am more confirmed now as I note the complacency in creative mediocrity which prevails in the categories I have cited.

Whatever laws of popular appeal television may have derived from the cinema, there is one which it may not finally avoid. It is the law of 'importance also', the law which discovered that the Western was the more powerful for being an epic, the law that even Elizabeth Taylor is the better for being also Cleopatra. If, in its present organization, television cannot provide this 'importance also', the whole history of the cinema is there to say that the vacuum will be filled.

Now to the subject which fascinates me most in television—the nature of the television audience. As I have indicated, I believe that the same visual laws must affect the creative future of television—in certain categories—as have controlled the creative cinema and force television to make the appeals represented by the Film Societies, and the specialized cinemas as well as the popular emporia. But the exciting thing about the television audience is that it is a far more various phenomenon than we ever dreamt of in the cinema world, even in our most ambitious and various approaches to non-theatrical distribution. In some ways it is as various in its interests, curiosities and tastes as the readership of the newspapers and the magazines. Television inevitably follows their obvious lead and not least because it has been able to call richly on newspaper and radio skills and, above all, has

378

been able to meet many of these audience requirements cheaply. What has been less obvious is the thought that in certain aspects the television audience is not really an audience at all, much less a public audience.

This possibility has not been greatly grasped. You have that over-emphasis on T.A.M. ratings and the reduction of all programmes more or less to a simple quantitive measurement; and even the B.B.C., for all its great traditions, is guilty of this error, and in fact more guilty today than it was. I can realize why professional people who come in from show business are not likely to think otherwise, but I find it odd that people who come in from other quarters altogether and with other and different interests should fall so quickly for the thought that they are in the self-same way public figures with a similar public relationship. What if we are not public figures at all but strictly private ones in the television relationship? It could be an important distinction, not least because it would alter not only our expectations but also our attitudes, both in our television appearance and in our public one. I whisper the possibility that there is a point where publicity—which of course has some impact on our sponsors—may not be as useful as it would seem, and a point too where the old 'production value' is the one commodity which we least require. I add that in this other private realm of the television relationship even the letters we get may not give us a valid account of ourselves, and that the relationship with the people in the street which is inevitable may be in character far removed from the relationship very properly established by the public stars and the truly professional public performers.

I am, of course, following up on the notion that one essential, and it may be unique, aspect of the television relationship is that we are dealing with two or three people gathered together, and in the very special circumstance and atmosphere of their home. These two or three people gathered together may be thought of not only in their domestic unity but as separate individuals: their ages different, their experience different, their range of interests different, their sensibilities sure to be different; the will to see and appreciate varying accordingly. They may be one as a family or as neighbours, but it is possible to think that each is seeing and listening quite privately, as when they read a book.

New modes of address and behaviour immediately suggest themselves, quite different from the ones we ordinarily adopt in show business or face to face with a large public. You will avoid a live audience in the studio like the plague, lest you, consciously or unconsciously, catch the mood and manner of addressing a public audience. You will behave, in short, like anyone entering someone else's home and measure your address to the normal courtesies. You will not take undue liberties and you will know that a show of cocksureness or arrogance or even of superiority can be deadly. You will in fact appreciate that it is not a situation in which you ordinarily preen yourself. Some do and the very nature of the embarrassment they induce is highly significant.

When you think further of this particular television relationship, you are bound to draw a sharp distinction between the practices of education on the one hand and, on the other, the arts of persuasion and finally of inspiration. Your educator, even your so-called popularizer, will not necessarily command these arts, but of course is wonderful when he does. As often as not, for all its earnest intention, the educational approach may actually appear in this connection patronizing and intrusive: the religious one apt to be the most painful of all.

If, as I think, the approach in this unique television relationship is by persuasion and inspiration, it is worth noting that the powers involved are not as unique as many—on both sides—suppose. The world of suggestion is one in which everyone operates to some extent. We can drop a hint or take it and a nod is as good as a wink. We know how to catch on and are fast or slow on the uptake as the case may be. We not only arrive at conclusions but jump to them. We can get wise to a situation, get the message or get with it; and of course a line is not the less effective for being thrown away. Indeed we have a hundred and one expressions by which we indicate our common power to appreciate from the merest nuance or innuendo—with, I notice, soupçon coming up fast on the horizon.

It is of course the profession of the publicists and propagandists to know their way around in this magic wood, but television is revealing another kind of operator—and from the most unexpected sources—who is even more subtly at home in it; and 'home' is the *mot juste*. Where more notably than in the home does the power of suggestion operate? It is the very citadel of suggestion, the one place where you don't have to spell things out and in fact would go up the wall if people did.

A fuller realization of the possibilities of this relationship must I imagine greatly enrich the whole operation of television. In the meantime there is much to admire and many exponents of them who positively delight. If I mention Michelmore specifically, it is only to indicate the sort of personal or relatively personal relationship involved. There are others who according to one's sensibility or fancy are equally our familiars, and so much so that an actual form of affection goes with them. I do a bit of a pitch myself in the territory and therefore know with a measure of specialized understanding how good they are; and this also means that I can talk more objectively than most about the affection they command. In the nature of things people talk to me just about everywhere as I get around, not only about my own programme but even more about others. It would be impossible not to catch a sense of the relationship they enjoy and the power they either command or potentially command as the result of it.

Mind you, there are differences of degree. If I myself make my pitch quite deliberately and almost exclusively to the two or three gathered together, this derives in part from personal predilection but also, in part, from the fact that it allows me one of the most economical gambits on television and therefore one of the freest. With another economic pattern I could interpret the relationship somewhat differently as indeed others do. The argument from the two or three gathered together applies similarly, if not equally, when you think of the neighbours of a local community, the familiars in a local pub or the private interchanges in a factory. I will swear that it is on this measurement and not the more grandiose measurement which applies to really public figures that we have the secret of our most warmly regarded television personalities.

The larger implication? That here, in the relatively intimate and devoted neighbourhood audience, much multiplied, is a fundamentally new factor in mass communication, to be prized, to be understood for what it is, for what it means and might mean. We may not be in the big big world of art, but we are certainly in the big big world of persuasion.

What have I myself learned from television? I have learned that in this league the law of Tao operates with deadly accuracy. 'He who stands on tiptoe does not stand firm; he who strains his stride does not walk well; and he who reveals himself is not luminous.' I have learned, and to my constant surprise, that we don't know very much about the powers of appreciation we confront; and that much more is possible than we ever dreamt of, in a medium which is God's gift to the operator who commands its relatively private relationships. I shall say also that it is a realm in which, as in sport, you recognize immediately and as of Providence the 'naturals'; and a realm in which you don't know much if you don't know how to admire and respect your betters. In this we are, blessedly, a world away from the catch as catch can of the show business we came from.

7 A Mind for the Future

The declaration of one's loyalties is always a very proper and agreeable duty. We are what our loyalties are. It means respect for origins, for the affections we were given, for the teachings we were given. We give a habitation and a place for the good things and the beautiful things that have given form and spirit to our lives. In other words we give thanks to our country for the particular attitudes with which it has equipped us for the busy and not inglorious business of being alive. A question you see of affections, a question of attitudes, which we think of as specially Scottish.

Of course there is nothing much to be argued about our affections. Every man to his own: to his own parents, to his own town or village, to his own schoolmasters, to his own work and his own workmates. I am the last to argue about them. I have spent a wandering life and the paradox of getting around is that you hold closer in the mind to where you come from. It is your first and original power of attorney. O. Henry wrote a wonderful short story which he called 'The Cosmopolite'. The Cosmopolite had been everywhere he said—in Paris, France, in Rome, Italy, and the like—and he couldn't bear he said all this local nonsense of New York, New York and Chicago, Ill. The men in the outer bar were profoundly impressed. He disappeared into the inner bar and there was suddenly a great outburst of violence. How come they asked. Oh they said, it was that Cosmopolite: somebody had knocked his home town. It turned out to be a very small town in the far far west.

No, your national affections will not stray much and distance will lend enchantment and all dreamers will behold their Hebrides. But as you wander, as you come up against other horizons, other peoples, other conditions of life, you do find yourself examining more and more the attitudes to life your country gave you.

There is one thing I am sure no one anywhere will want to deny us. We have made excellent emigrants, excellent mixers in the wide wide world away. We made good Canadians, good Americans. We didn't weep as certainly the Welsh did when it came to being good

Patagonians. Why, when it came to being Englishmen I regret to say that we made all too excellent Englishmen. And I think it's because they taught us that a man was a man for all that and that a man was sanctified by his work wherever he came from. Indeed the first thing that is said about the Scotsman abroad, and what everyone allowed, is that we were brought up to be a hard-headed people and got down to the work at hand whatever it was and fitted ourselves readily to whatever new conditions arose.

There is a lot more to be said, of course, about the Scot abroad and the attitude to life he so valuably took with him. But this capacity to come to terms speedily with new conditions and to make the most of them is what must interest us most today. For we at home find ourselves up against an economic situation which seems to test that very capacity as much as any new community the wide world over. You may think it a time when we might find some inspiration from our Scottish self abroad.

First let us have a closer look at this quality in our Scottish make-up which so greatly fitted us to be pioneers, explorers, emigrants and the like. Just where did it come from? Now the historians may not agree with me but this is the way I see it. We just have had to be self-reliant and for a long, long time. The English had the blessing of their Norman William and the great English rulers who came after him. They had Government; they had a rule of law that ran through the land. For hundreds of years we had nothing of the kind. The slogan of the Scots of the borders was 'Ready, aye ready'. Where there was no central authority to rely on they needs had to be and I don't think it any wonder that this self-reliance became a habit and an attitude of mind. When poor James VI set himself the task of repairing the damage, it was a lot too late. Our people had got to the point of doubting the efficacy not only of Government but of governance itself. Poor James, any man might buttonhole him to tell him he was only God's silly vassal. He couldn't get out to England fast enough and, until his death, the records say, he blushed and saw red every time the word Presbyter was mentioned.

So as I see it there are two sides to that self-reliance of ours. Splendid as it is in explorers and pioneers this scepticism of the efficacy of government, so deeply engrained in us, may not be so splendid as we react towards the ever more collective management of our economic and political life. Overseas we have had no choice. We couldn't contract out of the changing world or we would have been dead by the dyke-side; and there were other people all too eager to take over.

Here, it seems, we still have the illusion that we can contract out of the changing world and do and there is much in our tradition to confirm us in doing so. Just think of the pattern of our comedy, and not least of our Highland comedy—the confounding of the law, the upsetting of the grand schemes of the high heid yins elsewhere, the break down of all that is new or even modern.

A paradox it may be for a self-reliant people but we face the prospect of an even more highly organized economic future, very powerfully armed against it.

There is a variation on this scepticism towards change, this lack of will-power in regard to it. It is the fact that a people rooted in a tradition of self-reliance, rooted in the tradition of expecting little from Government, should in these new days tend to think that they have only to shout loud enough and this far away thing called Government will pass a miracle. And even when we do have our resources added to, the lethargy again. As we have seen in so many places just no great effort to make the most of them. Examples: well, the potential of the British Motor Corporation at Bathgate, the potential of the chemical complex at Grangemouth. What confuses me is that it is not exactly in the tradition of a hard-headed people to be going against the urgent fact of economic life. Indeed to go against the chiels that winna ding is for a Scot going against character altogether. It is not for me, because I am no economist, to say what the economic facts are, but we have been blessed in our country with highly authoritative analyses by the Scottish Council, by the Toothill report and by those excellently contrived addresses by Iain Stewart to his engineers. They tell us that mass production has concentrated in the south-east area of England, drawing ever-increasing vitality from an immediate great market and from closer and fast communications, mechanical and personal, with the creative centres of planning and research. It is allowed that we have made headway in the introduction of light industries, but it is clear that we are far behind with those industrial developments which are based on modern scientific invention. With this goes a disproportionate measure of unemployment, with twenty thousand of our best people every year emigrating elsewhere. In fact, Scotland is quite plainly failing to occupy the energies of its people at this particular juncture. Allowance for the fact that history has saddled us with the great burden of our past in heavy industry; allowance for our relative misfortune in the matter of communication, recognition that we are man for man as mature in skills and the capacity for acquiring skills as any people anywhere, but back always to the psychological problem

Merchant Seamen (British, 1941)
  Produced by Crown Film Unit: directed by Jack Holmes

Squadron 992 (British, 1940)
  Produced by G.P.O. Film Unit: directed by Harry Watt

The Brave Don't Cry (British, 1952)
  Produced by John Grierson: directed by Philip Leacock

Seawards the Great Ships (British, 1959)
  Produced by Templar (Glasgow) for Films of Scotland: directed by Hilary Harris

—the problem of why we do not react more vividly, more creatively, more urgently to the impact of scientific progress and economic development in this particular generation.

Now all of us have a certain duty in this matter and not least of course the economist, the industrialist, the planners and the politicians. But there are others, I think, more deeply concerned with the issue. If it is true that we are too set in our ways, too apt to cling to the old privilege, too apt to fear new methods, too unwilling to abandon old practices that have outlived their usefulness, if we are laggard in the application of new methods, we are concerned with attitudes. If, as Mr. Macmillan said, the most important thing in the life of the country today is the attitude to change itself, then everyone involved in the arts and practice of persuasion is involved.

Writers and newspaper men, the people of radio, films and television are all involved, for they cannot report or editorialize or criticize or create a picture of anything, without conveying explicitly or implicitly an attitude to the facts—and indeed, an attitude to life itself. They may confirm their audiences in old attitudes or direct them to new but certainly this business of attitudes is their business. And at a time like this it is their profound responsibility.

So if you will permit me I shall address myself to the writers and teachers and talkers and informers generally. I am suggesting that we might all be doing better for our country than we are now doing.

The first thing to say is that there is nothing peculiar to Scotland in the problem of making ourselves over. Even the countries most close to us in origin and language, countries like Canada, have been changing their mental patterns dramatically, as colonies become dominions and independent nations with their own self-rooted values and loyalties. In fact, the change we are making in Scotland today from an industrial economy rooted in the nineteenth century to an industrial economy rooted in the mid-twentieth century is a small matter relatively to the change Canada has made in twenty years or so from an agricultural economy to an industrial one. It would be difficult for anyone who last saw Canada during the war (1939–45) to recognize Edmonton today or even Vancouver. It would be impossible to recognize Kittymatt because it wasn't there and, like so many other communities in the north, has been created out of the wilderness in the few years between.

Changes and great changes are so much the normal order of life in the world today that our Scottish problem is neither peculiar nor peculiarly obstinate. There is a whole wide world of modern instances to demonstrate that the making over of minds even on a national scale is just another necessary activity in a world of change, and not only necessary but manageable. If on first appearance this thought is alienating it may be well to note that the most remarkable instances derive not from the Communist countries where such changes are planned and executed with an element of determination, but from America. American instances of change of attitude on a great scale are peculiarly pertinent to a country like ours because America too has represented the more romantic aspects of individualism. It too has had to change and change dramatically from a frontier outlook to one more suited to a highly complex economy based on mass production and scientific progress.

When I lived in America in the twenties the voice of the old romantic individualism was still loud in the land, but there were other voices too. 'What's new?' they would ask as the most common of salutations, implying that what was past was past and the new, however it came, was to be eagerly received. What interested me then and especially does now was the local even parochial manifestations of this spirit. You did not laugh at the new tractor and wait hopefully for its breakdown as we have all seen in the highlands. Not only was it front page news but there was scarcely a community of even hundreds that did not have a paper to give it headlines.

I remember being given an object lesson in how most locally we can create new attitudes, from the famous editor William Alan White of the *Emporia Gazette*. He took me through a local department store to tell me where everything came from. He said it was a part of the civic pride of Emporia, Kansas, to be getting things from all over the world and keeping up-sides with whatever was new anywhere. He said that a department store could be a powerful influence on the imagination and a powerful spur to the future simply because it talked a language everyone understood and was talking it each day and every day all the time. I leave that thought with Sir Hugh Fraser. Obviously there are many points at the community level where the life-giving patterns of thought are created and re-created.

But, for me the most fundamental influence on that level must always be the teachers. The parents will have their say, but it is the teachers who represent the base of the pyramid of persuasion. As the twig is bent so it will grow and they are the first benders. They may think they are teaching subjects but what of course they are doing, for better or worse, is something far more important in the long run. They are instilling an attitude to subjects. This we all know, for who are

386

the teachers we best remember and honour long years after? Why, the teachers who, no matter what they told us, lit up for us the worlds of literature or science or history or economics or politics as the case might be. No matter their knowledge, what counted as we know was that they gave us an appetite for knowledge. No matter how local their horizons, it was what they did to inspire us to wider ones.

Now as you know we have a great tradition in education in Scotland and it is with us today. I myself cannot think of any more creative report than the one I think of as the Robertson report on Scottish education a few years ago. While we are obviously concerned with an increase in the teaching of the sciences, with acquiring the knowledge of new discoveries and learning the techniques that must derive from them, that Robertson report most rightly, as I think, held to the importance of the school as a community in which we learn the habits of a collective community, a community in which the teacher is still potentially prophet, and philosopher king, just as the old dominies tried to be.

Now I don't know enough to say if our teachers see it that way or not, though I have a simple faith, because I am out of teachers myself, that you must see it that way or they would not have undertaken the patience and persistence of being a teacher at all. In any case, a time like this does at the very least present a special challenge to them. For they have not only the facts of a changing world to teach but they have also the great power so to light up that changing world, that they impart a creative will towards it.

For teachers, at least some teachers, there are special professional hazards and temptations. Teaching is in some senses a sheltered profession, that is to say sheltered from the hurly burly of public pressures. It has in the enjoyment of learning an especial temptation to dwell in the past and even to feel at home in it. If the teachers bring the vitalities of the past to give life to the present all is well; but if their emphasis is such as to make their charges look backwards, all is not well. Literature and the Arts present yet another temptation to accept old-time judgments based on outdated patterns of thought and value, thereby instilling outdated patterns of thought and value. Behind many of them is a gentleman in a library concept and behind that again the concept of an aristocratic and static society which, if it ever existed, is certainly now gone with the wind. To my own schools I owe much but I recall that they equipped me but poorly for the appreciation of the new and wonderful in the painting and letters which were then

387

a-making. By God's grace I learned about them in the bistros, but, as the Balfour of Burleigh remarked, you can't be leaving everything to God's grace. Yes, there is a special challenge to the teachers. It is a time when they may well re-examine the principles on which we operate, a time also when they might reassert the importance of a profession which we can never sufficiently reward.

Here let me come to the wholesale approaches to the making of the mind over to fit the future; for the mass media must bear the brunt of what duty there may be. Again let us dismiss the notion that there is anything unnatural in thinking thus deliberately of making the mind over. All of us who operate in the worlds of information either confirm people in old attitudes or direct them to new; and if we don't do it explicitly we cannot avoid doing it implicitly in our every choice of material and in every judgment regarding it. All I suggest is that we examine a little more carefully what we are in fact doing with our media.

Let me give you a simple instance of this greater deliberation of approach. I once had the honour of serving Mr. Mackenzie King, the Prime Minister of Canada. On one occasion he said: 'Wouldn't it be a great pity if Canada were to lose her sense of dependence on the Mother Country only to fall into a sense of dependence on what we called at the time "our good neighbour to the South"; and what in fact were we going to do about it?' Well we did a lot of things. Just one of them was that we set about making the Canadians look to the north and, to that end, we began by changing the maps to focus on the North Pole. That is going to the very root in the changing of attitudes. Of course there were other things. We multiplied the expeditions into the north, we established better news services from the north, we started on what turned out to be an excellent series of films from the north. It happened that the facts of life were on our side. The aeroplane was reaching out into the wilderness and the Pole was becoming in cold hard fact a crossroads of the world. Then we struck uranium and nickel and other minerals. But the important thing for us is this: that in a short period of years the people of Canada were aided and abetted, and of deliberation, in realizing themselves as a people.

As far as they go, our newspapers in Scotland do very well, but only as far as they go. First we have our dramatic newspapers, and very lively they are. Indeed they are newspapermen's newspapers in the best professional sense. They are much accused of too much sensationalism. I, on the other hand, would criticize them for not being

388

sensational. I could think sometimes that, for all the flair of their make-up, they too have the illusion of living in a static society, whose perfect peace is only ever broken by the bells of the fire engines, the sirens of the ambulances and the strident whistles of a desperate police.

The great discovery of modern journalism was of course the use of the active verb; and I remind you that it came from the dynamic approach to life and reporting in America. But there it wasn't just a question of seeing the news in terms of stories. It was a question of building up a picture of events in which something was always happening to something else and somebody or other was always going places. Well, we inherited the active verb all right but I think not to dramatize the somethings and the somebodies that are really vital to our necessity. I know local papers in America that could give our great ones cards in spades in making the little important things seem great. In fact, I wish sometimes our newspapers would catch that American fever of asking and forever asking of their reporters 'What's new? What's new?' However, I am simple enough, or it may be logical enough, to believe that the popular newspapers will be the last to fail us at this juncture, for they are forced by definition to seek the interest of the young; and there can hardly ever have been a generation of young people less impressed than this one with the dying and decadent formulæ of their elders.

The more serious newspapers are of greater concern. These powerful sounding boards of Scottish thought and opinion are out there on the front line of what the poet Archie McLeish in his inspired phrase once called 'the war for men's minds'. First let me say that they serve us well and very, very well for a small country. In the matter of economic and industrial reporting, which is a basic need, we must be grateful. In the reporting and analysis of economic plans and economic drives and political action we are sure to be upsides with events. No one may doubt their devotion to the common weal. But just as the popular newspapers by their nature derive a certain vitality from their interest in the younger generation, the serious newspapers are tied, and it may be damnably, to the older generation they address.

This expresses itself in many ways which I for one often find tiresome and disappointing. In fact there is a basic contradiction between the vigour of their analyses of the factors governing our economic future and their reflection of social and mental attitudes in Scotland which not only cannot speed that future but, in many ways, prevent it. Theirs is the most difficult of all the dilemmas in Scottish information today and in my view the most important to resolve. In a small country like ours it is inevitable that, when you run radio or television or a national newspaper, all the lobbies and lobbyists of present power can get at you and do. The all too easy thing is to listen to them, as you must inevitably bear with them in the course of your social duty. The really difficult thing is to stand aside and subject them coldly, one and all, to the larger vision for which you are responsible.

Of all the lobbies the most dangerous ones in my view are the lobbies which in one way or another represent the *status quo* in ideas or, worse still, the ideas of the past. They come at you in their kilts and you are bound to show them a certain native affection. They come at you in their cassocks and you must show them a proper respect. They come in the name of learning and letters. Again we must take note of their badges and honour philosophy inasmuch as they even appear to guard it. The question however to ask, and it is not being asked nearly enough, is what, for all the time and attention we give them, they are adding unto us. Sometimes I think that there can never have been a museum with such a massive clutter of attendants as this my native land. For many of us the air is musty with what Flaubert called the *idées reçues*. They are the thoughts, once vital maybe, but now, as they say, old-fashioned, because the contact with reality, the fire of life has gone out of them.

I myself am grateful for much and not least for the progressive vigour of the film criticism over the years. I am sure the theatre people must be grateful too and now, at long long last, the painters are getting a bit of a break. But there is a lot of pot-boiling on the books and—why, oh why?—only one single whisper of bold and creative criticism about television. Then again we have our gentlemen in a library on a dozen important columns grinding out their memories of the dead and gone, inviting us to dream islands of the past that one may be pretty sure are desert islands. No, I don't think it is a living culture we are seeing reflected: a living culture out and about, like old Adam Smith in his day, in the living present, forging a mind for our tomorrows: rather a culture, all too often, of the cultural conceits and the culturally conceited.

It is, as I say, easy to understand why our great newspapers drift into a *laisser-faire* policy in the matter of social and cultural attitudes, even at a time when they affirm that a *laisser-faire* policy in our economic life is no longer possible. But I think they might well be surprised at the public response if they shifted ground. The younger people in every critical walk I know are certainly hungry for a change. So I am going to invite our Scottish editors to absent them from their felicities awhile and take to themselves the power of prophesy and be done with it. They have great examplars before them who have mastered and now master the self-same dilemma. I need only mention C. P. Scott of the *Guardian* and J. W. Dafoe of the *Winnipeg Free Press*. They might even think sometimes of old Sir George Waters of the *Scotsman*. He was a grim old Tory, and there was no great percentage in that, but by heavens he took this public role of the newspaper as seriously as ever a man did ; and I never heard it said that anyone could push him around in the line of duty. What delights me always about him was that he thought that to edit a national newspaper was the most exalting destiny to which the Almighty could call any man. And so say I.

In television we have the excuse of being very young in the game though, through radio and the figure of Lord Reith, we ought certainly to have inherited a sense of responsibility and of our power. We are of course subject to the same afflictions as the press, the pressure of the old-established lobbies for our time and attention. This pressure is all the greater because we command large audiences and more patent powers of publicity. Then again under the law we are required to demonstrate our sense of responsibility and we are vulnerable to any and every sort of nagging. What easier than to align ourselves patently and publicly with the old old things and the old old faces, however unreal they may be or unpleasant. It is just about the safest bet in the land that we shall spend more money and effort on the 14th Centenary of Iona than on any public occasion since the Coronation. Forget the Strip Mill. The cameras will be away out there in the wilds of the past and to whose advantage? Not the service of the future certainly.

Then again we are in show business and entertainment is certainly a large part of our role. The newspapers know, and the serious newspapers especially know, that it is a hard game to be serious and entertaining at the same time, though the documentary film development in the world at large has constantly demonstrated that it can be done and in the most stubborn matters of public affairs. I don't think anyone can question the achievement of our British television as a whole in following up the documentary film development. But where? I for one wouldn't think it was in Scotland, and I am more than sensitive on the point. Football reporting, yes, and why not when we are if nothing else a nation of superb football analysts—so much so that it seems to be difficult to get into the game with an English accent. But the hard stuff—no. Even in our dramatic adventures, the hard stuff—no. Just the well-tried pattern of comedy; and, on and on, the fifing and the jigging and the swinging of the kilts.

As I said, we are young at the game but even five years is a whole generation when it comes to finding new creative talent. Well, I have been watching for five years and what young masters of the future have we found? I wonder if we were looking hard enough. Now, as you know, such men only come out of great jobs to do and a sense of urgency and importance in the doing of them. They don't come off the sky, but only when the producers have a sense of mission and a powerful need for attendant missionaries.

Oh yes, we are good at the Public Relations all right, but, as with the editor, so with the producer. He has more important things to do: so important that he must face on occasion public relations which to say the least are dodgy. The point is that we can't play safe all the time and there are times when we must inevitably experiment as we turn more deeply to discover and reveal the new world which is making about us.

Now one last short word about films in Scotland: short because we have not yet organized or financed the film to be the national influence which of course it should be. You have only to think of the development of the film as a national influence in countries like New Zealand and Australia and Canada and Poland and Yugoslavia and even Ghana to realize how remiss we are. The best we can say for the present is that television with its documentary film magazines like 'Compass' and 'Here and Now' could do much more than they presently do to fill the gap. There is nothing I wish for more as a film man than that they should be more greatly encouraged to get out and about; that more time should be given to the visual observation of our current affairs, that more resources should be put at their disposition. Above all, they should be encouraged to be even more penetrating and effective in stirring up public interest and discussion.

I think of course of the film as capable of an even more lasting impact on the public imagination. Well, what have we? We have a Films of Scotland Committee financed in the first instance by the generosity of Sir Hugh Fraser;[1] but it has a hard, hard road to find the finance for its films from the local authorities and the local industries. It does very well in the circumstances but, as you might expect in Scotland, far too often the local groups can only think of a film as a catalogue of their local complacencies.

What we need is something better. The film will come to serve

[1] Now Lord Fraser of Allander.

A Mind for the Future

Scotland when we dig into our Scottish pockets and, in the name of all things vital and beautiful, make the film reach out to the great shapes, the dramatic and poetic shapes, which give depth to what we do. We are not so poor at all that we should be going along in our present beggarly way and a Film Foundation more really financed cannot be beyond the means of those who would patronize an art that matters. Why, only the other day I was invited by the Governor of North Carolina to sit in on the drafting of such a Foundation for his State. We started at nine o'clock in the morning and we had it formed and financed by telephone by eleven. A matter of superior wealth? Not a bit of it. Just a will to the future and no piking.

On that note I finish—a will to the future and no piking—with all of us who have power in one way or another over the images of the future dedicated to a more dashing account of our stewardship. Be sure the voices of the planners and the politicians will mean little without us.

We may well be a small country and the prophets of the future thin on the ground but I beg you remember that it was Andrew who brought in the lad with the five loaves and the two fishes and it was on his question that the miracle was performed. That I trust is an encouraging thought for St. Andrew's Day.

Postscript

I know that the dead bodies of coral insects make a South Sea island but I doubt if the dead bodies of old pieces make a book. The Scots doctrine has it that we are saved not by works 'but by grace' and, personally, I prefer books in the usual way, like locomotives with big journeys ahead of them. This is more like a night's shunting in the yards at Crewe.

I had some misgivings when my friend, Forsyth Hardy, wanted to make this selection. I never kept my stuff nor thought it important beyond the critical battles of the moment which, I am happy to say, were always plenty. It may be that I have hewn out some theory in my time, affecting the principles of education and affecting the use of the film as a vital instrument in public information. But writing, for all of us in the documentary movement, has been incidental to the business of making the word flesh. I must now, myself, have been associated in the making of maybe a thousand films or more. I have also had something to do with the machinery of their financing and distribution in different parts of the world, which is a greater labour still, considering the cross-purposes that attend the present phase of our somewhat romantic democracy.

Writing has no doubt helped us clear our heads and renew our spirits as we went along, but the most important point about the ideas on which we have speculated is that we have worked them out in practice. In fact, one must see the writing of the documentary group as somewhat strictly related to action. I have grown so weary of the distant nonsense of Laputa that I have almost come to believe it is the only kind of writing worth doing in our time.

In any case, I agreed to Forsyth Hardy's venture. I was moved that somebody should have gone to the labour of digging out my pieces from the old journals and the old files. But more conclusive was Hardy's insistence that a few people might get a better sense of what others, besides myself, have been driving at over the years. I hope they do and that Hardy's faith is in some measure justified.

It is clear that Hardy wanted this to be a serious book and myself

Postscript

a pretty serious character, and there is a way the Scots use the word 'purposive' with the accent on the second syllable, which rushes out of my diabolic infancy to frighten me everywhere I go. Among the best things for me in film have been the clowns and the comedians, the dancers, the horses, the poets and the dolls. By the witness of these pages I might never have delighted in W. C. Fields and Fred Astaire nor fallen in love for ever and a day with the great Miss West. The documentary group would not have gone very far if it had been all for public observation and reform and not started with an affection for the living quicksilver of the medium itself.

One special word should be said about the documentary movement. It has been greatly fortunate in its men and in its friends. We have held together as no independent movement in art has done in our generation: across the years and across the distances, physical and psychological, which separate nations. I could say it was the idea which held us, for it has at its core the secret of the co-operative spirit and no consciousness of boundaries to the common interest of mankind; but I have also the best reason to know how unselfish men can be.

Hardy emphasizes the long struggle to build a documentary movement and the intensity of effort it sometimes demanded. Certainly not all our decisions to open new horizons have been correctly understood or correctly supported. Certainly there were always people around, and in sometimes exaggerated estate, who, as they might say in Brooklyn, knew strictly and consistently from nothing. On the other hand, difficulties have been incidental to the fact that the British Government supported us throughout and over that long and necessary period which permitted us to mature our ideas as well as our techniques and our teams. In the light of events, that was crucial.

Some strength we may have got the hard way, by out-writing and out-speaking our opposition and, on occasion elbowing a piece of it into bankruptcy, after the gentle manner of Hammering Henry Armstrong, who was a principal inspiration of our day. But no one should forget the support we always enjoyed, and from the most unlikely sources, in both Whitehall and Parliament. Nor could we pay the debt we owe to the understanding of *The Times*, the *Manchester Guardian*, the *News Chronicle*, the *Express*, dear Lejeune's *Observer*, the *Sunday Times*, the *Yorkshire Post*, the *Spectator*, the *Glasgow Herald*, and Forsyth Hardy's own *Scotsman*; nor to the B.B.C.; nor to the trade papers, the *Cinema* and the *Kinematograph Weekly*, which, from 1929 on, were away ahead of the field in our support.

And what are you going to say when you have people about you

Postscript

like Stephen Tallents, Robert Nichols, Walter Elliot, Stafford Cripps, H. G. Wells, Charles and Lawrence Wright, Colonel Medlicott, Jack Beddington, S. C. Leslie, John Marshall, Niven McNicoll, Norman Wilson and, among the Canadians, Mackenzie King, Charles Cowan, J. W. Dafoe and George Ferguson? Each one of them has, at one point or another, made a fundamental contribution to the continuity of what, because of its continuity, is now called the documentary movement. I say: how could we have missed? I am glad indeed to have this chance to salute the people who trusted our purpose and pay them my affectionate due.

JOHN GRIERSON

1946

POSTSCRIPT TO THE NEW EDITION

In developing the documentary approach to film-making it is now obvious that we served a useful purpose and, it may be, more purposes in more places than we foresaw. A sense of purpose was certainly at the heart of the matter and, I think, still must be if the documentary film is to command wide and various public support and do justice to its æsthetic potential. While documentary's uses are today widely appreciated all over the world and even to the point of being taken for granted, the original driving force which pushed it over the years into some notable æsthetic achievements has weakened in some quarters. Indeed, any afterthought I have at this time is concerned not so much with the celebration of the world-wide success of the old campaigns, but with the failure on that one front, the æsthetic front, which has given some of us in the past our greatest satisfactions.

From the beginning it was clear, at least to me, that there was a limit to what could be expected from the commercial film industry. This, of course, was before the socialist countries had come to plan their film production in the constructive interest of their cause and community. In the West, the industry was concerned primarily, then as now, with mass entertainment, and the private profit motive, then as now, largely dictated its character and quality. A place was found, logically enough, for the 'actuality' film in newsreel and travelogue and in the format of lightweight film magazines. But there the road to realist observation stopped. There could be exceptional cases when exceptional films by exceptional men broke through to the public screens, but one was always conscious of the discomfort that went with

396

Postscript

it. The observation in depth which we hopefully thought possible was not welcome because the commercial industry, then as now, had no place for it. Even my own relatively pleasant experiences with distributors could not conceal the fact that there was no true economic root for the documentary idea in that quarter.

For me the greatest single discovery in the development of documentary came with the realization that its logical sponsorship lay with governments and with other bodies conscious of their public responsibilities. The second was with the realization that there was more seating capacity outside the commercial cinemas than inside them. In the event, television demonstrated that in this matter we were all too modest. It has provided an access to the means of production and distribution which has revolutionized the prospect for the documentary film and happily so, but only in direct proportion to the sense of public responsibility which has been forced upon it.

That first economic rule still sternly applies. Nowadays, backing for the documentary film in its journalistic, informational, educational and propagandist forms has become relatively easy to arrange; but it has still for its larger result to look for sponsorship where that larger result is actually wanted. This in turn involves it, now as then, in a constant effort to ensure that it is wanted. If these early writings have any significance it is in the measure that they reflect that effort. If we got anywhere—and we did—it was because, on every level of public persuasion including the ministerial, we saw to it that the documentary idea was taken seriously.

Looking about me, I merely note that the documentary men are not now organized as they once were for the purpose of ensuring their larger creative future, and themselves ensuring it. Their patient dependence on the fortuitous goodwill of the back-room species in government departments and television authorities, I sometimes find a trifle surprising. I could never get myself to believe in fortuitous goodwill from any source whatsoever. You get what you command.

Past experience would seem to suggest that one way out of that impasse is to make a cause of it, or better still many causes: the kind of hooks you can hang big hats on. The better economic circumstances which permit so many good things on the lighter levels should fool no one. The fact is that in some countries which should know better the great things we once expected are not being made; or, when they are, they are as rare and accidental as in the primitive days.

None the less while the difference between sponsorship in the socialist countries and the private enterprise countries is profound, it

397

Postscript

can be misleading. By and large, the best documentary production on the æsthetic level is today in Poland, Czechoslovakia, Yugoslavia and Hungary which is to say that more good things get done there and as a general rule than anywhere else. On the other hand the record of the British Government was at one time excellent as the record of the Canadian Government is excellent and to this day. The industrial sponsorship of great international companies such as Shell has been, and as a general rule, inspired. However they manage it in the by guess and by God conditions which govern their sponsorship of the arts, these odd ones round the corner in France and Italy, and Holland and America continuously demonstrate the power of the individual effort. It is a power that applies in socialist countries as in others, just as complacency there can be as enervating as anywhere else.

My own prejudice is for régimes which have abandoned the by guess and by God approaches. I am for what they call in the best quarters 'the regular development of society', including the sort of contribution to it the documentary film can make, though I hold an absolute reservation in favour of the especial freedoms due to seers and artists. Obviously in one régime or another much will always depend on the powers of persuasion of individuals on the film side and on the creative goodwill of individuals among the sponsors. In the documentary development I know best good work has always derived from these special personal relationships. But in the last resort I would insist that they are better based on genuine national aspirations and such. If there is a truly creative understanding the art will look after itself. In short, we either belong to the creative mainstream of our society or we do not. If we do, it is for us to assert where and how we do belong and speak and act with a due sense of our role in the social leadership.

JOHN GRIERSON

Kinsale
12th September 1965

398

Appendix

The dates and original sources of the articles, reviews, and other writings and addresses of John Grierson included in this volume are listed below.

PART 1: BACKGROUND TO DOCUMENTARY

THE LOGIC OF COMEDY:

City Lights by Charles Chaplin: *Artwork*, Autumn 1931.
Modern Times by Charles Chaplin: *World Film News*, April 1936.
Sous les Toits de Paris by René Clair: *The Clarion*, January 1931.
Laurel and Hardy: *Everyman*, 29th October 1931.
Animal Crackers with the Marx Brothers: *The Clarion*, December 1930.
Monkey Business with the Marx Brothers: *Everyman*, 15th October 1931.
The Passionate Plumber with Buster Keaton: *Everyman*, 28th April 1932.

DIRECTORS OF THE THIRTIES:

Shanghai Express by Josef von Sternberg: *Everyman*, 14th April 1932 and *The Clarion*, May 1932.
The Lost Squadron with Erich von Stroheim: *Everyman*, 26th May 1932.
A House Divided by William Wyler: *Everyman*, 24th March 1932.
Dynamite by Cecil B. de Mille: *The Clarion*, May 1930.
Kameradschaft by G. W. Pabst: *The Clarion*, March 1932.
M by Fritz Lang: *Everyman*, 16th June 1932.
The Man I Killed by Ernst Lubitsch: *Everyman*, 23rd June 1932.
Le Million by René Clair: *Everyman*, 18th February 1932.
Murder by Alfred Hitchcock: *The Clarion*, October 1930.
Rich and Strange by Alfred Hitchcock: *Everyman*, 24th December 1931.
Tell England by Anthony Asquith: *The Clarion*, May 1931.

399

Appendix

Dance Pretty Lady by Anthony Asquith: *Everyman,* 31st December 1931.

Quick Millions by Roland Brown: *The Clarion,* November 1931.

Hallelujah! by King Vidor: *The Clarion,* February 1930.

Tabu by F. W. Murnau: *The Clarion,* October 1931.

HOLLYWOOD LOOKS AT LIFE:

The Champ by King Vidor: *Everyman,* 14th January 1932.

Street Scene by King Vidor: *Everyman,* 21st January 1932.

Three Cornered Moon by Elliott Nugent: *New Britain,* 20th September 1933.

Tom Mix: *New Britain,* 2nd August 1933.

Cimarron by Wesley Ruggles: *The Clarion,* March 1931.

Enemies of the Public by William Wellman: *The New Clarion,* 2nd July 1932.

The Mayor of Hell with James Cagney: *New Britain,* 29th November 1933.

Gabriel Over the White House by Gregory La Cava: *New Britain,* 14th June 1933.

Arrowsmith by John Ford: *Everyman,* 7th April 1932.

I'm No Angel with Mae West: *New Britain,* 6th December 1933.

THE CINEMA OF IDEAS:

Things to Come by H. G. Wells: *Glasgow Herald,* 29th October 1935.

Don Quixote by G. W. Pabst: *New Britain,* 7th June 1933.

The Skin Game by Alfred Hitchcock: *The Clarion,* November 1931.

All Quiet on the Western Front by Lewis Milestone: *The Clarion,* July 1930.

Frankenstein by James Whale: *Everyman,* 4th February 1932.

The Life of Emile Zola by William Dieterle: *World Film News,* November 1937.

Dead End by William Wyler: *World Film News,* January 1938.

The Vessel of Wrath by Erich Pommer: *World Film News,* April 1938.

Captains Courageous by Victor Fleming: *World Film News,* December 1937.

THE RUSSIAN EXAMPLE:

One Family: The Clarion, August 1930.

Earth by Dovzhenko: *The Clarion,* November 1930.

The Man with a Movie Camera by Dziga Vertov: *The Clarion,* February 1931.

Appendix

Enthusiasm by Dziga Vertov: *The Clarion,* December 1931.
Deserter by Pudovkin: *New Britain,* 25th December 1933.
Thunder Over Mexico by S. M. Eisenstein: *New Britain,* 24th February 1934.

PART 2: A MOVEMENT IS FOUNDED

Drifters by John Grierson: *The Clarion,* October 1929.
Flaherty: *Artwork,* Autumn 1931; *Cinema Quarterly,* Autumn 1932.
First Principles of Documentary: *Cinema Quarterly,* Winter 1932; *Cinema Quarterly,* Spring 1933; *Cinema Quarterly,* Spring 1934.
Creative Use of Sound: *Sight and Sound,* Autumn 1934.
The E.M.B. Film Unit: *Cinema Quarterly,* Summer 1933.
Summary and Survey: 1935: *The Arts Today,* London, 1935.

PART 3: DOCUMENTARY ACHIEVEMENT

Films and the Community: Comprising 'The Use of Radio and Films in the Classroom', an address to the National Union of Teachers, Southport, England, 1936, and 'The Film in the Service of Religion', *World Film News,* October 1938.
The Course of Realism: *Footnotes to the Film,* Peter Davies, London, 1937.
A Scottish Experiment: *The Spectator,* 6th May 1938.
Battle for Authenticity: *Documentary News Letter,* 1939.
Metropolitan: (*The City,* by Ralph Steiner and Willard van Dyke): *Films,* Vol. 1, No. 1, 1939.

PART 4: DEVELOPMENT IN CANADA

The Film at War: Broadcast from Ottawa, 30th November 1940.
Searchlight on Democracy: *Documentary News Letter,* 1939.
The Nature of Propaganda: *Documentary News Letter,* 1942.
The Documentary Idea: 1942: *Documentary News Letter,* 1942.

PART 5: EDUCATION: A NEW CONCEPT

Education and the New Order: The 'Democracy and Citizenship' series, pamphlet No. 7, 1941, published by the Canadian Association for Adult Education.
Education and Total Effort: An address at Winnipeg, Canada, 1941.

Appendix

Propaganda and Education: An address before the Winnipeg Canadian Club, 19th October 1943.

The Library in an International World: An address before the American Library Association, Buffalo, New York, June 1946.

PART 6: FUTURE FOR DOCUMENTARY

Films and the I.L.O.: An address before the International Labour Organization, Philadelphia, 26th April 1944.

The Challenge of Peace: An address to the Conference of the Arts, Sciences, and Professions in the Post-War World, New York, June 1945.

Report from America: *Theatre Arts Monthly*, December 1946.

PART 7: INTERNATIONAL

Documentary, the Bright Example: *Documentary 47*: The Edinburgh International Festival of Documentary Films, 1947.

Edinburgh and the Documentary Idea: *Documentary News Letter*, August 1948.

Progress and Prospect: *Documentary 49*: The Edinburgh International Festival of Documentary Films, 1949.

The Malaise of Disillusionment: *Documentary 51*: The Edinburgh Film Festival, 1951.

Documentary: A World Perspective.

Learning from Television: *Contrast*, Summer 1963.

A Mind for the Future: The St. Andrew's Day lecture, 1962: The Scottish Home Service of the British Broadcasting Corporation.

Index

Index

404

Index

Daly, Tom, 26
Dance Pretty Lady, 79, 80
Dand, Charles, 32
Danish Films, 200
Dante's Inferno, 200
Darrow, Clarence, 95
Davidson, J. N. G., 168
Davy, Charles, 20
Daybreak in Udi, 350, 351, 354
Dead End, 115–16
Death Valley, 90
de Mille, Cecil B., 64–6, 104, 169
Dent, Arthur, 198
Depinet, Ned, 204
Descartes, 295, 300
Deserter, The, 104, 113, 130, 154, 182, 208
Desert Victory, 24, 289
Desire under the Elms, 64
Destiny, 172
Dickson, Paul, 32
Dietrich, Marlene, 60–2, 173
Disney, Walt, 58, 146, 160, 170, 178, 354
Dix, Richard, 92
Docks of New York, The, 49, 61
Documentary Newsletter, 369
Documentary film, the: aesthetic, 22, 29–30, 121, 140–2, 185, 205, 249–50, 289; first principles, 145–56; and industry, 206–7; and governments, 207–8, 349, 397; and social problems, 215–17; in wars, 223–6, 239, 243, 252, 317; force for internationalism, 29, 30, 32, 309–16, 361, 365, 369
Dog's Life, A, 51
Donellan, Phillip, 370
Don Quixote, 101, 105–7
Dos Passos, John, 73
Dostoievsky, 130, 350
Douce France, La, 101
Douglas, George, 64
Dovzhenko, 123–6, 182
Drake, Charlie, 375
Dreyer, Carl, 173
Drifters, 17, 18, 19, 135–8, 152, 153, 167, 205, 206, 213, 216, 366
Durante, Jimmy, 177
Durham University, 14
Durrane, Maggie, 177
Düsseldorf murders, the, 68
Dyer, Ernest, 20
Dynamite, 65

Earth, 66, 113, 123, 145, 208

East Germany, 365
Edinburgh Film Festival, 34, 337, 346–8, 351, 357
Education, 14, 15, 34, 189–94, 228–37, 261–71, 272–9, 299, 304–5, 321, 324–8
Educational Foundation for Visual Aids, 352
Egypt, 369
Eisenstein, Sergei, 17, 122, 123, 130–2, 133, 182, 184, 203, 205
Ekstase, 155, 161, 175
Eldridge, John, 32, 33
Elephant Boy, 203, 204
Eliot, T. S., 374
Elliot, Walter, 214, 366, 396
Elton, Sir Arthur, 18, 19, 23, 167, 168, 180, 208, 215, 348, 354, 369
E.M.B. Film Unit, 18, 19, 20, 31, 69, 133, 164–8, 176, 180, 181, 361
Emmott, Basil, 17
Empire Film Library, 19, 27
Empire Marketing Board, 16, 17, 19, 20, 164, 180, 206, 207, 208, 251, 366
End of St. Petersburg, The, 130, 161, 181
Enemies of the Public, 93, 94
England, 139, 168, 211, 218, 225, 242, 251, 258, 383
Enough to Eat, 22
En Rade, 205
Enthusiasm, 128, 129, 182
Epic, the, 170, 178
Epstein, Jean, 179
Ermler, F., 182
Ervine, St. John, 176
Evans, Ernestine, 310, 311
Exquisite Sinner, The, 49, 59

Face of Scotland, The, 214
Fairbanks, Douglas, 101, 173
Family Portrait, 32
Fellini, Frederico, 374
Ferguson, George, 230, 396
Field, Mary, 202
Fields, Gracie, 210
Fields, W. C., 177, 395
Fight for Life, The, 24, 330
Film Centre, 23, 367, 369
Film Society (London), 17, 102, 207
Finance, film, 165, 167, 169, 170
Finch, Peter, 34
Finlayson, James, 212
Fitzpatrick, James, 146
Five Star Final, 175

405

Index

406

Index

Index

408

Index

Index

Index

411